*Guide to Manuscripts
in the
Western History Collections
of the
University of Oklahoma*

GUIDE TO MANUSCRIPTS
in the
WESTERN HISTORY COLLECTIONS
of the
UNIVERSITY OF OKLAHOMA

∼

Compiled by
KRISTINA L. SOUTHWELL

Foreword by
DAVID L. BOREN

Introduction by DONALD J. PISANI
and DONALD L. DeWITT

UNIVERSITY OF OKLAHOMA PRESS · NORMAN

Library of Congress Cataloging-in-Publication Data available through the Library of Congress.

ISBN 978-0-8061-3473-4 (paper)

This guide was published in part with funds provided by the Associates of the Western History Collections. The Associates of the Western History Collections is a support group dedicated to helping the Western History Collections maintain its national and international reputation for research excellence.

The paper in this book meets the guidelines for permanence and durability of the Committee on Production Guidelines for Book Longevity of the Council on Library Resources, Inc. ∞

Copyright © 2002 by the University of Oklahoma Press, Norman, Publishing Division of the University, Red River Books edition. All rights reserved. Manufactured in the U.S.A.

CONTENTS

List of Illustrations	vii
Foreword	ix
Preface	xi
How to Use the Guide	xiv
Acknowledgments	xvi
Introduction	xvii
Manuscript Collections	3
Index	377

ILLUSTRATIONS

An allotment certificate for Chickasaw Nation
lands issued in 1904   39

The diary of Charles Kroff, 1861–1865   75

Charter of the Fairview, Oklahoma Territory,
Anti-Horse Thief Association, 1895   113

Correspondence of General Matthew Arbuckle to
Cherokee Nation Principal Chief John Ross, 1839   145

Miller Brothers 101 Ranch Wild West
Show pamphlet, 1927   178

The diary of U.S. Army surgeon James Reagles, Jr.,
1864–1867   213

Ledger drawing of the Battle of the
Rosebud River in Montana, 1876   251

An issue of *Siwinowe Kesibwi*
(*The Shawnee Sun*), 1841   283

The diary of Samuel Murray Stover, 1849   321

Scrapbook of 8th Route Army
activities in China, 1937   360

FOREWORD

by David L. Boren

Upon arriving at the University of Oklahoma, I felt it was important for others to understand and be exposed to our heritage, so I turned to the Western History Collections' staff, who soon furnished hundreds of early photographs depicting life on campus and in Oklahoma. We created a university-wide photo album of sorts by putting up historic photographs throughout the buildings on campus. These photographs, now prominently displayed in lecture halls, departmental offices, libraries, and residence halls, give our diverse student body a common "family history" and will help later generations understand the courage and vision of those who preceded them. All who view these pictures will admire the spirit of those men and women who came to a treeless prairie, in some ways barren and uninviting, and saw in it limitless possibilities, which they were determined to realize. The landscape itself became an actor in history, inspiring hopes and nurturing dreams of those who sought new opportunities as unlimited as the unbroken horizon.

The Western History Collections includes some of the University of Oklahoma's crown jewels. Housed in historic Monnet Hall, they are among the best collections of their kind in the United States. Nearly two thousand collections are held in the Manuscripts Division alone. It includes the region's premier Native American manuscript resource. Here one can find journals, correspondence, legal documents, drawings, and sound recordings of some of the most influential tribal leaders of the last century. This division also preserves more than five thousand maps of Indian and Oklahoma territories. The transportation manuscript collection, which includes research materials related to railroads and aviation, is virtually unmatched by any library in the area.

Perhaps the Western History Collections' best-known resource is the Photographic Archives, which contains over eight hundred thousand prints and negatives. It features the work of some of the great early frontier photographers, such as William S. Prettyman, Andrew A. Forbes, William Soule, and W. A. Flowers. Oklahoma's great events and eras, such as the land runs, the growth of agriculture and cattle trade, and the development of the petroleum industry are captured on film and made available for research.

The Library Division contains the Frank Phillips Collection and eleven other named collections with some of the world's most impressive holdings on Native American culture. Here one can also find artifacts and literature on Abraham Lincoln, the Civil War, the Louisiana Purchase, the St. Louis World's Fair, and a host of other events in our nation's history.

The Western History Collections plays a vital role in our university, the state of Oklahoma, and the nation as a whole. Its collections help preserve our heritage and provide a tremendously valuable resource for researchers of the American West. These collections give us an insight into ourselves and the core values that define us as Americans. I invite all to experience these collections and discover our past.

PREFACE

by Kristina L. Southwell

In the year 2002, the Western History Collections at the University of Oklahoma Libraries marks its seventy-fifth anniversary. This set of guides to the manuscripts and photographs in the Western History Collections is published to celebrate the Diamond Jubilee and to make these resources more widely known within the research community.

The Western History Collections is a special collection within the University of Oklahoma Libraries on the main campus in Norman, Oklahoma. The mission of the collection is to collect, preserve, and make available rare and special research materials for scholars in the fields of history of the American West, Oklahoma history, Native American studies, and anthropology. As a member of the University Libraries, part of the Western History Collections' purpose is to support the research and teaching programs of the University of Oklahoma. The materials collected are made available to university students, faculty and staff, as well as the general public.

Three main departments comprise the Western History Collections: the Library Division, the Manuscripts Division, and the Photographic Archives. The Library Division holds over 60,000 volumes, made up of a central collection known as the Frank Phillips Collection, plus a dozen family library collections which focus on such diverse topics as military history, the life of Abraham Lincoln, and the 1904 St. Louis World's Fair. The Manuscripts Division holds approximately 11,000 linear feet of textual primary materials. In addition, the Manuscripts Division administers 5,200 maps, 1,500 sound recordings, 800 posters, and over 1,000 series of microforms. The Photographic Archives, the most heavily used of the three divisions, maintains 841,000 images. Strengths of the Photographic Archives include the works of frontier photographers such as W. S. Prettyman and A. A. Forbes, photographs of Native Americans in Oklahoma and the Southwest, and images of the range cattle industry in the West.

The Western History Collections began in 1927, when University of Oklahoma history professor Edward E. Dale started the Frank Phillips Collection of books on western history. Although the collection was originally comprised mostly of published materials, Dale and university archivist Gaston Litton gradually expanded the Phillips Collection to include primary documentation as well. Through their efforts, the core collections that are the foundation of the Western History Collections Division of Manuscripts were acquired. Primary materials in the Division of Manuscripts currently number 1,535 discrete collections. The subjects covered by these collections are diverse, including records of the Five Tribes settled in Oklahoma, expansion and settlement of the American West, and businesses that contributed to the development of the Trans-Mississippi West region.

Among the materials most frequently requested by researchers are the over three hundred Indian-related collections. Documents reflecting the history of the Cherokee, Chickasaw, Choctaw, Creek, and Seminole Nations are all represented by official records, family papers, diaries, and printed materials. The largest of these collections is the Cherokee Nation Papers, documenting the development of the Cherokee Nation in Oklahoma from 1830 to 1907. Of special interest in the Cherokee Nation Papers is the correspondence of the prominent Cherokee families of Stand and Sarah C. Watie, James Madison Bell, and the Ridge and Boudinot families. The Cherokee Nation Papers has recently been complemented by the addition of the Wilma Mankiller Collection. In 1985, Mankiller became the first female principal chief of the Cherokee Nation. Her papers, reflecting the complex operations of a contemporary tribal government, are useful for comparing the Cherokee Nation government of yesterday and today.

Other Indian-related collections of note include the Choctaw Nation Papers, the Peter P. Pitchlynn Collection, and the Green McCurtain Collection, all of which document the history of the Choctaw Nation; the Jerry Whistler Snow Collection of Sac and Fox family correspondence; and the Duke Indian Oral History Collection and the Indian Pioneer Papers Collection, both of which contain interviews with early Oklahoma Indians and settlers.

Collections related to Oklahoma business and industry comprise a large portion of the materials in the Manuscripts Division. Early town merchants such as Spiro's Redwine Trading Company and Atoka's Zweigel Mercantile Company are well represented, as are larger companies such as the Cities Service Oil and Gas Corporation, and the Chicago, Rock Island, and Pacific Railway Company. These records help document the expansion of key industries throughout Oklahoma and the region, and often provide historical information on the development of surrounding cities and towns. In addition, more than four hundred linear feet of Oklahoma banking records are held by the Manuscripts Division.

Collections of authors' papers are another rich resource at the Western History Collections. The papers of western authors Walter Stanley Campbell and B. M. Bower are present, as are children's authors Harold Keith and Lois Lenski. Authors' papers often include variant drafts of their published works, subject files of materials gathered during the research process, and research notes that may be used to trace the development of a thesis or idea into a full-fledged monograph.

The popularity of the Western History Collections' resources on wild west shows of the early 1900s is evidenced by patrons' frequent requests for them. Three collections focus on this form of entertainment: the Miller Brothers 101 Ranch and Wild West Show Collection, the Gordon W. Lillie Collection, and the D. Vernon Tantlinger Collection. The materials represented in these collections range from performers' scrapbooks, posters, and memorabilia to company correspondence and financial records.

Collections of governors' papers at the Western History Collections offer many opportunities for research on Oklahoma politics. Seven governors are represented, including territorial governors Thompson B. Ferguson and Abraham J. Seay. State governors' collections are those of Raymond D. Gary, Charles N. Haskell, Henry S. Johnston, Johnston Murray, Leon C. Phillips, James B. A. Robertson, and John C. Walton. The political history of Oklahoma can also be studied in the papers of judges, members of the state legislature and U.S. Congress, and state officers.

Original correspondence and diaries written by pioneers, missionaries, and settlers are perhaps some of the most unusual treasures to be found in manuscript repositories. These first hand accounts of life on the western frontier offer a glimpse of life that seems far removed from that of contemporary society. The diary of Cassandra Sawyer Lockwood (1833–1835) in the Roberta Robey Collection describes daily life at Dwight Mission, Indian Territory, and missionary work with Cherokee Indians. Lockwood also touches briefly on the subject of freeing slaves kept by local settlers in the area. Similarly, in the Kathleen Faux Collection, the letters of Presbyterian missionaries Joseph Leiper, Fanny Leiper, and Margaret McCarrell illustrate the constant difficulties they experienced in attempting to provide religious and academic instruction to the local Cherokee children. These and other collections provide researchers with vivid depictions of frontier and pioneer life as it actually was.

A natural strength of the collection is the history of the University of Oklahoma. The Western History Collections maintains over sixty collections from university presidents, faculty, staff, and alumni. For example, the papers of history professor Morris L. Wardell contain correspondence regarding all aspects of university life during the 1930s and 1940s, including history studies, university committees, World War II curriculum changes, Extension Division programs, and student life. Collections such as these provide historical data and personal narratives that can be used to form an understanding of the development of the University of Oklahoma into the academic institution it is today.

Since 1927, hundreds of manuscript collections have been acquired for the Western History Collections through the combined efforts of its curators, James Babcock, Edward E. Dale, Donald L. DeWitt, John S. Ezell, Jack Haley, Abraham Hoffman, Bradford Koplowitz, Gaston Litton, and John R. Lovett, Jr. These collections serve to complement the resources of the Library and Photographic Archives with first-person accounts of history, and in so doing, they significantly enhance the scope of opportunities for scholarly research in western history at the University of Oklahoma.

HOW TO USE THE GUIDE

The 1,535 collections in this guide are arranged alphabetically by collection title. Each entry includes up to seven information fields to help researchers analyze collections. The following figure illustrates a typical entry and identifies each of the fields. Following the section that describes the collections is an index, keyed to each collection's entry number. Entry numbers appearing in the index in boldface type refer to a collection by the same name. Numbers not in boldface type indicate that the referenced entry contains some information by or about that specific person, place, subject, or event. To find all collections containing information on a specific subject, turn first to the index, find the desired subject listing, and note the entry numbers following it. Then turn to the specific entries cited and read the summary to see if the collection merits further examination. The finding aid statement that is included at the end of collection entries indicates whether a published or unpublished finding aid is available to researchers. Finding aids provide detailed information about the materials included in a collection, and are particularly helpful in locating specific items in large collections. Unpublished finding aids are available onsite at the Western History Collections' reading room. Published finding aids are available for sale at the Western History Collections, or from the publisher.

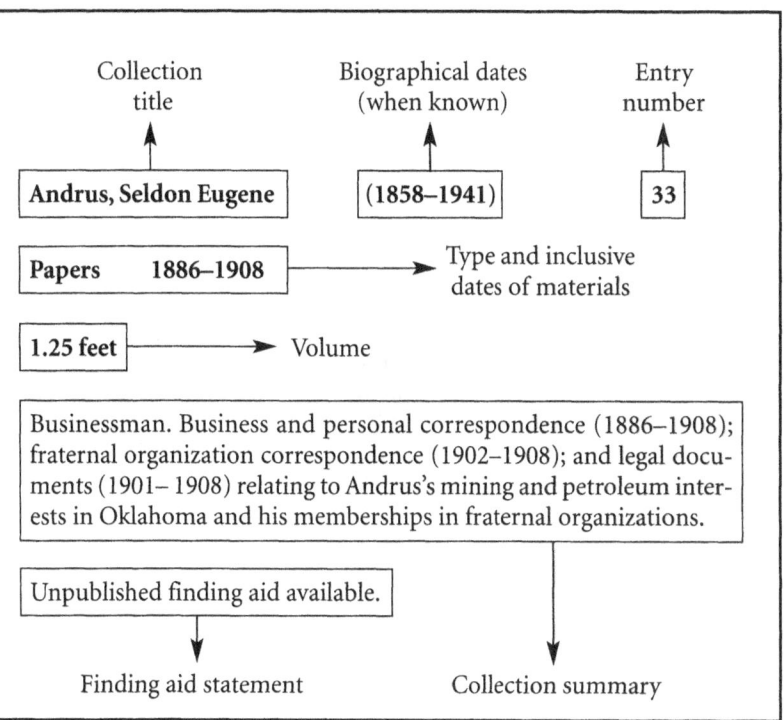

INFORMATION FIELDS FOR COLLECTION ENTRIES

ACKNOWLEDGMENTS

The compilation of this seventy-fifth anniversary edition of the guide to the Western History Collections' manuscript collections has been made possible by the assistance of many people. Curator Donald L. DeWitt performed the arduous task of compiling the original 1994 edition of this guide, with the invaluable assistance of former assistant curator Bradford Koplowitz and former staff assistant Shirley Clark. Their work laid the foundation upon which the current guide was created. Both Donald L. DeWitt and staff assistant Stacie L. Graves provided generous editorial assistance during the manuscript revision process, and provided well-considered advice and direction for an often unwieldy project. Special thanks are due to the Associates of the Western History Collections and to the president of the Associates, Donald J. Pisani, for sustained support of the mission and programs of the Western History Collections. In addition, the work of all former curators and staff of the Western History Collections is to be acknowledged. This guide would not be possible without their knowledgeable guidance and stewardship of the collections over the years.

INTRODUCTION

by Donald J. Pisani and Donald L. DeWitt

First-rate universities need good students, an accomplished faculty, and outstanding libraries. The Western History Collections at the University of Oklahoma has provided the university with a national reputation in the study of Oklahoma, the Great Plains, the American Southwest, and the Far West. Publication of this guide commemorates the seventy-fifth anniversary of the founding of the collections. The guide is a testament to the vision and devotion of people inside and outside the university. The vision and devotion of E. E. Dale and Frank Phillips in the 1920s endure today in the many benefactors, library staff, and faculty who consider the Western History Collections vital to the intellectual life of this state and region.

That many of the most notable western history collections date to the early decades of the twentieth century is not accidental. The definition of the American West as a distinct region depended on the widely held belief, developed during the 1890s, that the frontier phase of United States history had ended. Simultaneously, the Spanish American War (1898) marked the emergence of the United States as a world power. The United States entered a militant, nationalist period of its history, and Latin America assumed far greater importance in American diplomacy. Therefore, American universities began to place more emphasis on the history of Mexico, Latin America, and the Southwest, as well as the West. Only when the West was incorporated into the nation, and only when the United States began to look overseas, did the region's history begin to attract historians as well as collectors.

Only a handful of distinguished university libraries focus on the study of the American West. They include the Beinecke Library at Yale University, the Bancroft Library at the University of California, Berkeley, the Barker Texas History Collection at the University of Texas, and the Western History Collections at the University of Oklahoma. These institutions have much in common. All depended on the dreams and shared values of dedicated faculty members, private donors, university administrators, and library staff. Without that common purpose, many collections would have been broken up and scattered before they could be consolidated and made available to scholars. Most began as private collections. For example, William Robertson Coe gave the core of Yale's celebrated Western Americana Collection, a treasure of rare books, maps, and manuscripts related to the Trans-Mississippi West, to the Yale Library in annual installments beginning in 1942. Yale had several advantages over other American universities in the acquisition of western materials. First, the university had been in existence for nearly two and a half centuries when Coe made his gift; therefore, it already possessed a large number of books and manuscripts pertaining to the West. It was logical for private collectors like Coe to turn to Yale rather than newer universities in the West. Second, many Yale faculty members, including Benjamin Silliman, Jr., William H. Brewer, and Othniel Marsh, had been active in exploring and developing the West. Finally, many Yale alumni had collected significant libraries that they or their heirs transferred to the university. The Frederick W. Beinecke collections, which were particularly rich in the area of the Great Plains, Rockies, and Spanish Southwest, complemented as well as built on the Coe Collection, which contained little on the Spanish Southwest outside Texas.

Only one public institution in the West can compete with the collections at Yale. The Bancroft Library at the University of California also owes its existence to private collectors. In an age when few westerners had any interest in preserving documents pertaining to the settlement of the Far West, Hubert Howe Bancroft was the great exception. After trying his hand at a variety of jobs in the gold fields of California, he went into the stationery and book business in San Francisco. But he soon became an academic entrepreneur as well as a collector. His great dream was to write a comprehensive history of the Pacific Coast. To lay the foundation for that project, he began collecting everything he could find on the American West. Within a decade he had acquired sixteen thousand volumes, some of which he acquired on trips east and to Europe. Not only did Bancroft accumulate books, maps, pamphlets, manuscripts, and periodicals, he had an army of copyists transcribe documents in private hands and in government and church archives. Her was also one of the first to transcribe the memories of pioneers. In the 1870s and 1880s, his staff interviewed virtually every important pioneer in the history of California. His "history factory," as he called it, produced dozens of volumes on Northern Mexico, Native Americans, and the settlement of the Far West and California. None of this work would have been possible without the documents he collected.

In 1905, at the end of his writing career, Bancroft, then in his early seventies, sold his collection to the University of California for $250,000. Bancroft reduced the price by giving the university $100,000 and permitting it to pay for the collection over three years. The library was a monument as much to the wisdom of the university president, Benjamin Ide Wheeler, and the university regents, as to Bancroft. Once acquired, the library's growth depended on Professors Herbert E. Bolton, George P. Hammond, and James D. Hart, who began to collect microfilm of Spanish and Mexican archives, as well as western art and literature, including the famous Mark Twain Collection.

At the University of Texas, the Barker Texas History Collection dates to 1899, when Lester G. Bugbee, a member of the history department, secured the transfer of the Bexar Archives to the University of Texas Library. This collection contained more than eighty thousand documents accumulated in San Antonio during the Spanish and Mexican periods (1700–1836). In 1906, the university wisely decided to cooperate, rather than compete, with other special collections libraries. It signed an agreement with the University of California, the Newberry Library in Chicago, and the Library of Congress to copy and share documents from the Mexican Archives and other repositories. The Stephen and Moses Austin Collections, acquired by the private collector Guy M. Price, also served as the foundation for the Barker Texas History Collection. As with the other libraries, the acquisition of major holdings immediately posed two problems: where to house them and how to catalog them. A full catalog of the Bexar Archives was not completed until 1932, three decades after the University acquired the first collections, and a public catalog to the entire Barker Texas History Collection was not ready until 1963. In this project, the University of Texas history department was greatly involved, particularly George P. Garrison and Eugene C. Barker.

The history of the Western History Collections at the University of Oklahoma has much in common with the experiences of Yale, the University of California, and the University of Texas. When Edward E. Dale, who came to Oklahoma as a boy and had been a doctoral student of Frederick Jackson Turner at Harvard, became chair of the University of Oklahoma Department of History in 1924, one of his goals was to build up the department's graduate program. Not only was Oklahoma rich in Indian history, but it was at the seams of the American West. One seam joined East and West; another joined South to West; and a third joined the Great Plains to the Rocky Mountain West. Since Oklahoma was one of the last American territories, and one of the last territories to enter the Union, its frontier past was still fresh in the minds of many of its residents. But Dale wanted to create a library devoted to the study of the entire Great Plains and Southwest, not just of Oklahoma.

Dale first attempted to secure an appropriation from the Oklahoma Legislature to create his library. That effort failed, and soon thereafter, with the help of the prominent Tulsa attorney Patrick J. Hurley, Dale approached Frank Phillips, an Oklahoma oilman who had begun to assemble a notable Oklahoma history collection during the 1920s. Phillips agreed to give limited financial support to Dale's proposal and, on April 5, 1927, the Frank Phillips Collection of Oklahoma and Indian History was established at the university.

The legal contract that created the new library outlined several goals for the collection. It was expected to celebrate and commemorate the past, not just serve impartial historians. The contract promised that the Phillips Collection would preserve "memorials of [Oklahoma's] pioneers, and romantic past"; demonstrate the state's progress in "industry, arts, civics, and literature, and all the elements of progressive civilization"; "institute and encourage historical inquiry"; "inculcate interest and pride in our history"; "mark the passing of a race of people and the genesis and growth of a new civilization"; and teach children "our debt to those who have gone before, and our responsibilities to the future." To accomplish these ends, Frank Phillips gave $2,000 annually for five years to acquire "letters, records, documents, books, pamphlets, manuscripts, maps, and prints, pertaining directly or indirectly to the history of that part of the Southwest now included within the state of Oklahoma . . . ."

The fund was to be administered by the president of the university, the head of the history department, and a third party to be appointed by Phillips. The first board consisted of President William Bennett Bizzell, Professor Dale, and Patrick Hurley. Initially, the books were housed in a glass case within Dale's Monnet Hall office. Subsequently, the collection was assigned to a room on the east side of the ground floor of Monnet Hall, and by 1936 its size required it to be moved into the main library building.

From the beginning, there was tension over whether the library would focus on Oklahoma, the Southwest, or the entire West. But E. E. Dale, who administered the collection until his retirement in 1952, insisted on taking the broader view. He believed in collecting not only materials pertaining to the entire West, but also materials pertaining to Native Americans outside Oklahoma. He was aided by the Brookings Institution, which contributed 625 volumes on Native Americans, these volumes had been collected in the 1920s to aid the work of the Merriam Commission, of which Dale was a member. Other acquisitions were serendipitous. For example, in 1933, Dale purchased three trunks of letters and Ridge-Watie-Boudinot family papers from a woman in Grove, Oklahoma, for $350. He considered this collection, along with the Indian-Pioneer Papers, and the Brookings Institution volumes as the most important acquisitions during his tenure as "director" from 1927 to 1952. When Dale retired, the collection he had built contained 8,500 books and pamphlets, 30,000 manuscripts, 4,500 photographs, and a wide assortment of typescripts, maps and newspapers.

By the 1940s, Dale recognized the need for a full-time curator and specialized staff to care for the Phillips Collection, but it languished during the 1950s. Cataloging proved impossible. The process had begun with high hopes in 1952, only to stall in 1955 because of financial problems. At the time, private donations had dried up, and the university's top priority was constructing a new library rather than expanding the special collections.

The 1940s, however, brought one significant development for the Phillips Collection. In 1948, the University of Oklahoma received a grant from the Rockefeller Foundation to establish a Division of Manuscripts within the University Library. Arthur McAnally, the university librarian, appointed Gaston Litton, one of Dale's former students, as archivist for the Division of Manuscripts. Litton proved to be a capable and aggressive collector of personal papers, maps, and photographs. By the time Litton left the University of Oklahoma in 1956, the Division of Manuscripts rivaled the Phillips Collection as a resource for historians.

Although the Division of Manuscripts and the Phillips Collection continued to operate independently of each other, Litton's resignation set the stage for a significant change in the administration of the two collections. In 1957, the University of Oklahoma appointed Arrell M. Gibson as curator of the Frank Phillips Collection and head of the Division of Manuscripts. Jack D. Haley joined Gibson as assistant archivist. Gibson enlisted the support of University of Oklahoma President George Lynn Cross, who hoped that with additional funding the Phillips Collection might one day rival the great collections on the American West at Yale, the University of Texas, and the University of California. Fundraising problems persisted, but the two collections were then under one director.

Despite generous gifts from the Phillips Foundation, the Phillips Collection still needed a permanent endowment. Considering the Phillips Collection a library rather than a specialized research facility, the Foundation placed a limit of $100 on any single item purchased with the money it gave the university; this limit precluded the purchase of manuscript collections as well as rare first editions. Earlier in the century, most collections were freely given to libraries, but such donations became less and less common as these collections increased in value, and as private collectors and libraries competed to acquire them. In 1958, for example, the Ramon Adams Collection went on sale in Dallas for $30,000. It contained documents on the range cattle industry as well as crime and law enforcement in the West. But before the university could find the benefactors needed to purchase the collection, it was sold to a private collector.

In 1967, in an attempt to provide better support for the two collections, the University Libraries' administration merged the Division of Manuscripts and the Phillips Collection into one unit called the Western History Collections. Since that time, the holdings of the Western History Collections have grown dramatically. These holdings now include the Mary P. Jayne Papers, which chronicle the activities of one of the first missionaries to serve among the Plains Indians; the official papers of the Cherokee, Choctaw, Chickasaw, and Creek nations; the personal papers of many notable Indian leaders, including D. W. Bushyhead and Lewis Downing of the Cherokees, Peter P. Pitchlynn and Green McCurtain of the Choctaws, J. M. Perryman and Pleasant Porter of the Creeks, and Cyrus Harris and William Byrd of the Chickasaws. The Indian-Pioneer Papers, a Depression-era oral history project consisting of 166 bound volumes of interviews, offer researchers the reminiscences of those white pioneers who took part in Oklahoma's land runs and of Native Americans who were already here.

The Western History Collections is particularly rich in material pertaining to the range cattle industry, agriculture, oil, banking, frontier trading, and other industries. For example, the Western History Collections contains the records of thirty-five representative Oklahoma banks during the territorial and early statehood periods. Scholars interested in Oklahoma agriculture can consult the records of the Oklahoma Wheat Growers Association or of the Pruitt Cotton Gin Company. Researchers seeking records can look at the Kali-Inla Coal Company or the Mullen Coal Company collections. Students of social history can consult the archives of the Episcopal Church of Oklahoma, the extensive files of missionaries, the papers of the State Medical Association, or the papers of such notable university presidents as William Bizzell and David Ross Boyd. But researchers interested in regions beyond the borders of Oklahoma also find plentiful material. The library has especially strong holdings of microfilmed records from the U.S. National Archives, the Mexican and Spanish archives of New Mexico, and from Mexican and Spanish archives related to the northern provinces of New Spain and New Mexico. Holdings of other universities are also available on microfilm, including the entire Bexar Archives from the University of Texas Barker Texas History Collection and the American Indian Periodicals Collection from Princeton University.

In addition to standard works on Oklahoma and Native Americans, the library contains numerous published government reports, including those of the Bureau of American Ethnology. It also contains many scholarly journals on the West, including *Western Historical Quarterly*, *Indian Historian*, and *Plains Anthropologist*, as well as rich holdings of twentieth-century Native American newspapers, such as the *Navajo Times*, *Jicarilla Chieftain*, and *Akwesasne Notes*.

In recent years, many other parts of the Western History Collections have captured attention across the nation. The Western History Collections' photographic archives contain over eight hundred thousand glass plate and acetate negatives from the entire West. These are frequently used in television productions and scholarly research. The cartographic section includes over five thousand maps related to Indian Territory, Oklahoma, the Southwest, and the Far West. The oral history section contains many Indian-related collections such as the Indian Oral History Collection, more than six hundred tapes financed by the Doris Duke Foundation in the 1960s; the "Indians for Indians Hour," sound recordings of a radio program that aired from the 1940s into the 1960s; and numerous other Indian-language recordings collected by linguists and anthropologists. The Western History Collections also contains many other notable audio collections ranging from a series of radio programs, entitled "Oklahoma School of the Air," to lectures by Edward Everett Dale and talks by prominent speakers at University of Oklahoma events. Recently, the Western History Collections has also begun to acquire collections of Native American art, and continues to acquire microfilm collections from the National Archives, Library of Congress, and commercial vendors.

All special collections pass through phases. They begin as the dream of a few academics and non-academics who value the past. Next, these founders search for a secure home for the core documents and for the staff to catalog and administer those documents. The founders then seek outside donors and hire archivists and curators who have the energy and talent to maintain the collections and manage an acquisition program. The Western History Collections has followed this pattern. Much has changed during the seventy-five-year history of the Western History Collections. What began as a specialized library of secondary literature has blossomed into a library and archive for all types of documentation of our past. Electronic catalogs have replaced the cumbersome card catalogs, and an increasing number of acquisitions are on microfilm, a medium which costs less, requires less time to catalog, lasts indefinitely, and requires less space to store than other media. Books remain important, but so do art, sound recordings, and Native American newspapers.

Fortunately, the Western History Collections has passed the days when success depended on a handful of individuals or a share of the University Libraries' budget. In the early 1970s, Curator John Ezell and Assistant Curator Jack Haley organized several friends of the Western History Collections into a small support group. Known as the Associates of the Western History Collections, the organization has grown to approximately 125 members and provided the Western History Collections with its own endowment. The Associates purchase rare books, photographs, and manuscripts for the Western History Collections and also support the publication of guides to manuscript collections and traveling exhibits of materials from the Western History Collections. The Western History Collections still depends heavily on state support, but private donors have made an enormous difference in the acquisitions program and the visibility of the library throughout the state.

The present volume will serve many purposes. The most important is to show scholars in Oklahoma and in the rest of the United States the rich and varied materials available at the University of Oklahoma for the study of the West, the Southwest, the Great Plains, and Oklahoma. This guide will also publicize the Western History Collections among potential donors. Anyone who thumbs through the pages of this set will be impressed with the histories yet to be written, anticipating the amateur and professional historians who will write the history of the West in the twenty-first century. Like the people who negotiated with Frank Phillips for that initial gift in 1927, today's readers may realize that these libraries are more about the future than the past.

*Guide to Manuscripts
in the
Western History Collections
of the
University of Oklahoma*

MANUSCRIPT COLLECTIONS

Abbott, J. H. 1
Papers 1937
1 item

Cowboy. A manuscript (1937) of "Reminiscences of J. H. Abbott," describing the settlement of No Man's Land (Oklahoma Territory), cowboys at the XIT Ranch in Texas, the Goodnight Pasture, and the Hi Koller Ranch. Also included is a list of ghost towns and defunct post offices from the early settlement of Beaver County, Oklahoma.

Abrams, Abner W. 2
Papers 1881–1916
.10 foot

Businessman. Correspondence (1893–1916) concerning lead and zinc mining in Oklahoma, the automotive business in Baxter Springs, Kansas, and real estate holdings, along with a program (1881) of a funeral service for Lucy Grey.

Adams, Arthur Barto 3
Papers 1924
1 item

Professor. A manuscript (1924) of "Economics of Business Cycles," written by Adams and published in 1925.

Adams, Joseph Quincy   4
Papers 1654–1911
.10 foot

Professor. An Elizabethan commonplace book (1654) with typescript; inventories (1870–1918) of the rare book collections of Adams Stevenson and Henry Stevenson; personal correspondence (1882– 1911) of E. J. Doggett, of Bristol, England, regarding rare book collecting; and an inventory (n.d.) of rare books at the William Bennett Bizzell Memorial Library, University of Oklahoma.

Adams, Ramon Frederick (1889–1976)   5
Papers 1942–1958
1.33 feet

Writer. Manuscripts of three of Adams's books, "A Genius in Chaps," "Cowboy Lingo," and "Come an' Get It," along with his correspondence (1942–1958) with other writers, collectors of western lore, fans, and publishers.

Unpublished finding aid available.

Aderhold, Thomas   6
Records 1921–1949
.33 foot

Superintendent. Minutes (1921–1935); statistical reports (1934–1949); and correspondence (1931–1942) of the El Reno Sanitarium, a general proprietary hospital, the first in Oklahoma to train and graduate a class from its school for nurses.

Adkins, (Mrs.) Jim   7
Records 1907
1 item

Collector. An invoice from a St. Louis, Missouri, wholesale firm to a general store in Walters, Oklahoma, for the purchase of buggy whips and lamp burners.

Advertising Card Collection   8
Papers 1884–1918
.33 foot

Subject collection. Advertising cards (1884–1918) from businesses in Arkansas, Illinois, Indian Territory, Missouri, New York, Oklahoma, Pennsylvania, and Texas.

Albert Pike Hospital Collection   9
Records 1917–1948
12 feet

Hospital for women and handicapped children. Admittance records and ledgers (1917–1948) of the Albert Pike Hospital, McAlester General Hospital, and All Saints Hospital, all in McAlester, Oklahoma. Also included in the collection is a certificate of incorporation (1928) granted by the state of Oklahoma to the Albert Pike Hospital.

[5]

Unpublished finding aid available.

Alcorn, Ken, and Steven Alcorn   10
Papers 1914
2 items

Collectors. A copy and transcript (ca. 1914) of correspondence from John A. Sutter of New Helvetia, California, to William A. Leidesdorff concerning the discovery of gold by Sutter, dated March 15, 1848.

Alexander, Ira Olyen (b. 1906)   11
Papers 1950–1952
.10 foot

Collector. Genealogical material (1950–1952) concerning the Alexander, Sellers, Chisum, and Bourland families; notes (ca. 1952) on the early histories of Paris, Texas, and Bennington, Oklahoma; and printed material (1950–1951) on organized labor in Oklahoma.

Allen, Clarence   12
Papers 1952–1968
5 items

Cartoonist. An autographed print of a painting of Will Rogers by Clarence Allen, newspaper clippings regarding Allen, several cartoons by Allen from the *Tulsa Tribune*, and a social club event program that spoofs Oklahoma politics and politicians of 1968.

Allen, Neva   13
Ledgers 1911–1912
2 items

Hosteler. Two registers (1911–1912) from the Hotel Dewey in Dewey, Oklahoma.

Allen, Susie Keefer   14
Papers 1911–1940
8 items

Collector. An obituary (ca. 1925) of Lewis Keefer; a discharge certificate (1911); pension certificates (1914–1926) for Keefer and his widow, Ann; a statement (ca. 1940) by former state senator Walter Bruce Allen concerning conditions at the Granite (Oklahoma) Penitentiary; and copies of two letters (1940) from Allen concerning the death of former state senator Ralph Busey.

Alley, Charles   15
Diary 1861–1865
1 item

Soldier. A typescript of a diary (1861–1863, 1865) kept by Lt. Charles Alley, Company "C," Fifth Iowa Cavalry, with an appendix containing the regiment's organization and strength.

Alley, John   16
Papers 1890–1940
2.50 feet

University professor. A letter (1912) to Alley from Victor M. Locke, Jr., principal chief of the Choctaws, listing present and former principal chiefs of the Five Civilized Tribes, and discussing the status of the Choctaw government; a four-page manuscript (n.d.) entitled "For the First Time: The True Story of the Last Oklahoma Indian Uprising as Told by the Man Who Put It Down," as related to Alley by Col. Roy V. Hoffman of the Oklahoma National Guard; Hoffman's official reports (1909) concerning the Crazy Snake Rebellion, along with Governor Charles N. Haskell's orders (1909); correspondence (1926–1942) concerning Kingfisher College; documents (n.d.) about the Dalton family; and miscellaneous research notes and professional correspondence (1920–1942) accumulated by Alley as a professor of government.

Unpublished finding aid available.

Allman, George   17
Papers 1917–1952
.33 foot

Oil field worker. Personal correspondence (1945–1950); war ration books, bills, and receipts (1944–1948); Catholic church programs (1951);

road maps and travel guides; farmers' handbooks (1947–1951); and telephone directories (1928–1950) from Oklahoma and Texas towns.

Alpha Chi Sigma Collection   18
Records 1921–1969
4 feet

Professional chemistry fraternity. Records of the Alpha Chi Sigma fraternity, including reports (1921–1966), minutes (1922–1956), correspondence (1946–1969), subject files (1904–1968), membership records (1931–1968), financial records (1917–1967), newsletters entitled, "Proceedings of the Grand Chapter of Alpha Chi Sigma," (1930–1968), "The Chrome and the Blue," (1941–1944), and other publications of the organization, along with a scrapbook.

Unpublished finding aid available.

Alpha Epsilon Delta Collection   19
Records 1932–1951
1.33 feet

Professional organization for pre-medical students. Correspondence (1938) of the officers of the University of Oklahoma Kappa Chapter of Alpha Epsilon Delta; biographical data forms (1936–1946) for each member of the organization; petitions (1947–1948) from local collegiate chapters nationwide requesting admittance to the national organization; publications (1932–1951), including *The Scalpel*, published by the national organization; and brochures (1946), with form letters enclosed, explaining the Graduate Record Examination, a scholastic aptitude test for graduate students.

Unpublished finding aid available.

American Association of University Women Collection   20
Records 1923–1949
9 feet

Professional organization. Minutes (1920–1949) and correspondence (1934–1946), along with other records (1923–1949) including membership lists, reports, newspaper articles, bulletins, yearbooks, histories, bylaws, and related materials from the state of Oklahoma chapter and the University of Oklahoma chapter of the American Association of University Women.

American Indian Aid Association Collection 21
Papers 1859
1 item

Organization. A list of officers, members of the executive committee, and the objectives of the American Indian Aid Association.

American Indian File Collection 22
Printed materials 1939–1975
.75 foot

Subject file. Publications (1939–1975) of the Bureau of Indian Affairs and other state and federal government agencies, along with reprints of articles regarding the American Indian. Included in the collection is a report (1970) entitled "President Nixon's Indian Legislative Program."

Unpublished finding aid available.

American Indian Institute Collection 23
Records 1956–1974
8 feet

Indian advocacy organization. Minutes (1958–1960) of annual conferences; correspondence (1956–1974); and newsletters and other publications (1956–1974), all concerning Indian education, civil rights, tribal council proceedings, and Indian youth programs.

Unpublished finding aid available.

American Legion Post 303 Collection 24
Records 1944–1950
5.50 feet

Veterans organization. Awards, bulletins, and committee reports (1946–1950); correspondence (1946–1950); financial records (1946–1950); minutes of meetings (1944–1950); membership applications (1946–1949); and scrapbooks (n.d.) of the University of Oklahoma American Legion post.

Unpublished finding aid available.

American Red Cross of Beckham County Collection 25
Records 1916–1921
2 feet

Local Red Cross chapter. Correspondence (1916–1921); minutes (1917–1921); financial records (1917–1921); and a history of the Beckham County (Oklahoma) chapter formed during World War I.

Unpublished finding aid available.

American Red Cross of Cleveland County Collection 26
Records 1917–1919
1 item

Local Red Cross chapter. A scrapbook history of the Cleveland County (Oklahoma) chapter formed during World War I.

Ames, Charles Bismark (1870–1935) 27
Printed material 1902–1920
.66 foot

Judge. Promotional literature and a speech (1902–1903) by Ames on Oklahoma statehood; pamphlets (1915–1918) regarding American involvement in World War I; reports (1914) of earnings and expenses of the Oklahoma City *Times* Company; and correspondence (1907–1919) regarding Oklahoma and Oklahoma City politics.

Unpublished finding aid available.

Ames, H. B. (b. 1873) 28
Records 1901–1934
3 feet

Physician. Office records (1901–1934), including ledgers, bills, patient case histories, correspondence, and insurance papers, documenting Ames's practice of medicine in Alva, Oklahoma.

Unpublished finding aid available.

Amos, French Stanton Evans 29
Papers 1928–1937
.10 foot

Professor. Grade books (1929–1937) from Amos's courses in government and an unpublished manuscript (1928) by Amos entitled "The Yazoo Land Frauds."

Anderson, R. M. 30
Papers 1893
1 item

Physician. Lecture notes (1893) taken by Anderson while a medical student.

Anderson, R. R. (1851–ca. 1930) 31
Papers 1887–1923
2 items

Physician. A daybook (1918–1923) and a medical notebook (ca. 1887) of diseases and treatments.

Anderson, Richard T. 32
Printed material 1800
1 item

Collector. A reprint of the *Ulster County Gazette* (January 4, 1800) of Kingston, New York.

Andrus, Selden Eugene (1858–1941) 33
Papers 1886–1908
1.25 feet

Businessman. Business and personal correspondence (1886–1908); fraternal organization correspondence (1902–1908); and legal documents (1901–1908) relating to Andrus's mining and petroleum interests in Oklahoma and his memberships in fraternal organizations.

Unpublished finding aid available.

Anthony, Travis Dan (1914–1993) 34
Papers 1926–1989
.75 foot

Teacher. Correspondence (1926, 1974–1989); newspaper articles (1982–1989); manuscripts (n.d.); and publications (1935–1987) either by or about Travis D. Anthony, and relating to Anthony's family, his life in rural Oklahoma, and his student experiences at the University of Oklahoma in the 1930s.

Unpublished finding aid available.

Anti-Horse Thief Association Collection 35
Records 1892–1902
.25 foot

Vigilante group. Constitutions (1892–1895); rosters (n.d.); minutes (1895–1902); and proceedings (1895–1901) of Chapter 35 of the Anti-Horse Thief Association located in Fairview, Oklahoma Territory.

Unpublished finding aid available.

Apushmataha 36
Printed material 1906
1 item

Indian chief. A typescript of an article from *Sturm's Oklahoma Magazine* (1906) regarding the life of Apushmataha.

Ardrey, Helen 37
Records 1962–1968
.25 foot

Collector. Financial records (1962–1968) from Union Banque Suisses regarding Helen Ardrey's account.

Arnold, Ben 38
Scrapbook 1938–1950
1 item

Lawyer and judge. A scrapbook of news clippings (1938–1950) documenting Arnold's career as an attorney and judge.

Arthur, Patti Joy 39
Scrapbook 1915–1917
1 item

Collector. A scrapbook (1915–1917) kept by Patti Arthur, who graduated from the University of Oklahoma in 1917, about her college experiences.

Asahl, John 40
Ledger 1903–1904
1 item

Merchant. An account book (1903–1904) from Asahl's hardware store in Ramona, Indian Territory.

Ashbrook, William 41
Records 1853–1855
3 items

Collector. Deeds (1853–1855) to land in Missouri.

[12]

Ashley, Charles 42
Manuscript ca. 1951
1 item

City clerk. A list of mayors of Claremore, Oklahoma, from 1900 to 1949, including the index numbers to city record books where their records can be found.

Atoka Lions Club Collection 43
Records 1927–1930
.10 foot

Service organization. Meeting minutes, accounts ledger, officer and membership lists, financial reports, and correspondence (1927–1930) of the Atoka, Oklahoma, Lions Club.

Atoka State Bank Collection 44
Records 1905–1935
25 feet

Bank. Records (1905–1935), including tellers' daily balance books, discount rate books, draft registers, daily statement books, tellers' cash journals, reconciliation registers, and a photocopy of the bank's articles of incorporation.

Austin, William Claude (1880–1946) 45
Papers 1920–1943
71.33 feet

Lawyer. Case and client files (1920–1943) from Austin's law firm in Altus, Oklahoma, in which Robert B. Harbison and David Ross Rutherford were associate members.

Unpublished finding aid available.

Ayer, Hugh M. 46
Printed materials 1952–1953
4 items

Historian. Reprints (1952–1953) from the *Indiana Magazine of His-*

tory, and a paper read at a historical society convention, all written by Ayer, concerning the medical career of Joseph Rodes Buchanan.

Babcock, James M. (b. 1926)   **47**
Papers 1900–1953
.10 foot

Archivist. Correspondence (1951–1953) concerning the University of Oklahoma's Western History Collections and the nomination of Luther H. Evans for the post of Librarian of Congress, along with history-related printed materials (1900–1953).

Bacon, Charles W.   **48**
Records 1891–1917
11 items

Pharmacist. Certificates and diplomas (1891–1917) awarded to Bacon during his career as a pharmacist in Oklahoma.

Badger, Ina   **49**
Papers 1898–ca. 1925
5 items

Collector. A yearbook (1898–1899) of the Pioneer Club, a women's club in Chickasha, Oklahoma; two letters (n.d.); notes (ca. 1925) about early settlers on Bitter Creek near Chickasha; and a notebook (n.d.) of recipes.

Baehl, Zelma I.   **50**
Papers 1918–1964
.10 foot

Collector. Correspondence (1926–1930), newspaper clippings (1927–1964), and printed materials (n.d.) regarding the life and career of Colonel George H. Wark, Prohibition Director of Kansas, and U.S. Prohibition Administrator for the Fifteenth District (Missouri, Kansas, Oklahoma, and Arkansas).

Bailey, Hurshel   **51**
Records 1846–1930
1.66 feet

Collector. Bills, land deeds, leases, and correspondence of the Cocke family (1846–1930) and of the Ben Lafayette and Brothers Company (1900–1910) of Checotah, Indian Territory.

Unpublished finding aid available.

Baker, Frances   52
Printed material 1916
1 item

Author. A copy of an appeal syllabus (1916) of Duncan vs. Cactus Mining Company, a personal injury lawsuit.

[14]

Baker, Jesse Albert (1853–1925)   53
Papers 1853–1928
.10 foot

Judge. An election certificate (1906) and a letter (1907) from William H. Murray regarding Baker's service as a delegate to the Oklahoma Constitutional Convention; letters (1898–1922) from territorial governor Cassius M. Barnes, Oklahoma governor J. B. A. Robertson and state supreme court justice Summers Hardy; a transcript (ca. 1890) of the story of Baker's participation in the run into the Cherokee Strip; and one copy of *The Barking Water* (1928), a magazine published in Wewoka, Oklahoma.

Baldwin, Delmar H.   54
Papers 1820–1950
.33 foot

Collector. One letter (1937) from former U.S. marshal Chris Madsen; a proclamation by Oklahoma Territory governor Cassius M. Barnes welcoming Theodore Roosevelt; a reprint (n.d.) of a publication entitled *Opening of Kiowa, Comanche, Apache and Wichita Indian Lands in the Territory of Oklahoma*; a program of the Roosevelt Rough Rider Reunion of 1900 in Oklahoma City, Oklahoma Territory; a typescript (n.d.) entitled "Oklahoma Criminals with a History, 1889–1933"; a copy of a magazine (1899) entitled *Buffalo Bill's Wild West and Congress of Rough Riders of the World*; and a textbook (n.d) entitled *The American Spelling Book* by Noah Webster.

Balenti, Bill, and Lucille Balenti   55
Papers 1904–1975
.33 foot

Collectors. Newspaper clippings and photocopied images (1904–1975) regarding the Balenti family, and manuscript and typescript narratives (n.d.) of Indian legends by Arapaho, Shoshone, Cherokee, Cheyenne, and Seneca Indians, among others.

Balyeat, Frank Allen (1886–1971)   56
Printed materials 1774–1960
.33 foot

Educator. Typescripts and notes (1926–1957) regarding Baptist missionaries to the Indians; a history (1960) of schools in Kiowa County, Oklahoma; publications (1953–1957) of the Bureau of Indian Affairs concerning American Indians and Indian education; a booklet (n.d.) on Sequoyah and the Cherokee syllabary; notes and correspondence (1926) concerning Joseph Samuel Murrow and Bacone College; a leaflet (1958) describing El Meta Bond College; and correspondence (1960) concerning Oklahoma post offices.

Bandy, Mary   57
Records 1890–1931
1.25 feet

Collector. Land title abstracts of property (1890–1931) located in Kingfisher County, Oklahoma.

Bank of Udall Collection   58
Records 1891–1896
1 item

Bank. A daybook (1891–1896) of individual accounts from the Bank of Udall, Oklahoma.

**Barbour, John (1872–1950), and
Robert Barbour (1871–1953)**   59
Records 1889–1952
40.66 feet

Pharmacists. Ledgers and account books (1889–1952); business correspondence (1900–1916); a drug registration record book (1900–1945); and sports literature (1911–1918) from the Barbour Drug Store, which John and Robert Barbour opened in Norman, Oklahoma Territory, in 1889.

Unpublished finding aid available.

Barker, N. L.   60
Ledger 1945
1 item

Physician. A daybook (1945) listing appointments from Barker's medical practice in Paris, Texas.

[15]

Barnes, Arch 61
Papers 1877–1900
.10 foot

Collector. Correspondence (1877–1900) concerning Barnes's family matters and property taxes.

Barnes, D. Elijah (b. ca. 1850) 62
Papers 1876–1879
2 items

Physician. A diploma (1876) awarded to Barnes by the University of Louisville, granting him a degree in medicine and a certificate (1879) licensing Barnes to practice medicine in Texas.

Barnes, Sudie McAlester (1873–1953) 63
Papers 1875–1920
.33 foot

Homemaker. A diary (1880s) kept by Barnes while at Baird College in Clinton, Missouri; a published letter (n.d.) from J. J. McAlester, founder of McAlester, Oklahoma, and a prominent figure in territorial politics, to the Dawes Commission and the Choctaw Commissioners; and correspondence (1900–1929) relating to Barnes and her family's business and personal affairs.

Barrett, Hershel 64
Manuscript 1850–1890
1 item

Pioneer. A short, typewritten manuscript (n.d.) entitled "Frontier Experiences of Hershel Barrett" recounting Barrett's participation in the Oklahoma land run of 1889 and subsequent life in Earlsboro, Oklahoma Territory.

Barrett, Paula Colby 65
Printed materials 1981–1984
2 items

Author. Two magazine articles (1981–1984) by Paula Colby Barrett regarding the Colby Motor Company of Iowa and its product, the Colby automobile.

Bartell, E. C. 66
Papers 1862
1 item

Traveler. Typescript of a letter (1862) from E. C. Bartell to his wife regarding his experiences traveling from Springfield, Illinois, to Kansas to attend a trial. Bartell primarily describes the land in the Topeka, Kansas, area.

Bass, Althea Leah Bierbower (1892–1988) 67
Papers 1847–ca. 1960
.33 foot

Historian. Essays (1847–1850) written by Sarah Worcester, a daughter of missionaries to the Cherokees, while a student at Mount Holyoke Female Seminary; unpublished manuscripts (ca. 1950–1960) by Althea Bass, entitled "The Inheritance of Alice Robertson," "I Raise This Glass to Jennie," "Harriet Bunce Wright, a Charleston Lady Among the Choctaws," "A Summer Thanksgiving-the Seneca Green Corn Festival," and "Standing Bear of the Ponca Nation," along with correspondence and research notes (ca. 1957) regarding William L. Bear and his role in the founding of Osborne, Kansas.

Bass, Henry Benjamin (1897–1975) 68
Papers 1861–1966
12 feet

Historian and collector. Materials (1962–1965) from Bass's participation with the Oklahoma Civil War Centennial Commission, including general correspondence and correspondence regarding Abraham Lincoln; and subject files regarding Civil War historical sites, events, personalities, and programs received from other state commissions. Also included in the collection are Bass's travel diaries (1943–1966); correspondence (1933–1936) to and from patriotic societies; correspondence (1935–1940) from J. Edgar Hoover regarding conferences on crime; speeches (1935–1940) by Hoover; and reports (1933–1936) from conferences regarding crime.

Unpublished finding aid available.

Bates, S. R. 69
Records 1930–1943
1 foot

Physician. Patient account ledgers (1930–1943) and other financial records from Bates's medical practice in Wagoner, Oklahoma.

Battenburg Press Collection 70
Printed materials ca. 1950–1955
.10 foot

Commercial press. Books (1951–1954), pamphlets, calling cards, Christmas cards, announcements, and other items printed by the Battenburg Press in Norman, Oklahoma.

Battey, Thomas C. 71
Papers 1824–1897
.33 foot

Teacher. Battey's diaries (1872–1884) and correspondence with family members (1873–1874) regarding his experience as a teacher of Indians, along with a book (1876) by Battey entitled *Life and Adventures of a Quaker Among the Indians*, containing substantial manuscript revision. The collection also includes newspaper articles (1897) regarding Battey, and copies of Sac and Fox treaties (1824-1868) with the United States.

Baum, F. J. 72
Printed materials 1899–1925
.25 foot

Physician. An account book (1899–1901) from his medical practice and a manuscript and printed copy (1925) of an article by Baum entitled "The Modern Management of Acute Gonorrhoea."

Baumgartner, Frederick M., and A. Marguerite Baumgartner 73
Papers 1930–1987
4 feet

Ornithologists. Correspondence (1930–1978), research notes (1930–1978) and preliminary manuscripts (1979–1987) regarding the habits and species of birds indigenous to Oklahoma and accumulated by the Baumgartners while writing their book, *Oklahoma Bird Life*.

Unpublished finding aid available.

Beaird, Thomas Marion (b. ca. 1897) 74
Papers 1921
2 items

University administrator. Certificates (1921) granting Beaird membership into the University of Oklahoma chapters of the Delta Sigma Rho and Pi Kappa Alpha fraternities.

Beam, J. P. 75
Records 1929–1941
2 items

Physician. Two ledgers (1929–1941) relating to Beam's medical practice.

Beck Family Collection 76
Papers 1907–1944
1 foot

Family collection. Two accounts receivable ledgers (1907–1908) from the G. W. Beck General Merchandise Company; three scrapbooks (1912–1944) kept by Ethel Beck, containing correspondence and mementos from her high school days, and clippings regarding local events in the Miami, Oklahoma, area; and a high school diploma for Mabel Beck, Miami, Oklahoma.

Bell, Earl L. 77
Papers 1869–1966
.33 foot

Collector. Receipts (1869–1909) for business transactions between Thomas J. Stephenson and merchants of Vicksburg, Mississippi; contracts (1881) with the Northern Pacific Railroad Company for the sale of land in Washington and Idaho territories; and letters (1876–1930) to the railroad from homesteaders regarding their purchases of land from the railroad.

Bell, Jack 78
Papers 1937–1970
2.66 feet

Journalist. Manuscripts and galley proofs (1960–1962) of books by Bell, including *The Johnson Treatment*, *Mr. Conservative: Barry Goldwater*, and *The Splendid Misery*; and typescripts of interviews (1960–1965) with Hubert H. Humphrey, Lyndon B. Johnson, John F. Kennedy, and Robert F. Kennedy. Bell's correspondence (1945–1970) with political figures, including Dwight D. Eisenhower, Everett Dirksen, Barry Goldwater, J. Edgar Hoover, Hubert H. Humphrey, Lyndon B. Johnson, Edward M. Kennedy, Richard M. Nixon, William Proxmire, Douglas MacArthur, Nelson A. Rockefeller, Harry S. Truman, and Adlai E. Stevenson is in the collection, along with newspaper articles (1937–1970) written by Bell on various topics.

Unpublished finding aid available.

Bell, Robert E. 79
Papers 1936–1977
.25 foot

Anthropologist. Correspondence (1949); notes (n.d.); and publications (1948–1951) concerning a field trip headed by Bell in 1949 to the Harlan Site, near Fort Gibson, Cherokee County, Oklahoma. Included in the collection are notes (1950) by Kenneth Orr concerning the Spiro Site in LeFlore County, Oklahoma, and minutes (1939–1942), along with related records (1936–1943) of the Oklahoma State Archaeological Society.

Belt, Robert V. 80
Papers 1885–1898
.33 foot

Government employee and attorney. Five letter books (1885–1898) containing correspondence from Belt, an assistant commissioner of Indian affairs, to government officials regarding the administration of federal Indian policy and legal matters of his private law practice.

Belvin, G. N. 81
Papers 1874–1929
.33 foot

Collector. A collection of documents (1874–1929), most in English, but many in the Choctaw and Creek Indian languages. The papers include correspondence, postcards, bankbooks, mortgages, wills, speeches, allotment certificates, homestead patents, deeds, licenses, and printed materials. The documents in English indicate that much of the collection concerns the Four Mothers Society.

Benedict, John D. 82
Papers 1912–1931
.10 foot

Physician. Personal correspondence of John D. Benedict (1912–1930); a program (1931) from the First Presbyterian Church of Muskogee; and a booklet depicting the life of Herbert Hoover.

Bennett, (Mrs.) Harold R. 83
Papers 1903
15 items

Collector. Eleven checks (1903) drawn on the Bank of Commerce,

Okmulgee, Indian Territory; and four receipts (1903) regarding the building of a church.

Benson, Mildred June Tompkins (1915–1981)   84
Papers 1948–1981
27 feet

Mayor. Correspondence (1954–1981), certificates (1953–1981), municipal reports (1948–1961), and agendas and minutes (1954–1981) of the Norman, Oklahoma, city council and of several city government boards, including those governing environmental and noise pollution and the quality of water; publications, including newsletters and brochures, published by the League of Women Voters of the United States; and one manuscript, jointly authored by Benson and Cortez A. M. Ewing, regarding presidential nominating politics in 1952. Benson was active in Norman politics and her papers reflect the governance of the municipality for the period 1954–1981.

Unpublished finding aid available.

Benson, Oliver (1911–1999)   85
Papers 1932–1978
13 feet

Professor. Research files (ca. 1950–1978), correspondence (1949–1968), student composition books and notes (1932–1937), publications and manuscripts (ca. 1960–1976), and related materials concerning the life and career of Oliver Benson, a professor of political science at the University of Oklahoma, 1936–1981. Benson taught and studied in the areas of political science, statistics, and international relations.

Unpublished finding aid available.

Benson, Robert R.   86
Papers 1890–1962
2.33 feet

Historian. Manuscripts and typescripts (n.d.) by Benson regarding Lee Vining Creek, California; the boundaries of New Mexico, Colorado, and No Man's Land and the panhandle of Oklahoma; the Pecos River; the tri-state corner of Oklahoma, New Mexico and Colorado; Charles Goodnight's trail; and several other locales in the American West, along with a history (n.d.) of the American Garden Service.

Unpublished finding aid available.

Benton, Joseph Horace (1898–1975) 87
Papers 1815–1970
1.66 feet

Professor. Correspondence (1815–1893) from Benton's family; correspondence (1892–1896) from Giuseppe Verdi and Francesco Tamagno; memorabilia (1913–1970) concerning Lynn Riggs; scores (1911–1926) of Franz Joseph Haydn's "The Seasons" and Felix Mendelssohn's "Elijah"; four Japanese music books, one autographed by Giacomo Puccini; programs (1899–1968) from various musical productions; scrapbooks (1900–1967) of reviews and programs; clippings (1924–1939); and posters (1924–1934) advertising the performances of Benton, a University of Oklahoma professor of voice who sang professionally under the name of Joseph Bentonelli.

Unpublished finding aid available.

Berry, Everett, and Jean Berry 88
Papers 1893–1926
.66 foot

Collectors. Correspondence (1926) between Glenn C. Clark and Emil R. Kraettli; a speech (1926) by Glenn C. Clark for the inauguration of William B. Bizzell as president of the University of Oklahoma; and publications (1905, 1926), including *The Trail*, the Norman, Oklahoma, high school yearbook, and clippings from Norman, Oklahoma, newspapers.

Berry, Josie Craig 89
Letter 1937
1 item

Collector. A letter (1937) written to Josie Craig Berry from Ralph Ellison, Pulitzer-Prize-winning author of *Invisible Man*.

Berry, Roger M. 90
Printed materials 1909–1939
3 items

Collector. An annual report of the city of Norman, Oklahoma, (1938–1939); a news clipping regarding early University of Oklahoma faculty member Vernon Louis Parrington; and a scrapbook of photos, programs, calendars, and brochures (1909–1914) depicting student life at the University of Oklahoma.

Berry, Virgil (1866–1954)   91
Papers 1895–1953
.50 foot

Physician. Clippings (1951–1953) of Berry's column in the *Okmulgee Daily Times*; copies of the American Medical Association delegates handbook and program (1908); and a typescript memoir entitled "Experiences of a Pioneer Doctor in Indian Territory," in which Berry describes his medical practice in Chouteau, Indian Territory, 1890; his experiences as the first physician in Wagoner, Indian Territory, 1891–1898; as a physician to the Seminole tribe, 1898–1901; and as a physician in Wetumka, Oklahoma, 1901–1909, and Okmulgee, Oklahoma, 1909–1947.

Berry, William Aylor (b. 1915)   92
Papers 1941–1950
1 foot

Lawyer. Campaign material (1950) from Berry's race for the Democratic nomination to the fifth Oklahoma congressional district, including press releases, radio spots, speeches, and three scrapbooks of newspaper clippings, along with a scrapbook (1941–1946) containing material about Berry's experiences as a prisoner of war of the Japanese in the Philippine Islands.

Berthrong, Donald J.   93
Papers 1750–1879
13 feet

Professor. Photocopies of correspondence (1786–1918) of government officials regarding Great Plains Indian tribes and their relations and treaties with the United States; treaties (1803–1875) between these tribes and the United States; maps (1750–1876) of treaty areas; and manuscripts (1965) regarding the Indians of the Great Plains.

Unpublished finding aid available.

Bethany Nazarene College Collection   94
Printed materials 1952–1954
3 items

College. Issues of *The B-PC Historian* (1952–1954) published by the Bethany-Peniel College Historical Society.

[23]

Betts, D. C. 95
Records 1916–1941
1.33 feet

Merchant. Business correspondence (1927–1940); ledgers recording cash sales (1918–1928); business accounts (1916–1941); and expenses (1917–1934) from the D. C. Betts Supply Company, suppliers of mining equipment, in Quapaw, Oklahoma.

Unpublished finding aid available.

Betzinez, Jason (b. 1860) 96
Manuscript 1942
1 item

Farmer. A 145–page manuscript (1942) entitled "My People—A Story of the Apaches."

Bevan, Wilbur Harrison 97
Papers 1907–1942
1 item

Collector. A journal (1914–1918) containing quotations, poetry, lecture notes, and notes for self-improvement collected during Bevan's service in World War I, along with lists of personal property (1936–1938), school memorabilia (1907–1911), and correspondence (1942).

Bienfang, Ralph David (1905–1975) 98
Papers 1900–1945
2 feet

Pharmacist and professor. Bound sketchbooks (1933–1952) of animals and plants; manuscripts (1956–1957), notebooks (1932–1948), and workbooks (1939–1941) written by Bienfang and relating to pharmacognosy; correspondence (1942) and printed material (1944–1945) relating to the role of pharmacy in military history; and Bienfang's collection of postage stamps and seals (ca. 1930–1960).

Unpublished finding aid available.

Biggers, Jesse, and Helen Biggers 99
Printed materials 1892–1940
1.10 feet

Collectors. Travel brochures (ca. 1920–1940); postcards, greeting cards, and calendars (1892–1908); books (ca. 1920–1930), including cookbooks and do-it-yourself guides, and University of Oklahoma directories and programs (ca. 1900).

Unpublished finding aid available.

Billings, James F.   100
Papers 1878–1897
.10 foot

School superintendent. Correspondence (1878–1897) from James F. Billings, city magistrate and superintendent of schools in Clay Center, Kansas, to his family concerning business affairs, illnesses, social events, and daily life in several Kansas towns.

Bingham, George   101
Printed material 1909
1 item

Photographer. A calendar (1909) featuring a photograph of Bingham Photograph Gallery in Rogers, Arkansas.

Bittle, William E. (b. 1926)   102
Papers 1949–1965
2.33 feet

Professor and anthropologist. Typescripts of anthropological field notes and oral interviews (1949–1965) collected by William E. Bittle and his students about the Kiowa-Apache tribe of Oklahoma. Topics addressed include culture, customs, games, kinship, ethnobotany, and others.

Unpublished finding aid available.

Bizzell, William Bennett (1876–1944)   103
Papers 1910–1945
11.25 feet

University president. Personal and business correspondence (1910–1945), including correspondence from Bizzell's tenure as president of Texas A&M College, his association with Drury College in Springfield, Missouri, and letters of condolence to his family upon his death; official correspondence (1925–1941) from Bizzell's tenure as president of the University of Oklahoma; University of Oklahoma sociology department lecture notes and class materials (1941–1943); correspondence, circulars, and reports (1941–1944) from Bizzell's tenure as a director of the Federal Home Loan Bank of Topeka, Kansas; reprints (n.d.); manuscripts of articles and speeches (n.d.) by Bizzell; correspondence (1940–1944) concerning Bizzell's publications; a genealogy of the Bizzell family; and class notes (ca. 1920) taken by Bizzell while attending Baylor and Columbia universities.

Unpublished finding aid available.

**Blachly, Lucile Spire, and
Charles Dallas Blachly (1883–1959)**   104
**Papers 1924–1955
6 feet**

Physicians. Correspondence (1924–1955) regarding personal affairs and selected national affairs such as health care, socialized medicine, the threat of nuclear weapons, and the U.S. government's response to those issues. The correspondence also refers to the Oklahoma County Consumers Council, a depression-era federal agency established by the National Emergency Council. Other series include manuscripts (ca. 1915–1935) by the Blachlys on various aspects of national health, and a short autobiography of Lucile Blachly; certificates and diplomas (1928–1950) awarded the Blachlys for the practice of medicine; minutes (1934–1936) of the meetings of the Oklahoma County Consumers Council and of its committees; and publications (ca. 1932–1936) of the Oklahoma County Consumers Council regarding the results of surveys by that agency investigating the prices of food and the availability and quality of housing and health care in the Oklahoma City, Oklahoma, area. Correspondents include Eleanor Roosevelt and Pitirim Sarokin.

Unpublished finding aid available.

Black, Albert Hamilton (1936–)   105
**Manuscript 1492–1985
1 item**

Tribal historian. A typewritten manuscript (ca. 1985) by Black entitled "Ceremony of the Earth People," regarding the history and religious ceremonies of the Cheyenne and Arapaho Indians from the time of first contact with Europeans to the 1980s. The author details the procedures and appropriate time of each ceremony.

Blakemore, Jesse Lee (1862–1953)   106
Records 1913–1931
2.66 feet

Physician. Account books (1913–1929) and daybooks (1916–1931) from Blakemore's medical practice in Muskogee, Oklahoma.

[27]

Blanchard, James Lyon   107
Letter 1852
1 item

Pioneer. A copy of a letter (1852) by Blanchard describing his journey to the California gold-mining camp of Placerville and events in the camp.

Blanding, Donald Benson (1894–1957)   108
Papers 1938–1946
.10 foot

Poet and author. Correspondence (1940–1946) of Don and Dorothy Blanding regarding his books and poetry, and their travels and friends; postcards (1940–1946) from the Blandings sent from various points in their travels; newspaper clippings (n.d.) regarding Blanding and his books; and poetry (n.d.) by Blanding.

Blanton, (Mrs.) James T., Jr.   109
Papers 1827–1941
3 items

Collector. A biographical sketch (1939) of Smith Paul, who was raised by the Chickasaw Indians and for whom Pauls Valley, Oklahoma, is named, along with two lists (ca. 1941) of inscriptions taken from tombstones in the old Indian cemeteries at Pauls Valley and at Whitebead, a historic village in the Chickasaw Nation and now in Garvin County, Oklahoma.

Blew, W. Bryan   110
Records 1949–1950
1 foot

Collector. Records (1949–1950), including correspondence and scrapbooks of Oklahoma Lions clubs during Blew's term as a district governor.

Blinn, Richard F.   111
Papers 1861–1991
.33 foot

Pioneer. Correspondence, newspaper clippings, photographs, governmental reports, maps, copies of claims, a transcript of a diary, and related research notes (1861–1991) regarding the life of Richard F. Blinn and his family. The wife and child of Blinn were taken captive by Cheyenne Indians in 1868.

Blomshield, John   112
Papers 1947
2 items

Writer. An article (1947) by John Blomshield about artist Philip Evergood, for *47: The Magazine of the Year*, along with a letter from Evergood regarding the article.

Boatman, Andrew Nimrod "Jack" (b. 1887)   113
Papers 1922–1951
.10 foot

Attorney. Correspondence (1922–1951) regarding the University of Oklahoma Alumni Association, of which Boatman was president in 1924 and 1925, and Oklahoma politics.

Bodine, John James   114
Papers 1956–1957
.10 foot

Ethnologist. Three letters (1956–1957) describing Bodine's travels in Mexico and Guatemala. He was employed as a manager of a large ranch in Guatemala, and one letter (n.d.) describes the ranch and its native employees.

Boggs, Herbert Otho   115
Papers 1830–1889
8 items

Collector. Photocopies of Choctaw Indian documents including an occupation permit (1889); a sales brochure (n.d.) from the Sacred Heart Abbey in Sacred Heart, Oklahoma; a letter (1845) from George Harkins describing the conditions among the Choctaws since their removal from Mississippi to Indian Territory; and a letter (1874) from Peter Pitchlynn to his nephew W. B. Pitchlynn regarding Choctaw politics.

Boirun, G. D.   116
Papers 1897–1921
3 items

Farmer. A ledger (1897–1901) of prices and kinds of liquor sold in a saloon in Burnett, Indian Territory; a ledger (1917–1921) in which Boirun chronicled the weather and day-by-day activities on his farm near Burnett, including a record of farm sales and purchases (1897–1902); and a letter (1908) from Mrs. Boirun's sister describing the problems of farming in the Van Alstyne, Texas, area.

[29]

Boke, Norman   117
Papers n.d.
1 item

Botanist. A brief manuscript (n.d.) on the *Cycas circinalis* (Sago palm) in the Marianas Islands of the South Pacific Ocean.

Bollinger, Clyde John   118
Papers 1915–1978
8 feet

Professor. Papers (1915–1978), including correspondence between geography professor Clye John Bollinger and other geographers; research notes with calculations for Bollinger's solar atlas; and reprints of eight articles by Bollinger.

Unpublished finding aid available.

Bond, (Mrs.) A. L.   119
Printed materials 1912
3 items

Collector. Typescripts of newspaper articles regarding Oklahoma history and the Five Civilized Tribes' role in the U.S. Civil War.

Bond, George M. (1847–1922)   120
Printed materials 1916–1951
5 items

Judge. An obituary (1922) of Bond, the first county judge of Jefferson County, Oklahoma; a list (n.d.) of Bond's brothers and sisters and their birth dates; a certificate of election (1916) to the Oklahoma legislature; and two broadsides (1951) advertising the sale of a Hereford bull.

Bone, Kathleen 121
Papers 1903–1906
7 items

Collector. Allotment certificates (1903–1906) for land in the Chickasaw Nation, Indian Territory.

Bonner, Thomas N. 122
Printed material 1953
1 item

Physician. A reprint (1953) of an article by Bonner, entitled "The Social and Political Ideas of Midwestern Physicians 1840–1940: Chicago as a Case History."

Boomer Literature Collection 123
Printed materials 1859–1905
1 foot

Subject collection. Flyers, leaflets, and handbills (1859–1905) advertising land in Oklahoma, both settled and unsettled, along with booklets, leaflets and handbills (1859–1905) advertising the new cities, counties, and regions of the territory. The collection also contains a proclamation (1893) by territorial Governor William Renfrow, and a commencement ceremony program (1882) from Indian University in Muskogee, Indian Territory.

Unpublished finding aid available.

Boone, Charles A. 124
Records 1925–1966
3 feet

Pharmacist. Financial ledgers (1925–1966) recording daily purchases and sales of a drug store in Sentinel, Oklahoma.

Booth, G. R. 125
Records 1905–1915
.25 foot

Physician. Four daybooks (1906–1910) and one account ledger (1911–1915) from Booth's medical practice near Hughes, Oklahoma.

Boren, David L. (1941–) 126
Papers and artifacts 1905–2001
.66 foot

University president. Correspondence from University of Oklahoma alumni and political figures to University of Oklahoma president David L. Boren regarding OU events and history; artifacts and a scrapbook regarding OU sports and OU history; the OU commencement address by Sam Nunn; and publications regarding OU history and OU personalities. The collection also contains items such as a set of photograph printing plates of OU administrators and professors; a U.S. flag bearing forty-six stars; an engineering student's set of drafting tools; photographs of OU president emeritus Joseph Brandt and of the bombed Alfred P. Murrah Federal Building in Oklahoma City; and printed programs of the Y.M.C.A. and the Y.W.C.A.

Unpublished finding aid available.

Boswell, H. D. 127
Printed materials 1950–1952
6 items

Physician. Newspaper clippings regarding Boswell's tenure as company physician for the Eagle-Picher Mining and Smelting Company at the Henryetta, Oklahoma, smelter.

Bosworth, Caroline M. 128
Printed materials 1942–1945
7 items

Collector. Seven World War II ration books (1942–1945) issued by the Oklahoma City, Oklahoma, ration board.

Boudinot, Frank J. (b. 1866) 129
Printed materials 1893–1910
.25 foot

Politician. Typescripts of newspaper editorials and articles (1893–1910) regarding the activities of Boudinot, an attorney and political leader in the Cherokee Nation and the Keetoowah Society.

Boudinot, W. P. (d. 1898)   130
Printed materials 1870–1899
.25 foot

Editor. Typescripts of articles (1870–1899) by or about W. P. Boudinot, from various Cherokee Indian newspapers and relating to the Indian policy of the federal government, the Cherokee Orphan Asylum, land transfers, and railroads in Indian Territory.

Bowen, Myrtle Evans (1898–1975)   131
Papers 1898–1975
.10 foot

Pioneer. Biographical and genealogical material (1898–1975) written by Bowen describing frontier and pioneer life in Oklahoma Territory and Indian Territory.

Bower, B. M. (1871–1940)   132
Papers 1882–1951
1.5 feet

Author. Business and personal correspondence (1924–1941) of western fiction writer B. M. Bower and family members; manuscripts and research notes (1904–1940) for books by Bower; publishing and copyright contracts (1904–1951); and photographs (1882–1911) of the Bower family.

Unpublished finding aid available.

Bowling, Clara Ellen Merkel   133
Printed materials 1937–1944
2 items

Collector. Two copies of the *Pauls Valley Enterprise* (1937, 1944), one of which contains an account of the death of R. E. Bowling.

Boyd, David Ross (1853–1936)   134
Papers 1899–1957
.75 foot

University president. Correspondence (1899–1943) between Boyd, his family, and others, including Edward E. Dale, William B. Bizzell, and George B. Parker, regarding the establishment of the University of Oklahoma, its formative years, and the tenure of Boyd as its first president; speeches (n.d.) delivered by Boyd regarding the university and its early faculty and personalities; newspaper clippings (n.d.) regarding Boyd and the university; contracts (1892) signed by Boyd and the university's Board of Regents hiring him as president; certificates (1903–1924) of appreciation and recognition awarded Boyd by institutions and organizations; obituaries and memorials (1936–1937) of Boyd; genealogies of the Boyd and Ross families; event programs (1900–1909) recording university fine arts, athletic, baccalaureate and commencement activities, as well as those of the Norman, Oklahoma, chapters of the Y.M.C.A. and Y.W.C.A.; songs, music, and yells (ca. 1905) of the University of Oklahoma; and posters (1902–1907) advertising University of Oklahoma football games and fine arts events. Also included in this collection is a manuscript by Mary Alice Boyd, daughter of David Ross Boyd, describing the Boyds' life in Arkansas City, Kansas, their move to Oklahoma Territory, and their impressions of and experiences in early Norman, Oklahoma, and at the University of Oklahoma, with accounts of tornadoes, lawless Indians, racial tension, and personalities.

Unpublished finding aid available.

Boydston, Samuel M. (b. 1884) 135
Papers 1908–1927
.25 foot

Union activist. Financial secretary's ledger (1908–1911) for United Mine Workers Local #1864 (Wilburton, Oklahoma); correspondence (1916–1922) concerning Boydston's activities as an Oklahoma United Mine Workers board member from Sub-District #1, U.M.W. #21, including member complaints submitted for arbitration.

Boyer, Dave (b. 1874) 136
Papers 1913–1946
.25 foot

Politician. Correspondence (1913–1946) regarding Boyer's term in the Oklahoma state senate, a political appointment for his son Wilfred (1931), and his own appointment as senate auditor (1933).

Braden, John 137
Printed materials 1938–1948
.10 foot

Philatelist. Thirty-one envelopes bearing cancelled stamps, mostly commemorating the first day of issue of the 1948 stamp honoring Will Rogers, along with one noting National Air Mail Week in 1938. Many of the envelopes commemorating Rogers have scenes of Claremore, Oklahoma, Rogers's home town.

Bragg, Arthur Norris (b. 1898) 138
Papers 1934–1968
10.33 feet

Zoologist. Correspondence (1946–1967) with colleagues and associates regarding Bragg's research and publications; reprints of articles (1934–1968) in his subject field, along with galley proofs and book manuscripts (n.d.) by Bragg regarding amphibians and the zoology of Oklahoma.

Unpublished finding aid available.

Brandt, Joseph August (1899–1981) 139
Papers 1915–1980
4 feet

University president. Correspondence (1940–1980) with professors, academic deans and administrators of the University of Oklahoma, the University of Oklahoma Press, and others; speeches (1948–1950) by Brandt; and articles (1940–1948) written or collected by Brandt.

Unpublished finding aid available.

Branen, Joseph L. 140
Records 1941–1949
1 foot

Collector. Chapter reports (1948–1949) and correspondence (1948–1949) from Branen's term as district governor of Oklahoma Lions clubs, along with programs (1941) for the fiftieth anniversary of the Marshall (Oklahoma) Christian Church.

Unpublished finding aid available.

Branson, Carl Colton (1906–1975) 141
Papers 1900–1975
8 feet

Geologist. Correspondence (1900–1975) regarding the geology of Oklahoma and the affairs of the Oklahoma Geological Survey, of which Branson was a longtime director.

Unpublished finding aid available.

John Bray Society Collection 142
Printed materials 1979–1980
.33 foot

Heritage organization. Newspaper clippings (1979–1980) regarding people, places, and functions, from Oklahoma newspapers the *Cordell Beacon*, the *Blanchard News*, and the *Moore Monitor*.

Brazell, James C. (1868–1948) 143
Papers 1911–1948
.10 foot

Oilman and aviator. A scrapbook (1932–1948) of photographs, clippings, and memorabilia relating to Brazell's interest in flying, along with a copy of an account (1911) of the Civil War experiences of Brazell's father, J. H. Brazell.

Breeding, (Mrs.) W. K. 144
Printed materials 1932
4 items

Songwriter. Musical scores and lyrics of two songs (1932) by Breeding, entitled "My Dearest" and "Life I Love Best."

Brennan, John 145
Letter 1867
1 item

Soldier. A letter (1867) by Brennan concerning his service in the Confederate States Army during the Civil War.

Bressie, R. M. (b. 1848) 146
Papers 1885–1975
.10 foot

Rancher. Genealogical papers (1885–1975) of the Bressie family, including correspondence (1885–1975), news clippings (1950–1960), and reminiscences (1963) concerning the local history of Bressie, Oklahoma, and Ford, Oklahoma.

Brewster, Edythe Pearl 147
Papers 1860–1950
.10 foot

Collector. Two biographical typescripts (n.d.) recounting the life of Anna Amelia Doubleday Stanton and her family history. One of the typescripts contains several cowboy-related stories.

Brillhart, Norman W. 148
Printed materials 1960–1974
.33 foot

Collector. Newspaper clippings on forts, battles, monuments, and trails (1960–1974), with an emphasis on George Armstrong Custer. Three items describe the 1965 dedication of the restored Fort Washita, Oklahoma.

Brinkley, William C. 149
Papers 1938–1993
17 feet

Author and journalist. Brinkley's manuscripts and galley proofs (1948–1988); clippings, reviews, and business letters (1945–1993); *Life* magazine (1950–1957) materials, including text pieces, background notes, and picture stories; biographical information and correspondence with publishers and agents (1938–1993); and a diary kept by Brinkley during World War II. Also in the collection are magazine articles (1952–1963) from *Life* and *Holiday* and newspaper clippings (1939–1944) of articles written by Brinkley and published in Oklahoma newspapers.

Briscoe, Isaac 150
Letters 1849–1850
2 items

Pioneer. Two letters (1849–1850) from Isaac Briscoe to his wife, Nancy, describing his situation in the California gold fields near Sacramento.

Broaddus, Bower (1888–1949) 151
Papers 1930–1949
6.66 feet

Judge. Findings of fact, conclusions of law, and case files (1940–1949) from Broaddus's tenure as a judge for the eastern, northern, and western districts of the Tenth Federal District Court; case files (1933–1940) from Broaddus's law practice in Muskogee, Oklahoma; business and personal correspondence (1930–1949); and speeches (n.d.) of Broaddus and others.

Unpublished finding aid available.

Broken Bow Lions Club Collection 152
Printed materials 1959
5 items

Service organization. Programs, newspaper clippings, and a membership list of the Broken Bow (Oklahoma) Lions Club.

Bronson, Edgar S. (1858–1924) 153
Scrapbook 1917–1927
1 item

Editor. A scrapbook (ca. 1927) of newspaper clippings by and about Bronson, who was editor of the El Reno *American* and secretary of the Oklahoma State Press Association.

Brooks, Stratton Duluth (1870–1949) 154
Papers 1918–1919
.33 foot

University president. A scrapbook (1918–1919) containing letters and photographs sent to Brooks from Oklahomans who were fighting in World War I. The letters describe military life, fighting, and the writers' reactions to the war.

Broome, Bertram C. 155
Papers 1890–1937
.66 foot

Author. Manuscripts (n.d.) of fictional stories by Broome, set in the American Southwest in the late 1800s and entitled "Pagan of the Mesa," "Navajo Gold," "Injun Toll," and "Trail Dust." The collection also includes correspondence (1927–1934) and watercolor and ink drawings by Broome.

Brown-Wilcox Family Collection   156
Papers 1809–1994
5 feet

Family collection. Genealogical and historical documents regarding the Brown-Wilcox family and the history of Clinton, Custer County, Oklahoma, and western Oklahoma. The Brown-Wilcox family papers consist of eighty-seven volumes of copied documents including recollections, letters and cards, poems, essays, newspaper clippings, stories, drawings, invitations, obituaries, bulletins, business cards, political posters, certificates, programs, recipes, legal documents, land records, sale bills, histories, diaries, military records, coats of arms, telegrams, speeches, catalogs, calendars, and photographs.

Brown, Benjamin H.   157
Papers 1914–1920
3 items

Physician. A reprint of an article (1914) published by the Muskogee County (Oklahoma) Medical Society and entitled "Report of the Committee on Tuberculosis and Tuberculosis Anti-Sera"; a typescript of a speech (1919) by Brown to the Oklahoma State Medical Association, entitled "Diagnosis of the Pathological Heart"; and a typescript (ca. 1920) entitled "An Analysis of the Hospital Situation in Muskogee."

Brown, Hugh   158
Printed materials 1821–1865
2 items

Collector. Two typescript copies of a journal (1821–1865) recounting John Brown's study of law in Lexington, Kentucky, 1821–1822, and his activities and expenses as a planter, lawyer, and insurance agent in Camden, Arkansas, 1852–1865.

Brown, John F. (1843–1919)   159
Printed materials 1870–1907
.25 foot

Indian chief. Typescripts of news articles (1870–1907) relating to mining and grazing leases, Dawes Commission proceedings, tribal government, and politics of the Seminole Nation, along with editorials concerning John F. Brown, a businessman and principal chief of the Seminoles from 1877–1902.

[38]

An allotment certificate issued in 1904 for lands located in the Chickasaw Nation. From the Kathleen Bone Collection.

Brown, Phillip (ca. 1867–1951) 160
Papers 1898–1933
6.66 feet

Merchant. Correspondence (1898–1933); cotton record books (1904–1928); journals (1917–1933); ledgers (1904, 1921–1922); and daybooks (1923–1925) relating to the Brown Brothers Mercantile Store in Eufaula, Oklahoma, which bought cotton and invested in real estate. Unpublished finding aid available.

Brown, Samuel H. 161
Printed materials 1958
.10 foot

Indian chief. Newspaper articles regarding the death of Yuchi chief Sam W. Brown, and the return of the Yuchi Tribe to its ancestral lands in the Chattahoochee Valley, Alabama.

Brown, W. H. 162
Manuscript 1933–1969
1 item

Judge. A typescript (ca. 1969) by Brown chronicling the invention of the parking meter in Oklahoma City, Oklahoma, and Brown's role in its development.

Bryan, Frank 163
Papers 1928–1958
.33 foot

Geologist. Correspondence (1928–1932) with Gilbert Floyd of England and others concerning arrowheads and contemporary affairs, along with two manuscripts (ca. 1958) entitled "The Llano Estacado" and "Lewisville: Its Place in the Pleistocene Picture."

Bryan, J. R. 164
Papers 1896–1917
12 items

Physician. Notebooks (1906–1907) containing descriptions of diseases, cures, treatments and remedies; and diplomas and certificates (1896–1917) awarded Bryan by medical schools and the Selective Service office of Caddo County, Oklahoma.

Bryan, John   165
Papers 1864–1983
1 foot

Collector. Correspondence (1889–1891) between U.S. Supreme Court justice Joseph P. Bradley and Calvin W. Bradley; news clippings and magazine articles (1915–1973) regarding World War II, the movie *Gone With The Wind*, Martha Graham, Anna Pavlova, Will Rogers, and Wiley Post; discharge and pension papers (1864, 1908) of Civil War veteran Benjamin Ittner; a notebook (n.d.) regarding the Bertolt Brecht play "Mother Courage and Her Children"; a notebook concerning stage actresses; five notebooks (n.d.) for directors and set designers containing notes about nineteenth century fashions, glass, jewelry, furniture, and interior design; and five publications (1936–1938) produced by the National Play Bureau of the Federal Theater Project.

Bryan, John A.   166
Records 1882–1909, 1944
.25 foot

Collector. Two ledgers (1882–1909) from the post office at Nelson, Indian Territory, listing materials received and delivered, and a roster of members (1944) of the Oklahoma State Medical Association.

Bryant, William J.   167
Printed materials 1875–1878
2 items

Indian chief. Two typescripts of news articles (1875–1878) from Choctaw Nation newspapers. One concerns the nomination of Bryant for principal chief; the other deals with Bryant's approval of a Choctaw Nation law.

Buchanan, F. R.   168
Records 1915–1941
.66 foot

Physician. Daybooks (1921–1922) and ledgers (1915–1941) from Buchanan's medical practice in Canton, Oklahoma. The collection also includes an inventory (1941) of office equipment and medical instruments.

[42]

Buchanan, James Shannon   169
Papers 1850–1937
2 feet

Professor and university president. Correspondence (1902) related to Buchanan's attempts to have power and water companies established in Norman, Oklahoma; lecture notes (n.d.) for history classes; draft copies (n.d.) of his book, *The History of Oklahoma*; lecture notes (n.d.) of Katherine Buchanan, a teacher at University High School, Norman, Oklahoma; papers (1912) relating to the history of the University of Oklahoma; personal correspondence and legal papers (1893–1927) of the Buchanan family; printed propositions, journals, and committee reports (1906–1907) to the Oklahoma Constitutional Convention; guides (n.d.) for the study and teaching of English; and Delta Kappa Gamma bulletins (1936–1937).

Unpublished finding aid available.

Buffett, Richard H.   170
Papers 1918–1927
12 items

Collector. Correspondence (1918) with Havemeyers-Seamans Oil Company and Seamans Oil Company, both of Oklahoma City, Oklahoma, concerning Alvah H. Buffett's stock purchases. Also included in the collection are five stock certificates (1921–1927) from the Continental Asphalt and Petroleum Company and the Healdton Petroleum Company.

Burch, Don   171
Printed materials ca. 1982
3 items

Collector. Typescripts (1982) listing Union and Confederate commanding officers (1861–1865) who served west of the Mississippi River, and minor military operations of the region. Also in this collection is a photocopy of the *Journal of the Senate of the Confederate Legislature of Missouri* (1861).

Burchardt, August Gustave (1906–1988)   172
Records 1952–1955
.66 foot

Collector. Correspondence, publications, bulletins and membership lists, all dated 1952–1955, from international and Oklahoma Lions Club organizations, of which Burchardt was a district governor.

Burchardt, George M. 173
Directory 1926
1 item

Collector. A city telephone directory (1926) for Frederick, Oklahoma.

Burchardt, William 174 [43]
Papers 1960–1965
3.33 feet

Author. Correspondence (1960–1965) to and from Burchardt concerning the Western Writers of America. The collection also contains numerous manuscripts (n.d.) of short stories and articles by Burchardt dealing with the American West.

Unpublished finding aid available.

Burdine, C. A. 175
Papers 1903–1909
.10 foot

Government employee. Letters (1903–1909) from Burdine to his wife describing life in Indian Territory, especially in the town of Tishomingo, and his work as a member of the Dawes Commission.

Burditt, Mary Edna 176
Papers 1879–1980
.33 foot

Teacher. General correspondence (1892–1972) between members of Edna Lewis Burditt's family, including letters received from Burditt's brother, William Lewis, while principal of Farris Public School, Farris, Oklahoma, and during army training, Camp Travis, Texas; public school report cards (1912–1913, n.d.); Garvin County teacher's contract (1924); a copy of *The East Centralite*, Ada, Oklahoma (1919); newspaper clippings; a handwritten school notebook (n.d.); and school textbooks, including *Ray's Elementary Arithmetic* and several revised editions of *McGuffey's Eclectic Reader*.

Bureau of Government Research Collection 177
Papers 1889–1962
6 feet

University research bureau. Proceedings and debates of the Oklahoma Constitutional Convention (1906–1907); reports of studies made by the Oklahoma State Planning Board (1936–1938), the Oklahoma Tax

Commission (1935–1936), the Oklahoma State Legislative Council (1947–1952), the University of Oklahoma College of Business Administration (1950), and the Bureau of Government Research (1951–1961); typescripts (1910–1931) of newspaper articles relating to the Socialist Party of Oklahoma; and a chart (1962) showing the organization of Oklahoma state government.

Unpublished finding aid available.

Burney, B. C. 178
Printed materials 1878–1891
6 items

Indian chief. Typescripts of editorials (1878–1891) on Burney's governorship of the Chickasaw Nation from 1878 to 1880, and of his messages to the Chickasaw Nation legislature, which originally appeared in the *Star Vindicator,* the *Cherokee Advocate,* and the *Purcell Register.*

Burns, David A. 179
Papers 1920–1968
5 items

Collector. Photocopies of articles (1920–1960) concerning Governor Ernest W. Marland and Lew Wentz; a photocopy of a speech (1932) by Marland regarding money trusts; and a college history class paper (1968) by Burns, entitled "Characterizations of E. W. Marland."

Burns, Samuel Lee (b. 1876) 180
Papers 1899–1905
3 items

Physician. Certificates (1899–1905) issued to Burns, authorizing him to practice medicine and surgery in the Creek Nation and in the southern district of Indian Territory.

Burton, Patricia 181
Printed materials 1960–1969
.33 foot

Collector. Newspaper articles (1960–1969) and related materials on the history and development of the Shetland pony breed.

Busby, Orel (ca. 1890–1965) 182
Papers 1918–1959
3 feet

Judge. Correspondence (1942), speeches (1942), and clippings (1942) concerning Busby's unsuccessful candidacy for the Democratic nomination for U.S. senator from Oklahoma; correspondence (1918) concerning Busby's successful candidacy for a judgeship in Pontotoc County, Oklahoma; correspondence (1924–1927) from Busby's term as a regent of the University of Oklahoma; and correspondence (1935–1937) concerning his unsuccessful bid for the nomination to a federal judgeship in Oklahoma.

[45]

Bush, (Mrs.) C. S. (b. ca. 1885) 183
Printed materials 1915–1951
7 items

Teacher. Clippings (1940–1950) from the *Oklahoma Daily* and the *Pauls Valley Enterprise* regarding the history of Oklahoma, Pauls Valley, and Central Christian College (Bartlesville, Oklahoma); and a printed invitation (1915) to a party at the "Girls' Club Room."

Bush, Charles C., II 184
Papers 1749–1965
5 feet

Professor. Instructional materials (1749–1965) for college history courses; student papers (1963); manuscripts (n.d.) and published materials (1941–1960) regarding historical events; and correspondence (1950–1965) to and from Bush regarding historical events and research, along with an original letter (1829) regarding Tecumseh and the Battle of the Thames in 1813, written by a soldier who participated.

Unpublished finding aid available.

Bush, Geoffrey 185
Papers 1957
1 item

Collector. Correspondence (1957) from Geoffrey Bush to Mr. Harrison in London, England, regarding a record album.

Bushyhead, Dennis Wolf (1826–1898)   186
Papers 1879–1922
.50 foot

Indian chief. Correspondence (1879–1897); annual messages (1879–1882); speeches (1879–1887); an autobiography (1880); proclamations (1879–1885); and other papers (1879–1922) relating to political matters in which Bushyhead was involved as principal chief of the Cherokee Nation, 1879–1887, and as a representative to the Dawes Commission; and papers relating to the controversies growing out of the Cherokee Strip Livestock Association's operations.

Butcher, Nahum Ellsworth (b. 1872)   187
Papers 1957
1 item

School superintendent. A transcript of an interview (1957) conducted by Frank A. Balyeat with Butcher, the first freshman enrolled at the University of Oklahoma (1893), recounting his experiences at the university and, later, as superintendent of West Norman (Oklahoma) schools.

Butcher, W. H.   188
Printed materials 1890–1930
.10 foot

Collector. Political pamphlets (1893–1916); a speech (1896) by William Jennings Bryan; and booklets (1890–1930) concerning social and labor organizations, such as the Masons, the American Federation of Labor, and the Knights of Labor.

Buttram, Frank (b. 1886)   189
Printed materials 1904–1911
5 items

Oilman. Publications of the University of Oklahoma featuring photographs of the campus in 1905–1906.

Byrd, Hiram, and Wallace Byrd   190
Printed materials 1915–1945
.10 foot

Physicians. Reprints of journal articles (1915–1945) by Hiram and Wallace Byrd regarding tuberculosis, glaucoma, cancer, and ganglia.

Byrd, William L. (b. 1844)   191
Printed materials 1888–1906
.25 foot

Indian chief. Typescripts of Byrd's messages (1889–1892) to the Chickasaw Nation legislature, along with editorials (1888–1891), interviews (1891), and articles (1891–1906) concerning Byrd as governor of the Chickasaw Nation from 1888 to 1894 and later as Chickasaw delegate to Washington, D.C.

Byrum, Rollie E. (b. ca. 1882)   192
Diploma 1899
1 item

Student. A high school diploma (1899) issued to Byrum by Greer County, Oklahoma Territory; an Oklahoma Teacher's County Certificate (1907) and a teacher's contract (1907) for Greer County, Oklahoma Territory.

Cable Temperance Union Collection   193
Records 1884–1886
1 item

Civic organization. A notebook containing the constitution, bylaws, and proceedings of the Cable Temperance Union of Cable, Illinois. The book also contains inspirational songs and readings.

Caddo County Education Archives Collection   194
Printed materials 1945–1946
2 items

Subject collection. A Caddo County Educational Directory (1945–1946) and a Caddo County Teachers' Convention program (1945).

Caddo County Medical Association Collection   195
Papers 1904–1941
2 items

Professional organization. Ledgers (1904–1941) containing minutes of the Caddo County (Oklahoma) Medical Society, from its inception through its evolution into the Caddo County Medical Association.

Calloway, John R. 196
Papers 1920–1945
.10 foot

Physician. Note cards (1920–1930) recording patient accounts from Calloway's medical practice in Pauls Valley, Oklahoma, and abstracts of lectures (1940–1945) on surgical diagnosis and pediatrics, published by the Oklahoma State Medical Association.

Camp Supply Collection 197
Letterbook 1869–1878
1 item

Military post. A letterbook (1869–1878) containing copies of letters sent; lists of names of captured Cheyenne and Arapaho Indians; data relating to their provisioning and outfitting; and reports on hostile bands kept by the commissary supply officer at Camp Supply, Indian Territory, which was established in 1868 as a base for operations against the plains Indian tribes.

Camp, Earl F. (b. 1892) 198
Records 1922–1940
5 items

Physician. Ledgers (1922–1940) recording Camp's patient treatment and billing records for both his medical practice and the hospital he operated in Buffalo, Oklahoma.

Campbell, Anson 199
Papers 1965–1967
2 items

Collector. A letter (1967) regarding the Campbell family history and a typescript (ca. 1965) regarding the Bullock family of Lindsay, Oklahoma, and the family's contribution to the development of early Lindsay.

Campbell, Charles Duncan (b. 1877) 200
Papers 1901–1921
.10 foot

Oilman and postmaster. Correspondence (1905–1907) from Wilbur E. Campbell concerning his oil company and the Prairie Oil Company, his purchase of a Tulsa, Oklahoma, sub-division, and the introduction of a land-purchasing bill into the 1907 Oklahoma legislature. The collection also includes a letter (1907) from T. S. Boyers concerning Boyers's family history, and letters (1901) from W. T. Flynn concerning Campbell's appointment as postmaster of Apache, Oklahoma Territory.

Campbell, J. F. (1876–1934) 201
Records 1906–1934
5 feet

Physician. Ledgers (1906–1934) and daybooks (1921–1934), in which fees and services from J. F. Campbell's Mangum, Oklahoma, medical practice were recorded.

Campbell, John McKoy 202
Printed materials 1920
4 items

Judge. Program (1920) of the initiation and installation ceremony of Phi Beta Kappa, University of Oklahoma chapter; and pins and medals (ca. 1918) awarded to John McKoy Campbell by the University of Oklahoma.

Campbell, John Sidney, Sr. (1875–1961) 203
Records 1899–1934
8 feet

Businessman. Account ledgers of the Campbell Hardware Store (1909–1934) and the Campbell Funeral Home (1899–1918), both of Fairland, Indian Territory, and Oklahoma. The funeral home ledgers record the names of the deceased persons for whom undertaking services were provided and include some biographical and cause-of-death information.

Campbell, Robert Boyers 204
Papers 1907–1948
.10 foot

Collector. A letter (1907) from W. E. Campbell to his son, R. B. Campbell, describing the successes of the elder Campbell's oil company; news clippings regarding oil in Oklahoma; and a reprint (1948) of an article regarding the elder Campbell.

Campbell, S. W. (b. ca. 1850) 205
Manuscript 1926
1 item

Collector. A manuscript (1926) recounting a journey made in 1857 by Campbell's family over the Oregon Trail to Colorado to prospect for silver.

Campbell, W. H. L. 206
Printed materials 1909–1910
2 items

Clerk. Pamphlet (1909) regarding a decision by the Oklahoma Supreme Court on the legal liability of physicians and surgeons; and a political advertisement (1910) for the re-election of W. H. L. Campbell as clerk of the Oklahoma Supreme Court.

Campbell, Walter Stanley (1887–1957) 207
Papers 1800–1964
77 feet

Professor. Personal correspondence (1897–1957); correspondence with Campbell's relatives (1822–1896); correspondence with publishers and literary agents (1920–1958); literary manuscripts (ca. 1914–1957); diaries, notebooks, and journals (1901–1926); and business papers (ca. 1925–1959) regarding Campbell's writings on the West, Indians, and Oklahoma, with emphasis on transportation, fortifications, cowboys, wars and battles, criminals and outlaws, and Indian chiefs, along with original Indian art by Carl Sweezy.

Published finding aid available.

Canton, Frank M. (d. 1927) 208
Papers 1886–1927
3 feet

Lawman. Canton's correspondence (1893–1927) while a U.S. deputy marshal and Oklahoma adjutant general; reminiscences (n.d.) of his experiences in Texas, Oklahoma, Wyoming, and Alaska; newspaper clippings (n.d.) about his experiences; and related artifacts (1896–1915). The collection also contains both biographical and autobiographical material on Canton.

Unpublished finding aid available.

Cantonment Indian Agency Collection 209
Records 1902–1931
2 feet

Indian agency. Records of the Cantonment (Oklahoma) Indian Agency and Cantonment Training School, including general and official correspondence (1903–1923) regarding agency affairs, the school and its students, along with financial records such as billing and account statements, invoices and receipts, property vouchers, and applications for renewal of Indian trader licenses; applicant files (1910–1926) regarding the agency superintendent's approval and disbursal of funds of individual Indians; subject files (1902–1931) containing lease records, property cards, land patents and deeds, and miscellaneous records regarding the Seger Indian Agency, Colony, Oklahoma; and checking account stubs and receipts from the Office of the Assistant Treasurer of the U.S. (1902–1920).

[51]

Capshaw, Madison T. J. (1856–1920) 210
Papers 1884–1920
4 items

Physician. Handwritten accounts (1890–1920) of Capshaw's experiences as a physician in Norman, Oklahoma Territory, and during the World War I influenza epidemic; and of the childhood of his son, Walter Capshaw. The collection also contains a diploma (1884) issued to Madison T. J. Capshaw by the Memphis Medical College in Tennessee, granting him the M.D. degree.

Carlisle Barracks Collection 211
Papers n.d.
2 items

Collector. Hand-printed, bound manuscripts (n.d.) in the Ethiopian/Amharic language, brought to the United States from Africa during World War II and believed to be a regional religious text.

Carlock, Arlie Ernest (1873–1936) 212
Papers 1896–1936
3 items

Physician. A news clipping (1896) announcing Carlock's graduation from the Missouri Medical College in St. Louis, Missouri; a letter (1897) from a former classmate regarding the alumni of the class of

1896 and the destruction of the college by fire; and a biographical sketch (1936) of Carlock, detailing his long career as a physician in Indian Territory and Oklahoma, with an account of the establishment of a hospital at Hartshorne, Oklahoma, and the reasons for its failure.

Carmen First National Bank Collection 213
Records 1903–1934
4 feet

Bank. Ledgers (1903–1934); tellers' cash books (1905–1908); and discount and collection registers (1905–1917) from the First National Bank of Carmen, Oklahoma.

Carpenter, Everett 214
Papers 1911–1977
.10 foot

Petroleum geologist. Correspondence (1950–1977) between Dan H. Carpenter and Everett Carpenter's associates regarding Everett's fiftieth anniversary as a petroleum geologist. Some letters concern the history of petroleum geology. Other materials in the collection include Everett Carpenter's geology thesis (1911) and petroleum-related publications.

Carpenter, Paul Simon (1895–1949) 215
Papers 1910–1956
2.66 feet

Professor. Correspondence (1910–1956) to and from Carpenter regarding his university studies at the National Conservatory in Paris, his 1914 appointment to the faculty of the University of Oklahoma, his 1946 appointment as Dean of Fine Arts at the University of Oklahoma, the designation of a university building as Carpenter Hall, and his book *Music, An Art and a Business*, which was unfinished at the time of his death; Carpenter's financial records (1940–1949), including cancelled checks, bills, and receipts; note cards (n.d.) containing a bibliography of music books; scrapbooks (n.d.) containing musical scores with accompanying research notes; and publications (1870–1954) including musical scores, performance programs, and journals. Also included in the collection is a two-page genealogical listing (ca. 1949) tracing the Carpenter family history from 1675 to 1949.

Unpublished finding aid available.

Carriker, Robert C. (1940–) 216
Manuscript 1970
1 item

Historian. A manuscript (1970) of Carriker's book *Fort Supply, Indian Territory: Frontier Outpost on the Plains*, published by the University of Oklahoma Press.

Carseloway, James Manford 217
Papers 1859–1937
3 items

Historian. A manuscript (1883) containing instructions to the Cherokee National Council's Washington, D.C., delegation, as approved by D. W. Bushyhead, principal chief; a typescript concerning a flowing oil well brought in during 1859 in the Cherokee Nation; and correspondence (1937) describing the history of Grand River Dam in Oklahoma.

Carson, Frank L. 218
Papers 1902–1918
.10 foot

Physician. Lecture notes used at Tulane University (1902) and the Mayo Clinic (1906); correspondence (1917–1918) concerning Carson's service in World War I; and a professional paper by Carson about the treatment of tetanus.

Carson, Lamoine S. 219
Papers 1922–1926
.25 foot

Student. Scrapbook (1922–1926) compiled by Lamoine S. Carson as a student at the University of Oklahoma. The scrapbook contains newspaper clippings, photographs, invitations, and programs for social and athletic events.

Carter, Frank C. (1862–1954) 220
Papers 1930–1956
1 foot

Politician. Correspondence (1938–1956) regarding farm mortgages, Carter's campaigns and election as state auditor in 1938 and as Oklahoma secretary of state in 1942, his retirement from political office in 1946, and his death in 1954; a scrapbook (1930–1948) of clippings and correspondence about Carter's political career; and a certificate (n.d.) from the Oklahoma Sheriffs and Peace Officers Association, honoring him for a lifetime of service to Oklahoma law enforcement.

Carter, M. L. (d. 1923) 221
Records 1911–1924
.10 foot

Physician. An account book (1911–1913) in which Carter recorded house calls he made in Choctaw County, Oklahoma, the services rendered to each patient, and the fees charged, along with an account ledger (1923–1924) in which Carter recorded the same information for treatment in his office.

Casey, Alvin Harold 222
Records 1933–1955
.25 foot

Collector. Correspondence (1944); committee assignments (1954–1955); financial statements (1933–1946); and annual reports (1946–1954) of the Guthrie, Oklahoma, Lions Club.

Cass, Lewis 223
Papers 1825–1839
.10 foot

Army officer and statesman. Copies of letters (1825–1839) from Gen. Matthew Arbuckle, Montfort Stokes, and Jean Pierre Chouteau, written at military posts in Indian Territory to Secretary of War Lewis Cass, concerning the attempt to gather the plains Indian tribes at Camp Mason on the Canadian River for a peace conference, along with other detailed observations on Indian affairs.

Cate, Roscoe Simmons (1876–1954) 224
Papers 1819–1970
5.33 feet

Indian attorney. Diaries (1939–1949) kept by Cate; manuscripts (1876–1924) in the Creek language; copies of correspondence (1838–1937) in English, signed by officials connected with Indian affairs, including Maj. Gen. Thomas S. Jessup, Opothleyaholo, and Albert Pike; and a compilation of names and locations of Creek towns in Alabama and Oklahoma, along with briefs, trusts, and correspondence, all relating to the court case (1937–1938) concerning the estate of Jackson Barnett, one of Oklahoma's wealthiest Indians.

Unpublished finding aid available.

Cates, P. M.   225
Ledger 1927–1937
1 item

Merchant. An account ledger (1927–1937) showing the wages, wholesale purchases, and bank balances of Cates's dry-goods business in Maysville, Oklahoma.

Cattle Brands Collection   226
Poster n.d.
1 item

Subject collection. A poster (n.d.) entitled "Chart of Texas Cattle Brands Used Throughout the State with Attached Booklet Identifying Each Brand."

Caudron, Theophile (1880–1970)   227
Papers 1912–1970
1 foot

Priest. Clippings (1912–1970) concerning Monsignor Caudron's mediation in the labor disputes at Henryetta, Oklahoma, his long career as pastor of St. Michael's Catholic Church in Henryetta, his work as superintendent of the church school, his retirement in 1965, his return to his native Belgium, the subsequent closing of the school, and Caudron's death in 1970; correspondence (1965) to and from Caudron concerning the closing of the upper six grades at St. Michael's Catholic School in Henryetta; and telegrams from prominent political figures, including a letter from President Franklin D. Roosevelt.

Cayuga Nation Papers   228
Papers 1895–1953
.10 foot

Indian tribe. Correspondence (1895–1953) concerning claims by the Cayuga Indians against the state of New York, the United States, and the St. Lawrence Power Company.

Centennial Collection 229
Papers 1920–1991
1.33 feet

Subject collection. Correspondence (1988–1991), memoirs (1920–1991), scrapbooks (1920–1937), and photographs (1920–1991) collected for a special Centennial Celebration issue of *Sooner Magazine* (Volume 11, No. 2, Spring 1991). The materials document the student experiences of various OU alumni.

Unpublished finding aid available.

Center For Studies in Higher Education Collection 230
Records 1970–1986
10 feet

Research center. Records (1970–1986), including correspondence, reports, and subject files from the Oklahoma Center for Studies in Higher Education regarding the center's operation and mission as well as its participation in a number of special projects, including a training program (1972–1979) for education administrators from Saudi Arabia. Also in the collection are records relating to higher education colloquiums sponsored by the center and relating to the University of Oklahoma Budget Council, the Athletics Council, the University of Oklahoma seal, accreditation programs, and program audits.

Unpublished finding aid available.

Central State University Collection 231
Printed materials 1976
.33 foot

University. Newspaper clippings and printed materials (1976) from Central State University and Edmond, Oklahoma's celebration of the United States bicentennial in 1976. The collection also includes a score from *Oklahoma, U.S.A.: A Historical Pageant with Original Music*, with words and lyrics by Stan Hoig, and music by Bob Dillon.

Certificates and Diplomas Collection 232
Printed materials 1847–1994
4 feet

Series collection. Certificates, diplomas, and awards (1847–1994) issued by governmental entities, private and public institutions, and organizations to individuals as awards, academic degrees, appointments to office, acknowledgments of service, and expressions of appreciation.

Unpublished finding aid available.

Chaat, Robert P. 233
Records 1900–1908, 1939–1948
.10 foot

Clergyman. A minute book (1900–1908) kept by the secretary of the Apache Indian Mission at Fort Sill, Oklahoma; manuscripts (n.d.) concerning the history of the Dutch Reformed church schools, the Comanche Mission, the Warm Springs Apaches, and Indian conversion to Christianity, along with booklets, pamphlets, and newsletters (1939–1948) regarding the history and constitution of the Dutch Reformed Church, and the evils of narcotics.

[57]

Chandler National Bank Collection 234
Records 1894–1910
8 feet

Bank. Ledgers (1898–1909); note ledgers (1907–1910); journals (1894–1908); remittance registers (1894–1900); and discount registers (1895–1898) recording daily business transactions of the Chandler National Bank of Chandler, Oklahoma Territory.

Chaney, Warren P. (b. 1878) 235
Papers 1864–1935
.10 foot

Government employee. Correspondence (1904–1908); recollections (1955); allotment records (1908); Civil War papers (1864); and published materials (1932–1954) relating to Indian Territory events of the early twentieth century and reflecting Chaney's experiences while traveling through the Choctaw and Chickasaw nations as clerk-in-charge of the Choctaw-Chickasaw allotment division of the Dawes Commission.

Chapman, Berlin Basil (1900–1994) 236
Papers 1889–1955
1 foot

Historian. Photocopies of correspondence, reports, and news articles (1889–1955) by Chapman regarding the history of Oklahoma Territory, including Lincoln County, the towns of Chandler, Mountain View, and Stillwater, and the Boomers led by David L. Payne. The collection also contains material relating to Oklahoma State University and the loyalty oaths required of the state's college and university faculties during the early 1950s. Also included is a proclamation (1923) by Governor J. C. Walton declaring martial law in Okmulgee County, Oklahoma.

Unpublished finding aid available.

Chapman, T. Shelby 237
Records 1895–1911
1 foot

Physician. A typewritten account of the first meeting of the Indian Territory Medical Association in 1899; certificates (ca. 1900); copies of magazines (ca. 1910–1930); three letters (1904) of condolence on the death of Chapman's son; and seven account books (1895–1911) from his medical practice in McAlester, Oklahoma.

Checote, Samuel (1819–1884) 238
Printed materials 1867–1886
.25 foot

Indian chief. Typescripts of messages (1875–1883) of Checote, first principal chief of the Creek Nation under the Muskogee Constitution of 1867, to the House of Kings and Warriors; newspaper editorials (1872–1883) on Checote and George W. Grayson from the *Vindicator* and the *Cherokee Advocate*, along with a biographical sketch (1926) of Checote.

Chelsea (Indian Territory) Town Records Collection 239
Records 1893–1899
.33 foot

Municipality. Minutes of the Chelsea, Indian Territory, city council (1893–1896); city assessments for 1899; summons for witnesses (1896–1897); and a warrant (1899) for disturbing the peace.

Cherokee Advocate Collection 240
Printed materials 1881–1905
2 feet

Newspaper. Original issues of the *Cherokee Advocate* (1881–1905) published at Tahlequah, Cherokee Nation, Indian Territory. The newspaper was published in Cherokee and English.

Cherokee Bibliography Project Collection 241
Papers ca. 1984
15 feet

Research project. Notes and bibliographic materials (ca. 1984) used in the compilation of an unpublished bibliography regarding the Cherokee Indians and Cherokee Nation.

Unpublished finding aid available.

Cherokee Bilingual Education Project Collection 242
Printed materials 1972–1976
1 foot

Educational project. Publications (1972–1976) of the Cherokee Bilingual Education Project of Tahlequah, Oklahoma, including teacher's guides and student's primers in both Cherokee syllabary and Roman script. The collection includes sample materials from a similar project from Mississippi, produced for Cherokee Indians in that state.

[59]

Cherokee Nation Papers 243
Papers 1801–1982
83 feet

Indian tribe. Official correspondence, letter books, reports, chiefs' messages, speeches of delegates, proceedings, laws, court decisions, acts, leases, election returns, registers of removal claims, and clippings relating to the affairs of the Cherokee Nation. Specifically included are groups of records and papers relating to the *Cherokee Advocate* (1869–1906); the Cherokee boundary survey (1871–1873); the Cherokee census (1868–1901); the Cherokee Outlet (1871–1896); citizenship (1856–1904); the Creek War or the William Cobb murder case (1880–1885); the Dawes Commission (1894–1907); delegations, agents, and attorneys (1816–1910); the Eastern (North Carolina) Cherokee (1871–1906); education (1856–1906); elections (1856–1901); the insane asylum (1874–1907); intruders (1868–1902); legislative affairs (1837–1905); licenses, permits, and fees (1856–1902); United States–Cherokee disputes (1874–1899); executive documents (1801– 1909); financial records (1868–1909); national officers (1856–1902); the national prison and high sheriff (1870–1900); Old Settlers Band (1875–1902); pardons and commutations (1876–1897); per-capita payments (1875–1902); railroads (1866–1900); rewards and extraditions (1877–1888); smallpox (1882–1900); suspensions (1877–1896); town lots (1858–1911); the Vann murder case (1879–1881); Cherokee Nation printed documents (1800–1982); Stand and Sarah C. Watie papers (1832–1881); Ridge and Boudinot family papers (1835–1890); James Madison Bell papers (1836–1908); general correspondence (1836–1908); Cherokee Treaty Fund claims (1837–1850); Civil War records (1861–1866); and general documents (1824–1893).

Published finding aid available.

Cherokee Phoenix Collection 244
Printed materials 1828–1832
1 foot

Newspaper. Original issues of the *Cherokee Phoenix* (1828–1832), published at New Echota, Cherokee Nation, Indian Territory. This newspaper was published in Cherokee and English.

Chi Delta Phi Collection 245
Records ca. 1934–1948
.33 foot

Literary society. Two scrapbooks (1934–1948) containing correspondence and reports (1936–1948), membership records (1934–1948), bylaws (1939) and event programs of the University of Oklahoma Alpha Sigma chapter of Chi Delta Phi, a national collegiate literary society.

Chi Upsilon Collection 246
Records 1919–1955
.50 foot

Professional geology society for women. Correspondence (1921–1941); minutes of meetings (1920–1921); constitutions and bylaws (1920–1955); newspaper articles (n.d.); and manuscripts (1919–1937) regarding the establishment, history, members, and operation of the Alpha chapter (University of Oklahoma) of Chi Upsilon.

Chicago, Rock Island and Pacific Railroad Collection 247
Records 1853–1984
520 feet

Railroad company. Corporate records arranged in the five functional subgroups of executive files; legal files; engineering records; property accounting; and real estate and industrial development records. Record series of the executive subgroup include minutes (1905–1915, 1947–1975); annual reports (1884–1908, 1915–1932, 1941, 1948–1975); subject files (1900–1984); Executive Committee minutes (1953–1955, 1971–1974); monthly letters to the Board of Directors (1921–1972); correspondence (1913–1976); corporate files of associated railroads (1910–1975); liquidation files (1968–1984); and stock ledgers (1853–1864, 1906–1933). In the legal subgroup are subject files (ca. 1925–1979); correspondence (1969–1976); contracts (1900–1910, 1930, 1950–1960); merger files, Union Pacific (1963–1975); merger files, other railroads (1920–1980); litigation files (1930–1980); legislation files-state level (1908–1920); and liquidation files (1975–1984). The engineering subgroup consists of projects files (1890–1975); graphics, including maps, tables, station blueprints, track layouts, bridges, engines and cars, total-system diagrams, and statistical charts (ca. 1890– 1980); structural notes (1916–1917); and capital expenditures (1940– 1941, 1947, 1966–1968). In the property accounting subgroup are grand summaries (1942–1972); valuations (1915–1981); money control files (1903–1904, 1935–1942); original cost data files (1934– 1941); general balance sheet statements (1959–1964); and revenues and expenditures files (1902–1903, 1928–1944). The real estate and industrial development subgroup includes real estate sales files (1937– 1974); abstracts of title (1859–1902, 1911–1931); industrial area files (1956– 1977); lease records (1902–1925); quit claim deeds and tax records (1890–1907); land contracts (1941–1943); and station master files (1979).

Unpublished finding aid available.

Chickasaw Nation Collection 248
Papers 1871–1933
.25 foot

Indian tribe. Typescripts of laws (1871–1881) and newspaper articles (1874–1933) relating to the lands, institutions, and affairs of the Chickasaw Nation, Indian Territory.

Chickasha Milling Company Collection 249
Records 1899–1952
452 feet

Grain milling company. Correspondence (1914–1952); financial records (1899–1952); and associated agricultural and economic historical materials, all pertaining to the operation of the Chickasha Milling Company of Chickasha, Oklahoma. Also included in the collection is a typewritten history (1899–1952) of the company.

Unpublished finding aid available.

Childs, (Mrs.) William Oscar (1868–1957) 250
Papers 1926–1956
.66 foot

Philanthropist. Correspondence (1926–1955) concerning the Childs family's move to Oklahoma in the 1920s and William O. Childs's subsequent involvement in the Oklahoma oil industry, as well as his membership in the Scottish Rite of Freemasonry, his death in 1936, and Mrs. Childs's memorial gifts of chime carillons to the Scottish Rite Temple, Guthrie, Oklahoma, and to the University of Oklahoma in 1955. Included are the acceptance speech (1956) at the University of Oklahoma's dedication of the chimes and an original purchase agreement (1955) for one of the three chimes Mrs. Childs donated.

Choate, May Treadwell (b. 1884) 251
Papers ca. 1750–1927
.25 foot

Collector. The collection contains five books, including an eighteenth-century Bible; receipts and promissory notes (1809–1889); tax receipts (1871–1929); and a recipe for medicine (1839), all from the family of May Treadwell Choate, who settled first in Texas in the 1850s and then came to Oklahoma in 1905.

Choctaw Nation Papers 252
Records and printed materials 1868–1936
17 feet

Indian tribe. Acts, laws, bills, and resolutions (1896–1910) of the Choctaw Nation; typescripts of newspaper articles (1868–1936), mainly about political matters such as elections, allotment, and the Dawes Commission, along with four ledgers (1902–1911) which were the journals of record and contain the minutes of the Choctaw Nation Council.

Unpublished finding aid available.

Choska Trading Company Collection 253
Records 1902–1907
2 items

Trading company. Ledgers (1902–1907) recording the daily commerce of the Choska Trading Company, a general merchandise store which operated in the Creek Nation villages of Choska and Porter, Indian Territory.

Chouteau, Myra Yvonne (ca. 1929–) 254
Printed materials 1932–1950
.33 foot

Ballerina. Articles (1932–1950) concerning Chouteau's direct ancestor and first white settler in Oklahoma, Jean Pierre Chouteau, and his brother, Auguste Chouteau, founder of St. Louis, Missouri; also articles concerning her dance career, from childhood appearances at such events as Pioneer Day parades to membership in the Ballet Russe de Monte Carlo, and her acquaintance with Oklahoma political figures such as Governor Ernest W. Marland.

[63]

Christopher, Ernest Randell (1897–1967)   255
Records ca. 1940–1959
82 feet

Postmaster. Records (ca. 1940–1959) of the U.S. post office in Bartlesville, Oklahoma, of which Christopher was postmaster, including employee records and correspondence with the U.S. Post Office Department in Washington, D.C., regarding service in Bartlesville, Oklahoma. Also publications and correspondence (ca. 1950–1959) of the American Legion organization and its posts in Oklahoma, including information regarding its National American Commission, of which Christopher was a member, and "Man of the Year" awards, which he received.

Christopher, Joe R.   256
Papers 1980–2001
10 feet

Professor. Chapbooks (1993–2001) by Joe R. Christopher and other authors; Tarleton State University records (1989–1995); student themes and lecture notes (1987–1991); conference minutes (1980–1986), correspondence and grant files (1994–1997); and the Christopher family's Christmas newsletter (1992–1998).

Unpublished finding aid available.

Chupco, John (d. 1881)   257
Typescript 1874
1 item

Indian chief. A typescript of a news article (1874) from the *Cherokee Advocate*, entitled "A Protest by John Chupco, P. P. Pitchlynn, et al.," in which Chupco, Pitchlynn, and a number of Indian leaders protest efforts by white men to stop the formation of a ruling general council of Indians for Indian Territory, as provided by the Treaty of 1866, and efforts to extend a federal territorial government over Indian Territory.

Ciba Pharmaceutical Collection   258
Printed materials 1940–1951
27 items

Drug company. This collection consists of twenty-seven issues (1940–1951) of *CIBA Symposia*. Each issue is devoted to specialized topics in the history of medicine, including information on pregnancy and childbirth among Native Americans.

Ciereszko, Leon   259
Printed materials and artifacts 1915–1917
.33 foot

Collector. Camp Fire Girl instruction manuals for leather and pine needle crafts, a Camp Fire Girl ceremonial dress, and beaded choke necklace. Also included is a booklet from the Camp Fire Outfitting Company describing the ceremonial dress.

Cities Service Oil and Gas Corporation Collection   260
Records 1896–1982
40 feet

Petroleum-related corporation. Administrative reports (1913–1980) and publications (1923–1982) regarding the history and operations (1896–1982), both domestic and international, of the Cities Service Oil Company, later the Cities Service Oil and Gas Corporation, as well as of other energy industry companies. Also included are biographical sketches of corporate officers such as Arthur W. Ambrose, Singer B. Irelan, J. Edgar Heston, Robert L. Kidd, and Henry Doherty.

Unpublished finding aid available.

Civil Rights Commission Collection   261
Records 1957–1961
.50 foot

Federal commission. Minutes (1960) of the Oklahoma Advisory Committee, along with correspondence (1958–1961) and publications (1957–1961) of the U.S. Commission on Civil Rights and the Oklahoma Advisory Committee, all relating to civil rights in Oklahoma.

Claremore Chamber of Commerce Collection   262
Printed materials ca. 1948
1 item

City chamber of commerce. This collection consists of a marketing and media brochure (ca. 1948) sent to industries, featuring population figures, zoning areas, and labor force and trade figures for Claremore, Oklahoma.

Clarita Farmers State Bank Collection 263
Records 1913–1944
3 feet

Bank. Ledgers and cash account books (1922–1944) recording the daily business of the bank and also containing the bylaws, articles of incorporation, and minutes (1913) of stockholders' meetings of the "96" Ballard Oil and Gas Company of Inola, Oklahoma.

Clark, Ben 264
Papers 1863–1907
.10 feet

Interpreter and scout. Military orders and personal correspondence (1863–1907), most notably from Gen. Nelson A. Miles, received by Clark while serving as an interpreter and scout for the U.S. Army at Fort Reno, Indian Territory.

Clark, Carter Blue 265
Printed materials 1922–1974
.33 feet

Historian. Photocopies of articles (1923–1927) from Ku Klux Klan journals such as *Kourier Magazine* and *Imperial Night-Hawk*, including many with articles about the Klan in Oklahoma; newspaper articles (1922–1924) on the Klan in Oklahoma; papers (1923–1924) relating to Oklahoma Governor John C. Walton and the Klan; Klan pamphlets and handbooks (1920s) and interview transcripts (1972–1974) with Ira M. Finley, Albert S. Giles, and Leon Hirsch regarding the Klan in Oklahoma.

Clark, Joseph J. 266
Papers 1908–1935
.10 foot

Physician. Correspondence (1933) to Clark from friends; receipts (1935) for goods purchased by Clark; a notebook (n.d.) of medical notes recorded by Clark; a daily journal (1934); and one ledger (1934–1935) in which Clark recorded patient accounts.

Clarke, (Mrs.) Hulbert S. 267
Printed materials 1924–1959
.50 foot

Professional golfer. A scrapbook (1926–1930) containing photographs, news clippings, and correspondence regarding Georgia Lee Clarke's career as a professional golfer.

Clarke, John R. 268
Papers 1926–1932
.10 foot

Politician. Correspondence (1926) to Clarke from Henry S. Johnston and others concerning political issues and Clarke's campaign for the 1926 gubernatorial election in Oklahoma; pamphlets (1926) from Clarke's campaign, and Henry S. Johnston's platform for the same race; and an article (1926) from the *Muskogee Daily Phoenix*, giving the election results by county. The collection also includes a letter (1932) to Clarke from Franklin D. Roosevelt concerning Clarke's platform.

Clarkson, Addie W. (1869–1950) 269
Papers 1908–1926
.10 foot

Physician. Account ledgers (1908) from Clarkson's medical practice at the Wheelock Academy in Millington, Oklahoma, and at Valliant, Oklahoma. The collection also includes class notes (1926) his son, A. M. Clarkson, while a student at the University of Oklahoma.

Classen, Anton H. (1861–1922) 270
Papers 1900
4 items

Realtor. Correspondence (1900) between Classen and Governor Theodore Roosevelt of New York, regarding Roosevelt's attendance at the Rough Riders' reunion of 1900 in Oklahoma City, Oklahoma Territory.

Cleckler, Frank Stuart (1922–1978) 271
Papers 1922–1978
8 feet

Philanthropist. Correspondence (1923–1974); financial records (1922–1978); travel logs and manuscripts (1964–1978) of trips to Australia, Oceania, the Near East, and the Far East; and posters (ca. 1940) by British Railways advertising the policy at its Preston, England, station of forbidding local boys from "engine spotting" from the platform. Also included in this collection are publications (1941–1963), including a dedication program of a U.S. naval air station in the Philippines and travel booklets advertising Hong Kong and the Federation of South Africa, as well as one booklet published by the U.S. embassy in Teheran, Iran, regarding the pleasures of travel there.

Unpublished finding aid available.

Clemens, Samuel Langhorne (1835–1910)   272
Papers n.d.
1 item

Author. One page of handwritten notes (n.d.) attributed to Samuel L. Clemens, also known as Mark Twain.

Clements, Frank B. (1896–1955)   273
Papers 1933–1953
2.66 feet

Collector. Correspondence (1933–1953) of Clements regarding Lions International activities in Tulsa, Oklahoma, and in the state of Oklahoma, and publications, including *The Roar*, newsletter of the Tulsa Lions Club, and the *Official Proceedings* (1936–1947) of the Lions International conventions.

Unpublished finding aid available.

Cleo State Bank Collection   274
Ledgers 1900–1933
12 feet

Bank. General ledgers (1902–1932); reconciliation books (1916–1925); trial balances (1901–1903); bills receivable registers (1900–1914); collection registers (1900–1913); draft registers (1900–1915); remittance registers (1900–1908); cash sales books (1907–1914); tellers' cash books (1900–1933); and cash books (1914–1920), all documenting the accounting functions of the Cleo State Bank in Cleo Springs, Oklahoma.

Unpublished finding aid available.

Cleveland, Arlyss, and Paula Cleveland   275
Printed materials 1977–1983
.25 foot

Collectors. Printed materials (1977–1983) used in a course taught at

Yavapai College, Prescott, Arizona, entitled Oral Traditions of Pueblo Indians, including newspaper articles on the Navajo–Hopi land dispute, tribal feuds, Apache culture, and Zuni pilgrimages; articles on basket making, medicinal plants, musical instruments, prayer sticks, rugs, and pottery; and biographical sketches of Ganado Mucho, Henry Chee Dodge, Yukioma, Carlos Montezuma, Atsidi Sani, Mangas Coloradas, Popé, Julian Martinez, Hosteen Klah, and Manuelito.

Cleveland County (Oklahoma) Children's Clinic Collection 276
Records 1927–1956
.10 foot

Medical facility. Correspondence (1949–1956); board meeting minutes (1937–1945); a clinic history (n.d.); and financial records (1938–1953) relating to the operation of this children's clinic.

Clifton, Robert T. 277
Manuscripts 1970
2 items

Author. Two manuscript copies (1970) of Clifton's book, *Barbs, Prongs, Points, Prickers and Stickers: A Complete and Illustrated Catalogue of Antique Barbed Wire*, published by the University of Oklahoma Press.

Cline, (Mrs.) B. F. 278
Records ca. 1920–1940
.33 foot

Merchant. An account ledger (1920–1940) from Cline's Department Store in Medford, Oklahoma.

Co-operative Publishing Company Collection 279
Records ca. 1900
3 items

Publishing company. Unpublished manuscripts (ca. 1900) entitled "Early History of the Co-operative Publishing Company," concerning the beginning of the company, its executives, and early gains and losses; "History of the State Capitol," describing the State Capitol Printing Company's printing plant from founding to incorporation and including names of early executives; and "An Historical and Economical Brief of Guthrie and Logan County, Oklahoma," which includes sketches of the area's industry and scenic beauty, along with a description of the 89'er Celebration, an annual event recognizing pioneers of the 1889 land run into Oklahoma Territory.

Coachman, Ward   280
Printed materials 1877–1878
3 items

Indian chief. Typescripts of messages (1877) and an editorial (1878) concerning an attempt to unite Creek political factions and promote the Creek constitution of 1867.

Cobb, Isabel (1858–1947)   281
Papers 1893–1913, 1959
2 items

Physician. A record book (1893–1913) listing Cobb's patients and house calls and a brief biography of Cobb, written by her nephew.

Cobean, Samuel E. (1913–1951)   282
Printed materials 1946
.10 foot

Cartoonist. A newspaper clipping regarding the career and work of Samuel E. Cobean, an Oklahoma cartoonist who worked for *The New Yorker* magazine.

Coffey, John L. (b. 1898)   283
Record 1725
1 item

Collector. A document (1725) of proceedings before a royal notary concerning the death of a member of the Fourche family and his New World estate. The document is in French with no translation.

Coins, Tokens, and Money Collection   284
Artifacts 1816–1924
.10 foot

Numismatic collection. Trade tokens (1892–1920) issued by retail stores in Oklahoma Territory, Indian Territory, and the state of Oklahoma, along with currency issued by the Bank of Augusta, Georgia (1816), the Confederate States of America (1863–1864), the states of Arkansas (1863) and North Carolina (1862), and by the Church of Jesus Christ of Latter Day Saints in Salt Lake City, Utah (1896).

Colbert, Winchester (1810–1880) 285
Printed materials 1866–1908
2 items

Politician. A typescript of a letter (1866) from Colbert to Stand Watie, along with a brief biography (1908) of Colbert.

Colby, John 286
Papers 1942–1995
2 feet

Collector. Correspondence, hand-drawn maps, and other data (1942–1995) John Colby used in writing a history of the U.S. Army's 357th Infantry Regiment, 90th Division. The collection also contains articles about the 90th Division; memoirs of Colby's former comrades; field artillery and regiment unit journals; cassette tape recordings of soldiers discussing the role of the 90th Division; and maps of the Koenigsmacher and Metz areas of France and the Dillingen area of Germany.

Unpublished finding aid available.

Colcord, Charles Francis (1859–1934) 287
Papers 1885–1935
15.33 feet

Civic leader and businessman. Correspondence (1901–1935) relating to Colcord's oil and other business activities; general correspondence (1909–1930) to Colcord; and correspondence (1909–1930) from Colcord, his wife, Harriet Scoresby Colcord, his sons, Ray and Sidney Colcord, and his brother, Will C. Colcord; genealogical material (n.d.) concerning the Colcord family; scrapbooks and newspaper clippings (1910–1934) relating to Colcord, including some concerning the 1934 Charles F. Urschel kidnapping case, for which Colcord offered a reward; miscellaneous printed material (1920–1934) collected by Colcord; and a manuscript of his autobiography, published in 1970.

Unpublished finding aid available.

Coldiron, Daisy Lemon (1876–1946) 288
Papers 1918–1950
1 foot

Poet. Correspondence (1918–1941) of Daisy Lemon Coldiron with her publishers, with the Oklahoma Tuberculosis Association, and with local political candidates about women's suffrage; a ledger (1924–1937) listing poem titles, publishers, and payments; and scrapbooks (1920–1941) containing published and unpublished poems, essays, and greeting card manuscripts, copies of Coldiron's column called "Letters From Aunt Sallie," and articles from literary and political sources on issues such as suffrage, prohibition, censorship, and eugenics. Also included in the collection is a typed manuscript of "Ballads of the Plains," published posthumously in 1950.

Unpublished finding aid available.

Cole, Coleman 289
Printed materials 1875–1879
.33 foot

Indian chief. Typescripts of correspondence (1875–1879) relating to Choctaw participation in the proposed Indian Union growing out of the Okmulgee Council; published speeches (1877–1878); Choctaw Tribal Council proceedings (1873–1878); accounts of Choctaw court cases (1877); and other papers (1875–1879) pertaining to the problem of intruders, tribal citizenship, and royalties from Choctaw coal lands, all during the period of Cole's tenure as principal chief, 1874–1878.

Cole, Redmond S. (1881–1959) 290
Papers 1894–1956
38 feet

Judge. Correspondence (1894–1947) regarding the personal affairs of Cole, politics and government at both the state and local levels, and legal cases before the Oklahoma court system; legal briefs (1909–1925) of Oklahoma cases; publications (1908–1956) regarding politics and government at the local, state, and national levels; and speeches (n.d.) delivered by Cole before civic, fraternal, and other groups.

Unpublished finding aid available.

Coleman, Emma Alberta White (1863–1949) 291
Printed materials 1889–1927
2 feet

Photographer. Business and personal correspondence (1890–1910), along with advertisements and mail-order catalogs (1889–1927) for photography, art, needlework, garden supplies, household products, patent medicines, and women's clothing and dress patterns. The bulk of the material dates from 1903 to 1914.

Unpublished finding aid available.

Collins Coal Company Collection 292
Records 1938–1949
2 feet

Coal company. Employee records, including wage reports (1938–1942), payrolls (1940–1947), records of orders and employees' pay (1939–1948), and a time book (1942–1947); shipment records (1943–1947); correspondence (1941–1949); financial reports (1940–1947); expenses and sales accounts (1937–1946); and Bituminous Coal Producers Board reports (1939–1942), all from the Collins Coal Company in Krebs, Oklahoma.

Unpublished finding aid available.

Collins Hardware Store Collection 293
Records 1902–1920
1.50 feet

Hardware store. Ledgers (1902–1920) from this retail business in Hydro, Oklahoma, along with catalogs (1902–1920) of jewelry, saddlery, stoves, and other hardware store merchandise.

Unpublished finding aid available.

Collins, Arza Bailey, and John O. Arnold 294
Papers 1907–1936
.75 foot

Government employees. Diaries (1912–1933) kept by Collins recording his travel and activities as a U.S. farmer for the Sac and Fox Indian Agency; correspondence (1924–1929) relating to lease disputes; weekly reports (1922–1925) to the Shawnee Indian agent; and other records (1907–1936) relating to the Sac and Fox and Iowa Indians in Oklahoma.

Collums, D. B., and Garner G. Collums 295
Papers ca. 1915–1976
6 feet

Collectors. Unpublished manuscripts (n.d.) by Garner G. Collums; correspondence (ca. 1940–1955), including personal, military, and rejection letters from publishers; newspaper clippings (ca. 1930–1950); certificates and diplomas of D. B. and Garner G. Collums; and posters and photographs.

Unpublished finding aid available.

Collums, (Mrs.) Garner G.   296
Printed materials 1947–1950
.33 foot

Collector. Invitations (1947–1950); newspaper clippings (1948–1950); newsletters (1949–1950); and directories (1947–1948) from Norman, Oklahoma, clubs and organizations such as the University of Oklahoma Faculty Club, the University Women's Club, the Y.W.C.A., the Girl Scouts, and the Red Cross.

Colonial Dames Collection   297
Papers 1852–1894
1.33 feet

Collector. Correspondence (1859–1862) regarding the Choctaw Indians and Spencer Academy; correspondence (1864–1871) concerning the Omaha Indian mission in Nebraska; correspondence (1861–1864) dealing with the Civil War, and correspondence (1852–1894) from Charles S. Rogers to Mrs. Orlando S. Lee, mostly regarding student life, family illnesses, and duties as a minister.

Unpublished finding aid available.

Comanche County Historical Society Collection   298
Printed materials 1901–1903, 1955
3 items

Historical society. Copy of the first issue of *The Chronicles of Comanche County* (1955) and two land titles (1901–1903) for lots in Lawton, Oklahoma.

Combest, George Marion (1866–1926)   299
Papers 1899–1927
.10 foot

Physician. A diary (1899) detailing Combest's participation in the Spanish-American War; certificates (1896–1906) of honorable discharge from military service, of registration as a physician in Indian Territory, and of pension eligibility from previous military service; articles (1918–1926) concerning Combest's enlistment into the medical reserve force in 1918; his obituary in 1926; and medals earned during his military career. The collection also includes an unpublished biography (n.d.) entitled "Life and Works of George Marion Combest: Oklahoma Pioneer Medical Doctor," by Christine Combest Millsap.

Commerce First State Bank Collection 300
Records 1911–1950
17 feet

Bank. General ledgers (1918–1921); collection registers (1919–1926); discount registers (1915–1936); tellers' cash books (1917–1929); journals (1915–1920); voucher registers (1913–1916); distribution of expense ledgers (1917–1938); and overdraft registers (1944–1950) from the First State Bank of Commerce, Oklahoma, along with records (1915–1935) of the city of Commerce; a treasurer's register (1917– 1919) from Ottawa County, Oklahoma; and business records (1911– 1930) from a lumber company and a drugstore, apparently in Miami, Oklahoma.

Unpublished finding aid available.

Commercial National Bank Collection 301
Ledger 1935–1936
1 item

Bank. An account ledger (1935–1936) from the Commercial National Bank of Muskogee, Oklahoma.

Condit, (Mrs.) J. A. 302
Records 1908
1 item

Collector. A cancelled check (1908) issued to W. A. Condit and written on the Bartlesville National Bank, Bartlesville, Oklahoma.

Confederate States of America Indian Affairs Collection 303
Papers 1861–1864
.25 foot

Subject collection. Provisions returns (1861); memoranda (1861–1862); and correspondence (1862), all regarding the provision of rations by the Confederate States of America to the Five Civilized Tribes, and to the Osage, Comanche, and Caddo Indians.

Conklin, Richard A. (1885–1952) 304
Papers 1914–1953
.10 foot

Petroleum geologist. Correspondence (1921–1922) to Conklin from his colleagues concerning personnel changes at Roxana Petroleum Corporation, Ardmore, Oklahoma, including Conklin's resignation as head geologist in 1922 and his subsequent employment; an employment

The diary of Charles Kroff, Company F, Eleventh Indiana Volunteer Infantry. Kroff's diary covers his service in the Eleventh Indiana from July 12, 1861, to August 11, 1865. His entries record not only the battles and campaigns, but the hard marches, short rations, and long, boring, but dangerous days in the trenches. The most significant portion of his diary contains a detailed account of the final phase of General Ulysses S. Grant's Vicksburg campaign. From the Sherry Marie Cress Collection.

contract (1914) between Conklin and the Bataafsche Petroleum Maatshappij, an allied corporation of Roxana Petroleum based in the Netherlands; and certificates (1929–1946) issued to Conklin by the University of Oklahoma. Also included is a reprint of a biographical article (1952) written by Albert S. Clinkscales shortly after Conklin's death.

Conlan, Madeline Czarina Colbert 305
Papers 1756–1932
.33 foot

Historian. Typewritten manuscripts (1920–1938), including research notes, speeches, and reports on the history and culture of Oklahoma's Indian tribes and their leaders, with an emphasis on the Choctaws.

Conn, J. L. 306
Papers 1895
2 items

Collector. Copies of two letters (1895) from Amos Ewing to William McKinley concerning an upcoming Oklahoma territorial convention, the Free Home bill, and delegates to the St. Louis convention at which McKinley would be nominated for the presidency of the United States.

Connelley, William Elsey (1855–1930) 307
Papers 1854–1925
2.33 feet

Author. Correspondence (ca. 1923) regarding the Benders of Kansas and the genealogy of families in Big Sandy Valley, Kentucky; notebooks (ca. 1854–1913) concerning the Civil War, William Quantrill, Indians, linguistics, border wars, Kansas history prior to the twentieth century, and the genealogy of families of Big Sandy Valley, Kentucky; clippings (ca. 1855–1900) concerning Indian mythology, legends, and relations with whites, the Civil War within Kansas and adjoining states, as well as other Kansas history; manuscripts (ca. 1902) concerning politics, Indian mythology, folklore, linguistics, and relations with whites, John Brown, William Quantrill, and Kansas history; and pamphlets (1857–1925) concerning politics within and between Indian and white groups, Indian mythology, folklore, linguistics, "Wild Bill" Hickok, and John Brown. The collection also includes diaries (1858–1911) of Connelley and of George Ela, who writes of Kansas farm life, local Indian groups and their linguistics, and his Civil War experiences at Pine Bluff, Arkansas.

Unpublished finding aid available.

Connors State Agricultural College Collection   308
Typescript 1951
1 item

State college. A transcript of the proceedings (1951) of the opening ceremony for the Jacob Johnson Library at Connors State Agricultural College in Warner, Oklahoma.

Constant, Alberta Anne Wilson   309
Papers 1930–1983
9 feet

Author. Correspondence (1930–1983) of Edwin and Alberta Constant with friends, admirers, publishing companies, and agents regarding family affairs of the Constants, the authorship, publication, and distribution of her works, and public appearances by Alberta Constant; publicity items (n.d.) generated by Constant's writings; subject and reference files (n.d.) of Constant regarding topics of interest or on which she wrote; manuscripts (n.d.) of the fiction and non-fiction works by Constant; and publications (1945–1953), including newsletters, magazines, and journals, containing articles or stories by Constant.

    Unpublished finding aid available.

Cook, Benjamin R.   310
Records 1872–1948
1 foot

Collector. Three account books (1872–1874) and a fire insurance policy (1889), along with statements and receipts (1879–1880) from the Hester Mercantile Store, Boggy Depot, Indian Territory, owned by George B. Hester. The collection also contains printed election returns (1930–1948) from Atoka County, Oklahoma.

Cook, F. L. (d. 1950)   311
Manuscript n.d.
1 item

Physician. A manuscript (n.d.) by Cook describing the symptoms, progression, and treatment of syphilis.

Cooksey, Harold S.   312
Papers 1954–1970
9 feet

State employee. Oklahoma Wildlife Conservation Commission minutes (1961–1969); monthly reports (1958–1969); financial reports (1963–1969); budgets (1962–1970); federal aid budgets (1966–1970); correspondence (1961–1970); fisheries reports (1962–1968); deer and game reports (1958–1969); legislation (1962–1968); wildlife and conservation publications, and government documents relating to the Little River Reservoir (Lake Thunderbird), all accumulated by Cooksey while he was a member of the above commission.

Unpublished finding aid available.

Cooper, Ann Mayer   313
Manuscript 1949
1 item

Pioneer. A typewritten manuscript (1949) written by Cooper concerning the history of Lincoln County, Oklahoma, and including information on early county officials and the land runs into the Sac and Fox, Iowa, and Kickapoo Indian reserves.

Copeland, Fayette, Jr.   314
Papers 1915–1971
5.50 feet

Professor. Correspondence (1841–1968); research notes (1835–1914); reference materials (1910–1961), including book reviews; publications (1886–1971); and manuscripts (1892–1953) by Fayette and Edith Copeland regarding the University of Oklahoma and its School of Journalism, the history of journalism in general, and the lives of social reformer Kate Barnard and journalist George Wilkins Kendall. The collection also includes copies of Kendall's correspondence, financial records, and personal journals.

Unpublished finding aid available.

Coppadge, Ethel (1882–1965)   315
Printed materials 1883–1965
.33 foot

Collector. A membership roster (1942), convention proceedings (1906–1929), and other materials (1883–1965) relating to Oklahoma's Woman's Relief Corps and specifically to the Stillwater, Oklahoma, chapter.

Cornell, Doris   316
Papers 1933–1979
.33 foot

Collector. Bank statements and financial records (1934–1971); Cities Service Oil Company contracts and correspondence (1954–1962); tax returns and filings for Lewis E. Rape and Mrs. C. C. Custer (1933–1951); a Cosgrove Fire Protection, Inc., promissory note and purchase agreement (1973); and correspondence (1917) from Frank Phillips to Lewis E. Rape regarding a well drilling near Salter, Oklahoma.

Cornell, Kearns Bryon (b. ca. 1890)   317
Printed materials ca. 1950
3 items

Politician. An article (1950) concerning the announcement of Cornell's candidacy for the U.S. Congress and explaining his platform, which included advocacy of a return of prohibition; a pamphlet (ca. 1950) in comic book format, entitled "Here's What A Republican Congress Did For You"; and a letter (1950) to James Babcock, giving a brief personal history of Cornell.

Cornish, Melven (b. ca. 1870)   318
Papers 1876–1940
20 feet

Attorney. Case files (1903–1904) and letterbooks (1900–1905) relating to Choctaw and Chickasaw Indians' citizenship claims; dockets (1903–1904) for the central and southern divisions of the U.S. District Court; an account book (1899); and a record book (1876) entitled *Proceedings of the Court of Claims, Choctaw Nation*, along with clippings (1896–1907) and published court documents (1900–1940) relating to Chickasaw and Choctaw Indian cases represented by the law firm of Mansfield, McMurray, and Cornish in U.S. courts.

Unpublished finding aid available.

Court, Nathan Altshiller (1881–1968)   319
Printed materials 1896–1950
.33 feet

Mathematician. A biography (n.d.) of Court and a bibliography (n.d.) of his writings and publications; school inspection reports and certificates (1896–1905) from Poland; and articles (1923–1950) by Court regarding the fields of mathematics and geometry.

Covey, Arthur S. (1877–ca. 1960) 320
Printed materials 1877–1960
3 feet

Artist. Publications (1925–1960) describing Covey's art, sketches, and lithographs.

Unpublished finding aid available.

Covington, J. A. 321
Diaries 1863–1900
.10 feet

Government employee. Photocopies of diaries (1863–1900) kept by Covington and describing his work at the Cheyenne-Arapaho Indian Agency and his travels to Alaska during the Klondike gold rush.

Crawford, L. E. 322
Papers 1885–ca. 1949
.10 foot

Author. Manuscripts (n.d.) of articles dealing with cattle branding and cowboy life and work, and lists of cattle brands used in western Oklahoma, the Texas panhandle, and western Kansas.

Creek Indian Museum Collection 323
Printed materials 1957
2 items

Museum. Two pamphlets (1957) entitled "History and Legends of the Creek Indians of Oklahoma" and "Creek Nation Capitol and Indian Museum, Okmulgee, Oklahoma."

Creek Nation Collection 324
Papers 1849–1943
.33 foot

Indian tribe. Court decisions, treasury warrants, and related legal documents (1868–1900); correspondence (1873–1898); and typescripts of newspaper articles (1849–1943). All relate to land, institutions, and the affairs of the Creek Nation, Indian Territory. Correspondents include Samuel Checote, Ward Coachman, Joseph M. Perryman, and Isparhecher.

Cress, Sherry Marie   325
Papers 1861–1956
.10 foot

Collector. The diary (1861–1865) of Charles Kroff, recording his experiences as a soldier in the Eleventh Indiana Volunteer Infantry during the Civil War and detailing his participation in the battles of Shiloh, Fort Donelson, and Corinth. Also included are letters (1885–1956) about the diary.

Crittendon, William Dial   326
Legal document 1690
1 item

Collector. A vellum document (1690), in French, regarding the sale of an orchard near Orleans, France.

Cronkhite, Kitty   327
Papers 1836–1872
6 items

Collector. Land titles from Illinois (1836–1872); copies of the United States Constitution printed to mark its centennial in 1876; and an issue (1864) of *The Wenona Sentinel* of Wenona, Illinois.

Crook, Kenneth E.   328
Printed materials 1918
2 items

Professor. Publications (1918) of the Committee on Public Information (Creel Committee) regarding World War I and Germany's reasons for war.

Cross, George Lynn (1905–1998)   329
Manuscript 1926
1 item

University president. A copy of Cross's M.A. thesis (1926), entitled "The Ontogeny of the Vascular Elements in Zea Mays."

Crouch, Aziel Henry (b. ca. 1866)   330
Papers 1904–1916
3 items

Physician. Certificates (1904–1916) authorizing Crouch to practice medicine in Oklahoma and appointing him a medical examiner for the Aetna Life Insurance Company and a camp physician for the Modern Woodmen of America.

Cruce, Cruce, and Bleakmore Collection 331
Papers 1899–1935
25 feet

Law firm. Legal documents and correspondence from the law firms Cruce, Cruce, and Cruce (1899–1901); Cruce, Cruce, and Bleakmore (1901–1912); and Potter and Cruce (1912–1928) reflecting the firm's practice representing Chickasaw Indian citizenship and allotment claims, banking interests, and oil and gas companies. Also in the collection are correspondence and speeches from Lee Cruce's gubernatorial campaign of 1907 and his senatorial campaign of 1930.

Unpublished finding aid available.

Crumbo, Woody (b. 1912) 332
Art prints n.d.
2 feet

Artist. Prints (n.d.) of works by Potawatomi Indian artist Woody Crumbo.

Cuddeback, Frank J. (b. ca. 1904) 333
Manuscript 1926–1940
1 item

Mining engineer. A typescript (n.d.) describing the lead and zinc mining operations, 1926–1940, in the tri-state district of Oklahoma, Kansas, and Missouri.

Culwell, Frankie 334
Certificate 1909
1 item

Collector. A copy of an allotment certificate (1909) for Willie Inex Kirkendall, signed by Green McCurtain, principal chief of the Choctaws.

Cunningham, Robert O'Darrell 335
Printed materials 1952
4 items

Politician. Articles (1952) regarding Oklahoma state representative Cunningham's proposal for a 1952 road bond, including details of the proposal and favorable editorial comments.

Curry, Arthur R.   336
Notebook 1921–1923
1 item

Librarian. A notebook (1921–1923) labeled "To My Successor," in which Curry lists his activities, functions, and duties as the reference librarian for the University of Oklahoma library.

Cushing Refining and Gasoline Company Collection   337
Records 1927–1945
2 feet

Refining and gasoline company. Correspondence (1927–1945) to and from other petroleum companies regarding orders and shipments of petroleum products, and from federal agencies concerning the rationing and price regulation of gasoline during World War II; pamphlets (1941–1943) from federal agencies concerning gasoline rationing and price controls during World War II; and additional business records (ca. 1935–1945) concerning Cushing's production. Also included in this collection is a blueprint (n.d.) of an underground oil tank.

Unpublished finding aid available.

Custer County Medical Society Collection   338
Ledger 1904–1909
1 item

Professional organization. A ledger (1904–1909) containing the minutes, roll of membership, and financial accounts of the Custer County (Oklahoma) Medical Society.

Custer County State Bank Collection   339
Records 1900–1938
27 feet

Bank. Balance ledgers (1900–1920); collection registers (1911); daily statement books (1900–1938); deposit ledgers (1906–1920); discount registers (1901–1933); distribution ledgers (1911–1912); general ledgers (1926–1935); transfer ledgers (1906–1936); tellers' cash books

(1900–1932); and related records, all detailing the daily financial transactions of the Custer County State Bank of Arapaho, Oklahoma, and Oklahoma Territory.

Unpublished finding aid available.

Cutler, Violona 340
Printed materials 1929–1953
.10 foot

Collector. Publications (1929–1953) and manuscripts (1950) regarding social work among the aged, young, and physically handicapped in Oklahoma.

Cutlip, C. Guy (1881–1938) 341
Papers 1867–1967
5 feet

Judge. Records (1930–1931) of the Oklahoma Bar Association's board of governors; speeches (1927–1936) by Cutlip; manuscripts (n.d.) regarding the history of Seminole County, Oklahoma, Wewoka, Oklahoma, and the Seminole Indian Nation; Seminole Indian land allotment certificates (1901–1902); Cutlip's travel diaries and personal diaries (1920–1936); records (1905–1910) of the Wewoka Masonic Lodge; and a financial ledger (1867–1872) of the Wewoka Trading Company.

Unpublished finding aid available.

Dahlberg, Sophie Little Bear 342
Papers 1861–1979
.25 foot

Collector. Photocopies of birth and death certificates and related genealogical materials of members of the Little Bear family, including Bacon Rind, Haynes Little Bear, Dora Pah Se To Pah, Jack Portillo, Sophie Little Bear Dahlberg, Edward L. Chouteau, and Rosalie Capitaine Chouteau. Also in the collection are tombstone inscriptions from the Kiowa Indian cemetery near Duncan, Oklahoma, and the Deyo Mission cemetery near Lawton, Oklahoma, along with a checklist of Osage Indian songs in the Library of Congress and published information about Osage Indian traditions.

Dale, Edward Everett (1879–1972)   343
Papers 1865–1948
80 feet

Professor and historian. Correspondence (1902–1972), student papers (n.d.), theses and dissertations (1932–1933), and personal research materials (1832–1967) regarding the history of Oklahoma, Oklahoma Territory, and Indian Territory, the Indians of North America, and the American Southwest; teaching materials used by Dale at Harvard (1913–1920) and the University of Oklahoma (1921–1952); administrative and other files (1936–1941) of the Works Progress Administration's Indian-Pioneer History Project for Oklahoma; U.S. government documents (1897–1957); and presidential papers of University of Oklahoma presidents James Shannon Buchanan (1911–1929) and Stratton D. Brooks (1915–1922).

Unpublished finding aid available.

Danforth, Thatcher O.   344
Letter 1863
1 item

Soldier. A letter from Union soldier Thatcher Danforth to his mother, written from somewhere near Vicksburg, Mississippi. He comments on the excitement caused by a naval battle on the Mississippi River and adds that he expects to be moved south of Vicksburg soon.

Dangerfield, Royden James (1902–1969)   345
Papers 1914–1948
3 feet

Professor. Reprints (1914–1940) and manuscripts (ca. 1930–1948) of both published and unpublished works by Dangerfield, including a history of Oklahoma political campaign platforms from 1890 to 1914; *The Hidden Weapon: The Story of Economic Warfare*, and other works dealing with international relations, Oklahoma state and local government, and national and foreign affairs; and research notes (ca. 1930–1948) concerning the Oklahoma land run of 1889, Oklahoma politics, international law, and international relations, including research material relating to the allied blockade of Germany during World War II.

Unpublished finding aid available.

[85]

Daniel, Harley A. 346
Papers 1936–1956
2 feet

Collector. Correspondence (1936–1954) regarding the Lions Club organization in Oklahoma; a poster (1953) advertising Daniel's campaign for governor of his district Lions Club; publications (1952–1954) of the Lions Club; and club reports (1954) from towns and cities throughout Oklahoma, listing membership and activities.

Unpublished finding aid available.

Daniels, Opherita Eugenia 347
Papers 1920–1979
.10 foot

Teacher. An autobiographical manuscript (ca. 1979) by Daniels, the first African-American to enter the University of Oklahoma's School of Social Work, along with news articles (1920–1979) regarding her attendance at the University of Oklahoma.

Dannelly, Paul Edward (b. 1919) 348
Printed materials 1972–1974
1 item

Professor. A collage of newspaper headlines (1972–1974) regarding the Watergate scandal and the resignation of president Richard M. Nixon, collected by journalism professor, Paul Edward Dannelly.

Danner, Clyde 349
Papers 1894–1945
.10 foot

Collector. Teaching contracts (1894–1926) for P. M. Danner's employment in Arkansas and in Beckham and Caddo counties, Oklahoma. Also included are a land patent (1906), a warranty deed (1915) to land in Caddo County, and newspaper clippings (1940s) from World War II.

Darnell, E. E. 350
Records 1911–1953
.50 foot

Physician. Journals and ledgers (1911–1953) from Darnell's medical practice in Colony, Oklahoma, along with a copy of a report (1923) of the Oklahoma Commissioners of Charities and Corrections.

Daugherty, Charles L.   351
Papers 1907–1913
.66 feet

State official. Circulars, pamphlets, and labor regulations (1907–1913); and correspondence to and from Charles L. Daugherty, Oklahoma's first commissioner of labor, on issues such as labor legislation, organized labor, open and closed shops, child labor, the Democratic Party, local elections, and political appointments.

Daughters of the American Revolution Collection   352
Records 1914–1957
.50 foot

Women's club. Minutes (1914–1944) and publications (1919–1957) of the Daughters of the American Revolution, Black Beaver chapter, Norman, Oklahoma.

Davenport, James S. (1864–1940)   353
Printed material 1900
1 item

Attorney. Typescript of an article from the *Daily Chieftain* (Vinita, Oklahoma) giving biographical information on Davenport and an account of his appointment to the Cherokee National Council.

Davis, Alice Brown (1852–1935)   354
Printed materials 1905–1935
6 items

Indian chief. Typescripts of newspaper articles (1905–1935) regarding Alice Brown Davis, Seminole land claims in Mexico, and Seminole schools.

Davis, Robert Murray   355
Papers 1965–1995
.50 foot

Professor. Manuscripts and articles (1965–1995) by University of Oklahoma professor of English, Robert Murray Davis; critiques (1965–1995) of literary works by Evelyn Waugh; and research materials (1968–1971) regarding Waugh's works, as well as those by Donald Barthelme, Charles Molesworth, and Matthew Bruccoli.

Davison, Oscar William (b. 1905) 356
Printed materials 1940–1949
.66 foot

Collector. Publications (1940–1949), including reports, circulars, press releases, newsletters, and clippings relating to legislative programs sponsored by the Oklahoma Education Association.

Dawkins, (Mrs.) Ernest 357
Printed materials 1883–1903
2 items

Collector. Complimentary card (1883) to a carnival ball in New Orleans; and a program (1903) of the Sulphur Chautauqua at Sulphur, Indian Territory.

Dawson, Herron Victor (b. ca. 1905) 358
Papers ca. 1950–1981
.33 foot

Composer. Manuscript songs (n.d.) written and published by Dawson.

Dawson, Winnie M. 359
Papers 1911–1967
4.33 feet

Teacher. Manuscripts (1952–1967) regarding the history of Wanette, Oklahoma, and its schools, along with Protestant religious song books (1911–1913).

Unpublished finding aid available.

Day, John Lewis 360
Printed materials 1910–1941
.10 foot

Physician. A daybook (1910–1911); a pamphlet (1913) on preparation for childbirth; reprints of two articles (1932, 1941) by Day; and a copy of *Harlow's Weekly* (1935) containing a story about Day.

De Camp Consolidated Glass Casket Company Collection 361
Printed materials 1938
1 item

Business. A sales catalog (1938) describing and illustrating casket models offered by the De Camp Consolidated Glass Casket Company.

Dean, Samuel C.   362
Papers 1896–1906
.10 foot

Physician. A ledger (1902–1906); a memorial to Charles D. Frick (1902); and an indexed ledger of class notes (1896–1900) taken by Dean while a student at Barnes Medical College, St. Louis, Missouri.

DeBarr, Edwin C. (1859–1950)   363
Papers 1870–1950
1.33 feet

Professor and chemist. Correspondence and reports (1897–1950) regarding essays, autopsies, chemical analyses, and consultations conducted by DeBarr; services rendered by DeBarr as expert witness in legal cases; the DeBarr family and personal affairs; members of the University of Oklahoma faculty and Board of Regents; and the construction and laboratory fittings of the University of Oklahoma's chemistry building, including a report (1870–1872) on the survey of the Indian Meridian boundary through Indian Territory.

Unpublished finding aid available.

Debo, Angie Elbertha (1890–1988)   364
Papers 1953–1976
.66 feet

Historian. A galley proof and original typescript for the book *Geronimo* (University of Oklahoma Press, 1976); correspondence (1967–1972) written by Debo on behalf of Alaskan Indians to regain their tribal lands; and newspaper clippings (1953–1954) of Debo's column in the *Daily Oklahoman*.

Decker, Charles Elijah (1868–1958)   365
Papers 1861–1957
5.33 feet

Professor. General correspondence (1911–1957); papers (1923–1950) regarding the University of Oklahoma chapter of the geology fraternity, Sigma Gamma Epsilon; correspondence (1925–1942), membership lists, and expense records (1934–1935) from the Oklahoma

Academy of Science; manuscripts, reprints, and research correspondence (1932–1934) from Decker's research on the geology of Oklahoma and on grapholites; correspondence (1925–1946) and notebooks (n.d.) concerning the Methodist Episcopal Church in Norman, Oklahoma; correspondence and printed material (1931–1952) concerning the University of Oklahoma; and correspondence and printed material (1913–1955) from geological associations and other universities.

Unpublished finding aid available.

DeKnight, Emma H. 366
Diary 1886–1892
1 item

Teacher. A diary (1886–1892) kept by DeKnight and relating her experience as a teacher at the Chilocco Indian School and the Oto school at the Red Rock Indian Agency. The diary emphasizes the time DeKnight spent among the Otos and includes a list (1887) of her Oto students.

Delaware Indian Agency Collection 367
Records 1867–1874
2 items

Indian tribal agency. A manuscript allotment list (1867) prepared by the federal government when the Delaware Indians moved from their reservation in Kansas to settle along the Caney River, Indian Territory, along with a printed Delaware allotment list published in 1874.

Delta Tau Delta Collection 368
Ledger 1922–1958
1 item

College social fraternity. A ledger (1922–1958) containing rosters of initiates of the University of Oklahoma Delta Alpha chapter of Delta Tau Delta fraternity.

DeMoss, Robert 369
Papers 1993–1994
.10 foot

Historian. Correspondence (1993) from Berlin B. Chapman to Robert DeMoss regarding Opothleyaholo and the location of an 1861 battlefield; and two articles (n.d.) by DeMoss, on the Battle of Caving Banks (Indian Territory), and Opothleyaholo.

Dennis, Frank Landt, Sr. (b. 1907) 370
Papers 1928–1988
.75 foot

Journalist and attorney. Correspondence (1933–1988); certificates (1933–1941); ribbons and patches (1929–1947); cartoons (n.d.); publications (1928–1988); newspaper clippings (1928–1939); and a scrapbook (1928–1935) chronicling the life of Frank Dennis as a student at the University of Oklahoma and as an editor. Also included in the collection are teletype printouts (1962) from an unidentified wire service detailing news of the United States' first human orbital space flight by John Glenn in the space capsule *Friendship*.

Denver, James William (1817–1892) 371
Papers 1849–1891
.50 foot

Lawyer and U.S. Army general. Correspondence (1855–1888) from the Denver family, from politicians concerning national politics and political appointments, and from Denver's legal practice, including cases involving damage claims for cotton illegally seized by the U.S. government during the Civil War; a manuscript account (n.d.) of Denver's activities as a Union brigadier general, 1861–1863; a pamphlet (1884) endorsing Denver as a Democratic nominee for the presidency; typescripts of a journal (1850) kept by Denver during an overland journey from Fort Leavenworth, Kansas Territory, to California; pamphlets (1865–1891) of speeches by Denver and others; bills for legislation in which Denver had an interest; and a genealogical chart (n.d.) of the Francis Xavier Rombach family.

Denver and Salt Lake Railroad Collection 372
Printed materials 1911
1 item

Railroad company. A booklet entitled "Over the 'Moffat Road' to the Top of the World," by Tom Jones.

Department of the West Collection 373
Papers 1861
1 item

U.S. military division. A bound copy of telegrams, military reports and dispatches, letters, orders, and other papers (1861) following the progress and development of affairs in the Department of the West while under the command of Major General J. C. Fremont.

DeRosier, Arthur H. 374
Papers 1780–1903
.10 foot

Collector. Photocopies of correspondence (1780–1842) between William and Diana Dunbar regarding the American Revolution, New Orleans, Louisiana, and the Napoleonic wars in Europe, along with correspondence (1901–1903) between the U.S. Department of the Interior and its surveyor, Charles L. Wood, regarding townsite locations and surveys in Indian Territory.

Des Champs, John Lefeber 375
Papers 1905–1994
1 foot

Amateur historian. Typewritten and handwritten copies of manuscripts, reminiscences, and research materials (1905–1994) regarding the Des Champs and Lefeber families and various railroad companies, including the Midland Valley Railroad Company, the Kansas, Oklahoma, and Gulf Railway Company, and the Oklahoma City–Ada–Atoka Railway Company.

Unpublished finding aid available.

DeStwolinski, Louis C. 376
Papers 1844–1958
.10 foot

Amateur radio operator. Postcards (1933–1958) from amateur radio operators in numerous states and foreign countries, confirming radio contacts with DeStwolinski, along with a certificate (1844) of land purchase issued to Nathan Bass by the United States for land in Mineral Point, Wisconsin.

Detrick, C. H. 377
Papers 1880–1897
6 items

Interpreter. A Comanche–English dictionary (ca. 1895), with a Comanche alphabet and diacritical markings, compiled by Detrick while serving as an interpreter for the Red Store Trading Post at Fort Sill, Indian Territory. Also included in the collection are typescripts (n.d.) on the Comanche language, customs and conventions, the Lord's Prayer in Comanche, a translated Comanche reminiscence with language notes and explanations, and a typewritten memoir (ca. 1890) by Detrick about his work at the Red Store Trading Post.

DeVilliers, Myrtle 378
Papers 1891–1904
.10 foot

Collector. Quapaw tribal records (1891–1904) relating to governmental affairs, tribal schools, labor contracts, and farm leases, along with legal documents (1900) pertaining to the settlement of the estate of George Bingham, an early settler among the Quapaw Indians.

[93]

Devoe Family Collection 379
Papers 1867–1902
.33 foot

Subject collection. Genealogical records (n.d.) of the Cavnelos Devoe and Elizabeth Shaw family; and records (1867, 1902) regarding the Elizabeth Smead family.

Dewlen, Al 380
Papers 1961
.66 foot

Author. A manuscript (1961) of Dewlen's award-winning book, *Twilight of Honor*, with accompanying research notes.

Diamond Jubilee Commission Collection 381
Records 1982
1 foot

Official state commission. Records (1982) of the commission, including correspondence, proclamations, resolutions, and reports, along with calendars of commission-sponsored activities celebrating the seventy-fifth anniversary of Oklahoma's statehood.

Unpublished finding aid available.

Dill, C. A. 382
Typescript 1868–1869
1 item

Collector. A typescript of the journal (1868–1869) of Lt. P. V. Hardman, an officer on Gen. George Armstrong Custer's staff, Seventh U.S. Cavalry, detailing the Battle of the Washita, from the Osage scouts' reconnaissance to the departure of the Cheyenne prisoners for Fort Supply, Indian Territory.

Dinkler, Frank A. 383
Ledger 1893–1902
1 item

Pharmacist. An accounts receivable ledger (1893–1902) from the Jewel Drug Store in Hennessey, Oklahoma Territory. The book includes lists of the pharmaceuticals used and the prices paid for them.

Disney, Richard Lester (b. 1887) 384
Papers 1940–1951
3 feet

Judge. Majority and dissenting opinions (1940–1951) by Disney, on cases heard while serving on the U.S. Board of Tax Appeals from 1936 to 1951.

Ditzler, Walter Linginfelter (1892–ca. 1978) 385
Printed materials 1952–1967
2 items

Attorney. Poems (1952–1967) by Ditzler about his children and grandchildren, including some family data.

Division of Manuscripts Collection 386
Papers 1682–1969
4 feet

Subject collection. Letters, reports, publications, and manuscripts reflecting the history of Oklahoma and of its American Indian tribes and nations, including correspondence (1813–1839) from U.S. government officials concerning policy toward the Indians, especially in regard to the Indian removal, and correspondence (1862) from Confederate Army officer Albert Pike in regard to Confederate States of America policy toward the Indians. Also included in this collection is a group of French colonial documents (1682–1794), along with diaries and journals (1770–1877) of travelers on the American frontier. The collection contains material on a variety of topics; researchers are urged to consult the inventory to determine the full scope of the collection's contents.

Unpublished finding aid available.

Division of Manuscripts Map Collection 387
Printed materials 1630–1986
5,200 items

Map collection. Maps and atlases (1630–1986), both domestic and foreign, of North America, Oklahoma, Oklahoma and Indian territories, and the world. Included are maps of colonial French North America, of the locations of Indian tribes and reservations in the United States throughout its history, and of the early territorial west and southwest. Specific collections of Oklahoma interest include the Sanborn Fire Insurance Company maps of cities and towns of Oklahoma, and the Fred L. Wenner Collection of maps relating to the Cherokee Strip and the Territory of Oklahoma.

Unpublished finding aid available.

Dixon, A. 388
Records 1908–1944
1.25 feet

Physician. Patient account records from Dixon's medical practice in the Kingfisher County, Oklahoma, towns of Lacey (1908–1909), Kiel, now Loyal (1915–1917), and Hennessey (1920–1944), along with Dixon's records of births attended throughout the county and of drugs he prescribed (1917–1918).

Dolman, Lewis Samuel 389
Printed materials 1930
1 item

Attorney. An incomplete copy of the *Krohn Oil Review* (1930), with a map of the Madill, Oklahoma, oil field.

Donnelley, Herndon Ford (b. 1900) 390
Printed materials 1982
3 items

Collector. Correspondence and brochures (1982) regarding the establishment of the Individual Opportunity Achievement Ranch at Perkins, Oklahoma, along with a research paper (n.d.) about the Donnelley family, entitled "The Study of a Pioneering Seamstress," by Diana Inskip.

Doody, Maurice 391
Printed materials 1953–1954
3 items

Cobbler. A booklet (1954) by Doody, entitled *Modern Shoe and Foot Helps*, about tanning, the working of leather, and the making and repairing of shoes, along with two manuscripts (1953–1954) by Doody on the trend of education in the United States.

Doran, Lowry A. (1886–1966) 392
Typescripts 1892–1942
.50 foot

Collector. A typescript of the diary (1892–1893) kept by Abraham J. Seay, governor of Oklahoma Territory; typescripts of newspaper articles (1943) concerning foreign affairs and U.S. foreign policy; and two typescript copies of "How War Came," by Forrest Davis and Ernest K. Lindley, published in the *Ladies Home Journal* (1942) and concerning America's entrance into World War II.

Dorrance, Lemuel (1876–1921) 393
Papers 1896–1921
5 items

Pharmacist. A diploma (1896) from the University of Oklahoma School of Pharmacy, one of the first two diplomas granted by the university; two certificates (1896–1897) from the Oklahoma Board of Pharmacy and the Oklahoma Pharmaceutical Association; a log of correspondence (1920–1921) kept by Dorrance in Nicaragua; and a copy of *Southern Pharmaceutical Journal* (1955) with an 1896 photograph of Dorrance.

Dott, Robert Henry 394
Printed materials 1818
1 item

Geologist. A copy of *Liverpool Quarterly Magazine*, Volume 1, 1818.

Dowd, Jerome H. (b. 1864) 395
Papers 1891–1943
1.66 feet

Professor and sociologist. Personal correspondence (1930–1954) and manuscripts of books and articles written by Dowd while a sociology professor at the University of Oklahoma, 1907–1947. The manuscripts include two copies of Dowd's *The Negro in American Life* (1926); three unpublished manuscripts entitled "Seeing the World by Tramping and Ford Car" (1939), "The New World as Viewed by the Prophets and Interpreted by Jerome Dowd" (1943), and "Social Aspects of Art" (n.d.); and two article-length manuscripts dealing with Oklahoma prison reform and juvenile delinquency.

Unpublished finding aid available.

[97]

Drake, Noah Fields (1864–1945)   396
Papers 1894–1948
.10 foot

Professor and geologist. Geological reports (1916–1935) from oil and gas companies in Oklahoma; reprints of articles (1897–1945); and two field notebooks and a class notebook (1894–1895) belonging to Fields, a professor of geology and mining at the University of Arkansas.

DuBois Family Collection   397
Manuscript ca. 1849
1 item

Family collection. A brief history (ca. 1849) of the DuBois family, recounting the arrival of Louis DuBois in America in 1661, the purchase of land from Indians, the captivity of Catherine DuBois by Indians, and family participation in the American Revolution.

Duff, H. R.   398
Printed materials n.d.
2 items

Collector. Two buggy advertisements (n.d.) from the F. A. Ames Company, Inc., in Owensboro, Kentucky.

Duffy, Homer   399
Records 1943–1968
2 feet

Collector. Correspondence, tax records, audits, and financial statements (1943–1968) of the Oklahoma Farmers Union and of its subsidiary organizations, the Oklahoma Farmers Union Supply Association (1950–1957) and the Union Mutual Insurance Company (1947–1968); financial statements (1954–1955) of the Oklahoma Farmers Union Service Corporation and the Oklahoma Farmers Union Cooperative (1956–1960); financial reports (1961–1964) of the Mid-Continent Farmers Cooperative; and correspondence and financial reports (1949–1955) of the National Farmers Union.

Unpublished finding aid available.

Duke Indian Oral History Collection 400
Papers 1890–1968
20 feet

Oral history collection. Typescripts of interviews (1967–1972) conducted with hundreds of Indians in Oklahoma, regarding the histories and cultures of their respective nations and tribes. Related are accounts of Indian ceremonies, customs, social conditions, philosophies, and standards of living. Members of every tribe resident in Oklahoma were interviewed. The collection includes the original tapes on which the interviews were recorded, as well as microfiche copies of the typescripts.

Published finding aid available.

Duke, James Monroe 401
Records 1902–1926
5 items

Collector. Land deeds (1903–1908) issued by the Choctaw and Chickasaw nations; Choctaw Indian land allotment certificates (1903–1904); stock ownership certificates (1918–1923) issued by Oklahoma associations and companies; and a letter (1926) by Oklahoma congressman William W. Hastings in reply to charges made by his political opponent.

Dukes, Gilbert W. (b. 1849) 402
Printed materials 1877–1905
.25 foot

Indian chief. Typescripts of correspondence (1900–1901) written during Dukes's tenure as principal chief of the Choctaw Nation and relating to leases, stock raising, and Choctaw Indian schools; speeches (1900–1902); biographical information (1901); and political writings (1900–1905) reflecting the problems involved in the transition from tribal government to territorial, and, ultimately, state jurisdiction.

Duncan, Hank 403
Printed materials 1931, 1934
.33 foot

Sheriff and singer. Reprint of an article by Walter M. Harrison regarding Hank Duncan and the T-Bone Ranch, and a drawing of Hank Duncan.

Duncum, Floy 404
Papers 1941
3 items

Collector. Memoirs (n.d.) of James Louis Avant, relating his experiences as bailiff of the U.S. District Court for Western Arkansas at Fort Smith, Arkansas, and as disciplinarian of the Kiowa Indian schools at Anadarko, Oklahoma Territory, along with anecdotes of a hunting trip in the Kiamichi Mountains (Oklahoma), plus two obituaries (1941) of Avant.

Dungan, Eva Ellsworth 405
Papers 1898–1952
.33 foot

Music instructor. Personal correspondence (1917–1924); a poem (ca. 1924) regarding the South Canadian River; performance programs (1928) of the Oklahoma City Symphony Orchestra and of the University of Oklahoma Children's Sooner Orchestra (1917–1918); and newspaper clippings (1941–1945) regarding World War II.

Dunlap, S. T. 406
Certificate 1909
1 item

Collector. A homestead certificate (1909) issued to William O. Hartshorne, Jr., and bearing the signature of President William H. Taft, granting Hartshorne the right to homestead land in Kay County, Oklahoma.

Durant, William A. (1866–1952) 407
Printed materials 1926, 1937
2 items

Indian chief. Two typescripts of newspaper articles (1926, 1937) regarding the life and work of William A. Durant.

Duvall, Preston Van Buren 408
Manuscript 1938
1 item

Pioneer. A typed manuscript (1938) concerning the life of Preston Duvall and his experiences in the 1893 land run into the Cherokee Strip.

Dwight Mission Collection 409
Papers 1957
1 item

Subject collection. A biographical letter (1957) by Charles C. Torrey, in which the history of Dwight Mission is noted.

Eagle-Picher Mining and Smelting Company Collection 410
Records 1939–1974
4 feet

Mining company. Correspondence (1967–1974) related to geophysical consultants; equipment records and inventories (1939–1970) for the central mill; general ledgers (1940–1945, 1949–1951); a check ledger (1939–1945); and survey and drill records, all relating to the company's Oklahoma operations.

Unpublished finding aid available.

Eastman, Francis B. 411
Printed materials 1908–1909
2 items

Collector. Picture postcards (1908–1909) depicting a military parade through Sidney, Ohio, and a social gathering on the grounds of Fort George Wright, Spokane, Washington.

Edwards, Archibald Cason (b. ca. 1910) 412
Papers 1875–1987
104 feet

Investment broker. Correspondence (ca. 1875–1950) of the Robert James Edwards and J. S. Handy families; business correspondence (ca. 1890–1945) from Edwards's investment-securities firm, R. J. Edwards, Inc., including University of Oklahoma dormitory and Memorial Union building bonds (1946–1948); and concert and theater programs (1928–1987) from musical and theater productions throughout the United States and particularly in Oklahoma City and at the University of Oklahoma.

Unpublished finding aid available.

Edwards, Thomas Allison (1874–1955) 413
Manuscript 1949
1 item

Attorney. A twenty-page manuscript entitled "Early Days in the C & A," which was published in the *Chronicles of Oklahoma* (Summer, 1949) and in which Edwards recounts his experiences as a teacher and lawyer after coming to Washita County, Oklahoma Territory, in 1898.

Edwards, Virginia   414
Records 1940–1980
16 feet

Investment broker. Prospectuses (65 notebooks) for bond issues underwritten by R. J. Edwards, Inc. Includes a two-volume index to the prospectuses, as well as a three-volume index to audits of public entities such as cities and towns, hospitals, and colleges.

[101]

El Reno Citizens National Bank Collection   415
Records 1891–1930
15 feet

Bank. Financial records (1891–1930), including ledgers, journals, remittance registers, draft registers, loans and discount registers, collections registers, and daily balance books reflecting the daily commerce of the bank and that of its predecessor, the El Reno Bank of El Reno, Oklahoma.

Elder, Frederick Stanton (b. 1868)   416
Papers 1889–1904
.10 foot

Professor. Correspondence (1900–1902) and speeches (1902–1904) relating to Elder's involvement in the controversy over selling Oklahoma school lands.

Elk City Community Hospital Collection   417
Printed materials 1931–1953
5 items

Co-op health facility. Brochures (1931–1953) describing services provided by the Elk City, Oklahoma, hospital and the costs of each service.

Elk City Farmers National Bank Collection   418
Records 1920–1930
10 feet

Bank. Financial records (1920–1930), including correspondence, ledgers, journals, certificates of deposit registers, discount registers, and tellers' cash books, in which the daily business of the bank was recorded. The collection includes records of an institutional predecessor, the German State Bank, also in Elk City, Oklahoma.

Elk City First National Bank Collection   419
Printed materials 1901–1951
2 items

Bank. Booklets printed by the bank to mark its fiftieth anniversary (1951) and tracing the history of the bank and of Elk City, Oklahoma.

Elkins, Harrison M.   420
Papers 1952
2 items

Merchant. Poems (1952) by Harrison M. Elkins, including a work entitled "Sooners and Settlers."

Elliott, J. Ross   421
Papers 1975
4 items

Genealogist. A letter (1975) from Elliott commenting on the Boyd family, along with a manuscript (n.d.) and newspaper clippings (1975) tracing the genealogy of the David Ross Boyd family, including its coat of arms.

Ellison, (Mrs.) C. D.   422
Papers 1834–1956
4 items

Collector. A pamphlet (n.d.) entitled "Darlington, the Indian's Friend," which chronicles the life of the Cheyenne-Arapaho Indian agent and Quaker missionary, Brinton Darlington; a speech (1945) by Edgar S. Vaught, giving a brief history of Oklahoma; and a diary (1891–1893) kept by Caro Emerson while a student at Bethany College, Lindsborg, Kansas.

Embry, John   423
Papers 1908
1 item

Attorney. Legal brief by John Embry, an attorney of Guthrie, Oklahoma, to the U.S. Attorney General, regarding Kickapoo Indian land fraud and misappropriations in Oklahoma.

English, Frank Miller (1861–1931) 424
Papers 1901–1974
4 feet

Businessman and civic leader. Correspondence (1901–1914) relating to English's banking career and civic activities in Lawton, Oklahoma, along with personal financial records (1901–1924), including receipts and cancelled checks.

Unpublished finding aid available.

English, William M. 425
Papers 1935–1950
1 foot

Businessman. Correspondence and reports (1935–1939) relating to English's land sales and rentals in the Shattuck, Oklahoma, area, along with personal correspondence (1935–1950) with his family, friends, and civic organizations.

Unpublished finding aid available.

Epton, Hicks Byers (1906–1972) 426
Records 1860–1880
.10 foot

Collector. Discharge certificates (1860–1880) issued by the U.S. Army to Seminole freedmen, including David Bowlegs, for service rendered during and after the Civil War.

Erdmann, E. M. 427
Papers 1884–1891
2 items

Collector. An autograph book (n.d.) written in German and a class grade record book (1884–1891) by a German student.

Erwin, A. M. 428
Records ca. 1921–1942
.50 foot

Physician. Ledgers (1921–1928) and birth records (1925–1942) from Erwin's medical practice in Nowata County, Oklahoma.

Eta Kappa Nu Collection 429
Records 1942–1957
.25 foot

Professional society. Records of the University of Oklahoma Beta Xi chapter of Eta Kappa Nu, a national electrical engineering honorary fraternity, including the chapter's petition (1943) for admittance to the national body, and its correspondence (1943–1957).

Evans, Arthur W. (b. 1908) 430
Papers 1816–1968
.66 foot

Collector. Correspondence (1906–1968); certificates (1891–1918); and news clippings (1928–1939) regarding University of Oklahoma president Arthur Grant Evans, federal funding for schools in Indian Territory, the issue of separate statehood for Oklahoma and Indian territories, and Evans's participation in the United States' propaganda effort in World War I; a typescript regarding the history (1816–1831) of the Presbyterian church and missions in the eastern Cherokee Nation; a diary (1887) of A. G. Evans; and original records (1830–1857) of the New Echota Church in the Cherokee Nation, as recorded by Samuel A. Worcester, church clerk.

Evans, Charles 431
Correspondence 1862–1893
.10 foot

Collector. Correspondence (1862–1863) between Lt. Lyle Garrett of the Twenty-third Iowa Infantry and his wife, Mary Garrett. His letters describe camp life, attitudes toward officers, and troop movements in Missouri, Arkansas, Texas, Louisiana, Mississippi, and Alabama. Garrett also describes the general conduct of the war, soldiers' views about action in other theaters of the war, attitudes concerning the South, slavery, and the destruction caused by the war. The collection also contains three letters (1866–1893) regarding the Garrett family in general.

Evans, Melissa 432
Papers 1877
1 item

Collector. Correspondence (1877) to Melissa Evans from her husband, Elisha Evans, regarding his travels through Caddo, Indian Territory.

Evans, Oren F. 433
Papers. 1940–1950
.33 foot

Professor. Manuscripts (1940–1950) of geological articles and fiction stories written by professor of Geology, Oren F. Evans.

Ewing, Amos Alexander (1862–1937) 434
Papers 1891–1895
3 items

Politician. Correspondence (1895) and a certificate (1891) appointing Ewing a member of the Board of Regents of Oklahoma Agricultural and Mechanical College in the Territory of Oklahoma, and signed by territorial governor Abraham J. Seay.

Ewing, Cortez Arthur Milton (1896–1962) 435
Papers 1910–1951
20.33 feet

Professor. Manuscripts (1933–1961) of Ewing's papers on political theory and of his book *Essentials of American Government*; research materials (ca. 1930–1960), including information on impeachment and primary elections; lecture notes (ca. 1920–1930) and other teaching materials (ca. 1930–1960); correspondence (ca. 1930–1960); and speeches (ca. 1920–1950), all relating to American government.

Unpublished finding aid available.

Ewing, Finis W. 436
Printed materials 1942
3 items

Physician. A certificate (1942) awarded to Finis W. Ewing by the Oklahoma State Medical Association for study in internal medicine; a program (1942) for the Annual Meeting of the Fifth Counselor District of the Oklahoma State Medical Association; and one issue (1942) of *The Journal of the Oklahoma State Medical Association*.

Ezell, John Samuel (1917–2001) 437
Papers 1955–1984
.33 foot

Historian. A transcript of an oral history interview (1984) conducted by Herbert R. Hengst with John S. Ezell, recounting Ezell's tenure as dean of the University of Oklahoma College of Arts and Sciences; research and seminar papers (1955–1980) written by Ezell's students and colleagues, including three by Jack Ericson Eblen concerning the growth of the African-American slave population in nineteenth-century America and Cuba, and one by Gary L. Cunningham concerning gambling in frontier Kansas.

Fagin, Kay K. 438
Dissertation 1978
3 items

Anthropologist. A dissertation (1978) by Kay K. Fagin, entitled "Matrifocality in a Contemporary Cheyenne Community."

Fairland Municipal Records Collection 439
Records 1909–1945
4 feet

Municipality. Correspondence (1933–1936) relating to the finances of the city of Fairland, Oklahoma; copies of city ordinances (1935); a financial record book (1912–1926); two ledgers (1921–1924); a receipt book (1933); books of treasurer's warrants (1930–1936); and a daybook (ca. 1920) containing records of water bonds, electric bonds, and sinking funds.

Unpublished finding aid available.

Fairland National Bank Collection 440
Printed materials 1918–1926
.10 foot

Bank. Business correspondence (1923); sales catalogs (ca. 1920); and U.S. Treasury Department publications (1919–1922) regarding federal income tax laws and estate taxes.

Falconer, Ray, and Velma Falconer 441
Papers 1884–1923
.50 foot

Collectors. Diary (1886–1887) of Alice Cornish, and correspondence (1884–1923) of Cornish family members, including James Cornish (father), Esther Cornish (mother), and their six children, Alice, Mabel, Harry, Ed, George, and Arthur, reflecting family matters and photography studios of the late nineteenth and early twentieth centuries.

Farley, Alan W. 442
Papers 1833–1966
2.50 feet

Collector. A typewritten manuscript (n.d.) in which Homer W. Wheeler describes his life as a U.S. Army scout; numerous broadsides, newspapers, and handbills (1840–1966) regarding the settlement of Kansas, along with a wide variety of other documents (1833–1965) collected by Farley and relating to the Civil War, settlement of Kansas, Indian battles on the Great Plains, with an emphasis on Kansas and on the history of the West in general.

Unpublished finding aid available.

Farmers State Bank Collection 443
Ledger 1913–1918
1 item

Bank. A general ledger (1913–1918) from the Farmers State Bank of Park Hill, Oklahoma.

Farmers Union Cooperative Gin Company Collection 444
Records 1927–1948
.10 foot

Agricultural cooperative organization. Bylaws (1927) of the company; minutes (1927–1936) of the meetings of its members and directors; and a company financial statement (1948).

Farwell, John V., Jr. 445
Manuscript 1870–1938
1 item

Collector. Typescript (n.d.) regarding a trip by John V. Farwell, Jr., age eleven years, to Kansas in August of 1870 with his father, John D. Lang, and Vincent Collyer of the Board of Indian Commissioners.

Faux, Kathleen 446
Papers 1888–1995
.50 foot

Collector. Correspondence (1889–1890) of the Reverend and Mrs. Joseph Leiper and Margaret McCarrell, regarding their experiences as Presbyterian missionaries at Park Hill, Cherokee Nation, Indian Territory; notes (1935) written by Rev. Leiper regarding his life's work; a typewritten manuscript (1995) by Kathleen Faux regarding the letters of Rev. Leiper and Mrs. McCarrell; *Cherokee Pictorial Book with Catechism and Hymns*, compiled and translated by Rev. A. N. Chamberlin, 1888; and an article by Joseph McCarrell Leiper regarding the life and work of Rev. Joseph Leiper.

Fay, Robert O., and Helen S. Fay 447
Printed materials 1904–1982
.10 foot

Collectors. Correspondence and research materials (1977–1981) regarding the southwest Davis, Oklahoma, zinc field; and newspaper clippings (1968–1982) regarding primitive humans, including "Bigfoot" and the Tasaday Indians of the Philippines.

Feaver, John Clayton (1911–1995) 448
Papers 1968–1975
1.66 feet

Professor. Resource files (1974–1975) compiled by philosophy professor, John Clayton Feaver, while chairing the Commission on Curriculum for the University of Oklahoma College of Arts and Sciences, including correspondence and memoranda from outside consultants; information on curriculum programs at other universities; correspondence, memoranda, and reports from subcommittees; curriculum proposals; committee minutes; and copies of the final report. Also files (1968–1970) compiled by Feaver while chairing the University Constitution Drafting Committee, including correspondence, memoranda, drafts, faculty comments on drafts, bibliographies, notes, and clippings.

Unpublished finding aid available.

Felger, (Mrs.) J. H. 449
Papers 1946
1 item

Collector. A deed (1946) to a cemetery lot in the Independent Order of Odd Fellows Cemetery in Cleveland County, Oklahoma.

Ferguson, Milton James (1879–1954) 450
Grade book 1906
1 item

Librarian. A grade book for a course in bibliography taught by Ferguson at the University of Oklahoma in 1906.

Ferguson, Thompson Benton (1857–1921)   451
Papers 1901–1911
2.66 feet

Governor. Letterbooks of correspondence sent (1902–1911) and letters received (1901–1911) by Ferguson during his term as governor of Oklahoma Territory, along with a scrapbook containing newspaper clippings about Ferguson.

Unpublished finding aid available.

Ferguson, Walter Scott (1886–1936)   452
Papers 1863–1960
17.33 feet

Banker. Business and personal correspondence (1883–1951), the majority concerning Walter Ferguson's tenure as vice president of the Exchange National Bank in Tulsa, Oklahoma; a book-length manuscript (n.d.) on the Choctaw Indians; brand books (1906–1918) of Walter Ferguson; correspondence (1902–1906) to Thompson B. Ferguson, governor of Oklahoma Territory; typescripts of annual reports (1904–1905) of Thompson B. Ferguson as governor of Oklahoma Territory to the secretary of the interior; and correspondence (1928–1942) to Lucia Loomis Ferguson concerning her syndicated newspaper column, "One Woman's Opinion," along with manuscripts (ca. 1930–1962) and clippings (ca. 1928–1942) of her column.

Unpublished finding aid available.

Ferrell, Sally   453
Printed material 1982
1 item

Journalist. Newspaper clipping (1982) of an article written by Sally Ferrell for her column, "Historic Highlights," in the *Lincoln County News*, recounting news stories from Lincoln County, Oklahoma, in 1914.

Feuquay, Courtland Matson (1890–1949)   454
Papers 1885–1948
7 feet

Attorney and state senator. General correspondence (1915–1940) of Feuquay; his personal correspondence (1923–1925) as a state senator; Works Progress Administration work relief lists (1934–1935); case records (1917–1948) of railroad litigation in which Feuquay served as counsel; Selective Service directives (1941–1946); American Legion-related papers (1919–1924), including "40 et 8" materials; a diary (1885) of Feuquay's grandfather, W. B. Holland; and an account book (1905–1908) of Feuquay's father, J. W. Feuquay.

Unpublished finding aid available.

Field, J. Walker 455
Speech 1904
1 item

Assistant attorney general. A speech entitled "The Essentials of a Great Republic," written by Field in 1904 while a member of The Forum, a University of Oklahoma student literary and debating society.

Fillman, Irvin 456
Papers 1951
7 items

Treasure hunter. Correspondence (1951) from Fillman to Oklahoma governor Johnston Murray, describing excavations around Comanche, Oklahoma; from Murray to Fillman, forwarding Fillman's letter to Morris L. Wardell, a professor at the University of Oklahoma; and from Wardell to Fillman, and Wardell to Murray, acknowledging receipt of Fillman's original letter.

Findlay, James Franklin 457
Papers 1934–1938
.10 foot

Collector. Records (1934–1938) chronicling the origin, organization, and function of the Independent Men's Association of the University of Oklahoma, including typescripts (n.d.) regarding the history of the organization and a mailing list (n.d.) of persons to whom its publications were mailed, along with publications (1934–1938), including the local chapter newsletter *The Roundup*, and a program from the first national conference of the Independent Student's Association, held at the University of Oklahoma.

Fink, John Berlin (1886–1960) 458
Papers 1834–1957
6 feet

Collector. Correspondence (1933–1955); books (1833–1959) about railroads; printed material (1935–1960) also about railroads, including travel brochures and timetables; maps (1834–1883, ca. 1955) relating to early military posts in Oklahoma Territory and surrounding states; and notebooks (1934) kept by Fink.

Unpublished finding aid available.

Finney, Thomas McKean, and Frank Florer Finney   459
Papers 1827–1977
8 feet

Indian traders. Papers of Thomas M. Finney, Indian trader at Gray Horse, Osage Agency, Oklahoma Territory, and of Frank F. Finney, historian and employee of the Indian Territory Illuminating Oil Company, including correspondence (1925–1936) relating to T. M. Finney's book *Pioneer Days of the Osage Indians, West of '96*; historical materials (1827–1977) such as correspondence, news clippings, magazine articles, and bibliographic notes of Frank Finney on topics such as the Cherokee Strip, the Osage Indian Agency, Gray Horse Trading Post, the Dalton Gang, Kaw Indian Agency, Buffalo Bill, Pawnee Bill, peyotism, President Herbert Hoover's early days in Pawhuska, Oklahoma, and Maria Tallchief; field notebooks (1915–1949) kept by Frank Finney while an employee of the Indian Territory Illuminating Oil Company; finished and unfinished articles and stories (1891–1969) by Frank Finney, Thomas Finney, and J. E. Finney, including research notes, newspaper clippings, and magazine articles; and oil and gas files (1896–1972) of Frank Finney, with articles and documents primarily relating to the Indian Territory Illuminating Oil Company and oil and gas leases on Osage Indian lands.

Unpublished finding aid available.

First, Francis Ray, Sr. (b. 1887)   460
Ledger 1911–1915
1 item

Physician. A ledger (1911–1915) of patient accounts, in which patient ailments and the remedies prescribed were recorded. The last page tallies the number of abortions, births, deaths, and the causes of death.

Fisher, Daniel G.   461
Papers 1912–1937
.66 foot

Journalist. Correspondence (1912–1937) between Fisher and numerous authors regarding their contribution to literature and thoughts concerning their prominent works. The correspondents include Sherwood Anderson, Winston Churchill, Clarence Darrow, Hamlin Garland, Will James, Helen Keller, Ring Lardner, Charles A. Lindbergh, David Lloyd George, Robert Latham Owen, Burton Rascoe, Agnes Repplier, Sigfried Sassoon, Upton Sinclair, William Allen White, and Owen Wister.

Fisher, Te Ata (1895–1995) 462
Papers 1913–1983
6.50 feet

Performer. Correspondence (1934–1983) to and from Fisher, along with printed materials (1935–1976) she used as resource material for her performances as a storyteller and interpreter of Indian folklore and culture. The collection also includes a scrapbook (1936) of a Scandinavian tour, along with some correspondence (1922–1953) and printed material (1913–1936), mostly reprints, relating to Clyde Fisher, a naturalist and Te Ata Fisher's husband.

Unpublished finding aid available.

Fisk, Charles W. (ca. 1860–1939) 463
Papers 1902–1939
.10 foot

Physician. Official transactions (1906) of the joint session of the Oklahoma state and Indian Territory medical associations; official publications (1906–1935) of the Oklahoma State Medical Association; correspondence (1926–1939) regarding Fisk's appointment as consulting surgeon to the Chicago, Rock Island, and Pacific Railroad, and certificates of election (1902–1908) to the position of city councilman in Kingfisher, Oklahoma Territory, and Oklahoma.

Fite, Gilbert C. 464
Papers 1912–1967
6 feet

Historian. Reports, correspondence, and publications (1926–1952) regarding the Mount Rushmore national monument, including correspondence (1925–1940) from its creator, Gutzon Borglum; photocopies of Borglum's diary (1925); papers (1912–1948) regarding former governor of South Dakota, Peter Norbeck; a manuscript by Fite regarding consumer cooperatives; official files (1966–1967) of the search committee appointed to recommend a candidate to become the

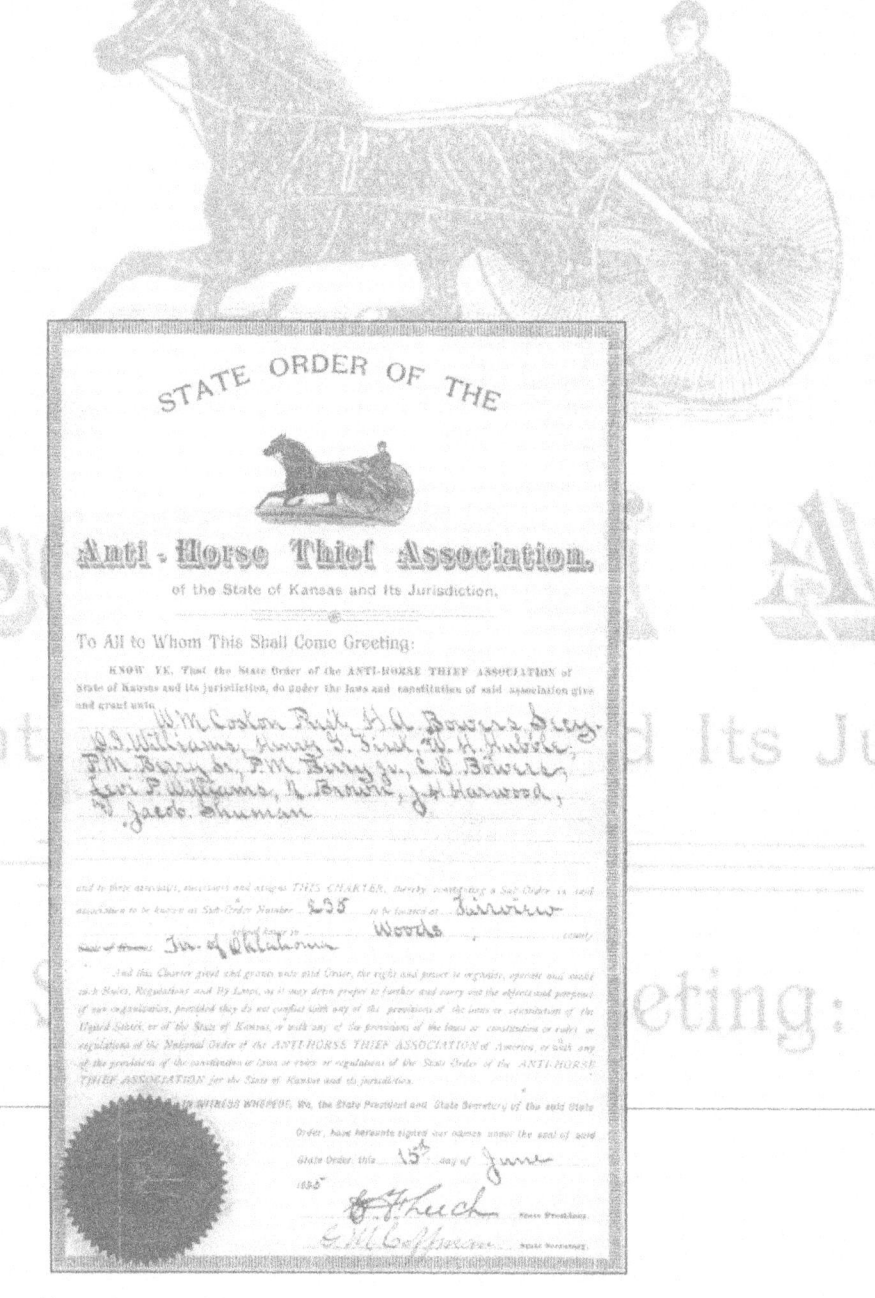

The official charter of the Fairview, Oklahoma Territory, Anti-Horse Thief Association was issued June 15, 1895. The charter was granted through the A.H.T.A. of Kansas, and bears the seal of the Kansas order. From the Anti-Horse Thief Association Collection.

eighth president of the University of Oklahoma; personal files regarding farm relief programs; and a typescript of George Peek's diary (1932–1933).

Unpublished finding aid available.

[114]

Fitzpatrick, H. L.   465
Papers 1955–1961
4 feet

Publisher. Resource files (1955–1961), including correspondence, newspaper clippings, tear sheets, drafts, and illustrations, all used by Fitzpatrick for publishing the *Oklahoma Almanac*.

Unpublished finding aid available.

Fletcher, Margaret Catherine   466
Diary 1879–1914
1 item

Homemaker. A bound photocopy of Margaret Catherine Fletcher's diary (1879–1914), which includes information regarding the history, politics, economics, and everyday life of the Flint District, Cherokee Nation; descriptions of early Tahlequah, Indian Territory, and Fort Smith, Arkansas; and detailed genealogical information concerning the Adair, Bixby, Fletcher, Guthrie, and Sanders families, including lineage charts and personal name indexes.

Flitch, Sylvester (1847–1900)   467
Printed materials 1881–1883
2 items

Cattleman. Guides (1881–1883) to cattle brands in the Cherokee Strip, Indian Territory, Kansas, and Texas, published by cattlemen's associations of those areas.

Flora, Snowden Dwight (1879–1957)   468
Papers 1920–1957
3 feet

Meteorologist. Printed materials on adverse weather conditions, especially hail and tornadoes, arranged by state; statistics and charts (ca. 1920–1950); weather maps (1930–1955); newspaper clippings (1935–

1955) and correspondence (1928–1957) concerning hail and tornadoes; clippings (1913–1955) by and about Flora; biographical materials, including Flora's awards and papers charting his career with the U.S. Weather Bureau; and a notebook (1899) Flora kept as a geography student.

Unpublished finding aid available.

Folsom, Lee W. 469
Papers 1867–1910
.66 foot

Journalist. Folsom family correspondence (1902–1908); a notebook (1897–1899) indicating the subjects studied by Folsom while a student at Atoka Baptist Seminary; and Folsom's personal account books (1905–1910). The collection also includes annual reports (1895–1900) of the U.S. Board of Indian Commissioners; a copy of the acts and resolutions (1897) of the general council of the Choctaw Nation; a hymnal (n.d.) written in Choctaw; two copies of the *Laws of the Choctaw Nation* (1866–1891) written in English and Choctaw; a Choctaw *New Testament* (1906); a Choctaw *Pentateuch* (1867); and a letter (1885) in Choctaw from Alfred Folsom to Rainie Winthrop.

Folsom Training School Collection 470
Records 1920–1986
1.5 feet

School. Business and legal records (1922–1975) of the Folsom Training School, a Methodist mission school for Indians, located in Smithville, Oklahoma; Folsom Reunion Association correspondence and mailing lists (1968, 1985–1986); history of Sealey Chapel Methodist Church, with announcements (1966, 1970, 1981–1986) of Folsom reunions; and an article concerning the school.

Unpublished finding aid available.

Foreman, Stephen (1807–1881) 471
Papers 1837–1881
.10 foot

Missionary. Typescripts of Foreman's journals (1862–1868) describing life in the Cherokee Nation during the Civil War, along with letters (1864–1881) written by Foreman regarding the same, and letters (1837–1881) to members of the Foreman family.

Forsyth, George Alexander (1837–1915) 472
Papers 1868–1915
10 items

Army officer. Photostatic copies of Forsyth's formal report (1869) of the Battle of Beecher Island; lists (1868) of casualties; general field orders (1868); and correspondence (1872–1915) concerning veterans of this 1868 battle with the Northern Cheyenne Indians.

Fort Clark, Texas Collection 473
Records 1887–1895
.25 foot

U.S. Army post. Ledgers entitled *Index to Letters Sent* (1890), with entries arranged alphabetically, and *Company Letter Book with Index* (1887, 1894–1895), listing officers and members of the Fort Clark Sunday School, members of the fort's library association, and titles of library books.

Fort Gibson First National Bank Collection 474
Records 1904–1930
18 feet

Bank. Financial records from the Fort Gibson (Oklahoma) First National Bank, including a cash book (1908); cashiers' check registers (1919–1938); a circulation register (1917–1935); a collection register (1911–1916); commission books (1922–1930); a daily balance ledger (1904–1906); daily statement ledgers (1907–1941); daybooks (1913–1924); discount registers (1904–1920); general ledgers (1904–1932); journals (1904–1939); letters of credit books (1908–1924); liability ledgers (1922–1937); a minute book (1906–1922); notary records (1911–1916); order books (1906–1921); a payment ledger (1916–1917); reconcilement registers (1909–1937); record of checks cashed ledgers (1924–1926); bonds registers (1918–1919); tellers' cash books (1906–1937); and a time certificates of deposit ledger (1911–1929). The collection also includes a town treasurer's monthly report ledger (1923–1926) and the Muskogee County treasurer's record ledger (1908–1909).

Unpublished finding aid available.

Fort Gibson Quartermaster Collection 475
Letterbooks 1879–1890
5 feet

Military post. Correspondence documenting Fort Gibson's significance in carrying out the U.S. government's Indian policy regarding the Indian pacification program following the Civil War. Included in the collection are letters sent (1879–1890), five volumes and one index volume; and registers of letters received (1879–1880 and 1886–1890), two volumes.

**Fort Smith, Subiaco, and Eastern Railway
Company Collection**   476
Records 1908–1916
.25 foot

Railroad company. A ledger (1908–1916) in which the finances of the Fort Smith, Subiaco, and Eastern Railway Company were recorded. The records show profits, losses, and business relations with other area railroads, including the Arkansas Central Railroad.

Fortescue, John W.   477
Papers 1930
.10 foot

Collector. Correspondence (1930) from John Fortescue regarding the career of Francis Gildart, a captain in the British Legion cavalry.

Foster, Del Oneita   478
Sheet music 1956
1 item

Amateur song writer. A collection of musical compositions written, arranged, and privately published (1956) by Del Oneita Foster.

Foster, Henry Vernon   479
Papers 1872–1990
7.5 feet

Oil producer. Henry Vernon Foster's correspondence and business records (1872–1990) which detail the Foster lease in the Osage Nation, initiated in 1896; early discoveries of oil in the Osage Nation; the history of the Indian Territory Illuminating Oil Company; Foster's discovery well in the Seminole field; and his Oklahoma #1 in the Oklahoma City field. Also included in the collection are contracts and other legal documents showing lease ownership and stock ownership of the I.T.I.O. Company (1900–1940); correspondence of Henry Foster (Henry Vernon Foster's father); a ledger of shares in the I.T.I.O. company regarding start-up and leases; documents regarding negotiations of separation between Cities Service Oil Company and Foster Petroleum; documents regarding Foster's businesses prior to his dealings in the Osage Nation; and business files (1900–1937) relating to Foster's ranching activities.

Unpublished finding aid available.

Fowler, David (b. 1877) 480
Printed materials 1889–1956
6 items

Labor leader. Printed reports (1951–1956) regarding a welfare and retirement fund for miners; handbills (n.d.) relating to miners' organizations; two printed copies of a speech (1952) by the United Mine Workers of America president; and two issues (1957) of the *United Mine Workers Journal*.

Fowler, Ezra 481
Papers 1862–1863
3 items

Soldier. Correspondence (1862–1863) from Ezra Fowler to his sister, Lucy, written during his service in the United States Army (Union forces) in the Civil War. Also included are transcripts of the letters.

Fowler, Richard Gildart (1916–1992) 482
Papers 1924–1980
12 feet

Professor. Correspondence (1924–1980); lecture notes and tests for classes in physics taught by Fowler at the University of Oklahoma; manuscripts (1958–1969) for textbooks authored by Fowler; correspondence with Fowler's publishers; research notes (1943–1979) arranged by research project; and project histories and documentation (1952–1972) for contracted research projects conducted by Fowler.

Unpublished finding aid available.

Francis, (Mrs.) William 483
Printed materials 1916
1 item

Collector. Pamphlet (1916) published by the *Elk City News-Democrat*, entitled "Elk City: Queen of the West."

Franklin, William Monroe (b. 1874)   484
Papers 1874–1956
.66 foot

Attorney and state senator. Printed materials (1926–1947) concerning the Oklahoma Farmers Union and Franklin's political campaigns; copies of laws (1905–1945) drafted by Franklin; his speeches (1915–1916); newspaper clippings (1943–1947) containing his editorials; and biographical material (1874–1958).

Frayser, E. B.   485
Ledger 1870–1872
1 item

Physician. A ledger (1870–1872) in which Frayser recorded lecture notes taken while a medical student in St. Louis, Missouri.

Frederickson, Mary Brownlee   486
Papers 1920–1930
.33 foot

Writer. Typescripts and manuscripts (1920–1930) of poetry and stories regarding the Oklahoma oil fields and oil industry, all by Mary B. Frederickson.

Freedom State Bank Collection   487
Ledger 1920–1933
1 item

Bank. A ledger (1920–1933) containing financial transactions of the Freedom State Bank in Freedom, Oklahoma.

Freeman, Margaret   488
Papers 1859–1872
.10 foot

Homemaker. Correspondence (1859–1872) between Margaret Freeman in Springfield, Illinois, and her children in Texas. The Freeman family owned land near Lancaster and Starlight, Texas, and was engaged in homesteading and cattle ranching. Many of the letters describe farm and ranch life, cattle drives, and family news. These letters also contain information about local politics and racial attitudes.

Freeny, Ellis 489
Records 1897–1903
.10 foot

Collector. Biographical and genealogical materials (1897–1903) gathered by Ellis Freeny regarding Peter Perkins Pitchlynn and the Pitchlynn family.

Freudenthal, Elsbeth Estelle (1902–1953) 490
Papers 1900–1953
8 feet

Economist and author. Correspondence (ca. 1940–1950); research notes (ca. 1900–1950); manuscripts (ca. 1900–1950); printed material (1930–1953); and a bibliography (ca. 1930), all relating to the history of aviation and Latin American aviation, with an emphasis on Alberto Santos-Dumont and Pan American Airways.

Unpublished finding aid available.

Fritts, Mary 491
Printed materials 1969–1972
1 foot

Collector. Copies of radical political magazines and pamphlets (1969–1972), covering such subjects as civil rights, ecology, and the Vietnam War.

Unpublished finding aid available.

Fuller, Agnes 492
Papers 1894–1923
.10 foot

Teacher. Certificates and teaching contracts (1894–1923); a teaching assignment (1907) from the U.S. Indian Service at McAlester, Indian Territory; and the Choctaw spelling book, *Chata Holisso* (n.d.), printed by the Richmond Presbyterian Committee of Publication, containing the alphabet, symbols, tables, vocabularies, the Ten Commandments and the Lord's Prayer, names of animals, money tables, and moral essays, all in the Choctaw language.

Fullerton, Samuel Clyde, Jr. 493
Printed materials 1951
3 items

Rancher. Two catalogs (1951) of cattle sales, and a copy of *The Ranchman* (1951), containing a biographical sketch of Judge Samuel Clyde Fullerton and information on Sunbeam Farms cattle.

Fulton, J. S. (d. 1950) 494
Papers 1904–1950
14 feet

Physician. Correspondence (1930–1950); medical records (1914–1950); and certificates and citations (1922–1948) relating to J. S. Fulton's medical practice in Atoka, Oklahoma, along with minutes (1904–1911) of the Atoka County Medical Society.

Unpublished finding aid available.

Funk, Rose 495
Papers 1886–1945
1 foot

Collector. Personal correspondence (1894–1908); diplomas (1894–1905); and certificates (1910–1925) of the Funk family; books (1886–1899), including a *Majestic Cookbook* (1899) and a telegraphic code book; an autograph book (ca. 1900); a scrapbook (n.d.); and composition books (n.d.) belonging to Rose Funk; calendars (1898); printed invitations (1892–1902); greeting cards and postcards (ca. 1900); travel brochures (ca. 1920–1945); a cigar band collection (ca. 1914); and legal papers (1894–1906) from the files of attorney John Funk.

Unpublished finding aid available.

Funnell, Roberta Ann Paris 496
Papers 1972–1998
.66 foot

Lobbyist. Correspondence (1975–1998), printed materials (1972–1998), newspaper clippings (1975–1995), and legal research files (1976–1998) concerning the work of Roberta Ann Paris Funnell, founder of the Oklahoma People's Lobby and lobbyist for legislative reform for consumer protection in the health care, nuclear power, and legal industries.

Unpublished finding aid available.

Gaillardia Garden Club Collection 497
Records 1927–1954
3 items

Women's club. Notebooks (1927–1954) containing programs, membership lists, and minutes, along with a history of this Norman, Oklahoma, club that sponsored local beautification projects.

Gaither, Edna 498
Printed materials 1860–1956
.33 foot

Collector. Newspaper clippings (1860–1956) regarding the history of the Missouri-Kansas-Arkansas-Oklahoma border area, including information on Indians, border industries, monuments and landmarks, the Civil War, and individuals such as George W. Carver and Belle Starr.

Galen Society Collection 499
Records 1932–1952
.10 foot

Professional organization. Correspondence (1933–1948); the club constitution (1948); membership lists (1932–1948); minutes (1938–1939); account ledgers (1932–1950); and memorabilia of this pharmacy-related organization at the University of Oklahoma.

Gallaher, William M. (1877–1955) 500
Papers 1925–1954
1.66 feet

Physician. Correspondence (1925–1950); manuscripts (n.d.) on medical topics; and account ledgers and daybooks (1925–1950) from Gallaher's general practice in Shawnee, Oklahoma; and publications (1950–1954) concerning Oklahoma medical laws and the health and pension plans of the Chicago, Rock Island, and Pacific Railroad.

Unpublished finding aid available.

Gamble, Richard Dalzell (b. 1925) 501
Printed materials 1853–1866
.33 foot

Professor. Photocopies of correspondence (1853–1854) from the letterbook of the commanding officer of Fort Union, New Mexico; typescript of the diary (1853–1854) of Caleb Burwell Rowan Kennerly, entitled "Diary of a Journey to California, 1853–1854"; photocopies of articles on the founding of D'Hanis, Texas, and on exploring expeditions through the American Southwest; and notecards (n.d.) made by Gamble while conducting historical research on the Southwest.

Gardner, Florence Guild Bruce (1900–1955)   502
Papers 1940–1953
1 foot

Author. Book manuscripts by Gardner, including "Woman: Her Power and Glory" and "Lillie of Six-Shooter Junction"; correspondence (1940–1953), a poster (1940), and scrapbooks and newspaper clippings (1940–1953) regarding Gardner and the release of her books; music scores (1942–1944) on the end of World War II, Gen. Douglas MacArthur, and the absence of Christianity in Great Britain; and publications (1940–1948), including Gardner's book *He is Risen: A History of the Wichita Mountains Easter Pageant*, and a copy of *The Official Peace Officer*, concerning the death of Anthony Mark Wallock, a minister who was a strong advocate of the pageant.

Unpublished finding aid available.

Gardner, Jefferson (ca. 1846–1906)   503
Printed materials 1894–1906
.10 foot

Indian chief. Typescripts of newspaper articles (1894–1906), including speeches and letters, by and about Gardner, a principal chief of the Choctaws, and also relating to such issues as slavery, financial affairs, tribal factionalism, and the allotment of land by the Dawes Commission.

Gardner, Oscar   504
Printed materials 1950–1955
5 items

Teacher. Booklets and brochures (1950–1955) describing the Goodland Indian Orphanage and School in Goodland, Oklahoma.

Garretson, Anna Kate   505
Diploma 1907
1 item

Student. A diploma (1907) awarded to Anna Kate Garretson from Spaulding Female College, Muskogee, Indian Territory.

Garretson, Henry David　　　　506
Records 1904–1923
.25 foot

Collector. Abstracts of title (1911–1919) for land in Pittsburg County, Oklahoma; an abstract of title (1904) for the townsite of Quinton, Indian Territory; and government bonds (1915–1923) from the Republic of Germany and the Kingdom of Hungary.

Garrity, Richard T.　　　　507
Printed materials 1986
4.33 feet

Collector. Newsletters of the Model Railroad Interest Group (1960–1985), for which Garrity served as editor, plus his notes and typescripts for the same. Also included are correspondence (1950– 1988); published and unpublished articles by Garrity and others, regarding railroad development around Ripley, Oklahoma, and Eureka Springs, Arkansas; Oklahoma natural history; Oklahoma local history; and solar energy. The collection also contains numerous sound recordings on cassette tapes.

Unpublished finding aid available.

Garvin, Isaac L.　　　　508
Printed materials 1877–1879
7 items

Indian chief. Typescripts of legislation (1877–1879) enacted by the Choctaw Nation council concerning the courts, schools, timberlands, and coal mining.

Gary, Raymond Dancel (1908–1993)　　　　509
Papers 1955–1958
41.66 feet

Oklahoma governor. Papers (1955–1958) of Oklahoma governor Raymond D. Gary, including commissions and appointments; correspondence concerning bills before the state legislature; radio speeches and press files; correspondence concerning the teachers' retirement referendum; alphabetical files of Gary's executive assistant, Clarence Burch; minutes of meetings and correspondence from the commissioners of the land office; files of the budget office, including payroll information; reports and correspondence concerning other individual state boards and committees; appointments and general correspondence of the governor's office; welfare files, including claims and correspondence organized by county; correspondence concerning padons, paroles and extraditions; and correspondence filed by organization, by personal name, and from out-of-state.

Unpublished finding aid available.

Gassaway, Percy Lee (b. 1885)   510
Certificates 1920–1934
7 items

Judge. Certificates (1920–1934) proclaiming Gassaway's admission to the Masonic Order, his election as a district judge, and his nomination by the Democratic Party of Oklahoma for congress.

Gatchell, Theodore Dodge   511
Papers 1881–1957
.50 foot

Collector. Manuscripts (1900–1901); typescripts (1880–1933); publications (1881–1957); and cartoons (1884–1942), all regarding the principal cotton expositions held throughout the southern United States from 1881 to 1937, including those at Charleston, Atlanta, Nashville, Jamestown, and New Orleans.

Gee, Robert L. (1878–1954)   512
Records 1926–1954
.33 foot

Physician. An account ledger (1929–1933); surgical supply catalogs (1926–1929); and an eyeglass catalog (1931) kept by Gee, an ear, nose, and throat specialist in Hugo, Oklahoma.

Geissler, Arthur H. (1877–1945)   513
Scrapbooks 1895–1928
1.50 feet

Diplomat. Scrapbooks containing news clippings, magazine articles, government documents, pamphlets, photographs, handbills, and memorabilia accumulated by Geissler while serving as U.S. ambassador to Guatemala and reflecting events throughout Central America for the period 1922–1928.

Unpublished finding aid available.

Gibson, Arrell Morgan (1921–1987) 514
Papers 1817–1871
.66 foot

Historian. A collection of research materials (1817–1871) gathered for use in writing projects. Most of the material deals with Fort Smith, Arkansas, and the Civil War in Indian Territory.

Gibson, Iva Thomas 515
Papers 1947–1960
.10 foot

Poet. Correspondence (1947–1958) to Gibson commenting on her progress as a lay teacher in the Methodist Church and on her inspirational poetry. Also included in this collection are published materials (1949–1951) from writers' organizations to which she belonged, along with magazines containing poems she wrote and announcing the publication of her poetry.

Giessmann, Gary 516
Papers and records 1862–1957
1 foot

Collector. Letters (1862–1863) from Union soldier Robert Stansberry to his family; business records (1904–1929) from the Southwest Merchandise Company; Sanders family correspondence and records (1870–1957); and a diary (1886) by an unknown author, recounting a trip from Carrolton, Arkansas, to Indian Territory.

Unpublished finding aid available.

Giffin, LaDonna 517
Papers 1898–1999
.33 foot

Collector. Unpublished autobiographical manuscript, "Years of Futility," by Fred C. Walters (n.d.) regarding his experiences as a child in Kansas; personal correspondence (1902–1969) of the Giffin family; compiled genealogical material (ca. 1999) on the Giffin-Owens family; and printed materials and memorabilia (1898–1988) of Giffin-Owens family members.

Unpublished finding aid available.

Gildart, W. B. 518
Letter 1899
1 item

Collector. A photocopy of a letter (1899) to W. B. Gildart of Stockbridge, Michigan, from J. B. Gildart of Austin, Texas, in which the latter comments extensively on the Gildart family and especially on the activities of the Gildarts who served in the Confederate States Army.

Gilkey, Jessie Lone Clarkson 519
Papers ca. 1936
2 items

Composer. A music manuscript of "The OU Chant," composed by Gilkey in 1936, along with a letter (n.d.) commenting on the composition.

Gilkey, John E. 520
Records 1903–1907
1 foot

Grocer. Ledgers (1903–1907) containing the names of customers, items bought, and amounts paid for goods from John Gilkey's Norman, Oklahoma, grocery and feed store.

Gill, (Mrs.) B. Franklin 521
Papers 1900–1932
.10 foot

Collector. Newspaper clippings (ca. 1932); a book (1922) entitled *Oklahoma and Oklahomans*, by Mrs. J. B. Harrell; and a button (ca. 1900) from Theodore Roosevelt's Rough Riders Convention.

Gillespie, F. E. 522
Manuscript 1951
1 item

Postmaster. A brief history (1951) of Kiowa County, Oklahoma, written by Gillespie.

Gillespie, John D. 523
Manuscript 1963
1 item

Collector. A typescript (1963) of several documents written in Cherokee, with a translation by Gillespie, one of which deals with the death of Sequoyah.

Gilliland, J. W. 524
Letter 1893
1 item

Collector. A photostatic copy of a letter (1893) by Newt Locke to his brother Tom, describing in detail his participation in the land run of 1893 into the Cherokee Strip, with accounts of the settlement of Hennessey, Oklahoma Territory, and Enid, Oklahoma Territory, and of the people who settled there, with a description of their modes of transportation. The letter concludes with Locke's decision to return to the United States, due to his disenchantment with Oklahoma Territory.

Gist, Chris 525
Papers 1836–1841
7 items

Collector. Military papers (1836–1841) of Brig. Gen. Greenup White, concerning his commissions from the state of Missouri.

Gittinger, Roy (1878–1957) 526
Papers 1864–1957
1.10 feet

Professor. Correspondence (1913–1955) regarding early faculty and student affairs at the University of Oklahoma, including enrollment, credit, and grading; hand-drawn maps (n.d.) of the American West; note cards (n.d.) containing information regarding the history of the University of Oklahoma; and publications (1914–1947) from schools, organizations, and associations in Oklahoma.

Unpublished finding aid available.

Gladney, Essa 527
Diaries 1925
2 items

Librarian. Two diaries kept by Gladney for January and February 1925. They briefly chronicle Gladney's daily activities for these two months.

Glasstone, Samuel 528
Papers 1968
2 feet

Professor. Book manuscripts (1968), including a rough draft, final manuscript, and galley proof for Glasstone's *The Book of Mars*, published by the National Aeronautics and Space Administration in 1968.

Glickman, Mendel   529
Papers 1932–1967
.10 foot

Architect. Correspondence (1932–1967) between Glickman and Frank Lloyd Wright concerning their collaboration on construction projects, along with a few unidentified blueprints.

Goddard, Eunice May Stewart (1923–)   530
Papers 1942–1978
.10 foot

Collector. Photocopies of U.S. government reports (1945–1959); publications (1945–1978); and notecards (n.d.) by Goddard, all in regard to the U.S. Naval Air Technical Training Center and the U.S. Naval Air Station in Norman, Oklahoma.

Golobie, John   531
Manuscript ca. 1865
1 item

Immigrant. A typescript of the autobiography (ca. 1865) of John Golobie, a nineteenth-century immigrant to America from Yugoslavia, with detailed description of life in his native country, his coming to America, and his impressions of the culture and people he found there.

Gomes, Pat   532
Papers 1864–1875
.10 foot

Collector. Photocopies of documents (1864–1875) relating to the Worcester Willey family and Dwight Mission, Indian Territory.

Gooch, Brison   533
Printed materials 1948–1963
1.6 feet

Historian. Pamphlets (1955–1960) regarding political affairs in France; and speeches (1957–1964) by French government officials.

Unpublished finding aid available.

Good, Nancye 534
Papers 1920–1922
.10 foot

Collector. Correspondence (1922) regarding the Oklahoma gubernatorial election campaign of 1922 and its coverage by the *Tulsa Tribune*; speaking itineraries (1922) of candidate John C. Walton; programs (1920–1922) of fine arts events at the University of Oklahoma; and one political campaign broadside, "John Writes Tate a Letter—and Tate Answers It," comparing the qualities of candidates John Fields and Jack Walton.

Goodland Indian School Collection 535
Printed materials 1940–1956
5 items

Indian school and orphanage. Newspaper clippings (1956); brochures (1950); pamphlets (1955); and a published history (1940) of the Goodland Indian School, a Presbyterian orphanage founded for Choctaw Indians, but later expanded to serve orphans from other tribes as well.

Goodrich, Harold Beach 536
Papers 1904–1943
.25 foot

Petroleum geologist. Correspondence (1931–1943) of Goodrich regarding his geological interests and research; blueprints and charts (ca. 1930) showing geological data, as well as one entitled "Graphic History of Oklahoma Oil Production, 1930," all compiled by Goodrich; news clippings (ca. 1940) regarding geological developments; data, in manuscript form, regarding the availability of oil in California; and a bibliography of sources regarding oil in California, compiled by Goodrich.

Gordon, Charles Ulysses 537
Printed material 1950
2 items

Postmaster. Mimeographed copies of Gordon's poem (1950), *The American Flag*, signed by the author.

Gordon-Van Tine Company Collection 538
Printed materials n.d.
1 item

Manufacturer. A catalog for Gordon-Van Tine manufactured housing, Davenport, Iowa.

Gould, Charles Newton (1868–1949) 539
Papers 1897–1948
11 feet

Geologist. Correspondence (1914–1941) regarding personal matters, Oklahoma place names, and the geology of Oklahoma; manuscripts (1907–1946), both book-length and shorter, and both published and unpublished, regarding the history, place names, and geology of Oklahoma; book reviews (n.d.) of Gould's works; poetry (n.d.) by Gould; speeches (n.d.) delivered by Gould; and newspaper clippings (1900–1946) regarding Gould's life and his writings.

Unpublished finding aid available.

Governor's Interstate Indian Council Collection 540
Minutes 1950
1 item

State organization. Minutes of the third meeting of the council, held December 7–8, 1950, in Oklahoma City, Oklahoma.

Graber, Stan L. 541
Printed materials 1991–1992
.10 foot

Cowboy. Eighteen articles by Stan L. Graber, published in *Grainews* (1991–1992), about the Matador Land and Cattle Company's cattle drive from its Saskatchewan ranch to Harlem, Montana.

Graham, Gideon Wesley (1867–1950) 542
Printed materials 1928–1949
.10 foot

Wildlife conservationist. Printed cards and one-page leaflets (1928–1949) expressing Graham's views concerning the conservation and protection of wildlife in Oklahoma. Also in this collection is one card advertising Graham's campaign (ca. 1930) to save the Cherokee Indian language.

Grass, Frank, and Patty Grass 543
Papers 1876–1957
.33 foot

Collectors. Correspondence (1876–1900) between members of the Helpenstein family, who settled in Oklahoma Territory in 1889; a scrapbook of newspaper articles (n.d.) concerning the history of Palo Pinto County, Texas; and a ledger (1907) belonging to L. E. Patterson.

Grayson Family Papers 544
Papers 1834–1919
1 foot

Family collection. Correspondence (1834–1919) regarding Creek Indian history, including tribal politics, tribal factionalism, the Green Peach War, sale of Creek lands in Alabama, removal, allotment of land, and related administrative matters. Correspondents include George W. Grayson, Washington Grayson, Pleasant Porter, Return J. Meigs, Samuel Checote, James A. Garfield, and Dennis W. Bushyhead.

Unpublished finding aid available.

Grayson, Ambrose T. 545
Papers 1905
2 items

Physician. A menu (1905) for a luncheon at the Hotel Threadgill, Oklahoma City, Oklahoma Territory, at which the Oklahoma County Medical Society was host to the Tri-State Medical Association; and a personal letter (1905) from Grayson to his family in Alabama.

Gregory, Arthur Leslie 546
Papers 1918
2 items

Physician. A diploma (1918) awarded to Arthur Leslie Gregory from the St. Louis College of Physicians and Surgeons, and a certificate (n.d.) for a post-graduate course in anatomy.

Griffith, Alfred 547
Records 1842–1931
.66 foot

U.S. Navy physician. Correspondence (1860–1913) to and from Griffith regarding his participation in the Civil War, his later membership in a U.S. Navy expedition to Darien, Panama, and also regarding the New Hope Seminary in the Choctaw Nation; diaries (1864–1870) regarding Griffith's naval travels abroad, his stay in Lisbon, Portugal, and his emigration to Indian Territory; naval medical reports and requisitions (1870–1871); a petition (1894) from the residents of Sans Bois, Choctaw Nation, requesting that Griffith become their physician; certificates (1900–1917) advising him of his election as superintendent of schools for the southern district of Indian Territory, and of his membership in medical associations; a passport (1871) issued to Griffith for travel in France; manuscripts (1864–1865) by Griffith, detailing his participation in Gen. William T. Sherman's march to the sea through Georgia and North Carolina during the Civil War; and publications (1888–1931), including Grand Army of the Republic encampment programs, a booklet entitled *Songs of the Darien Expedition*, and college graduation and event invitations.

Griffitts, James Addison (1859–1931)   548
Papers 1906–1940
.25 foot

Minister. Publications (1907–1940), including *The Christian Workers Magazine*, booklets produced by the American Friends (Quakers) regarding an African mission and national service efforts, and one textbook used at the Friends Hillside Mission in Indian Territory and Oklahoma; and minutes (1906–1907) of the ministry and oversight meetings held at the Friends mission at Vera, Indian Territory. The minutes of only two meetings are recorded. The collection also includes a biographical sketch of Griffitts.

Grimes, Mary E. (1891–1950)   549
Papers 1910–1950
8 feet

Teacher. Personal correspondence (1916–1950) and diaries (1919, 1941), along with photographs, scrapbooks, and sheet music reflecting her life and career as a teacher of music at the Walters, Oklahoma, high school, and her community service activities.

Unpublished finding aid available.

Grisso, D. Horton   550
Papers 1851–1865
.33 foot

Collector. Diaries (1851–1865) of John F. Lafferty, who enlisted in Company "E" of the Ohio militia and served during the Civil War. Included are hand-drawn maps of Union battlefield maneuvers and artillery batteries, as well as listings of daily rations given each soldier. The diaries are written almost exclusively in Pitman-style shorthand and have not been transcribed.

Grisso, Walker D. (1905–1965) 551
Papers 1953–1965
10 feet

Oil producer and lawyer. Correspondence (1953–1965) between Grisso, Arthur McAnally, and Col. John Virden on subjects such as the American Southwest, the Albert Jennings Fountain murder case, the Maxwell land grant, the University of Oklahoma Board of Regents, western saloons, and the oil industry in Oklahoma.

Unpublished finding aid available.

Gulledge, George Washington (1860–ca. 1955) 552
Printed materials 1895
5 items

Physician. Class rolls for the medical schools of the University of Nashville and Vanderbilt University (1895), and an obituary for George Washington Gulledge.

Gulliford, Andrew 553
Diary 1839–1840
1 item

Collector. Typescript of a diary (1839–1840) of John Bleecker Luce, a U.S. Indian agent to the Kaw Indians of Kansas, and later a subagent for other tribes in Indian Territory. The diary includes descriptions of daily life among the Kaw Indians; the Kaws' interactions with Pawnee Indians; and buffalo hunting. Also in the diary are lists of Indian words and signs (tribe unspecified) learned by Luce during his tenure as an Indian agent.

Gunning, R. Boyd 554
Papers 1947–1953
.33 foot

University administrator. Files (1947–1953) regarding the alumni development funds for several projects at the University of Oklahoma, Norman, Oklahoma, including the university museum, the Bizzell Memorial Library Fund, *Books Abroad*, and Max Westheimer Air Field.

Guthrie District Medical Association Collection 555
Minutes 1900–1940
1 item

Professional association. Minutes (1900–1940) of the Guthrie (Oklahoma) District Medical Association meetings, including a petition signed by association members requesting that schoolchildren be immunized.

Guy, William M. (1845–ca. 1907) 556
Printed materials 1887–1907
.10 foot

Indian chief. Typescripts of newspaper articles (1887–1907), including editorials and messages of Guy as governor of the Chickasaw Nation, on the issues of Chickasaw tribal legislation and the disputed gubernatorial election of 1888.

Guymon First National Bank Collection 557
Records 1906–1928
8 feet

Bank. General ledgers (1906–1918); journals (1907–1910); a discount register (1906–1910); daily balances (1908–1918); draft registers (1906–1907); expense ledgers (1906–1907); and tellers' cash books (1906–1928) from the First National Bank of Guymon, Oklahoma.

Haas, Mary R. 558
Printed materials 1941–1954
.10 foot

Anthropologist. Reprints (1941–1954), mostly relating to the Muskogean language, along with a dictionary (1953), compiled by Haas, of the Tunica Indian language.

Hackett, Helen 559
Artifacts 1888–1920
.33 foot

Collector. Ribbons, medals, and buttons (1888–1920) from various political campaigns and conventions, political parties, and fraternal organizations, plus a notary public seal.

[135]

Haddix, J. F. 560
Records 1921–1947
.66 foot

Collector. Minutes of stockholders' meetings (1921–1928); stock certificates (1921–1947); and a stock certificate register (1923–1933), all from the Farmers Cotton Gin Company of Maysville, Oklahoma.

Hadsell, Sardis Roy (1876–1942) 561
Papers 1900–1942
.50 foot

Professor. Correspondence (1916–1942); freshmen English placement exams and results (1936–1940); and English department circulars and course outlines (1929–1940) from the University of Oklahoma; a report of an audit (1905) of the university's finances; manuscript accounts by Hadsell of the early history of the University of Oklahoma, including "[Vernon L.] Parrington in Oklahoma" (n.d.), "A History of the University of Oklahoma" (1929), and "Twenty-Eight Years After" (1928), which relates Hadsell's experiences with the 1900 expedition of the Oklahoma Geological Survey, plus a typescript of Hadsell's diary from that expedition.

Hague, Lyle L. (b. 1895) 562
Papers 1930–1938
3.33 feet

Farmer. Personal and business correspondence (1930–1938); minutes (1930–1938); financial reports (1930–1933); journals (1930–1938); and printed material (1930–1938) relating to the Farmers National Grain Corporation, the Oklahoma Grain Growers Association, the Farm Credit Administration, the U.S. Department of Agriculture, and other farming organizations.

Unpublished finding aid available.

Hailey, Daniel Morris (1841–1919) 563
Printed materials 1912–1919
.10 foot

Physician. Newspaper clippings (1919) regarding the death of Daniel Morris Hailey, and two copies (1912, 1916) of *Confederate Veteran Association of the State of Oklahoma*.

Hainer, Bayard Taylor (1866–1933)   564
Papers 1887–1933
.50 foot

Judge. Correspondence (1906–1927); commissions and appointments (1898–1906) to the Oklahoma Territory supreme court; certifications as an attorney (1897–1909); and clippings (1900–1933) concerning Hainer's career as an Oklahoma Territory supreme court justice and Federal Trade Commission attorney.

Haines, Sarah Deborah (ca. 1891–ca. 1958)   565
Artifacts 1913
4 items

Collector. Four University of Oklahoma Class of 1913 pins belonging to Sarah Deborah Haines.

Hair, Fannie M. Townsend   566
Papers 1901–1911
10 items

Collector. Newspaper clippings (1901); certificates (1901–1911) from the U.S. Land Office, Lawton, Oklahoma; and a manuscript (n.d.) written by Fannie M. Townsend Hair concerning the naming and route of the Chisholm Trail in Oklahoma, with comments by Edwin C. McReynolds.

Hall, David   567
Papers 1970–1974
1.33 feet

Governor. Papers (1970–1974), including appointments, radio speeches, correspondence, and press files of Oklahoma governor David Hall concerning state prisons, federal disaster relief, agriculture, and politics.

Hall, Horace Mark (1854–1945)   568
Manuscript ca. 1958
1 item

Physician. A transcript of letters (1871–1873) written by Horace Mark Hall while he was working as a ranch hand in Texas. The letters are edited, with an introduction and detailed footnotes, by Joseph S. Hall.

Hallinen, Joseph E. (1859–1932) 569
Papers 1903–1973
.10 foot

Naturalist. Correspondence (1903–1973) concerning Hallinen's employment; a transcript of an interview (1973) with John A. Hallinen Jr., regarding Joseph E. Hallinen's life; legal documents (1903) regarding Andrew Hallinen's estate; and a catalog (1933) of Joseph E. Hallinen's library.

Halloran, Arthur F. 570
Printed materials 1941–1978
.10 foot

Biologist. Reprints of articles by Arthur F. Halloran regarding wildlife in southwestern Oklahoma, Arizona, and New Mexico, along with a complete index of all of Halloran's articles that appeared in the Lawton, Oklahoma, newspapers.

Halsell, Harold Hallet (b. 1892) 571
Papers 1930–1943
4 items

Merchant. Two typewritten manuscripts (1930, 1943) by Harold H. Halsell, concerning the life of his father, Oscar D. Halsell, and early Oklahoma City, Oklahoma, along with two letters (1932) concerning the Williamson, Halsell, Frasier Company.

Hamilton, (Mrs.) C. P. 572
Ledgers 1917–1925
2 items

Merchant. Two account books (1917, 1924–1925) from the Hamilton Hardware Store in Hollis, Oklahoma.

Hamilton, Charles W. 573
Papers 1909–1962
2.66 feet

Petroleum geologist. Correspondence with the Mexican Gulf Oil Company (1912–1922); Hamilton's family correspondence (1909–1926), including some (1914) concerning the Mexican Revolution; general business correspondence (1911–1923), including some with E. L.

DeGolyer; Hamilton's geology class notes (1914–1915); Hamilton's diary (1912–1914); printed material and reports (1913–1959) concerning oil production in Oklahoma, the Middle East, and Central and South America; and a draft of a book-length work by Hamilton, entitled "Americans in the Middle East."

Unpublished finding aid available.

Hamon, Earl (b. 1911)   574
Papers 1914
1 item

Collector. An architect's specifications (1914) for the construction of Newkirk High School, Newkirk, Oklahoma.

Hancock, William Box (1860–ca. 1934)   575
Memoirs 1812–1925
1 item

Cowboy. A typewritten autobiography (ca. 1925) of Hancock's life as a cowboy, primarily at the Woodard and Oge ranch near San Antonio, Texas. It also describes five of his trips driving cattle up the Western Trail, and the towns of San Antonio, Rockport, Fort Griffin, and Alpine, Texas, Camp Supply, and Fort Reno, Indian Territory, and Dodge City, Kansas, along with accounts of his work on ranches in Dakota Territory.

Harbison, Robert B.   576
Papers 1938–1942
1.66 feet

Lawyer. Correspondence (1938–1942) pertaining to Harbison's term as a senator representing district five, encompassing Jackson and Tillman counties, in the Oklahoma state senate.

Unpublished finding aid available.

Hardin, Joe   577
Manuscript 1952
1 item

Photographer. A poem (1952) written by Hardin, commemorating the Sons of the United Confederate Veterans.

Hargett, Jay L. 578
Papers 1792–1935
.66 foot

Collector. Typescripts of correspondence (1816–1870), mostly regarding missionary work among the Choctaw and Cherokee Indians; diaries (1914) recounting travel in the eastern United States and in the Galena, Kansas, area; a student's notebook (n.d.) containing class notes, poetry, and miscellaneous notes; an account book (1860s–1890s) recording purchases and daily expenses; and personal correspondence (1894–1902) between Edwin Ludlow, writing from Mexico as superintendent of the Mexican Coal and Coke Company, and his wife, who was residing in Hartshorne, Indian Territory. Correspondents writing about missionary activities include Cyrus Byington, Israel Folsom, David Folsom, Nathaniel Folsom, Peter Pitchlynn, Stand Watie, and Cyrus Kingsbury.

Hargrett, Lester (1902–1962) 579
Papers 1951
.50 foot

Writer and bibliographer. The manuscript, galley sheets, and page prints (1951) of *Oklahoma Imprints*; photocopies of manuscripts (1836, 1881) relating to the extension of the western boundary of Arkansas and the granting of rights-of-way to the Chicago, Texas, and Mexican Central Railway Company and to the St. Louis and San Francisco Railway Company.

Harjo, Lochar (d. 1879) 580
Printed materials 1875–1879
5 items

Indian chief. Typescripts of newspaper articles (1875–1879) of Harjo's inaugural speech as principal chief of the Creeks, on governmental affairs during his administration, and, subsequently, on his impeachment.

Harlow, James Gindling (b. 1912) 581
Printed material 1969–1976
1 foot

Educator. Promotional pamphlets (1968–1971) produced by the National Aeronautics and Space Administration concerning the Apollo

Space missions; pamphlets (1966) and photocopies of articles (1969–1975) concerning economics and management, along with calendars (1970–1976), desk diaries (1973–1976), and appointment calendars (1972–1975) belonging to Harlow and his wife.

Unpublished finding aid available.

Harlow, Victor E. (1876–1959) 582
Papers 1859–1950
1 foot

Publisher. Research materials (1859–1950) including notes and rough drafts of Harlow's book *Jesus the Man* and other religious monographs, along with a manuscript copy of Charles F. Colcord's memoirs.

Unpublished finding aid available.

Harper, Robert Henry (1869–ca. 1933) 583
Manuscript 1933
1 item

Physician. A six-page statement (1933) by Robert H. Harper, explaining why he requested that no religious services be held for him after his death.

Harrall, Stewart (1906–1964) 584
Printed materials 1947–1951
.10 foot

Publicity officer. Printed material, including reports and lists of participants from the Sixth Annual National Conference on Higher Education (1951); a clippings file (1947–1948) from the *Tulsa World* and the *Tulsa Tribune* concerning the University of Oklahoma; and publicity material (1950–1951) from Johnston Murray's 1950 gubernatorial campaign.

Harris, Colonel Johnson (1856–1921) 585
Printed materials 1892–1922
.66 foot

Indian chief. Typescripts of newspaper articles (1892–1922) on Cherokee Nation governmental issues such as allotment, the Dawes Commission, land transfers, and tribal politics during Harris's tenure as chief of the Cherokees and his service in the Cherokee senate.

Harris, Cyrus H. (1817–1888) 586
Printed materials 1872–1905
.10 foot

Indian chief. Typescripts of newspaper articles (1872–1905) on Chickasaw Nation governmental issues such as tribal factionalism, elections, schools, and the allotment of land during Harris's tenure as governor of the Chickasaw Nation.

Harris, Giles Edward (1878–1938) 587
Printed materials 1902–1938
.10 foot

Physician. A laboratory notebook (1902–1903); weekly public health reports for the United States (1909); a copy of the second biennial report (1910–1912) of the Oklahoma State Public Health Department; Harris's obituary; and a letter (1917) from Oklahoma governor Robert L. Williams regarding selective service registration.

Harris, James A. (1870–1947) 588
Papers 1853–1947
2 feet

Businessman. Correspondence (1900–1943) concerning Harris's activities with the Oklahoma Republican Party, of which he was state chairman from 1909 to 1924; legal correspondence, papers, deeds, and mortgages (1900–1947) from Harris's real estate business in Wagoner, Oklahoma; clippings (1914–1918); accounts and receipts (1853) from Harvey Harris, James Harris's father; and a genealogy (1924) of the Harris family.

Unpublished finding aid available.

Harris, Robert M. (1851–1927) 589
Printed materials 1896–1927
.33 foot

Governor. Typescripts of newspaper articles (1896–1927) regarding Harris's term as governor of the Chickasaw Nation from 1896 to 1898 and Chickasaw legislation, along with biographical information on Harris.

Harris, William Torrey (1835–1909) 590
Printed materials 1868–1929
.10 foot

Educator. Reprints and clippings of articles (1869–1904) by William Torrey Harris, United States Commissioner of Education, 1889–1906, concerning education, philosophy, and geography; and reprints and clippings (1908–1929) regarding Harris's life and work.

Harrison, Jacob 591
Printed materials 1905
3 items

Indian chief. Typescripts of newspaper articles (1905) regarding Harrison's impeachment and removal from office as chief of the Seminoles and regarding John Brown, his replacement.

Harrison, Walter M. (1888–1961) 592
Papers 1915–1961
10 feet

Journalist. Personal correspondence (1930–1961); military papers (1918–1959); political campaign materials (1949–1959); biographical materials (1915–1961); business correspondence (1931–1961); Pulitzer Prize Board materials (1938–1942); Will Rogers Memorial Commission papers (1938–1961); National Cowboy Hall of Fame files (1955); and Civil War Centennial Commission materials (1953–1961), all reflecting Harrison's personal affairs and his association with the above organizations while an editor for the *Daily Oklahoman* and the owner of *The North Star*, along with papers (1949–1959) regarding his service as a city councilman for Oklahoma City, Oklahoma.

Unpublished finding aid available.

Harrison, William H. (1876–1929) 593
Printed materials 1901–1937
5 items

Indian chief. Typescripts of speeches and correspondence (1901–1937) by Harrison, a principal chief of the Choctaws, on the subject of the allotment of Choctaw lands.

Harrod, Neva Belle 594
Papers 1901–1957
2 feet

Teacher. Correspondence (1917–1918) with U.S. soldiers during World War I; and newspaper clippings (1901–1957) concerning President

McKinley's assassination, World War I, Charles Lindbergh, World War II, and other major news stories of the twentieth century.

Unpublished finding aid available.

Harrold, Jack 595
Diary 1991
.25 foot

Professor. Diary (1991) of University of Oklahoma professor of music Jack Harrold. The diary details Harrold's travels and musical engagements in New York and Europe.

Hart, (Mrs.) Hugh 596
Manuscript 1887–1939
1 item

Writer. A history (ca. 1939) of the Presbyterian church in Pauls Valley, Oklahoma, written by Hart.

Haskell and LeFlore Counties Medical Society Collection 597
Records 1936–1951
.33 foot

Professional organization. Correspondence (1945–1952); minutes (1941–1952) of meetings; financial records (1939–1947); and miscellaneous printed materials (1936–1952) from the Haskell and LeFlore Counties (Oklahoma) Medical Society.

Haskell, Charles Nathaniel (1860–1933) 598
Papers 1863–1929
.50 foot

Governor. Correspondence (1863–1929) concerning Haskell's political career; speeches (1907–1952) made by Haskell; newspaper clippings (1908–1938); and notes (n.d.) concerning his involvement with the Oklahoma Constitutional Convention in 1906.

Hatfield, Edna Greer Porter 599
Papers 1831–1958
1 foot

Collector. Transcripts of interviews (ca. 1930–1958) with pioneers who took part in the 1893 land run into the Cherokee Strip. The interviews

No. 33.

Hd. Qrs. 2d Dept. W. Division,
Fort Gibson, 23d June 1839.

Dear Sir,

I received your letter of the 22d, late last evening, and independent of your express, sent your nephew to you, advising you to retire to this Post immediately, provided you did not feel yourself secure at your residence. I greatly regret the murder of Mr. Boudinot, and fear that the report of John Ridge having been killed, is also true; and if so, there is great danger of a civil war being commenced in your Nation. With every little delay I have therefore sent an express to the Chiefs, John Brown, John Looney and John Rogers, requesting them to repair to this Post with the least delay possible; and I judge they may be here by Tuesday next, when it is hoped some arrangements can be made by them, in conjunction with yourself, and other Principal Men of the late Emigrants, to put a stop to further acts of outrage and violence. Be so good as to let me hear from you by the return of the Express.

And believe me,
Dear sir, with
Great respect,
Your Obt Servant,
M. Arbuckle
Bvt Brigr Genl U.S.A.

To John Ross, Esq.
Principal Chief of the
Emigrant Cherokees.
&c &c

Correspondence of General Matthew Arbuckle to Cherokee Nation Principal Chief John Ross regarding the government of the Cherokee Nation and the Old Settler band of Cherokee Indians, 1839. From the Division of Manuscripts Collection.

contain descriptions of the land run, hardships encountered, sod houses and dugouts, agriculture, religion, schools, and other socioeconomic aspects of life in the Cherokee Strip. Township maps showing the location of original settlers in the Cherokee Strip accompany the interviews. The collection also includes historical, religious, social, and anecdotal information about the Indian tribes that lived in the eastern portion of the Cherokee Strip, such as the Tonkawa, Kansa (Kaw), and Ponca Indians. Correspondence (1871–1875) and field notebooks (1869–1871) written by Orville Smith and T. H. Barrett during a survey of the Sisseton and Wahpeton Indian reservations in Dakota Territory make up the final part of the Hatfield Collection.

Unpublished finding aid available.

Hathaway, A. H. 600
Records 1892–1954
3 feet

Physician. Ledgers and journals (1892–1954) in which patient accounts were recorded, along with Hathaway's observations on daily weather conditions, particularly those regarding the dust storms of the 1930s.

Hayes, James H. 601
Records 1903–1929
.10 foot

Physician. Ledgers (1903–1929) in which Hayes recorded patient accounts and fees charged. The collection also includes a booklet (1923) of poetry by Oklahoma poet Ina Gainer.

Haynes, Micajah P. (1851–1939) 602
Printed materials 1857–1897
6 items

Physician. A receipt (1857) for the sale of a slave, along with Haynes's enrollment forms (1897) establishing his eligibility for Cherokee citizenship.

Hayt, E. A. 603
Papers 1878–1879
.33 foot

Government official. Circular letters (1878–1879) written by E. A. Hayt as Commissioner of Indian Affairs.

Healy, Frank Dale, Jr. (b. 1897)   604
Manuscripts ca. 1920–1950
2 items

Rancher. Two manuscripts, one (1950) by Frank Dale Healy, Jr., concerning Healy family history and life in the Oklahoma panhandle area during territorial days, including a description of related photographs; and one (ca. 1920) written by George Henry Healy, concerning ranching on Padre Island, Texas.

Heck, Bessie Holland   605
Papers 1991
.33 foot

Author. Manuscripts, galleys, and author's advance copy with corrections of *Danger on the Homestead*, by Bessie Holland Heck, published by Levite of Apache, Norman, Oklahoma, in 1991.

Heffner, Edna Swenson   606
Papers 1947–1980
5 feet

Educator. Correspondence (1947–1980) and newsletters concerning missionary work and Bible translation, mainly in Peru and Nigeria, along with commencement programs from the University of Oklahoma (1947) and Central Grammar School (1953).

Unpublished finding aid available.

Heffner, Roy E. (1895–1949)   607
Papers 1874–1947
18 feet

Professor and photographer. Personal correspondence (1904–1940) of Heffner and his wife, much of it from missionaries; printed material (ca. 1920–1940) relating to missionary activities and to the University of Oklahoma; scrapbooks containing newspaper clippings and personal items; and posters publicizing church events.

Unpublished finding aid available.

Heflin, Cleo Eugene (1911–1986) 608
Papers 1950–1981
1.75 feet

Author. Correspondence (1950–1981); research notes (n.d.); journal articles (1915–1979); and one unpublished manuscript (n.d.), all regarding the Caddo Indians.

Unpublished finding aid available.

Heflin, Van (1910–1971) 609
Papers 1929–1971
.66 foot

Actor. Business and personal correspondence (1937–1971); contracts (1961–1969); financial statements (1959–1969); greeting cards and records of legal cases (1963–1969); newspaper clippings (1936–1968); playbills (1934–1963); records of stock transactions (1964–1969); and telegrams (1932–1938) from the life and career of Van Heflin.

Hefner, Robert Alexander (b. 1874) 610
Papers 1874–1947
.10 foot

Mayor. A biography (1874–1956) of Hefner, mayor of Oklahoma City, Oklahoma; a genealogy of the Hefner family; mayoral speeches (1947) to the city council of Oklahoma City; a first issue (1956) of the magazine *Independent Oil*; and a news magazine (1947) of the First National Bank Building in Oklahoma City.

Henderson, Arnold G. 611
Papers 1965–1970
11 feet

Professor. Source materials (1965–1970), including correspondence, research notes, interview forms, survey forms, and reports accumulated in compiling housing surveys and environmental studies of various Indian tribes, with an emphasis on the Cheyenne and Arapaho.

Unpublished finding aid available.

Hendricks, James R. (b. 1817) 612
Papers 1859–1902
1 foot

Judge. General and family correspondence (1865–1902); notebooks and journals (1862–1887); speeches (1866–1888); and legal documents

(1859–1894) dealing with the Cherokee National Party, the Cherokee Nation Blind Asylum, pensions, and Cherokee Indian medicines.

Unpublished finding aid available.

Hendrickson, Gwen (b. 1897) 613
Manuscript 1950
1 item

Homemaker. Gwen Hendrickson's reminiscences (1950) about her father, Samuel Harvey Hendrickson, who settled on the Cheyenne and Arapaho lands in 1892.

Hengst, Herbert Randall, Sr. 614
Papers and sound recordings 1951–1985
2.3 feet

Professor. This collection is an oral history project of the Center for Studies in Higher Education at the University of Oklahoma. The purpose of the project was to document the history of the University of Oklahoma through interviews with former administrators, faculty and staff members, regents, and alumni. The collection contains 131 cassette tapes and transcriptions of interviews (1979–1985), background information on the interviewees, and administrative records (1951–1985) of the project. This collection also contains Special Training Program Notebooks (1972–1979) of the Center for Studies in Higher Education's Special Training Program in Educational Administration for officials of the Ministry of Education of Saudi Arabia.

Unpublished finding aid available.

Henkle, George 615
Printed materials 1947
1 item

Collector. A souvenir program (1947) of the fiftieth anniversary of Bartlesville, Oklahoma.

Hennessey High School Collection 616
Papers 1880–1980
.10 foot

Public school. Term papers and reports (1980) regarding the history of Hennessey, Oklahoma, and surrounding communities, written by students in Hennessey High School's writing class, with an emphasis upon the Czechoslovakian immigrants who settled the area.

Hennings, A. E. 617
Records 1929–1950
.33 foot

Physician. A ledger (1929–1950) in which Hennings recorded patient accounts and services rendered, and a news clipping (1950) regarding a gift of land by Hennings to the Oklahoma Medical Research Foundation.

Hensley, Claude 618
Papers 1860–1940
.10 foot

Journalist. Typescripts of correspondence (1879) and memoirs (1860–1874) concerning Quanah Parker; the first telephone in Indian Territory; life at Fort Sill and Fort Reno, Oklahoma Territory; and the hunting of buffalo; along with an account (1940) by E. H. Linzee describing the development of Oklahoma Territory.

Herbert, Harold Harvey (1888–1980) 619
Papers 1918–1959
49 feet

Professor. Departmental and personal files (1918–1959) compiled by Herbert as director of the University of Oklahoma School of Journalism, concerning faculty, students, the College of Liberal Arts and Sciences, and general University of Oklahoma business, along with materials relating to committees and associations with which Herbert and the School of Journalism were connected.

Unpublished finding aid available.

Herring, Alvin J. (d. 1954) 620
Records 1922–1925
5 items

Collector. An account book (1923–1924) and notebooks (1922–1925) containing lists of photograph negatives from the Deal Studio in Chelsea, Oklahoma.

Hertzog, Anna Laura Brisky (1873–1963) 621
Papers 1904–1948
2 items

Educator and civic leader. A combination account book, scrapbook, and family diary (1904–1948) which includes descriptions of the mining boom in the Wichita Mountains and early school board meetings in Comanche County, Oklahoma, along with a manuscript (n.d.) entitled "Pioneer Days in Comanche Co."

Hewes, Leslie (1906–1999)   622
Papers 1901–1912, 1928–1998
11.3 feet

Professor. Research notes and township maps (ca. 1937) of the Cherokee Nation of Oklahoma, on which Hewes plotted the following data: which groups (categorized by degree of Indian blood, intermarried citizens, or freedmen) settled which allotments, along with the classification of these allotments and the appraised value per acre of each. Hewes used the information included on these maps to write his dissertation, "The Geography of the Cherokee Country of Oklahoma," at the University of California in 1940. Also included are research files (1928–1998), maps (1921–1987), and correspondence relating to Hewes's teaching and publications; research notes and data on the geography and agriculture of the Central Great Plains, irrigation, and land fencing; lecture notes from geography classes taught by Hewes and class notes taken by Hewes as a graduate student; biographical and other materials related to Hewes's professional career and studies at the University of California at Berkeley and the University of Oklahoma; and maps, photographs, lantern slides, and color slides related to Hewes's research.

Unpublished finding aid available.

Hewitt, Robert C.   623
Papers 1923–1953
.50 foot

Army officer. Personal correspondence (1942–1944) to family members regarding Hewitt's military service and war-related experiences as a bombardier in the U.S. Army Air Force; additional correspondence (1944–1953) to the Hewitt family from E. C. McCallum of Stanolind Oil and Gas Company; telegrams (1943–1944); medals (1944); personal records (1923–1946); and news clippings (1943–1946), all relating to Robert C. Hewitt up to the time of his death in 1944.

Heydrick, L. C.   624
Papers 1901–1953
.33 foot

Oil prospector. Correspondence (1901, 1931–1939, 1944, 1953) relating to Jesse A. Heydrick's discovery of oil in Red Fork, Oklahoma; a manuscript (1931) of unpublished chapters for John W. Flenner's *History of Early Oil Developments in Oklahoma*; legal papers (1901); newspaper clippings; and a bound report (1953) by Heydrick, entitled "Red Fork Discovery, June 1901."

Hicks, Jimmie   625
Manuscript 1990
1 item

Educator. An unpublished manuscript (1990) by Jimmie Hicks, entitled "A Critique of the PBS Television Program, 'Indians, Outlaws and Angie Debo,' The American Experience, #103." In this eighteen-page paper, Hicks introduces the principals, offers a point-by-point criticism of the program, discusses Debo's book, *And Still the Waters Run*, the controversy over its publication, and Joseph Brandt's effort to have it published, and defends Edward E. Dale's role in the controversy.

Hilbert-Price, Shirley   626
Papers 1963–1987
4.50 feet

Political activist. Legislative bills and resolutions (1975–1985); correspondence (1972–1986); publications (1972–1987); and memorabilia (n.d.), including banners, bumper stickers, pins, buttons, and sound recordings, all regarding the status of women's rights in Oklahoma and the United States and the campaign for the Equal Rights Amendment.

Unpublished finding aid available.

Hildebrand, Trudie Flanagan   627
Papers 1930–1933
.33 foot

Homemaker. Collection of recipes (1930), a handmade cookbook (1933), and an embroidered hand towel. Recipes in the cookbook are mounted on wallpaper and were collected during the Great Depression. One set of recipes is a collection of the favorite recipes of the western swing band, Bob Wills and the Texas Playboys, taken from a magazine. All pieces in the collection are from Trudie Hildebrand Flanagan's kitchen. Hildebrand was a woman of Cherokee descent born in Watova, Oklahoma.

Hill, Francis M. 628
Printed materials 1950–1951
2 items

Collector. Booklets (1950–1951) advertising the sale of Hereford cattle at the Honey Creek Ranch near Grove, Oklahoma. The booklets describe the stock-breeding techniques employed at Honey Creek Ranch, one of the first ranches in Oklahoma to adopt scientific breeding techniques.

Hill, George Washington (1834–1925) 629
Records 1858–1907
.10 foot

Merchant. Land titles and deeds (1858–1879) from Georgia and the Cherokee Nation, Indian Territory; an admission ticket to the 1900 Democratic Party national convention; minutes (1900) of the Vinita, Indian Territory, Democratic Club; an election poll list and tally sheet (1907) from Vinita, Indian Territory; and one court document (1886) of the Cooweescoowee District Court, Cherokee Nation.

Hill, Weldon 630
Papers 1957–1968
3.33 feet

Author. Book and short story manuscripts (1957–1968) regarding fictional themes, authored by Hill, using both his pen name, Weldon Hill, and his real name, William R. Scott. Titles include *Onionhead* (1957), *One of the Casualties* (1964), *The Long Summer of George Adams* (1961), *Rafe* (1966), and *A Man Could Get Killed That Way* (1967).

Unpublished finding aid available.

Hine, L. T. 631
Papers 1903–1935
.10 foot

Real estate agent. Correspondence (1925–1935), including legal and financial documents from Hine's real estate business in Purcell, Oklahoma; oil leases (1925); and correspondence and papers (1909–1926) relating to the Fraternal Order of Eagles, of which Hine was a member.

Hines, M. D. 632
Papers 1858–1942
.10 foot

Businessman. Financial agreements and correspondence (1858–1942) relating to family affairs and Hines's farm, cattle ranch, and nursery near Maysville, Arkansas. One letter (1868) describes preparations for a cattle drive from Boggy Depot, Indian Territory, to Maysville, Arkansas.

Hinkel, John W. 633
Papers 1894–1908
3 items

Collector. Correspondence (1894–1897) to and from Freeman E. Miller, a professor at Oklahoma Agricultural and Mechanical College, regarding Miller's publications; pamphlets (1896–1908); and printed advertisements from publishers.

Hinkhouse, Steven 634
Ledger 1889–1897
1 item

Collector. A Chicago, Rock Island, and Pacific Railroad Company station log from Durant, Iowa, for the period 1889–1897.

Hinsdale, Harriet 635
Papers 1895–1966
.10 foot

Collector and author. Manuscripts (ca. 1948) by Helen Hinsdale; copies of magazine articles (1895–1966), including some from an 1895 issue of *McClure's Magazine*; and newspaper clippings (1894–1966), all concerning Robert Louis Stevenson.

Hinton, S. E. (1949–) 636
Papers 1967–1995
.10 foot

Author. Uncorrected page proof (ca. 1967) of *The Outsiders* and related newspaper clippings (1982, 1995); and newsletters (1970, 1977) of the Oklahoma Student Librarians Association.

Hipes, Jessie James 637
Records 1908–1947
.66 foot

Physician. Records (1908–1947) from Hipes's medical practice, including prescriptions for glasses, patient case histories, and financial records, along with certificates (1911–1947) and diplomas (1908–1910) issued to Hipes by government health agencies and universities.

Hisel, (Mrs.) O. R. 638
Papers 1950–1951
3 items

Historian. Bound typescripts of three unpublished works by Hisel, entitled "Oklahoma Federation of Music Clubs" (1950); "Missionary Federation of Muskogee, Oklahoma" (1950); and "Presbyterian Pioneers and Personalities, 1825–1951" (1951).

Historic Oklahoma Collection 639
Printed material 1900–1998
19.33 feet

Vertical file. Newspaper clippings and brochures containing information on selected subjects, events, and places significant to Oklahoma's history. The index to this guide includes each subject, event, or place, identified at the folder level in this collection.

Historic Oklahoma Collection: Biographies 640
Printed material 1900–1998
4.66 feet

Vertical file. Newspaper clippings and tear sheets containing biographical information on prominent and historically significant Oklahomans. The index to this guide includes the people documented in this collection.

Hixson, William F. 641
Papers 1939–1995
.33 foot

Economist. Published and unpublished articles (1938–1988) by William F. Hixson on economic issues; and correspondence (1981–1994) of Hixson with Paul Sweezy, James Galbraith, Guy Routh, Milton Friedman, Sidney Lens, and Leon Keyserling.

Hogarth, Andrew 642
Printed materials 1991–1992
.10 foot

Historian and author. Research materials (1991–1992) collected for *Cheyenne Hole: The Story of the Sappa Creek Massacre, 23rd April, 1875.*

Holbrook, Ralph Winfrey (ca. 1870–ca. 1952) 643
Records 1899–1944
.50 foot

Physician. Ledgers and notebooks (1899–1944); matriculation records (1896–1899); and birth memoranda for the years 1925–1941. These records document Holbrook's medical training and his medical practice in Payne County, Oklahoma, from 1896 to 1944.

Holbrook, Richard Burkey 644
Papers 1900–1915
1 foot

Editor. Correspondence (1900–1915) between Holbrook, his wife, Mabel Jackson Holbrook, and others regarding his editorship of the *Pawnee Dispatch*, family matters, and social life in Pawnee, Oklahoma.

Holdenville Schubert Music Club Collection 645
Scrapbook 1907–1957
1 item

Social club. A scrapbook (1907–1957) containing newspaper clippings and memorabilia documenting the history of the Schubert Music Club of Holdenville, Oklahoma.

Hollem, Anna Iverson 646
Papers 1892–1935
.10 foot

Collector. Correspondence, teaching certificates and examination scores, letters of recommendation, and tax receipts belonging to Charles L. Hollem, Anna Hollem's husband. All materials are from the years 1892–1901, except souvenirs from Hollem's lumberyard and letters describing Hollem's funeral in 1935. The papers reflect Hollem's activities as a schoolteacher in Oklahoma Territory and as owner of the first lumberyard in Lawton, Oklahoma.

Holmberg, Gustaf Fredrik (d. 1936)   647
Papers 1921–1936
.10 foot

Professor. Correspondence (1921–1935); manuscripts (n.d.); speeches (n.d.); and newspaper clippings (n.d.) relating to Holmberg's career as dean of the University of Oklahoma School of Fine Arts, 1907–1936.

Holmes, Helen F.   648
Papers 1876–1996
8 feet

Historian and politician. Subject files (1876–1996) containing Helen Holmes's research notes and materials regarding the history of Guthrie, Oklahoma, and Logan County, Oklahoma. Also included in the collection are research materials on the history of Abell, Cashion, Cimarron City, Coulter, Coyle, Crescent, Langston, and Mulhall, Oklahoma. Specialized subject files include research materials on historic homes in and around Guthrie and on cemeteries, schools, and churches in Guthrie and Logan County, as well as annual narrative reports of extension work (1935–1961) reporting the activities of African-American 4–H clubs in Logan County.

Unpublished finding aid available.

Holt, Smith Lewis, and James Doepel Holt   649
Papers 1829–1870
5 items

Collectors. An account book (n.d.) of W. M. Lewis; a ciphering book (1829) belonging to Samuel D. Jackson; a deposition and petition (1870) of Elizabeth and Angeline Carter; and a warrant (1870) issued by George W. Campbell.

Holtzendorff, Crichton Brooks (1886–1958)   650
Papers 1919–1922
.10 foot

Attorney. Financial records (1919–1922); notes (1920–1922); correspondence (1921–1922); legal documents (1920); and a newspaper clipping (1922), all relating to a legal dispute over utility rates between the city of Claremore, Oklahoma, and the Oklahoma Natural Gas Company.

Hood, F. Redding 651
Printed materials 1891
1 item

Physician. A partial transcript of a congressional debate regarding the sale of the Cherokee Outlet to the U.S. government and the price per acre.

Hooper's Printing Collection 652
Printed materials 1951–1952
3 items

Printer. Three samples of printing by Hooper's Printing of Norman, Oklahoma, including a program (1951) for the Junior-Senior Banquet at Noble High School; a program (1951–1952) for the Parent-Teacher Association of Noble, Oklahoma; and a handbook (1952) for the Order of the Coif.

Hoops, Mary Griffith (1842–1898) 653
Manuscript 1864–1866
1 item

Pioneer. A photocopy of a typewritten memoir (1887) by Mary Griffith Hoops, published in the *Marion Record* in 1925, and describing the 1864–1866 settlement of her family in Marion, Kansas. It includes information on the early history of the area, life on the frontier, a meeting with Kit Carson, and a trading post on the Santa Fe Trail.

Hoover, Earl R. 654
Printed materials 1941–1968
.10 foot

Judge. Printed materials (1941–1968) regarding composer Benjamin R. Hanby; and printed materials (1956–1966) regarding the work of Earl R. Hoover.

Hopeton State Bank Collection 655
Records 1903–1910
2 items

Bank. Two general ledgers (1903–1910) of the Hopeton State Bank in Hopeton, Oklahoma.

Hopson, Etta Roberts 656
Papers 1998–2000
.15 foot

University of Oklahoma alumna. Correspondence (1998–2000) and newspaper articles (1998–1999) regarding the life of Etta Roberts Hopson, a 1930 graduate of the University of Oklahoma College of Arts and Sciences. The collection includes reminiscences of her days as a child in Oklahoma Territory, as a student at the University of Oklahoma, and as an Oklahoma public school teacher, as well as notes on her friendship with the George H. W. Bush family.

Horton, Guy K. (b. 1912) 657
Manuscript ca. 1979
1 item

Attorney and state legislator. An unpublished, typewritten memoir (ca. 1979) of Horton's life in southwestern Oklahoma as an attorney and state legislator. The memoir contains references to his family, his boyhood, his college years, and especially to Oklahoma politics and his career as a state legislator.

Hoskinson, William Earl (b. 1887) 658
Papers 1873–1973
2 feet

Collector. Correspondence (1914–1973); financial and tax records (1901); clippings (n.d.); and family memorabilia (ca. 1905–1950) of William E. Hoskinson. The collection also includes hymnals (1873–1907) and a family history (1970), entitled "Thomas Bowman Hoskinson of Ohio, Texas, and California."

Unpublished finding aid available.

Hoss, Henry Sessler (ca. 1882–1921) 659
Papers 1898–1931
.10 foot

Physician. An account book (1917); notes (1904) from a course of lectures on obstetrics; two letters (1898, n.d.); and obituaries of Hoss, who practiced medicine in Muskogee, Oklahoma, from 1906 to 1921. The collection includes an appointment book (1931) of A. R. Gregory.

Hosterman, Jacob (1831–1903)   660
Ledger 1859–1862
1 item

Shoemaker. An account book (1859–1862) kept by Hosterman, who practiced his shoemaking trade in and around Mechanicsville, Iowa, during the years 1859–1862. A recipe for ink is included at the back of the book.

Hotchkiss and Cronkhite Loan and Investment Company Collection   661
Ledger 1905–1914
1 item

Financial institution. A daybook (1905–1914) of the Hotchkiss and Cronkhite Loan and Investment Company of Watonga, Oklahoma.

Hotema, Solomon E.   662
Manuscript 1907
1 item

Indian chief and minister. A typescript of an article (1907) concerning Hotema, a Choctaw chief and Presbyterian minister, and his release from prison.

Houghton, Fred Ernest (1854–1943)   663
Records 1901–1943
.25 foot

Merchant. A daily account book (1919–1920); a trade token advertising Houghton's stores; and photocopies of other financial records (1901–1943) belonging to Houghton, who owned general merchandise stores in the towns of Guthrie, Coyle, Cashion, Meridian, and Goodnight, Oklahoma.

House, Roy Temple (b. 1878)   664
Papers 1939–1951
.33 foot

Professor. Manuscripts (n.d.) of short stories by Roy Temple House, Emil Lucka (in German), José de la Cuadra, and others; and correspondence (1939–1951) concerning House's work with the University of Oklahoma and *Books Abroad*, much of it from Ada P. McCormick.

Housh, Earl C. 665
Papers 1920–1936
2 items

Collector. Certificates entitled "The Imperial Council of the Ancient Order of the Nobles of the Mystic Shrine" (1928) and "Lake Texoma College of Hunting and Fishing Diploma" (n.d.)

Houston, Temple (1860–1905) 666
Speech 1898
1 item

Attorney. A typescript of a speech (1898) by Temple Houston at the laying of the cornerstone of Northwestern State Teachers College, Alva, Oklahoma.

Howard, Walter Alonzo (1883–1970) 667
Papers 1919–1928
1 foot

Physician. Correspondence (1924–1927) from Howard's tenure as secretary-treasurer of the Rogers County (Oklahoma) Medical Society; military examination records (1920–1927) created while Howard was a designated medical examiner for the U.S. Veterans Bureau; and personal correspondence (1918–1927) regarding Howard's activities with the American Legion and the American Red Cross, along with reprints of articles on medical subjects.

Howe, A. N. 668
Manuscript 1883–1938
1 item

Cowboy. Transcript (n.d.) of a personal reminiscence by Howe regarding his experiences in the West, including visits to Dodge City, Kansas, Beaver County, Oklahoma, and No Man's Land (the Oklahoma panhandle). Also included are words to a song entitled "The Little Old Sod Shanty on My Claim."

Howell, Jesse V. (b. 1891) 669
Papers 1934–1952
3 items

Geologist. A reprint (1934) of an article by Jesse V. Howell; and a letter (1952) to the National Science Foundation from the Glossary Committee of the American Geological Institute, requesting funds to prepare a glossary of geological terms.

Howell, O. E. (b. 1877)   670
Papers 1907–1946
4 items

Physician. A copy of a speech (1946) by Howell, in which he recounts his experiences as a country physician in Oktaha, Oklahoma (1904–1929). Also included are copies of the *Saturday Evening Post* (1907), the *Illustrated London News* (1915), and a flyer advertising the movie *Ashes of Vengeance*, starring Norma Talmage.

Hudson, Waddie (b. ca. 1865)   671
Papers 1847–1951
.33 foot

Collector. Papers (1847–1951) of the Hudson family, including letters (1855, 1860) from Jefferson Davis and L. Q. C. Lamar to Thomas J. Hudson; Hudson's commission (1861) as a major in the Confederate States Army; and a letter to Hudson from M. H. Thomson concerning the prices of household goods. Also included in this collection are eight notebooks of official notary records (1905–1907) of William F. Rasmus of Tahlequah, Indian Territory; a ledger (1870) from Rasmus's general store in Flint, Indian Territory; two funeral registers (1903–1909) from John W. Stapler and Son; and a scrapbook (n.d.) prepared by Waddie Hudson for his grandson, Gordon Hudson Council.

Huff, Thomas J. (b. 1884)   672
Printed materials 1907–1949
.10 foot

Collector. Programs (1907–1949) from musical recitals, concerts, and plays performed in central Oklahoma, along with valentines and political flyers (n.d.).

Huffman, John   673
Records 1864–1871
6 items

Collector. An account book (1864–1871) of Jacob C. Huffman's personal expenditures; and five advertising cards.

Huggard, Christopher James (1954–)   674
Thesis 1828–1910
2 items

Historian. Huggard's thesis (1987), entitled "The Role of the Family in Settling the Cherokee Outlet," with chapters regarding the land run of 1893, settlement and housing patterns, and interaction with neighbors. Also in this collection is an unpublished paper by Huggard, entitled "Culture Mixing, Everyday Life Among the Choctaw in the Mid-Nineteenth Century."

[163]

Hughes, Jim   675
Papers 1948–1957
.33 foot

Labor official. Scrapbooks (1948–1957) of newspaper clippings concerning investigations of labor problems, legislation, and strikes; copies of the *United Mine Workers Journal* (1957); a typescript of a speech (1957) Hughes presented to the Oklahoma State Federation of Labor; a labor convention program (1957); and a contract for the publication of "A Labor History of Oklahoma."

Hughes, John Elmer (1878–1947)   676
Printed material 1906–1951
1 item

Physician. A published memoir (1951) in which Hughes describes his medical practice in Shawnee, Oklahoma, beginning in 1906, and his travels in Alaska, Europe, South America, Africa, and Indochina.

Hughes, Josephine S.   677
Printed materials 1939
2 items

Writer. Two copies of *"Unto the Least of These"; A Sketch of the Life of the Late Charles Page, Sand Springs, Oklahoma*, (1939) by Josephine S. Hughes.

Hume, Carlton Ross (1878–1960)   678
Papers 1838–1948
10.50 feet

Attorney. Personal and business correspondence (1893–1948) relating to Hume's family, his attendance at the University of Oklahoma, his contact with the university as an alumnus, and his law practice as an attorney for the Caddo Indians. Also included are numerous legal documents (1838–1948) relating to Indian claims and the Indians of Oklahoma, the Shirley Trading Post, the Anadarko, Oklahoma, area and the University of Oklahoma.

Unpublished finding aid available.

Hundley, John (b. 1872)   679
Records 1900–1942
7 feet

Businessman. Account books (1913–1937); daily statement ledgers (1914–1918); correspondence (1913–1919); tax receipts (1912–1917); stock inventories (1923–1942); and financial records (1920–1937) from Hundley's general store, plus assorted business papers (1900– 1936), all relating to Hundley's enterprises in and around Calvin, Oklahoma.

Unpublished finding aid available.

Hunt, Blanche Seale   680
Papers 1936–1951
.33 foot

Author. A scrapbook containing a complete set of Hunt's *Little Brown Koko* children's stories (1936–1951), clipped from magazines.

Hunt, J. O.   681
Records 1853–1903
7 items

Physician. An account book (1898–1903); a notebook (1876) of medicinal recipes and accounts; and matriculation and lecture tickets (1853) from the Medical College of Georgia, all belonging to Hunt or relating to Hunt's medical practice in Wallis, Indian Territory.

Hunter, H. A.   682
Ledger 1912
1 item

Collector. A ledger entitled "List of real estate owned by J. E. Campbell and E. B. Lawson jointly. November 25th, 1912."

Hunter, Thomas W.   **683**
Printed materials 1902–1903
3 items

Indian leader. Typescripts of newspaper articles (1902–1903) concerning Hunter's appointment of E. P. Pitchlynn as a light horseman and his authority to do so.

Huntley, A. A. (d. 1933)   **684**
Papers 1897–ca. 1900
2 items

Physician. A manuscript of a paper (1900) read by Huntley before the Beckham County (Oklahoma) Medical Society, and a reprint of an article (1897) written by Huntley and Delano Ames.

Hurley, Patrick Jay (1883–1956)   **685**
Papers 1900–1956
188 feet

U.S. ambassador. Correspondence, reports, and articles (1900–1956) regarding Hurley's positions as national attorney for the Choctaw Nation, including enrollments, land questions, and the Mississippi Choctaw Indians; as assistant U.S. secretary of war and U.S. secretary of war; as a special presidential representative to the Soviet Union, Great Britain, Afghanistan, and the Middle East; and as U.S. ambassador to China during World War II, including correspondence regarding American and Allied efforts in the Far Eastern theater. Correspondents include Winston Churchill, Franklin D. Roosevelt, Louis Mountbatten, Mao Tse-Tung, Chiang Kai-Shek, Herbert Hoover, Douglas MacArthur, Henry A. Wallace, Joseph Stilwell, Helen Keller, and Cordell Hull, as well as officials of the diplomatic corps, such as Averell Harriman and Harry Hopkins.

Unpublished finding aid available.

Hurst, Irvin   **686**
Manuscript 1957
1 item

Writer. An annotated manuscript (1957) for Hurst's book, *The 46th Star*, a history of Oklahoma's Constitutional Convention.

Hutchison, L. L. 687
Papers 1909–1911
.33 foot

Geologist. Correspondence (1910–1911) recommending Hutchison for employment as a consulting geologist; geological analyses (1911); and publications by Hutchison.

Hutto, Robert W. (b. 1885) 688
Papers 1929–1946
.66 foot

Banker. Business correspondence (1929–1946) and printed materials (1944–1946) relating to the Norman, Oklahoma, Chamber of Commerce, and to the Oklahoma Bankers Association, plus bound copies (1944–1946) of *The Oklahoma Banker*.

Hyde, Clayton H. (1868–1950) 689
Papers 1881–1946
13.66 feet

Farmer. Personal correspondence (1881–1946) of Clayton H. Hyde, including copies of speeches and public statements; correspondence (1909–1939) with local, state, and national farm, business, and political organizations, together with informational circulars on their activities.

Unpublished finding aid available.

Hyde, Sadie M. 690
Papers 1961–1985
.10 foot

Secretary. Correspondence (1961, 1964) from Robert F. Kennedy; invitations (1962) from the president's cabinet to attend various events; and a birthday card (1985) from Ronald and Nancy Reagan.

Hydro First National Bank Collection 691
Records 1903–1951
25 feet

Bank. Financial records (1903–1951), including correspondence, ledgers, draft registers, daily statements, distribution of expenses, and insurance records of the Bank of Hydro, the Hydro First National Bank, and the Farmers National Bank, all of Hydro, Oklahoma.

Ice, Rodney D.   692
Papers 1980
.10 foot

Collector. A notebook (1980) comprised of genealogical records of the Ice family, which has resided in Oklahoma since the territorial period.

Impson, Hiram   693
Letter 1940
1 item

Collector. A letter (1940) written by Paul McKennon, recounting his experiences in the Seminole Nation (1894–1896), with an explanation of how criminals were punished under Seminole law.

Independent Order of Odd Fellows Collection   694
Printed materials 1904–1911
7 items

Fraternal organization. Publications of Independent Order of Odd Fellows lodges in Indian and Oklahoma territories (1904–1907), and in the state of Oklahoma (1907–1911).

Indian Claims Commission Collection   695
Papers 1951–1958
.33 foot

Subject collection. Litigation brought before the Indian Claims Commission by the Kickapoo, Miami, Peoria, and Potawatomi tribes. The litigation pertains to treaties and land petitions for tribes in Oklahoma, Michigan, and Kansas.

Indian-Pioneer Papers Collection   696
Papers 1861–1936
22 feet

Oral history collection. Typescripts of interviews conducted during the 1930s by government workers with thousands of Oklahomans regarding the settlement of Oklahoma and Indian territories, as well as the condition and conduct of life there. Consisting of approximately 80,000 entries, the index to this collection may be accessed via personal name, place name, or subject.

Unpublished finding aid available.

Indian Territory Medical Association Collection   697
Records 1881–1904
.33 foot

Professional organization. Minute books (1881–1904) recording the proceedings of the Indian Territory Medical Association; and a college term paper (1956) regarding the history, origin, and governance of the Indian Territory Medical Association.

Indian War Veterans Collection   698
Papers 1937–1956
.50 foot

Veterans' organization. Correspondence (1930–1954), including personal data sheets on veterans of Indian wars and letters requesting assistance in obtaining pensions; diary extracts (1866–1893) describing experiences in various Indian wars, especially from 1860 to 1900, against the Apaches, Arapahos, Cheyennes, Comanches, Dakotas, Kiowas, and Paiutes; a manuscript (n.d.) written by Gen. T. H. Slavens, entitled "San Carlos, Arizona in the Eighties; The Land of the Apache," describing Indian activity in the San Carlos area, 1849–1894; and publications including issues of *Winners of the West* (1937–1944), *The Veteran Corps Bulletin* (1952, 1954), *The William McKinley Camp Bulletin* (1954), *War Path* (1955–1956), and the *Proceedings* of the twenty-fifth annual convention of veterans of Indian wars.

Indians of the Northwest Collection   699
Papers 1854–1859, 1966
.33 foot

Indian tribes. Facsimiles of treaties between the United States and Indian tribes of the Pacific Northwest, including Dwamish, Suquamish, Nisqualli, Yakima, and Makah tribes.

Ingram, Edwin L.   700
Papers 1910–1964
6 feet

Businessman. Correspondence and commercial literature (1910–1964) regarding investment opportunities throughout the United States, especially mining in the western states; and clippings and printed materials (1924–1925) regarding the Ku Klux Klan, its activities, and its political candidates. Ingram was an anti-Klan activist in the Cherokee, Oklahoma, area.

Unpublished finding aid available.

Internal Provinces of New Spain Collection   701
Papers 1704–1789
1 foot

Spanish colonial governmental unit. Copies of documents (1704–1789) from the Spanish archives of New Mexico relating to Indian relations, military defense, trade, and general colonial conditions in New Mexico, with notes from Ralph Emerson Twitchell's guide, *The Spanish Archives of New Mexico*.

Unpublished finding aid available.

Isparhecher (1828–1902)   702
Printed material 1884–1908
.25 foot

Indian chief. Typescripts of letters (1891–1898); speeches (1884–1898); editorials (1896–1906); and biographical accounts (1903–1908), all relating to Isparhecher, a principal chief of the Creek Nation, and covering subjects such as tribal factionalism, finance, land titles, and related government affairs.

Jackson, C. C.   703
Papers 1904
1 item

Surveyor. A certificate of allotment (1904) issued to Charles Wilson by the Cherokee Land Office at Tahlequah, Indian Territory.

Jackson, Hedy Steincamp   704
Papers 1872–1958
.50 foot

Collector. Correspondence and postcards (1883–1956), newspaper clippings, and marriage and death announcements (1872) regarding the Heagy family and the related families of Adams, Minniear, and Lord.

Jackson, Jacob Battiest (b. 1845)   705
Printed material 1896
1 item

Indian chief. A typescript of a newspaper article (1896) regarding Jackson's election as a principal chief of the Choctaw Nation.

Jackson, Robert Edward, Jr. (b. 1891)   706
Papers 1906–1907
3 items

Collector. An autograph book (1906) kept by Jackson while a page at the 1906 Oklahoma Constitutional Convention, containing the names of each delegate attending; a printed copy (1907) of the new Oklahoma constitution, along with county boundaries and election ordinances; and one parliamentary procedures manual (1906) entitled *Rules, Roster and Standing Committees of the Constitutional Convention*, used by Jackson during the convention.

Jacobson, Oscar Brousse (1882–1966)   707
Papers 1916–1945
1 foot

Professor. Newspaper editorial cartoons (1918–1930) regarding World War I and the post-war period; civilian defense correspondence (1917–1920) and publications (1942–1945), including plans, papers, and blueprints detailing civilian defense of the University of Oklahoma in the event of enemy attack; biographies (n.d.); and Jacobson's unpublished manuscript (ca. 1954) regarding Oklahoma artists and the status of art in Oklahoma through 1930.

Unpublished finding aid available.

Jaffe, Eli (d. 2001)   708
Papers 1935–1995
.66 foot

Labor organizer and author. Subject files (1935–1995), including newspaper clippings, magazine articles, and original correspondence relating to Jaffe's activities as an organizer for the Workers Alliance in depression-era Oklahoma. This collection also includes published and unpublished writings by Jaffe on his experiences in Oklahoma, his four-month imprisonment in the Oklahoma County jail, and the history of the Albert Einstein College of Medicine.

Jameson, John (b. 1897)   709
Records 1891–1911
1 item

Rancher. A ledger (1891–1911) containing financial transactions of the Jameson ranch in Indian Territory, along with personal and family information. Included is a home remedy for "weak lung," using as ingredients glycerin, whiskey, and white rock candy.

Jamieson, W. C.   710
Papers 1915–1937
.10 foot

Farmer. Bulletins (1918–1921) released by the National Board of Farm Organizations; a letter detailing an automobile journey through Oklahoma in 1930; a letter regarding presidential candidate Alfred M. Landon; and correspondence (1919–1920) regarding the creation of a dairy farmers' league for the Oklahoma City, Oklahoma, market.

[171]

Jarboe, (Mrs.) W. C.   711
Manuscript 1890–1913
1 item

Pioneer. In 1913 Jarboe wrote this account of her family's move from Texas into Indian Territory, and their subsequent move to Greer County, Oklahoma. The manuscript contains anecdotes about their experiences with Choctaw and Kiowa Indians, as well as a general description of hardships faced by pioneers.

Jayne, Mary Prosser   712
Papers 1896–1924
.33 foot

Missionary. Correspondence (1915) and pamphlets (1924) of missionary Robert Hamilton, stationed in Shawnee, Oklahoma, regarding his work there; and manuscript notes (n.d.) by Jayne, regarding missionary work at the Cheyenne and Arapaho Indian Baptist Mission and the class of 1896 of the Baptist Missionary Training School.

Jazhe, Benedict   713
Printed materials 1680–1963
.10 foot

Collector. Maps (1680–1963); government documents (1917–1960); a bibliography (n.d.) of sources; and a checklist of names (n.d), all relating to the Fort Sill Apache Indians.

Joblin, Walter Ridgway (1873–1950)   714
Records 1902–1943
6.33 feet

Physician. Records of Joblin's medical practice in Porter, Indian Territory, and Oklahoma, including ledgers listing patients and fees (1902–

1943); narcotics purchased and administered (1933–1939); and personal and household expenses (1933–1942).

Unpublished finding aid available.

John, Walter N.   715
Records 1894–1949
.10 foot

Physician. Ledgers (1923–1938) in which John recorded patient visits and services rendered; a diploma (1894) issued to John; and a biography and news clippings (1894–1949) regarding his life and career.

Johnson, B. F.   716
Records 1898–1954
2 items

Physician. Ledgers (1898–1954) listing patient visits and charges from Johnson's practice as a physician and pharmacist in Fairview, Oklahoma.

Johnson, Bob   717
Papers 1849–1873, 1908
.10 foot

Collector. A short, typewritten copy of a travel diary (1908) describing a trip through Kansas and Oklahoma, along with copies of three letters (1849–1873). One letter is from Beni Wingate, writing from Ft. Gibson, Indian Territory, in 1850 about family matters; the second is from George Mower, writing from the Platte River in Nebraska Territory in 1849 and commenting on what he has seen since leaving St. Joseph, Missouri; and the third (1873) is a brief letter of introduction for a salesman operating out of Denison, Texas.

Johnson, Dorothy   718
Papers 1876–1970
.50 foot

Collector. Stories (n.d.) written by Matie Mowbray Thomas regarding the exploits of Deputy U.S. Marshal Heck Thomas; a transcription of a letter written by Isaac Parker recommending Thomas's appointment as marshal of U.S. courts for Oklahoma; correspondence (1876–1960) regarding Heck Thomas, including a letter to Thomas from U.S. Senator Tom P. Gore, a letter to Bill Doolin from his wife, Edith, and a letter to Matie Thomas from Chris Madsen; magazine articles (1935) recounting the exploits of Heck Thomas as a railroad express messenger in Texas and as U.S. deputy marshal in Indian Territory; and diaries (1889–1895) kept by Heck Thomas that include notations about cases, witnesses, etc.

Johnson, Edgar Allen (1880–ca. 1955)   719
Records 1919–1950
13 feet

Physician. Case histories (1934–1950); fee books (1919–1950); and obstetric records (1934–1950) from Johnson's practice as a specialist in obstetrics and radiology in Hugo, Oklahoma.

Johnson, Edith Cherry (b. 1879)   720
Papers 1919–1951
2 feet

Journalist. Correspondence (1922–1945) from Johnson's readers concerning their personal problems and their opinions about her editorials and columns in the *Daily Oklahoman*; typescripts (1934–1948) of articles by Johnson; clippings (1919–1951) of her columns and of articles about her; letters (1921) endorsing Oklahoma senator John Golobie for the post of U.S. minister to Yugoslavia; and papers (1949–1950) from Johnson's tenure as secretary of Oklahoma Goodwill Industries, Inc.

Johnson, Edward Bryant (1865–1935)   721
Papers 1882–1929
7 feet

Banker and rancher. Correspondence (1882–1929); legal and financial records (1896–1928); diaries (1928–1929); and related biographical items concerning the banking, ranching, oil interests, and life of Edward Johnson, a Chickasaw Indian businessman and banker in Norman, Oklahoma.

Johnson, Henry Lee   722
Printed material 1945
1 item

Physician. A copy of *A Standard Practice Manual for Use in State Hospitals for Mental Disorders*, a manual (1945) written by Johnson while serving as the assistant superintendent for the Western Oklahoma Hospital, a psychiatric hospital at Fort Supply, Oklahoma.

Johnson, James T. 723
Papers 1882
1 item

Collector. A deed transferring land sold to James T. Johnson by Walter W. Durham in Hunt County, Texas.

Johnson, Martha Sherwood Finch 724
Papers 1954
3 items

Poet. Copies of three letters (1954) from Johnson to Mrs. Copeland, possibly Edith Copeland.

Johnson, Oscar Warren 725
Diploma ca. 1900
1 item

Pharmacist. A diploma (ca. 1900) issued to Oscar Warren Johnson by the Pharmaceutical Department of the University of Oklahoma.

Johnson, William E. 726
Papers 1912–1917
.10 foot

Government employee. A letter (1914) describing Johnson's trip to Russia, along with newspaper clippings (1912–1917) of stories about Johnson and his work to prevent the sale of alcoholic beverages to Indians. Among the clippings is a two-page article (1917) written by Johnson and entitled "Ten Years of Prohibition in Oklahoma."

Johnston, Douglas H. (1858–ca. 1940) 727
Printed materials 1896–1936
1 foot

Indian chief. Typescripts of newspaper articles and editorials (1896–1936) regarding Johnston as governor of the Chickasaw Nation and issues such as tribal government, land, mineral resources, finances, claims, education, and the ownership of slaves.

Unpublished finding aid available.

Johnston, Henry Simpson (1870–1965) 728
Papers 1891–1960
51 feet

Governor. Correspondence (1900–1960) relating to Henry Simpson Johnston's political and legal careers, and to his affiliation with various fraternal organizations; legal papers (1909–1934) documenting court cases with which Johnston was involved; speeches and other papers (1914–1930) relating to his political campaigns; and printed material and newspaper clippings (1920–1960) collected by Johnston.

Unpublished finding aid available.

Johnston, Marshall   729
Papers 1832–1878
6 items

Collector. Business and personal correspondence (1877–1878) and a land grant certificate (1832) issued to Robinson Frieman for a plot in Cherokee County, Georgia.

Johnston, Paul Imbrie (b. 1886)   730
Records 1927–1973
3 feet

Business executive. Corporate records (1934–1973), including articles of incorporation and minutes of the Oklahoma Public Services Corporation, the Oklahoma-Kansas Natural Gas Company, the Atlantic Oil Corporation, and the Continental Investment Corporation; operating manuals and brochures (1927–1930) of the Eason Oil Company, the Mid-Continent Petroleum Corporation, the Independent Oil and Gas Company, and the Transcontinental Oil Company; and a notebook (1957) labelled "Proxy Contest," including lists of stock sales and stockholders for the Atlantic Oil Corporation.

Unpublished finding aid available.

Jones, Daniel C.   731
Papers 1941–1944
.10 foot

Airman. Correspondence (1941–1944) from Daniel C. Jones to his mother, Cecilia Jones of Kent, Ohio. Daniel C. Jones was in military training at the Army Air Force Technical School at Seymour Johnson Field, North Carolina; at Peterson Field, Colorado Springs, Colorado; and at Will Rogers Field, Oklahoma City, Oklahoma. Jones's letters describe his basic training, daily routine, family relations, and his medical discharge from service.

Jones, Dovie   732
Papers 1870–1892
2 items

Collector. A ledger (1870) with entries in the Choctaw language, belonging to Wilson N. Jones, a principal chief of the Choctaws, and containing information regarding a general store he operated in Cade, Indian Territory. Also included is a copy of a speech (1892) by Jones to the Choctaw general council.

Jones, Gomer (1914–1971)   733
Printed material 1971
1 item

Athletic director. A copy of Oklahoma Senate Concurrent Resolution No. 29 (1971), regarding the death of University of Oklahoma athletic director Gomer Jones.

Jones, John Paul   734
Ledger 1923–1924
1 item

Physician. A ledger (1923–1924) in which Jones recorded services rendered and fees charged.

Jones, Lydia Caroline Baggett (1843–1934)   735
Papers ca. 1900–1988
5 items

Pioneer. Photocopies of Jones's account of pioneer life in early Montague County, Texas, from 1854 to approximately 1867, describing early settlers and raids by Comanche Indians; census returns from 1860 and 1870 for the Jones and Baggett families, taken from *Early Records of Montague County, Texas* (1982); an obituary (1934) of Jones; a roll of the Nacogdoches (Texas) Mounted Volunteers; and notes (1988) on the genealogy of the Jones and Baggett families.

Jones, Stephen (1940–)   736
Papers 1964–1977
8 feet

Lawyer. Correspondence (1971–1973) of the American Civil Liberties

Union and the Oklahoma Civil Liberties Union; court records (1971–1973); testimony (1972–1973); transcripts, prisoners' petitions, and prison records (1971–1977); and publications (1964–1976) of the American and Oklahoma civil liberties unions, all relating to Jones's service as general counsel to the Oklahoma chapter of the American Civil Liberties Union and his successful representation of Bobby Battle in the landmark case *Battle vs. Park Anderson.*

Unpublished finding aid available.

Jones, Wilson N. (ca. 1831–1901) 737
Printed materials 1890–1935
.10 foot

Indian chief. Typescripts of newspaper articles (1890–1935), including speeches, editorials, and official documents which focus on Choctaw tribal politics, land allotment, and mineral rights on Choctaw Indian lands.

Jordan, Glenn 738
Printed materials 1860–1977
.50 foot

Historian. Research materials (1860–1977) gathered by Jordan while preparing his dissertation on Joseph S. Murrow and Bacone College, including photocopies of Murrow's diary (1867–1869).

Jordan, J. F. 739
Records 1921–1928
.50 foot

Pharmacist. Prescriptions filled at the Jordan Drugstore pharmacy, Oklahoma City, Oklahoma, for the period 1921–1928.

Jordan, John D. 740
Papers 1839–1903
.10 foot

Collector. A typescript letter (1842) to Stand Watie from John R. Ridge regarding the Ross faction and the death of James Foreman; and a biography (n.d.) of Stand Watie, compiled by the Daughters of the Confederacy.

This cover of a 1927 publicity pamphlet for the Miller Brothers 101 Ranch Wild West Show features illustrations of show highlights. From the Miller Brothers 101 Ranch Collection.

Jordan, Omar L. 741
Records 1940–1948
.66 foot

Collector. Correspondence (1941–1948) regarding Oklahoma Lions Club business, and publications (1940–1941) issued by the Lions Club, including a history of Oklahoma club district 3–A.

Journeycake, Charles (1817–1894) 742
Printed materials 1936–1964
.10 foot

Indian chief. A typescript of a biography (n.d.) of Delaware chief Charles Journeycake, and newspaper clippings (1936–1964) regarding the Journeycake home and his career.

Judd, Neil Merton 743
Papers 1964–1967
.33 foot

Archaeologist. Manuscripts (1964–1967) by Neil Merton Judd regarding Pueblo Bonito in Mexico and natural bridges in U.S. national parks.

Judy, Thomas J. (1861–1936) 744
Manuscript 1884–1936
1 item

Rancher. A typewritten, twenty-seven page memoir (ca. 1936) of Judy's life as a pioneer rancher in No Man's Land (the Oklahoma panhandle area). The memoir recounts the hardships of ranching in what is now Beaver County, Oklahoma, and the lawlessness of that area.

Jumper, John (1823–1896) 745
Printed materials 1874–1928
.10 foot

Indian chief. Typescripts of newspaper articles (1874–1929) by and about Jumper, and about the Peace Council of 1874 and the status of Christian missions in the Seminole Nation.

Kagey, Joseph Newton (1890–1959) 746
Papers 1850–1959
.10 foot

Educator. Newspaper clippings (1946–1959) and a history (1954) of the Seneca Indian School; a pamphlet (1950) and booklet (ca. 1951) regarding the history of the Goodland Indian Mission; and an obituary (1959) of Kagey.

Kali-Inla Coal Company Collection 747
Records 1903–1944
219 feet

Coal mining company. Correspondence, financial reports, leases, legal reports, and general reports, all dated 1903–1944, regarding the operation and management of the Kali-Inla Coal Company of Hartshorne, Indian Territory, and Oklahoma, and that of its subsidiary coal companies and related firms. Special correspondence files include those regarding labor union activity, mining accidents, company housing, relations with railroads, and insurance. Also included in this collection are equipment catalogs (ca. 1910–1944) containing advertisements and information regarding miner and mining supplies. In addition to reflecting the mining industry in Oklahoma, the collection also contains information on mining operations in Colorado, West Virginia, and Arkansas.

Unpublished finding aid available.

Kaufman, Kenneth Carlyle (1887–1945) 748
Papers 1908–1942
.10 foot

Professor and editor. Manuscripts (1929–1940) of poetry, short stories, and plays; printed material (1930–1942), including literary publications; a bibliography (n.d.) of Oklahoma writers; and certificates and diplomas (1908–1926) received by Kaufman.

Kaw Indian Agency Collection 749
Records 1887–1939
15.33 feet

Indian agency. Farming and grazing leases (1903–1937); oil and gas leases (1913–1932); allotment records (1902–1936); financial and property records (1887–1927); employee records (1903–1918); correspondence (1901–1939); and general subject files (1895–1932) of the agency for the Kansa (Kaw) Indians.

Unpublished finding aid available.

Kay County State Bank Collection   750
Records 1898–1901
4 feet

Bank. Four deposit ledgers (1898–1901) from the Kay County (Oklahoma) State Bank.

[181]

Keiger, Charles Guy (b. ca. 1891)   751
Papers 1904–1908
5 items

University student. Newspaper clippings (1904) of prose and poetry written by the students of the Pond Creek (Oklahoma) High School class of 1904; and an event program (1908) for the senior banquet of the University of Oklahoma class of 1908, signed by the senior class members.

Keith, Harold (1903–1998)   752
Papers 1900–1993
20 feet

Author and publicist. Professional correspondence (1928–1992); personal correspondence (1922–1987); personal records (1903–1987); author subject files (1900–1984); typescripts and manuscripts (1938–1986); publications (1928–1987); financial records (1930–1993); and memorabilia from the life and career of Harold Keith, author of children's stories *Rifles for Watie* and *Boys' Life of Will Rogers*, and sports information director of the University of Oklahoma. Also included are programs (1930–1970) of University of Oklahoma athletic events, and correspondence (1942–1946) from University of Oklahoma students and alumni, mostly athletes who were serving in the U.S. Army during World War II, to Harold Keith and members of the University of Oklahoma Athletic Department.

Unpublished finding aid available.

Keller-Clarke Seed Store Collection   753
Records 1908–1953
4 feet

Retail business. Ledgers (1927–1929); receipts, invoices, and bank books (1920–1921); legal papers (1920); correspondence (1930–1943); and blueprints (1920), all concerning the Keller-Clarke Seed Store in Shawnee, Oklahoma, together with reports (n.d.) of Oklahoma agricultural colleges; typescripts (n.d.) of radio advertisements; and minutes (1908) of the Shawnee (Oklahoma) Fanciers Association.

Unpublished finding aid available.

Kennedy, John 754
Certificate 1906
1 item

Collector. License (1906) issued to W. S. Kennedy to practice pharmacy in Indian Territory.

Kennedy, John C. (1910–1993) 755
Papers 1906–1990
4 feet

Insurance executive. Correspondence (1957–1990); speeches (1959–1983); Democratic political campaign literature and memorabilia (1960–1980); scrapbooks (1938–1955); and newspaper clippings (1906 1993) relating to Kennedy's businesses and investments, his support of the Democratic Party in Oklahoma and nationally, his appointment as an alternate delegate to the U.S. mission to the United Nations, his service as a commissioner of the Oklahoma State Highway Department, and his travels in the U.S. and worldwide.

Unpublished finding aid available.

Kennedy, John Fitzgerald (1917–1963) 756
Printed materials 1963
.33 foot

Subject collection. Newspapers and news magazines (1963) published in the United States and the Federal Republic of Germany, regarding Kennedy's visit to West Germany and West Berlin in June, 1963, and his assassination in November, 1963. All items in this collection bear cover stories regarding, or are special editions devoted to, President Kennedy and his death.

Kennedy, Kay Don 757
Records 1903
3 items

Collector. Three $500 bonds (1903) issued to fund the Oklahoma Territorial University, the Agricultural and Mechanical College, and the Normal School.

Kennedy, L. P. 758
Letter 1887
1 item

Clergyman. A letter (1887) from Judge Isaac C. Parker advising Kennedy as to the legality in Texas of marriages performed in Indian Territory.

Kenton, Simon   759
Paper 1798
1 item

Collector. A document (1798) regarding a payment in Kentucky currency from Simon and John Kenton to William McDonald.

Keown, William H.   760
Printed materials 1951–1977
.33 foot

Collector. Publications regarding aspects of the oil industry including water, flooding, and conservation; abstracts of real estate titles from Oklahoma counties; and directories from both the East Texas and Oklahoma City petroleum landmen associations.

Kerley, J. W.   761
Ledger 1903–1922
1 item

Physician. An account and prescription ledger (1903–1922) from Kerley's medical practice in Cordell, Oklahoma.

Kerr, Harrison (1897–1978)   762
Papers 1904–1978
30 feet

Composer and university dean. Correspondence (1904–1976) with wife Jeanne Kerr and colleague George Exline; musical scores (1916–1977) written by Harrison Kerr and other composers, both printed and manuscript form, including Kerr's 1960 opera *The Tower of Kel*; manuscripts (1932–1978) of writings by Kerr on music, including his 1976 monograph, *The Musical Experience*, as well as articles from his tenure as editor of *Trend*; teaching and class materials (1964–1968) reflecting his work as dean of the University of Oklahoma College of Fine Arts; and newspaper clippings (1920–1972) regarding Kerr's career and interests.

Unpublished finding aid available.

Kerr-McGee Corporation Collection 763
Printed material 1928–1978
.66 foot

Energy corporation. Photocopies and printed material (1928–1978) issued by the public relations department of the Kerr-McGee Corporation, including biographical information on Robert S. Kerr and Dean A. McGee; reports (1976–1977) to the Securities and Exchange Commission; reference material (n.d.) used for the report on drilling operations in the corporation's annual reports (1960–1966); chronologies of corporate history and general statistics (1962–1977); an index (1977) to the minutes of the board of trustees meetings; and clippings and press releases (1975–1977), including information on Karen Silkwood.

Kessler, Edwin, III 764
Printed materials 1942–1944
.50 foot

Collector. Newspapers and news magazines published for the benefit of U.S. servicemen stationed in the China–Burma–India theater of World War II, including *Yank* (1942–1944) and *C.B.I. Roundup*, as well as an edition of the private tabloid, *The Times of India* (1944), published in Bombay, India.

Kibbey, W. Beckford 765
Manuscript 1929
1 item

Rancher. A typewritten, ten-page daily account (1929) of Kibbey's activities to defend his hacienda in northern Sonora, Mexico, against revolutionary forces and the counter demands of Mexican federal troops during a short-lived revolt in 1929.

Kibler, Nell 766
Papers 1828–1888
5 items

Collector. An oath of allegiance (1862) to the United States; a history (1863) of the Confederate States Army's Dublin Provost Guard; a letter (1828) from an ancestor of Kibler regarding the hardships of life in Michigan Territory; and schoolbooks (1885–1888).

Kiebler, W. G. 767
Records 1920–1927
.10 foot

Physician. Five journals (1920–1927) recording patients' names and fees charged, from Kiebler's medical practice in Enid, Oklahoma; and a 1927 edition of *The Skeleton*, a yearbook from the training school for nurses in Enid, Oklahoma.

Kincaid, John W. 768
Ledger 1867–1887
1 item

Collector. A ledger book of accounts (1867–1887) kept by attorney Jonathan Gore of Shawnee, Kansas. The second half of the ledger book is comprised of diary entries by Gore (1867–1869) concerning daily life in Shawnee, Kansas; Gore's legal practice and related cases; and observances regarding members of the local Shawnee tribe.

Kinder, George 769
Printed materials 1904–1950
2 items

Collector. A booklet (1904–1905) entitled *Souvenir*, listing the teacher and pupils of Mount Pleasant School in Blaine County, Oklahoma Territory; and one entrance ticket to the 1950 Sugar Bowl football game in New Orleans, Louisiana, at which the University of Oklahoma football team won its first national championship.

King, (Mrs.) A. J. 770
Papers 1856–1876
.10 foot

Collector. Typescripts of letters (1856–1865) by Abraham J. Seay, second governor of Oklahoma Territory, regarding the role of the American Party in Missouri and Seay's experience and views regarding the Civil War; and a typed manuscript (1856–1876) regarding the history of Seay's parents and family.

King, Charles Francis Xavier (d. ca. 1981) 771
Papers 1960–1975
2 feet

Professor. Unpublished manuscripts (1951–1975) on western history themes, including the Battle of the Washita in 1868, the establishment of Fort Gibson, Indian Territory, and its cemetery, and the westward migration of the Cherokees; and lecture notes (n.d.) used by King to teach American, European, and Russian history.

Unpublished finding aid available.

King, Donald   772
Papers 1897–1914
.25 foot

Collector. Issues of the *Colony Mercantile Company Store News* (1912–1914), an in-house newsletter of a retail store run by the King family and serving the Cheyenne-Arapaho reservation, plus an issue of the *Colony Courier* (1910); and three commencement and wedding invitations (1897–1910).

Kingfisher College Collection   773
Records 1894–1964
1 foot

College. Administrative records (1894–1964), including a report (1917) of the president; administrative correspondence (1921–1928); constitutions of the college (1895–1964); papers of the college's board of trustees; alumni ballots (1927) regarding the future of the college; and a certificate of amended incorporation. Also included are publications such as *The Halcyon*, a yearbook (1914); *The Kingfisher*, a newsletter (1903–1909); and the *Kingfisher College Bulletin* (1903– 1921).

Unpublished finding aid available.

Kingsbury, Cyrus (1786–1870)   774
Records 1819–1869
1.50 feet

Missionary. Photocopies of the correspondence (1818–1869) and reports (1820–1859) of Cyrus Kingsbury, Presbyterian missionary among the Choctaw Indians, regarding the Choctaw removal to the Indian Territory, the Civil War, and slavery.

Unpublished finding aid available.

Kiowa County Historical Society Collection   775
Manuscripts 1911–1945
7 items

Historical society. Anonymous manuscripts (1911–1945) regarding crime and criminals, and specifically concerning Frank Nash, a bank robber and murderer from Hobart, Oklahoma.

Kirk, Betty (1904–1984)   776
Papers ca. 1940–1970
10 feet

Journalist. Manuscripts of articles; correspondence; research notes; and reprints (all ca. 1940–1970) used by Elizabeth Mahala Kirk Boyer, who wrote under the name Betty Kirk, in writing her articles and books concerning U.S. politics, Mexico, and international relations.

Unpublished finding aid available.

Kirkpatrick, Albert J.   777
Papers ca. 1932–1968
.50 foot

Pianist. Musical score (n.d.) entitled "Grand River Suite," written for string orchestra by S. A. McReynolds, along with original compositions (1932–1968), travel sketches, and short stories (ca. 1963–1968) by Kirkpatrick. Also included are sound recordings (ca. 1990) of Kirkpatrick playing his compositions.

Klapp's Drug Store Collection   778
Records 1901–1913
.10 foot

Pharmacy. Two books (n.d.) containing formulae for home remedies, and a poison and narcotics register (1901–1913) from Klapp's Drugstore in Tecumseh, Oklahoma.

Kliewer, Heinrich   779
Papers 1892–1898
.10 foot

Government employee. Work reports (1892–1898) filed by Kliewer, a farmer employed by the Cheyenne-Arapaho Indian Agency, Darlington, Oklahoma Territory, to assist Indians in their agricultural activities. The reports include number of days worked, the number of Indians assisted, acres plowed, rods of fencing built or repaired, acres planted, houses improved or repaired, and the general condition of the Indians' stock and crops.

Knights Templar of Oklahoma Collection 780
Printed materials 1920–1934
.10 foot

Fraternal order. Official proceedings (1920–1934) of conclaves held by the Knights Templar of Oklahoma.

Knox, John J. 781
Papers 1875
2 items

U.S. Indian agent. Correspondence (1875) from John J. Knox to his brother, William W. Knox of Clarkston, Michigan. John Knox writes from the "South West Corner Pottawatomie Reserve 165 miles from Muscogee, Ind. Ter.," and describes the poor quality of the land on which Indians reside and their general living conditions.

Kobel, Raleigh (1877–1951) 782
Printed material 1915–1952
.10 foot

Merchant. Clippings (1915–1951) concerning John F. Wheeler and his descendants, the history of Sallisaw, Oklahoma, and the Cherokee Nation.

Korn, Anna Lee Brosius (b. ca. 1870) 783
Papers 1927–1955
.10 foot

Club woman. A typescript of a lecture (n.d.) entitled "Progress and Development of Missouri Since 1860 from Gleanings Here and There," for presentation to the Missouri division of the United Daughters of the Confederacy; a yearbook (1927) published by the National Society, United States Daughters of 1812 of Oklahoma; and programs and clippings (1930–1955) concerning Korn and her club activities.

Kraettli, Emil Rudolph (1890–1979) 784
Papers 1900–1959
.33 foot

University administrator. Reports (1900–1928) of the University of Oklahoma Board of Regents; financial papers (1906–1915); faculty lists

(1908–1913) of the university; and a letter (1933) from Oklahoma governor William H. Murray to Brig. Gen. Charles F. Barrett, ordering guards to be posted at the University of Oklahoma football stadium.

Krugers, Albert 785
Records 1838–1903
4 items

Investor. Three deeds (1838, 1857) for land in Vermont, and one deed (1903) for land in Oklahoma City, Oklahoma Territory.

Kruis, Roland (b. 1923) 786
Poster 1931
1 item

Collector. A poster (1931) announcing a benefit performance by Will Rogers at the University of Oklahoma.

Ku Klux Klan Women Collection 787
Records 1923–1928
.66 foot

Women's organization. Official correspondence (1926–1928); membership lists (1924–1928); minutes (1924–1928); booklets (1923–1928); song sheets (n.d.); flyers (n.d.); and memorabilia (1923–1928) from this Alfalfa County, Oklahoma, women's group.

Kuyrkendall, Louis C. (d. 1956) 788
Records 1853–1955
12 feet

Physician. General correspondence (1906–1955); examination reports (1924–1944) of injured Missouri, Kansas, and Texas Railroad Company employees; examination reports (1943–1950) prepared for the Oklahoma Department of Public Welfare; correspondence (1929–1950) regarding workers compensation cases; examination reports (1940–1949) for the Civil Aeronautics Administration; and daybooks and account ledgers (1920–1948) from Kuyrkendall's medical practice in McAlester, Oklahoma. Also included in the collection are reprints of articles authored by Kuyrkendall and a prescription book (1853) belonging to Kuyrkendall's grandfather.

Kvaloy, Kare   789
Papers 1995
.10 foot

Graduate student. Papers (1995) written by Kare Kvaloy as part of course work while a student at the University of Oklahoma. The papers are entitled "Politically Active McIntoshes of the Creek Nation" and "The Creek Judicial System."

Ladies' Aid Society Collection   790
Records 1884–1913
.25 foot

Civic organization. A ledger (1884–1913) showing expenditures, dues, and account balances of the Ladies' Aid Society of Bismarck, North Dakota.

Lahman, Marion Sherwood (1872–1954)   791
Papers 1936–1950
.33 foot

Botanist. A manuscript (1950) with drawings, entitled "Some Cacti of Our Southwest," by Lahman; papers (1936) from the meetings of the Cactus and Succulent Society of Oklahoma City, Oklahoma; and paintings (1950) by Lahman of western wild flowers.

Lain, Everett S. (b. 1873)   792
Papers 1893–1952
.33 foot

Physician. A biography (1923) of Lain; a typescript of a speech (n.d.) by Lain to the Oklahoma State Medical Association; news clippings regarding medicine in Oklahoma; a patient accounts ledger (1900); and financial journals (1933, 1938) from Lain's medical practice. Also included in this collection are a publication of the Epworth Methodist Church of Oklahoma City, Oklahoma, entitled *The Epworth Spotlight*, and several articles which Lain wrote on herpes research, x-ray technology in Oklahoma, and skin diseases among Oklahoma Indians.

Lamb, Ellis   793
Records 1910–1915
.33 foot

Physician. Records (1910–1915), including ledgers, personal correspondence, and billing receipts from Lamb's medical practice in Clinton, Oklahoma.

Lane, Rose Wilder (1886–1968)   794
Papers 1924–1934
.10 foot

Author. Correspondence and biographical information (1924–1934) of Rose Wilder Lane, daughter of Laura Ingalls Wilder. The letters from Lane to Grant Carpenter were written from 1924 to 1934, primarily from Rocky Ridge Farm, Mansfield, Missouri. Two of the letters were written from Paris, France, and Tirana, Albania. The letters cover such topics as aging, literary gossip, American politics, and the world situation.

Langsford, William (b. 1869)   795
Records 1899–1939
2.33 feet

Physician. Records (1899–1939), including daybooks, patient hospital records, prescriptions, and certificates and licenses, all relating to Langsford's medical practice in Oklahoma City, Oklahoma.

Lansden, J. B. (1877–1953)   796
Records 1913–1939
.66 foot

Physician. Six ledgers (1913–1939) recording patients and fees from Lansden's medical practice in Granite, Oklahoma.

Las Dos Americas Collection   797
Records 1940–1951
.10 foot

Social club. Minutes (1940–1951) and correspondence (1940–1951), in Spanish, of Las Dos Americas, the University of Oklahoma Spanish club.

Latty, James Monroe (1861–1937)   798
Papers 1898
3 items

Farmer. A letter (1898), with typescript copies, by James M. Latty of Muskogee, Indian Territory, to his brother in Idaho, describing his intention to move west so that his children would receive a better education.

Lawton, Sherman Paxton (1908–1971)   799
Papers 1927–1968
2 feet

Professor. Television scripts and publicity (1951–1959) for "The Open Window"; radio scripts (1953) for "Labor's Side of the News" and "Wake Up to Yesterday"; correspondence (1945–1961); manuscripts (ca. 1935–1960) of articles and short stories; curriculum material (1934– 1960); and printed material (1927–1968) accumulated by Lawton while a professor of communication at the University of Oklahoma.

Unpublished finding aid available.

Layton, Helen Elizabeth Blackert   800
Papers 1840–1916
.33 feet

Collector. A manuscript of *Pilgrims of the Plains*, by Kate Smith Aplington, published in 1913; correspondence (1912–1914) concerning the publication of the book; a manuscript of "Life and Writings of Samuel A. Deming by his Brother" (1849); and newspaper clippings (1840–1916), all belonging to Helen Layton, niece of Kate Aplington.

Leckie, Shirley A. (1937–)   801
Papers 2000
1 item

Historian. An endnoted typescript of *Angie Debo: Pioneering Historian*, by Shirley A. Leckie, published by the University of Oklahoma Press (2000), as Volume 20 in the Western Biography Series.

Ledbetter, Eugene P.   802
Papers 1892–1952
2.33 feet

Attorney. Case files (1892–1952) of Ledbetter, an Oklahoma City, Oklahoma, attorney, concerning oil, gas, and railroad leases and stock; the payment of Oklahoma supreme court justices' salaries (1933–1935); and the payment of a reward offered for the arrest of George "Machine Gun" Kelly (1934).

Unpublished finding aid available.

Ledbetter, Walter A. (b. 1863) 803
Papers 1914
3 items

Attorney. A copy of the contract, bond, and specifications (1914) for the Oklahoma state capitol building in Oklahoma City, Oklahoma.

Lee, Ottie 804
Papers ca. 1936–1947
.10 foot

Collector. Newspaper clippings (1936–1947) relating to R. C. "Crockett" Lee; a typescript (n.d.) of an article on Lee by J. J. McAlester, grandson of Col. J. J. McAlester; a list (n.d.) of officials of the Missouri, Kansas, and Texas Railroad; and correspondence (1939–1946) to and from Lee concerning Oklahoma and national politics.

LeFlore, Carrie 805
Papers 1886–1892
.10 foot

Homemaker. Personal correspondence (1886–1892) with friends and family reflecting her life as the wife of Basil LeFlore, a principal chief of the Choctaw Indians, along with expressions of condolence on the death of her husband.

Lenski, Lois (1893–1974) 806
Papers 1907–1972
9 feet

Author and illustrator. Manuscripts (1918–1971) of works by Lenski; original art work (1917–1939); typescripts of speeches and articles (1932–1970) by Lenski; business and personal correspondence (1912–1972); biographical materials (1930–1970) on Lenski, including a scrapbook compiled by Letha Barde; and information (1956–1972) concerning other Lois Lenski collections.

Unpublished finding aid available.

Leslie, Samuel B. (b. 1874) 807
Records 1906–1952
.10 foot

Physician. Correspondence (1906–1952) relating to Leslie's service with the Oklahoma State Board of Medical Examiners, the Oklahoma State Medical Association, and the American Medical Association; and examination questions (1939–1945) used by the State Board of Medical Examiners to certify Oklahoma physicians.

Letterhead Collection 808
Printed materials 1865–1919
.25 foot

Subject collection. Samples of official letterheads and envelopes printed for the territorial and state governments of Oklahoma, Indian Territory, cities and towns, businesses, and organizations, all selected as representative of the stationery style of their period.

Lewallen, Wesley P. (1862–1943) 809
Records 1904–1932
1 foot

Physician. Patient account ledgers (1904–1932) and a daybook (1926–1930) from Lewallen's medical practice in Canadian, Oklahoma.

Lewis, Powell K. (1879–1955) 810
Records 1901–1954
1 foot

Physician. Daybooks (1936–1952); ledgers (1924, 1937–1942); receipt books (1946–1954); personal financial and legal records (1921–1938); a pamphlet of medical formulae (1912); and a *Guide to First Year Laboratory Work* (1901), all from Lewis's medical practice in Sapulpa, Oklahoma.

Lewis, Walter E. 811
Papers 1920–1991
.10 foot

Amateur ornithologist. Two manuscripts (ca. 1920) about birds in northwest Oklahoma (panhandle area); eight letters between Walter E. Lewis and Margaret Nice (1922–1932); four letters between John Tomer and Wayne S. Lewis (1990–1991); and a pamphlet (n.d.) about Walter Lewis as a candidate for the office of Oklahoma state representative.

Lewis and Clark Centennial Exposition Collection 812
Papers 1905
3 items

Exposition. Three copies of a brochure describing the Lewis and Clark Centennial Exposition in Portland, Oregon, 1905.

Liberty National Bank Collection   813
Records 1911–1930
24 feet

Bank. Financial records (1911–1930), including correspondence, general ledgers, a computation register, a distribution of expenses ledger, tellers' cash books, and an insurance policy register from the Stockyards National Bank and Guaranty Bank, which were absorbed by the Liberty National Bank of Oklahoma City, Oklahoma.

Ligon, Mary Louise   814
Papers 1906–1925
7 items

Collector. A manuscript (n.d.) describing a saloon fight; a typescript (n.d.) entitled "Fundamental Principles of Plant Breeding," by Isaac Renfro; newspaper clippings (1925); and a permit (1906) issued to Elkins, Webster, and Bayleas to sell insurance in Indian Territory.

Lilley, (Mrs.) John B.   815
Diary 1842–1857
1 item

Missionary. A typescript of a diary (1842–1857) kept by the wife of John B. Lilley, a Presbyterian missionary to the Seminole Nation. The diary describes the Lilleys' arrival among the Seminoles, the hardships of living in Indian Territory, problems with slaves, friction between the Creeks and the Seminoles, the departure of Wild Cat (Coocoochee) for Mexico, and tensions prior to the Civil War.

Lillie, Foress B. (1885–1926)   816
Papers 1872–1949
5 feet

Pharmacist. General correspondence (1887–1923); diaries (1886–1920); printed materials (ca. 1895–1934), including postcards, greeting cards, and magazines; scrapbooks (n.d.) regarding the history of Guthrie, Oklahoma; correspondence (1887–1889) relating to the passage of pharmacy laws in Oklahoma; a minute book (1889–1921) of the Oklahoma Territorial Board of Pharmacy; the constitution of the Oklahoma Pharmaceutical Association (1907); a report (1907) to the governor of Oklahoma on pharmacy in the state; and ledgers and correspondence (1887–1901) from Lillie's Drug Store, Guthrie, Oklahoma.

Unpublished finding aid available.

Lillie, Gordon William (1860–1942) — 817
Papers 1879–1945
8.5 feet

Rancher and businessman. Correspondence (1911–1943); legal and financial records (1879–1945); and printed materials (1893–1945) regarding G. W. Lillie, also known as "Pawnee Bill," his wild west show, and his ranching business. The collection includes wild west show memorabilia, an autobiographical sketch of Lillie, and references to several Indian chiefs.

Unpublished finding aid available.

Lincoln County Medical Society Collection — 818
Records 1904–1944
.10 foot

Professional organization. Society minute books (1904–1944); and correspondence (1928–1938) regarding the county medical Poor Fund and Cancer Committee, as well as society-sponsored proposals for improving medical care in Lincoln County, Oklahoma.

Lindsey, Newton Harvey (1870–1934) — 819
Papers 1951
2 items

Physician. A biographical sketch (1951) of Lindsey's life and his contribution to Pauls Valley, Oklahoma, along with an article (1951) by Kathleen Lindsey on being a physician's wife.

Lindsey, Ray H. — 820
Papers 1863–1864
.10 foot

Collector. Letters (1863–1864) written by Thomas G. Lindsey to his wife Laura during the Civil War, while he was serving with the Twenty-sixth Alabama Infantry Regiment in Virginia and Georgia.

Lininger, Herbert K. (d. 1953) 821
Papers 1621–1907
.10 foot

Collector. Deeds (1901–1907) issued in Oklahoma and Indian territories, and servant indentures (1621–1849) signed and issued in Great Britain.

Lininger, W. H. 822
Papers 1895–1932
3 items

Insurance agent. Two notebooks entitled "Comparative Agency Record for Fire Insurance Field Man" (1895–1904) for Kansas; and a brochure (1932) for the Guardian Funeral Home, Oklahoma City, Oklahoma.

Lions Club Collection 823
Records 1954–1955
.33 foot

Civic club. Membership and activity reports (1954–1955), and correspondence (1954–1955) with the local chapters of the Lions Clubs in district 3L, which included southwestern Oklahoma.

Lions International Collection 824
Printed materials 1954–1955
.10 foot

Civic club. Copies of the *Lions Club Official Directory* (1954–1955).

Lisa, Manuel 825
Papers 1796
1 item

Collector. A document (1796) regarding the payment of $1,000 to Henry Varderburg from John Small, Manuel Lisa, and John Baptiste Baroy of the County of Knox and Territory of the United States, Northwest of the Ohio.

[197]

Little, Jesse Samuel 826
Papers 1900–1930
.10 foot

Physician. Ledgers (1904); daybooks (1904–1908, 1930); and lecture notes, matriculation tickets, and lecture schedules (1900–1902) from Fort Worth University, all belonging to Little, who practiced medicine in Minco, Oklahoma.

Litton, Gaston (b. 1913) 827
Papers 1849–1987
9 feet

Archivist. Manuscripts and unpublished materials (1837–1940) relating to Douglas H. Johnston, governor of the Chickasaw Nation, the history of the Chickasaw and Choctaw Indian nations, and the enrollment of the Eastern Band of Cherokee Indians; lecture notes, class assignments and other materials (1950–1953) relating to courses Litton taught at the University of Oklahoma; radio scripts (1948–1949) from a program entitled "Great Men and Books," broadcast on WNAD, Norman, Oklahoma; and books, articles, and presentations (1955–1975) authored by Litton and relating to archival administration and librarianship in Latin America.

Unpublished finding aid available.

Livezey, William Edmund (b. 1903) 828
Papers 1932–1951
.66 foot

Professor. Letters (1932–1940) recommending senior students for admission to the University of Oklahoma President's Class; corrected manuscripts (n.d.) for *Mahan on Sea Power* (University of Oklahoma Press, 1947) and *The Philippines and the United States* (University of Oklahoma Press, 1951), the latter co-authored with Garel A. Grunder. The collection also includes correspondence and minutes (1939–1950) of the Oklahoma Memorial Union Board of Governors.

Locke, Victor M., Jr. 829
Papers 1900–1927
.10 foot

Indian chief. Typescript of newspaper articles (1900–1927) regarding the allotment of land in the Choctaw Nation and Locke's role in the Choctaw tribal government.

Logan, Bill 830
Records 1957
1 item

Legislator. Resolution (1957) of the Senate of Oklahoma memorializing Senator Bill Logan.

Logan County Road Record Collection 831
Records 1896–1905
.25 foot

County government. A ledger (1896–1905) containing applications for the construction of new roads in Logan County, Oklahoma Territory. Each application bears the applicant's justification for the road, along with a map plotting its exact course in relation to section, range, and township lines.

Logan, Leonard M. (1891–1974) 832
Papers 1925–1961
2.50 feet

Professor. Correspondence (1950–1958) with the U.S. Department of the Interior, congressmen, and the U.S. Bureau of Indian Affairs; reports (1956–1963); newspaper clippings (1925–1961) concerning Indian affairs; and manuscripts (1948) by Logan, entitled "The Care of Chronic and Convalescent Patients in Oklahoma" and "Norman and Cleveland County, A Resource Inventory."

Unpublished finding aid available.

Long, Charles Alexander (b. 1881) 833
Manuscript 1905–1971
1 item

Minister. Memoirs (1971) of Charles Alexander Long, who graduated from the University of Oklahoma in 1905 and served as a Methodist missionary to Brazil, 1911–1952.

Longstreet, James 834
Letter 1837
1 item

Army officer. A letter (1837) from Maj. James Longstreet in San

Antonio, Texas, to Maj. Gen. George Gibson, in which Longstreet requests $10,000 to purchase supplies for an upcoming campaign against the Indians.

Lottinville, Savoie (1906–1997)   835
Papers 1953–1977
1.33 feet

Editor. Edited manuscripts of "Travels in North America, 1822–1824," by Paul Wilhelm, Duke of Württemburg, and "Life of George Bent," by George E. Hyde; articles (1964–1977) by Lottinville on George Milburn, the University of Oklahoma seal, and the Rhodes Legal History Collection; a letter (1966) from E. N. Roberts to R. L. Disney, relating the meeting in 1883 of John Roberts with a woman claiming to be Sacajawea; and a notarized statement (1953) of Frank M. Wyncoop concerning the Sand Creek Massacre.

Love, Tom J.   836
Papers 1872–1949
7 items

Professor. Court documents (1879–1887) from the U.S. District Court, Western District of Arkansas, regarding the Choctaw Lighthorse, a search posse, and a death warrant; a list (1949) of Cherokee subjects including numerals, units of money, capital, districts, rivers, and important names; and correspondence (1872) of James Brizzolard and Judge William Story regarding an election in Sebastian County, Arkansas.

Lovelace, Bryan W.   837
Papers 1850–1858
.10 foot

Collector. A journal (1850) by Joseph R. Smith of New York, in which he recorded his experiences while on a surveying expedition through Indian Territory. Entries detail the expedition's encounters with hostile Comanches, friendly Osages, severe weather, and hordes of insects. Also included in this collection are photocopies of a legislative document (1858) and a published article (1850), both regarding Creek Nation boundaries.

Loy-McDonald Clinic Collection   838
Records 1938–1948
1 foot

Medical facility. Laboratory test results (1938–1939); receipt books (1945–1948); and an equipment catalog (1939) from the Loy-McDonald Clinic in Pawhuska, Oklahoma.

Lucka, Emil (1877–1941) 839
Papers ca. 1939
.10 foot

Author. Typescripts of unpublished essays (ca. 1939) by Lucka, an Austrian author who sent them to literary colleagues in Oklahoma for safekeeping after he fell into disfavor with the German forces in Austria.

Luster, Dewey William "Snorter" 840
Papers 1925–1980
1.33 feet

Coach. Correspondence (1941–1980); notebooks of football plays (1929–1945); and speech notes, reminiscences, and clippings (1925–1980) of Luster, the University of Oklahoma head football coach from 1941 to 1945.

Unpublished finding aid available.

Lyles, Harold L. 841
Printed materials 1912–1913
2 items

Collector. A pamphlet (1913) of speeches by U.S. Congressman Claude Weaver of Oklahoma in the U.S. House of Representatives; and a pamphlet (ca. 1912) containing excerpts of Weaver's speeches, including his closing speech in defense of William T. Peoples, charged with the murder of Eugene McLaughlin, at Peoples's trial in 1902.

MacDowell Club Collection 842
Records 1945–2001
1 foot

Fine arts organization. Meeting minutes (1947–1990); correspondence (1976–2001); newsletters (1977–2000); financial records (1945–1998); membership books (1973–1998); and scrapbooks (1946–1994) of the MacDowell Club of Norman, Oklahoma.

Unpublished finding aid available.

Mackenzie, Ranald Slidell
Printed materials 1897
1 item

843

U.S. Army officer. One issue of the *Journal of the United States Cavalry Association* (1897), containing two articles about Ranald Slidell Mackenzie.

Mackey, (Mrs.) Clifton Marion
Papers 1912–1977
1 foot

844

Homemaker. Correspondence (1912–1977) between Alice Hurley Mackey and her brother, Patrick Hurley, regarding Hurley's duties as the national attorney of the Choctaw Nation, as a colonel in the American Expeditionary Forces, as secretary of war during the Hoover administration, and as an ambassador during World War II. The collection contains Hurley's correspondence with Herbert Hoover, Henry Luce, Franklin D. Roosevelt, and Madame Chiang Kai-Shek. Also included is a diploma (1912) issued to Alice Hurley by the Sisters of Saint Joseph Carondelet in Missouri.

Unpublished finding aid available.

Madsen, Christian C. (b. 1850)
Papers 1886–1967
6 items

845

Soldier. Enlistment papers (1872–1886) and two letters (1926–1937) of Christian Madsen, who served with the Fifth Cavalry, U.S. Army. The collection also contains a letter (1967) to Jack D. Haley from John A. Minion, who claims that Madsen was with the Seventh Cavalry at the time of the Custer Massacre.

Maguire, Grace Adeline King (1880–1951)
Printed materials 1885–1935
2 feet

846

Professor and librarian. Newspaper clippings (1885–1935) concerning Abraham Lincoln, and of Maguire's weekly article, "Lights and Shadows"; books (1891–1927) and printed materials (1891–1906) relating to the Roman Catholic Church; a scrapbook (n.d.) kept by Maguire; documents (1902–1914) from the U.S. Land Office at Lawton, Oklahoma; and correspondence (1917) concerning the James D. Maguire Store in Norman, Oklahoma.

Unpublished finding aid available.

Malone, E. L.   847
Papers 1904–1905
.10 foot

Oil field worker. Letters (1904–1905) from E. L. Malone to his wife and son, describing oil field life and Oklahoma Territory boom towns.

Mankiller, Wilma Pearl (1945–)   848
Papers 1977–1995
45 feet

Indian chief. Official and personal correspondence, subject files, business records of the Cherokee Nation and Wilma Mankiller for the period 1977–1995. Includes personal correspondence (1993–1995); correspondence (1985–1995) with members of the U.S. Congress and the National Congress of American Indians; tribal council correspondence (1990–1994); Cherokee National Historical Society correspondence (1990–1995); and general correspondence (1982–1995). Subject files relating to the Native American Rights Fund (1989–1993); U.S. Bureau of Indian Affairs central office (1988–1995); U.S. Bureau of Indian Affairs Muskogee, Oklahoma, area office (1989–1995); Inter-Tribal Council of the Five Civilized Tribes (1977–1995); the National Congress of American Indians (1993–1995); the Tribal Election Commission (1985–1994); and tribal council meetings (1985–1993). Business and financial records of the Cherokee Nation concerning Cherokee Gardens (1981–1991); the Bingo Outpost (1989–1995); and Cherokee Nation Industries (1977–1995), along with budget, accounting, and audit papers. Education and training records of the Cherokee Nation concerning the Job Training Partnership Act (1993– 1995); Head Start (1985–1995); Oaks Mission School (1977– 1995); Sequoyah High School (1984–1995); and Talking Leaves Job Corps (1986-1995). Community development and housing files relating to block grants (1985–1995); the Community Loan Fund (1987–1994); the Bell Project (1981–1987); the Cherokee Housing Authority (1993–1994); and the Home Improvement Program (1985–1994). Health issue files relating to Indian health services (1991–1995) and the National Indian Health Board (1985–1992). Environmental program records relating to the Arkansas Riverbed Authority (1993–1994) and papers relating to Mankiller's books and other writings, with genealogical materials concerning her family.

Unpublished finding aid available.

Manos, Grace C. 849
Letter 1953
1 item

Business manager. A copy of a letter (1953) from Fred G. Cowles, part owner of the *McAlester News-Capital*, to Walter C. Johnson, briefly describing the history and ownership of the *McAlester News-Capital*.

Marable, Mary Hays (1889–1959) 850
Papers 1935–1954
6 feet

Librarian. Research notes (n.d.) and biographical information used in Marable's book *Handbook of Oklahoma Writers* (1959), along with bibliographic materials (n.d) and newspaper clippings (1935–1954) of book reviews written by Marable and others.

Unpublished finding aid available.

March, (Mrs.) Abe 851
Printed materials 1951–1952
.33 foot

Collector. Material from Lawton, Oklahoma's fiftieth anniversary celebration, including a script (1951) for a pageant entitled "Neath August Sun"; a copy of "Lawton's Golden Anniversary, 1901–1951" (ca. 1951); copies of the *Lawton Constitution* (August, 1951); programs (1951–1952); and the yearbook (1952) of the Lawton Pioneer Club, Inc.

Marland, Ernest Whitworth (1871–1941) 852
Papers 1937–1938
3 items

Governor. A letter (1938) supporting Marland's campaign for election to the U.S. senate; a promotional card (1938) from his campaign; and a printed speech (1937) by Governor Marland to the Oklahoma legislature.

Marquart, Vida 853
Papers 1892–1895
4 items

Collector. Invitations (1892–1895) to attend the exercises of Knights Templar at Guthrie, Oklahoma Territory, and Oklahoma City, and the 1895 graduation exercises of the University of Oklahoma.

Marriott, Alice (1910–1992) 854
Papers 1930–1976
21 feet

Anthropologist. Correspondence (1926–1976); manuscripts (n.d.) of Marriott's books and articles; research notes (n.d.); and printed materials (1930–1974) accumulated by Marriott in the course of her research for her numerous books and articles relating to Indians. Included in the collection are book-length manuscripts entitled "Maria, the Potter of San Ildefonso," "The Ten Grandmothers," "Indian Annie," and "The Valley Below."

Unpublished finding aid available.

[205]

Marriott, Sydney C. 855
Papers 1917–1941
.10 foot

Accountant. Programs (1927–1941) from conventions and meetings of the National Aid Life Association; one issue each of *The Highway Magazine* (1917) and *The N.A.L.A. News* (1927); and a handwritten musical composition (n.d.) entitled *Oklahoma, I'm Coming Back to You*.

Marriott-Rachlin Collection 856
Papers 1963–1975
3 feet

Anthropologists. Correspondence (1963–1975); research materials (1963–1975); and manuscripts (n.d.) of Alice Marriott and Carol Rachlin, accumulated during their collaboration on several essays and articles relating to Indian society, mythology, and peyotism.

Unpublished finding aid available.

Marrs, Frederica S. Dewey 857
Papers 1861–1912
.33 foot

Collector. Commissions, orders, and property reports (1881–1906) regarding Frederick Stanley Dewey's service as a contract surgeon and as an assistant surgeon with the U.S. Army in the Philippines; correspondence (1898–1912) regarding a lawsuit over a land claim in Oklahoma Territory; matriculation cards and notices of examination results (1877–1879) from St. Louis (Missouri) Medical College; and a journal

(1884), all belonging to Frederick S. Dewey. Also included are commissions, orders, property reports, and discharge papers (1861–1867) regarding George H. Dewey and his service as assistant surgeon with the 11th and 109th Illinois Volunteer Infantry regiments.

Marrs, James Wyatt (ca. 1896–ca. 1963)   858
Papers ca. 1922–1963
31 feet

Professor. Manuscripts, galley proofs, reviews, and letters (ca. 1940–1960) accumulated by Marrs for his book *The Man on Your Back*; research material on social parasitism (1930–1963); and sociology class materials (1922–1963), including lecture notes and student term papers from classes taught by Marrs, a University of Oklahoma sociology professor, 1922–1963.

Martin, Cy (1919–1980)   859
Papers 1966–1975
2.33 feet

Author. Manuscripts (1968) of "Your Horoscope," children's stories, and books (1973–1975), all written by Martin; magazines (1966–1975), some containing stories by Martin; and biographical information on Cy Martin, who wrote under the pen name of William Stillman Keezer.

Unpublished finding aid available.

Martin, Richard L. (b. 1847)   860
Papers 1860–1907
5 items

Rancher and postmaster. Two letter-size tablets containing rough drafts (1860–1907) of Martin's correspondence and a brief account of his experiences in Indian Territory during the Civil War. Some correspondence (1882–1907) concerns land allotment and Indian opposition to Oklahoma statehood.

Martin, Thomas Pugh, Jr.   861
Papers 1873–1952
1 foot

Banker. Programs of Oklahoma City businessmen's clubs, including the Oklahoma Club (1925–1931) and the Men's Dinner Club (1913–

1914); a program of an Oklahoma City banquet honoring Gen. John J. Pershing (1920); currency issued by the Confederate States of America (1864) and the federal and state governments of Mexico (1915–1916); programs of the inaugurals of Oklahoma governors Lee Cruce (1911) and John C. Walton (1923); a manuscript (1933) by Martin, regarding early telephone service in Marlow, Oklahoma; and showbills (1912–1920) of the Overholser Theatre in Oklahoma City, Oklahoma. Also in this collection are certificates of incorporation (1906–1909) of the Martin Mill and Elevator Company, and posters (ca. 1925) advocating use of the new airmail service, the latter picturing the dirigible *Shenandoah*, an early touring car, and an early open-cockpit airplane.

Unpublished finding aid available.

Mason, Viola 862
Records 1902–1915
2 items

Collector. Two farm leases (1902–1915) establishing guardianship for lands owned by orphaned Seneca Indian children.

Masonic Lodge of Oklahoma Collection 863
Printed materials 1911–1936
.66 foot

Fraternal society. Copies (1911, 1925–1936) of the *Annual Proceedings* of the Grand (Masonic) Lodge of Oklahoma, and the constitution and code (1927) of the Masonic Lodge of Oklahoma.

Massad, Ernest L. (1908–1993) 864
Papers 1926–1990
9 feet

U.S. Army officer. Correspondence and supporting reports and documents (1933–1969) regarding Massad's military service in the U.S. Army, especially his command of the Ninety-fifth Training Division and his service as deputy assistant secretary of defense for reserve affairs. The collection also includes correspondence and related papers (1929–1983) concerning his attendance and athletic career at the University of Oklahoma and his election to the Oklahoma Hall of Fame in 1971.

Unpublished finding aid available.

Matheney, James Curtis (b. 1880) 865
Papers 1908–1953
2 items

Physician. A letter (1953) by Matheney describing his experiences as a physician in Oklahoma between 1908 and 1953, and a news clipping (1951) regarding Matheney's retirement.

Matthews, Sam P. 866
Records 1890–1892
.10 foot

Collector. Four criminal-case docket books (1890–1892) from the court of A. D. Matthews, judge of the U.S. Circuit Court, Third Division, Indian Territory. The docket books record the names of defendants, the charges, the verdicts, and the penalties administered.

Maupin, Mary B. 867
Papers 1846–ca. 1930
.10 foot

Collector. Photocopies of Texas homestead documents (1867–1875); documents (1846–1857) concerning the estate of Lydia Loving, also from Texas; and photocopies of Guymon, Oklahoma, newspapers (ca. 1930).

Mayes, Joel Bryan (1833–1891) 868
Printed materials 1886–1905
.66 foot

Indian chief. Typescripts of newspaper articles and correspondence (1886–1905) of Mayes, a principal chief of the Cherokees, concerning tribal politics and the dissolution of tribal title to the Cherokee Strip.

Mayes, Samuel Houston (1845–1927) 869
Printed materials 1882–1928
.66 foot

Indian chief. Typescripts of newspaper articles (1882–1928) relating to Mayes's tenure as principal chief of the Cherokees, his negotiations with the Dawes Commission, the preparation of the tribal roll, and the assignment of lands.

McAlester Anniversary Incorporated Collection   870
Printed material 1949
2.33 feet

Civic organization. Programs, form letters, badges, circulars, and posters, plus nominations and voting coupons for the queen contest, all from McAlester Anniversary Incorporated, which sponsored this 1949 golden jubilee celebration in McAlester, Oklahoma.

Unpublished finding aid available.

McAlester, James Jackson (1842–1922)   871
Papers 1870–1908
58 feet

Businessman. Correspondence (1888–1908); store ledgers (1874–1903); daybooks (1870–1904); inventory books (n.d.); cash books (1889–1903); and supporting records from the J. J. McAlester Mercantile Company in McAlester, Indian Territory.

Unpublished finding aid available.

McBride, Earl D. (b. 1891)   872
Papers 1923–1954
.33 foot

Physician. Disability compensation reports (1950–1954); a copy of *Disability Evaluation* (1948) by McBride; and reprints (1923–1954) of articles by McBride, an orthopedic surgeon in Oklahoma City, Oklahoma.

McBride, Marguerite   873
Papers 1938–1943
.10 foot

Collector. Personal correspondence (1938–1943) to Marguerite McBride of Walters, Oklahoma, from Bob O'Brien, her New Zealand pen pal, plus memorabilia from New Zealand.

McCall, William (b. 1923)   874
Papers 1862–1863
2 items

Collector. Correspondence (1862–1863) from T. D. Horton, a Confederate soldier in the Civil War, to his wife and family, regarding life as a soldier and his participation in one of the Seven Days Battles at Malvern Hill (near Richmond), Virginia, a part of the 1862 Peninsular Campaign.

McCammon, J. D. 875
Papers ca. 1942
3 items

Journalist. Memoirs (n.d.) of McCammon's early career (ca. 1900) as a newspaper reporter; an article (n.d.) about Missouri judge Ernest S. Gantt; and a letter (1942) from Frank W. Taylor of the *Chicago Sun*, rejecting the article about Gantt.

Eugene McCarthy Campaign Collection 876
Papers 1968
.66 foot

Political campaign organization. Correspondence, press releases, speeches, position papers, clippings, and other campaign material (all 1968), concerning Eugene McCarthy's 1968 campaign to gain the Democratic presidential nomination, and particularly concerning the organization of the Oklahoma McCarthy for President Committee and the Oklahoma State Democratic Convention.

McCarthy, Thomas Joseph 877
Papers 1937
6 items

Broadcaster. Newspaper clippings from McCarthy's column in *The Washington Post* regarding his travels to, and observations of life in, the former mining boomtowns of Deadwood and Lead, South Dakota.

McCarville, Mike 878
Papers 1957–1965
7 items

Author. A manuscript account (n.d.) of a 1909 lynching in Ada, Oklahoma, written by McCarville; a copy (1957) of Oklahoma City's charter; a program (1965) for a dinner at the John Fitzgerald Kennedy Library in Oklahoma City, Oklahoma; and four pieces (n.d.) of U.S. military payment scrip.

McClure, Tecumseh A. (b. 1830)   879
Printed material 1894
1 item

Indian chief. A typescript of a newspaper article (1894) regarding McClure's call for a special session of the Chickasaw legislature to debate the Dawes Commission proposals for the allotment of Chickasaw lands.

McClure, William L. (1896–1930), and   880
    William C. McClure (1910–1953)
Papers 1860–1954
3 feet

Physicians. Correspondence (1860–1954); class notes (1912–1936); case histories (1937); annuals, diplomas and certificates (1912–1953); clippings (1914–1953); and medals and medical instruments of W. L. McClure, a surgeon at Massachusetts General Hospital, and W. C. McClure, a faculty member at the University of Oklahoma medical school.

Unpublished finding aid available.

McCornack, Ruth (b. ca. 1892)   881
Printed materials 1910–1932
.10 foot

Collector. Newspaper clippings, booklets, event programs, and broadsides (1910–1912) all regarding student life at Kingfisher College, Kingfisher, Oklahoma; an issue (1932) of the *Kingfisher College Alumni News*; and a yearbook (1913–1914) published by the Chaminade Club for the women of Oklahoma City, Oklahoma. The collection also includes two artifacts, an official emblem of Kingfisher College and a mortar board worn by McCornack in the college's 1912 commencement ceremony.

McCoy, A. M.   882
Papers 1878–1930
1 item

Collector. A typescript account by A. M. McCoy regarding early history of Beaver County, Oklahoma. McCoy describes the first house in Beaver, Oklahoma, and the first post offices to serve the Oklahoma panhandle area.

McCoy, James Stacy (1834–1862) 883
Papers 1859–1863
.10 foot

Soldier. Correspondence (1861–1863) to A. M. McCoy from her husband, James Stacy McCoy, captain of Company B, Twenty-sixth Alabama Infantry Regiment, and from Thomas McCoy, B. F. Thompson, and R. G. Wright; and a sales contract (1859) for slaves, stock, and farm implements sold to James Stacy McCoy by Baronett McCoy.

McCurtain, D. C. (b. 1873) 884
Printed materials 1899–1911
7 items

Indian statesman. Typescripts of newspaper articles (1899–1911) regarding McCurtain's views on schools, tribal government, and related issues confronting the Choctaw Nation.

McCurtain, Edmond (1842–1890) 885
Printed materials 1875–1901
.10 foot

Indian chief. Typescripts of McCurtain's annual messages (1884–1886) to the Choctaw Nation general council; letters (1875–1877) by McCurtain to newspapers regarding various issues, including railroad right-of-way and citizenship disputes; and an obituary (1890) of McCurtain.

McCurtain, Green (1848–1910) 886
Papers 1890–1916
14.50 feet

Indian chief. Correspondence (1890–1916) to and from McCurtain regarding Choctaw Nation railroads, administrative matters, politics, Choctaw Indian claims against the United States, and the issue of separate statehood for Indian Territory, including letters from the chiefs of the other major Indian tribes in the territory; maps (1876–1908) of railroad rights-of-way and towns in the Choctaw Nation; publications (1896–1913) by political parties and citizens groups in the Choctaw Nation regarding political and judicial events and issues; publications (1892–1916) of the U.S. government regarding mineral rights of the Choctaw Nation and Indian Territory; and McCurtain's personal expense accounts (1902–1910).

Unpublished finding aid available.

The diary of James Reagles, Jr., a U.S. Army surgeon who served in Virginia during the Civil War, and later with the Tenth U.S. Cavalry at Fort Arbuckle, Indian Territory. Reagles's diary (1864-1867) documents some of his Civil War experiences, as well as his post-war contacts with Choctaw, Chickasaw, Caddo, and Comanche Indians near Fort Arbuckle. From the James Reagles, Jr. Collection.

McCurtain, Jackson Frazier (1830–1885) 887
Printed materials 1875–1901
.10 foot

Indian chief. Typescripts of newspaper articles (1875–1901) regarding McCurtain and his State of the Choctaw Nation speeches (1881–1883) made before the general council while he was principal chief.

McEldowney, James 888
Papers 1922–1946
.33 foot

U.S. Army officer. Correspondence (1943–1945) from James McEldowney to relatives in Oklahoma regarding his experiences in the U.S. Army during World War II. The collection also contains correspondence (1922–1946) of James McEldowney and various family members regarding family matters, and newspaper clippings (1934–1938) and a scrapbook (1926–1927) regarding McEldowney's activities at Roosevelt Junior High and Classen High School in Oklahoma City, Oklahoma, and Pomona College in California.

McGee, C. R. 889
Papers 1992
.10 foot

Author. A manuscript (1992) entitled "Stories of Bethel and Other Adventures," by C. R. McGee, regarding Bethel, Oklahoma, during the period of 1916–1968.

McGhee, George 890
Records 1924–1980
20 feet

Oilman. Records of the McGhee Production Company in Dallas, Texas, including correspondence, abstracts of title, inventories, exploration program information, logs, and petroleum reserve data for fields in Louisiana, Texas, Oklahoma, and Pennsylvania, and notes about fields in other states.

Unpublished finding aid available.

McIntosh County Medical Society Collection 891
Records 1906–1948
1 foot

Professional society. Minutes of meetings (1906–1910, 1922–1923, 1939, 1943–1948); correspondence (1923–1949); resolutions and speeches from the medical society's programs; and membership records (1921–1948), all from the McIntosh County (Oklahoma) Medical Society, along with copies of the Oklahoma State Medical Association constitution and bylaws, and the American Medical Association newsletter (1948).

McIntosh, Roley Cub (1858–1920) 892
Printed materials 1835–1928
.10 foot

Indian chief. Typescripts of speeches by Creek chief Roley Cub McIntosh regarding the Creek Nation; and typescripts of newspaper articles (1871–1928) about McIntosh. The collection also includes an unidentified typescript speech to the Comanche and Wichita nations (1835) regarding the Camp Holmes Treaty.

McIntosh, William 893
Printed materials 1967–1993
.10 foot

Indian chief. Publications (1967–1993) regarding Creek Indian chief William McIntosh, the history of the McIntosh family and its Scottish ancestry, and the Mackintosh coat of arms.

McKenzie, (Mr. and Mrs.) W. H. 894
Printed materials ca. 1920–1938
9 items

Collectors. Clippings from the *Lawton Constitution* (1932) and the *Oklahoma News* (1938); Mother's Day cards (n.d.); a beauty-shop price list (1933); and postcard scenes (ca. 1920) of Lawton, Oklahoma.

McKeown, Roy J. (b. 1902) 895
Manuscript n.d.
1 item

Editor. A typescript (n.d.) entitled "Life History of Joannah Floyd Reed and William J. Reed, As Told by Joannah Floyd Reed," recounting their settling in Ada, Oklahoma, which was named after their eldest daughter, and where they operated several businesses.

McKinney, Raymond   896
Album ca. 1946
1 item

Collector. A Japanese picture album (ca. 1946) of World War II battle scenes in the Pacific theater, with the text in Japanese.

McKinney, Thompson   897
Printed materials 1886–1887
2 items

Indian chief. Typescripts of two newspaper articles (1886–1887). One is McKinney's inaugural address as principal chief of the Choctaws, and the other is an editorial on his handling of Choctaw Nation affairs.

McKinney, William H.   898
Manuscript 1878
1 item

Poet. A poem (1878) by McKinney, written in the Choctaw language and entitled *Iti Hishi Yama Isht Chit Haya Va Lihohe*, or *A Leaf That Reminds Me of Thee*. An English translation is included.

McLain, Raymond Stallings (1890–1954)   899
Papers 1920–1954
17.33 feet

U.S. Army officer. Correspondence (1929–1954) concerning McLain's personal and business affairs; orders, memoranda, reports (1920–1937), and correspondence (1939–1940) from McLain's service with the Oklahoma National Guard; speeches (1947–1954) made by McLain as chief of information for the U.S. Army and as a member of the National Security Training Commission; a typescript account (n.d.) by McLain of his participation as commander of the Forty-fifth Division artillery in the Allied invasion of Sicily during World War II; and a typescript account (n.d) by McLain of the Forty-fifth Division artillery's role in the Battle of the Aisne (1918) in World War I.

McMurray, John Frank   900
Printed materials 1898–1927
.50 foot

Lawyer. Published court records (1898–1926) and correspondence

(1900–1927) regarding McMurray's suit against the Choctaw and Chickasaw nations for expenses and legal fees incurred in McMurray's successful representation of Choctaw and Chickasaw Indians in a lawsuit regarding taxation of Indian lands.

McPhaul, Thomas C.   901
Records 1927–1936
2 items

Physician. Opium orders (1927) and a daybook (1935–1936) from McPhaul's Muskogee, Oklahoma, medical practice.

McReynolds, Edwin C. (1890–1967)   902
Papers ca. 1930–1967
13 feet

Professor. Correspondence (1945–1965); research notes on the southern United States, the Civil War, Missouri, and Oklahoma; manuscripts (1930–1967) of history-related books and articles; clippings and printed material (1963–1965) on President John F. Kennedy and on McReynolds, a University of Oklahoma history professor from 1943 to 1960.

Unpublished finding aid available.

McReynolds, S. A.   903
Papers 1924–1937
.33 foot

Composer. Manuscript copies of scores, including *Concerto in D Minor for Cello and Orchestra* (1936–1937), "Iron Mountain" (third movement of *Souvenirs*, string parts only, 1935), and *The Southwest* (suite for orchestra, 1924). The score and parts for *The Southwest* include "A Peace Council of the Redman," "La Fiesta," "Loading Cotton Bales," and "Restless Civilization."

Meacham, Ed, and James Watt   904
Printed materials 1982
.10 foot

Collectors. An autobiography by Florence Ellen Haynes Watt, entitled *When I Was a Little Girl*, describing many of her early life experiences in Jonesboro, Arkansas, and Clinton, Oklahoma, from 1904 to 1982, including notes on family life, education, entertainment, and local events.

Meacham, George A., III   **905**
Printed materials 1989
.10 foot

Collector. Family history entitled *The George A. Meacham Family*, by George A. Meacham, III, giving the history of the Meacham family in Custer County, Oklahoma, with notes on farming, family life, and early days in Clinton, Oklahoma.

Medford Progress Club Collection   **906**
Records 1931–1988
2 feet

Social organization. Minutes (1931–1946); annual reports (1934–1952); yearbooks (1931–1988); correspondence (1939–1951); scrapbooks (1931–1950); and clippings (1928–1950) from the Medford (Oklahoma) Progress Club.

Medicine Shows Collection   **907**
Printed materials 1887–1925
.25 foot

Subject collection. Correspondence and speeches (1911–1927); recipes for patent medicines, permanent waving solutions, and cleaning solutions; and advertisements (1887–1925) for patent medicines.

Memminger, Charles B.   **908**
Printed materials 1913–1914
8 items

Collector. Programs and invitations (1913–1914) for University of Oklahoma social events.

Menton, John William (d. 1928)   **909**
Papers 1903–1915
.10 foot

Businessman. Tax receipts (1903–1908); mortgages and stock certificates (1912–1923); and patents and deeds (1906–1915) of Menton, a Lehigh, Oklahoma, businessman.

Merrick, Henry Spencer   **910**
Printed materials 1953
1 item

Historian. One issue of *Corral Dust* (1958), published by the Potomac

Corral of the Westerners, featuring an article entitled "Recollections of the Last Frontier," by Henry Spencer Merrick.

Merrill, Maurice H. 911
Papers ca. 1903–1975
24.66 feet

Attorney. Correspondence (1903–1975) of Merrill; class notes (n.d.) taken by Maurice and Orpha Merrill; printed material, including copies of the *Phi Beta Kappa Key* (1911–1918), the *Supreme Court Reporter* (1964–1975), and *Proceedings* (1959–1975) of the National Conference of Commissioners of Uniform State Law.

Unpublished finding aid available.

Merriott, C. L. 912
Ledger 1937–1941
1 item

Merchant. An accounts ledger (1937–1941) from Merriott's Dry Goods Company in Walters, Oklahoma.

Mertes, John E. 913
Papers n.d.
.10 foot

A copy book (n.d.) kept by Mertes while a student at the University of Oklahoma, mostly containing biographical sketches of prominent literary figures.

Messenger, Eugene Fields (1866–1957) 914
Papers 1866–1957
2 items

Constitutional convention delegate. A typescript of Messenger's memoirs (1866–1957) detailing his role in the Oklahoma Constitutional Convention and the struggle to designate Holdenville, Oklahoma, as the county seat of Hughes County; and a newspaper obituary (1957) of Messenger.

Meyer, Leo 915
Papers 1906–1939
.25 foot

State auditor. Bound volumes of the rules of the Oklahoma Senate (1907–1908), the rules for the Oklahoma House of Representatives

(1911), the rules for the Oklahoma Constitutional Convention (1906–1907), and a printed copy of the constitution of the state of Oklahoma. The collection also includes a spiral-bound typescript of a tribute program (1939) given in honor of Leo Meyer by the Tulsa Lodge, B'nai B'rith #798, and two certificates (1910) for Meyer's election as state auditor.

[220] Meyer, William (1875–1956), and Apelona Meyer (b. 1883)   916
Papers 1852–1967
5 feet

Businessman and collector. Personal correspondence (1940–1965) of Apelona Meyer; certificates and awards (1882–1931) of William Meyer; greeting cards (1930–1960); travel pamphlets and brochures (1930–1960); and other printed materials (1914–1967) including invitations, programs, and newspapers, relating to U.S. society and social organization in Cuba; and service records (1852–1893) of Spanish Army soldiers in Cuba.

Unpublished finding aid available.

Miami Lumber Company Collection   917
Records 1911–1915
3 items

Retail business. Two account ledgers (1911) and one estimate ledger (1915) from the Miami (Oklahoma) Lumber Company.

Miami, Oklahoma, Municipal Records Collection   918
Ledger 1918–1920
1 item

Municipality. A daily balance ledger (1918–1920) for the assets of the city of Miami, Oklahoma.

Micco, Hulbutta (ca. 1835–1905)   919
Printed materials 1898–1905
.10 foot

Indian chief. Typescripts of newspaper articles (1898–1905) regarding the Seminole Nation and Hulbutta Micco, the last regularly elected principal chief of the Seminoles before statehood.

Midkiff, Charles F.   920
Records 1899–1917
3 items

Collector. A tax receipt (1907) for Midkiff's payment of taxes in Pauls Valley, Oklahoma, and a permit (1899) issued by the Chickasaw Nation for Midkiff, a non-Indian, to live in Indian Territory. The collection also includes a certificate (1917) from the United States Public Reserve.

Milbourn, Dolly   921
Papers 1915
2 items

Collector. Two account books (1915) from George F. Milbourn's grain business in Fairland, Oklahoma.

Milburn, George (1906–1966)   922
Papers 1912–1966
1.33 feet

Author. Correspondence (1912–1966), research notes, and manuscripts of articles (1931–1957) by Milburn; Little Blue Books (1926–1927) written by Milburn; periodicals (1929–1954) which include articles by Milburn; and clippings (1936–1966) concerning Milburn, a writer and native of Coweta, Oklahoma.

Unpublished finding aid available.

Miles, Charles   923
Printed materials 1921–1944
3 items

Collector. A book (ca. 1921) entitled *Oklahoma City*, published by Walker Taylor Printing Company; a pamphlet (1927), "Commemorating the 38th Anniversary of Oklahoma City and the American First National Bank"; and a program (ca. 1941) from the musical *Oklahoma*.

Mary Clarke Miley Foundation Collection   924
Papers 1900–1980
2 feet

Private foundation. Correspondence (1937–1954) of William Halliburton Miley and Mary Clarke Miley regarding personal matters and William's service in the U.S. Army during World War II and the Korean War. The letters include information regarding William's suicide in 1954, as well as the clemency case of Pvt. Eddie D. Slovic. Also in the collection are two scrapbooks (1900–1980) with clippings, programs, and photographs concerning Mary Clarke Miley, her career as a pianist, and the foundation she established; and an unpublished account by Grace Frances Campbell about life in Oklahoma Territory during the 1890s.

Miller Brothers 101 Ranch Collection 925
Records 1908–1936
39.66 feet

Ranch. General correspondence (1917–1936) and financial records (1923–1924) from the Miller Brothers 101 Ranch in Marland, Oklahoma; plus general correspondence (1908–1932), legal papers and contracts (1908–1932), route schedules (1910–1929), and scrapbooks (1908–1926) from the Miller Brothers 101 Ranch Wild West Show.

Unpublished finding aid available.

Miller, Florence Graves 926
Papers 1904–1968
4 feet

Professor. Correspondence (1942–1945) from former Eastern Oklahoma A & M College students serving in the armed forces during World War II; journals (1904–1950) recounting Miller's early experiences as an educator, first in Mississippi and, later in Oklahoma; teaching materials (n.d.); and clippings, poems, quotations, and sermons (1935–1968).

Unpublished finding aid available.

Miller, Floyd C. (b. 1912) 927
Papers ca. 1968
.33 foot

Author. Corrected manuscripts and galley proofs of Miller's book, *Bill Tilghman: Marshal of the Last Frontier*, published in 1968.

Miller, G. R. 928
Papers 1908–1936
.10 foot

Collector. Two account ledgers (1908–1920) from a Lawton, Oklahoma, business which sold goods primarily to Kiowa and Comanche Indians. The collection also contains a copy of the Comanche constitution (1936) and lists (1914–1915) of eligible Comanche voters and members of the Kiowa and Comanche tribes.

Miller, John Sinclaire (1876–1936) 929
Papers 1938
2 items

Physician. Miller's biographical data sheet (n.d.) from the Oklahoma State Medical Society, and a clipping (1938) concerning the founding of the Choctaw (Oklahoma) Medical Society, of which Miller was a founding member in 1905.

[223]

Miller, LaVerle 930
Printed materials 1989
.10 foot

Collector. Family history, *As My World Turns*, by Lena Rivers (Been) Miller. An autobiography of Lena Rivers (Been) Miller that describes her early life experiences in Clinton, Foss, and Parkersburg, Oklahoma, including notes on family life, education, entertainment, and local events. Also contains information on the Barnes and Been family genealogies.

Miller, Lillie Kate (b. ca. 1882) 931
Papers 1900–1904
.33 foot

Student. Class notebooks (1900–1904) kept by Miller while attending the University of Oklahoma; Miller's diploma (1904) from the University of Oklahoma; and a cookbook (1910) entitled *Home Helps: A Pure Food Cook Book*.

Miller, Robert L. 932
Papers 1960–1975
4 feet

University employee. Correspondence (1963–1975); reports (1962–1975); and printed materials (1960–1975) relating to Indian rights and Indian education, accumulated by Miller during his tenure as director of the Indian Education Center at the University of Oklahoma's American Indian Institute.

Unpublished finding aid available.

Miller, Stephen 933
Printed material 1942–1944
.10 foot

Collector. Copies of ships' newsletters and military newspapers entitled *Patrol* (1944), the *Midway Mirror* (1944), the *Fulton Bow Plane* (1942–1944), the *Fulton Flotsam* (1944), *History of the U.S.S. Caelum* (ca. 1945), and a *Resume of Shanghai* (n.d.) prepared for the crew of U.S.S. *Caelum*.

Mills, Walter Scott (b. 1872) 934
Papers 1930–1940
.10 foot

Attorney. Typescripts of articles (1930–1940) from Mills's column, "Hit or Miss," in the *Arapaho Bee*, which reflect on local and national political affairs.

Milsten, David Randolph 935
Printed material 1938
1 item

Attorney. A copy of Milsten's *Howdy Folks* (1938), the official Will Rogers poem.

Miner, Frederick William 936
Papers 1830–1947
1 foot

Attorney. Correspondence (1830–1947); legal documents concerning land (1860–1940); and school material (ca. 1880) of Miner, who moved from Virginia to Texas in 1859, and of his daughter, May Miner Dorchester.

Unpublished finding aid available.

Mitchell-Benham Collection 937
Papers 1942
1 item

Collector. A World War II ration book.

Mitchell, (Mrs.) Alfred   938
Printed materials 1895–1910
1 foot

Collector. Typescripts of articles (1895–1910) and poems (1901–1907) written by the Creek Indian poet Alex Posey. The articles include information on Posey's actions while he was a member of the Dawes Commission, the opposition to allotment by the Snake Clan of Creek Indians, and Creek Indian opposition to Oklahoma statehood.

Unpublished finding aid available.

Mitchell, Irene Eldridge   939
Printed materials 1906–1912
10 items

Collector. A freight train permit (1906); an authorization to dip cattle (1912); business cards from the Yaller Dawg Saloon; a five-dollar scrip note (1907) from the Guthrie Savings Bank; a receipt (1908) from the Fraternal Order of Eagles; and three newspaper clippings, all related to J. W. "Buck" Eldridge.

Mitchell, Robert Thurston   940
Papers 1937–1951
.10 foot

Collector. Memoirs (n.d.) of Robert L. Mitchell, a Vinita, Oklahoma, physician; correspondence (1938–1951) concerning the Mitchell family genealogy; newspaper clippings (1946–1951); research notes and materials relating to the Cherokee Nation, missions, education, roads, and schools in Indian Territory; and a typescript of an interview (1937) conducted by James S. Buchanan with Stanley A. Clark.

Mitchell, Sam W.   941
Papers 1899–1939
7 items

Mine worker. Contracts (1903–1939); a permit (1902); and leases (1899), all relating to the coal industry near McAlester, Oklahoma; plus a "Coal Mine Workmen's Compensation and Employers Liability Policy" (1922).

Mixon, A. M. (d. 1951)   942
Records 1914–1951
.25 foot

Physician. Account books (1914–1915, 1920); two issues of the *Oklahoma Cancer Bulletin* (n.d.); an anatomy chart (n.d.); and accounts (1951) turned over to the Interstate Reclamation Bureau for collection, all from Mixon's medical practice in Spiro, Oklahoma.

Monnet, Julien Charles (1868–1951)   943
Papers 1892–1913
.10 foot

University dean and professor. Newspaper clippings (1892–1913) relating to Julien C. Monnet's career at the University of Oklahoma; and speeches (1911) by Monnet.

Montezuma, Carlos (1858–1923)   944
Printed materials 1921–1923
5 items

Physician. Two pamphlets by Montezuma proposing the abolition of the U.S. Indian Service and entitled *Let My People Go* (1915) and *Abolish the Indian Bureau* (n.d.); two issues of a newsletter (1921–1922) by Montezuma, entitled *Wassaja: Freedom's Signal for the Indian*; and a pamphlet-length obituary (1923) of Montezuma.

Montgomery, Merle Aline (b. 1904)   945
Papers 1960–1978
2 feet

Musician. Subject files (1960–1978), including correspondence, clippings, programs, and newsletters arranged by state, from Montgomery's association with the National Federation of Music Clubs, both as president and as their representative to the United Nations.

Moore, Ercelle O'Brien Davis (b. 1903)   946
Papers 1947–1952
.33 foot

Author. Memoirs (n.d.) of Ercelle Moore; copies of journals (1947, 1975, 1982) with stories and poems by Moore; a teleplay set in Oklahoma, entitled "Christmas at Crossroads," by Moore; correspondence (1977) with Lawrence Kimble concerning the teleplay; and a copy of a screenplay (1975) by James McDonald and Robert Gerlach, written for the *Mary Tyler Moore Show* and entitled "The Seminar."

Moore, Ethel, and Chauncey O. Moore   947
Manuscript n.d.
1 item

Compilers. A manuscript (n.d.) entitled "Ballads and Songs of Oklahoma." An accompanying Ethel and Chauncey Moore Collection of tapes (n.d.) of American, British, and Scotch folk-songs recorded throughout Oklahoma is also in the Western History Collections.

Moore, Jessie Elizabeth Randolph (1871–1956)   948
Papers 1916–1930
6.66 feet

Court clerk. Correspondence (1927–1930) to and from Moore as clerk of the Oklahoma Criminal Court of Appeals and clerk of the Oklahoma Supreme Court; campaign material (1926–1930), including correspondence concerning Moore's campaign for election and re-election as court clerk; personal correspondence (1926); briefs (1916–1921) filed in the state supreme court while Moore was deputy clerk; and clippings (1926–1936) concerning Oklahoma history.

Unpublished finding aid available.

Moore, John D. (b. 1886)   949
Papers 1907–1955
3 items

Physician. A biographical data sheet (1955); a reminiscence (n.d.) of his first summer of medical practice at Swink, Indian Territory, in 1907; and Moore's license (1907) to practice medicine in Indian Territory.

Moore, John H. (1939–)   950
Papers 1880–1985
16 feet

Professor. Photocopies of field notes (1933) compiled by Fred Eggan during his studies of Cheyenne and Arapaho Indian kinship, bands, societies, marriage, genealogy, ceremonies, child care, and social customs; U.S. census coding sheets (1880, 1900); Cheyenne and Arapaho Indian censuses (1888–1977); computer printouts showing Cheyenne-

Arapaho allotments, census data, and kinship analyses (n.d.); printed materials and copies of records (1867–1982) relating to Northern Cheyenne Indians; printed material and copies of records (1864–1981) relating to Sand Creek Cheyenne Indians; copies of Cheyenne Indian probate records (1920s); and grant-related records (1975–1985).

Unpublished finding aid available.

Moore, Louise Beard — 951
Papers 1935–1984
7 feet

Professor and journalist. Correspondence and subject files (1935–1984) kept by Moore while supervisor of the *Oklahoma Daily*, the University of Oklahoma student newspaper, and University of Oklahoma yearbook *The Sooner*; correspondence (1968–1971) regarding the Oklahoma Memorial Association and Oklahoma Hall of Fame; Moore's classroom teaching files (1957–1972); manuscript copies of poetry by Kenneth C. Kaufman, entitled "Level Land," and volumes 1–3 of *Oklahoma Biographs*.

Unpublished finding aid available.

Moore, Robb — 952
Papers 1914–1949
.10 foot

Collector. Typewritten manuscripts (ca. 1949) by Ora Padgett, entitled "Thirty-two Years in the U.S. Indian Service" and "The American Reservation," both regarding his experiences in the Indian Service.

Mooreland Security State Bank Collection — 953
Records 1900–1920
11 feet

Bank. Financial records (1900–1920), including daily balance ledgers, account ledgers, and individual account ledgers, from the Security State Bank in Mooreland, Oklahoma.

Moorhead, Max Leon (b. 1914) — 954
Papers 1600–1976
18 feet

Historian. Correspondence (1962–1976); manuscripts (1960s); microfilmed and photocopied documents (1730–1790); research notes (n.d.); lectures (n.d.); student reports (n.d.); student research papers (n.d.); and printed materials (1853–1975), including book reviews and reprints, all relating to Moorhead's teaching of Latin American history at the University of Oklahoma, and to his publications about Jacobo de Ugarte, the presidio, other Spanish colonial institutions in the Southwest, and the Indians of Mexico and the southwestern United States.

Unpublished finding aid available.

Moorman, Lewis Jefferson (1875–1954) 955
Papers 1909–1953
1 foot

Physician. Typescripts of oral history interviews (1936–1937) conducted during the Indian-Pioneer Oral History Project; correspondence (1924–1953) concerning real estate transactions, Moorman's research on tuberculosis and Indian health, and other aspects of his medical career, including connections with the University of Oklahoma School of Medicine; and a stock certificate (1909) from Epworth College of Medicine in Oklahoma City, Oklahoma.

Unpublished finding aid available.

Mootz, Herman Edwin 956
Printed materials 1932–1944
6 items

Author. Two brochures (n.d.) promoting Mootz's books; two letters, one (1937) to Grace E. Ray from Grace V. Mootz, and one (1944) to Grace V. Mootz from Grace E. Ray; and two clippings (1932–1935) concerning Mootz.

Morford, Robert Boyd (b. 1876) 957
Papers 1909–1940
2 feet

Real estate agent. Business correspondence (1909–1929) concerning Morford's real estate business and the development of a cotton mill in Lawton, Oklahoma; political correspondence (1916–1929) with Senator John W. Harreld of Oklahoma, and others; Republican Party campaign literature (1936, 1940); and clippings (1913–1940).

Morgan, Clyde (b. 1886) 958
Printed materials 1899–1943
.10 foot

Collector. Newspaper clippings (1937–1938); bulletins (1936); a membership roster (n.d.); an annual reunion event program (1943); and a booklet about the U.S. Army Thirty-third Infantry Association, a veterans organization composed of members of the Thirty-third Infantry, who served in the Philippines and many of whom were from Oklahoma Territory.

Morgan, (Mrs.) Lawrence Nelson 959
Papers 1837–1925
.10 foot

Collector. Photocopies of correspondence (1865–1866) from John N. Edwards, a major in the Confederate States Army, who emigrated to Mexico after the Civil War, to family members, describing conditions in Mexico; a newspaper article (1925) about Edwards; and a copy of a treaty (1837) between the United States and the Sac and Fox Indians.

Morgan, Robert J. 960
Records 1894–1989
.33 foot

Collector. Two bound volumes (1894–1922) of handwritten minutes and reports of the trustees of Kingfisher College, Kingfisher, Oklahoma, as well as a copy of a historical newspaper article (1989) regarding Kingfisher College.

Morris, John Wesley (1907–1982) 961
Papers 1864–1982
6.66 feet

Professor and geographer. Correspondence (1939–1982); papers (1942–1956) concerning Morris's military service in the U.S. Navy and in the U.S. Army Reserve; certificates and diplomas (1864–1982); account books (1962–1969); and manuscripts, research notes, correspondence, and contracts (ca. 1950–1982) relating to books and articles written by Morris, a University of Oklahoma geography professor.

Unpublished finding aid available.

Morrison, Cammie   962
Papers 1949–1964
.33 foot

Sponsor. Cammie Morrison sponsored several Korean students in their studies at Oklahoma City University and the University of Oklahoma. The collection includes forty-three letters (1949–1961) written to Morrison by the students; Korean Christmas cards; Holt Adoption Program newsletters (1960–1962); and various Korean printed materials.

Morrison, G. A. (1853–1925), and Robin Leroy Morrison   963
Manuscript 1912
1 item

Physicians. A manuscript (1912) of an address by Mrs. G. A. Morrison regarding opportunities to provide educational and religious training for the African-American population of Poteau, Oklahoma.

Morrison, W. D., and James Morrison   964
Papers 1840–1920
8 feet

Historians. Research notes and related materials (1840–1920), many concerning Choctaw and Chickasaw tribal politics, allotment of lands, and Indian participation in the Civil War, gathered by the Morrisons for the purpose of writing a history of Bryan County, Oklahoma.

Unpublished finding aid available.

Morrow, John A. (b. 1875)   965
Papers 1953–1954
2 items

Physician. Memoirs (1954) of Morrow, recounting his early medical practice (1899–1912) in Indian Territory; and biographical newspaper clippings (1953).

Mosby, George Waldo (1875–1959)   966
Ledger 1913–1941
1 item

Businessman. A ledger (1913–1941) recording mortgages issued by the Mosby and Swartz Real Estate and Insurance Company of Frederick, Oklahoma.

Moseley, John Ohleyer 967
Papers 1931–1949
.50 foot

Professor. Notes (1931–1949) on Roman law and the decline of Greco-Roman civilization, including notes (1931) for a class on Roman law taught at the University of Oklahoma by Moseley; and a scrapbook of correspondence (1935) concerning Moseley's assumption of the presidency of Central State Teachers College in Edmond, Oklahoma.

Mosely, Palmer S. (1851–1908) 968
Printed materials 1894–1904
.10 foot

Indian chief. Typescripts of newspaper articles (1894–1904) concerning negotiations with the Dawes Commission and the allotment of Chickasaw Indian lands during Mosely's two terms, 1894–1896 and 1902–1904, as governor of the Chickasaw Nation.

Moulton, Herbert 969
Printed materials 1898–1934
13 items

Physician. Reprints (1898–1934) of articles by Herbert Moulton, an eye, ear, and nose specialist in Fort Smith, Arkansas.

Mountain Meadows Massacre Collection 970
Papers 1937
.33 foot

Historical event. This collection consists of typescript research materials regarding an attack upon a wagon train of California-bound emigrants from Arkansas in 1857 in the Territory of Utah. The research materials are comprised of correspondence (1858–1859) and printed materials (1937) about Utah, Mormonism, and the attack.

Mountain View Twentieth-Century Club Collection 971
Records 1904–1988
1.66 feet

Civic organization. Correspondence (1913–1946); minutes (1904–1951); account books (1903–1915); minutes of the Round Table Section (1904–1907); program calendars (1928–1950); yearbooks (1904–

1988); clippings (1956–1978); and copies of *History of Mountain View* (1970), from the Mountain View (Oklahoma) Twentieth-Century Club.

Mueller, Gustav Emil (b. 1898) 972
Papers 1914–1959
3 feet

Professor. Manuscripts (1945–1968) of Mueller's published and unpublished works in English and German, including philosophical treatises, a novel, a play, and poems; notes (1938–1963) from his philosophy classes; and newspaper clippings (1914–1942) of book reviews and other articles written by Mueller and others.

Unpublished finding aid available.

Muldrow, Henry Lowndes, Jr. (b. ca. 1905) 973
Papers 1857–1898
.66 foot

Collector. Correspondence (1857–1889) between Robert Muldrow, his wife, Annie Oliver Muldrow, and their children; and a journal (1898) of an expedition by Henry Lowndes Muldrow, Sr., to Alaska.

Mullen Coal Company Collection 974
Records 1900–1946
11.33 feet

Mining company. Correspondence (1902–1946); monthly account ledgers (1907–1945); payroll records (1931–1945); notebooks of production costs (1940–1943); bank statements (1909–1946); and bills and receipts (1900–1948) from the Mullen Coal Company, near McAlester, Oklahoma.

Unpublished finding aid available.

Munger, William Houston (1852–1926) 975
Records 1905–1941
.66 foot

Merchant. Account books (1906–1926); a letter book of outgoing correspondence (1917–1919); a record of funerals (1915–1921) from the W. H. Munger Hardware, Furniture & Undertaking Store in Watonga, Oklahoma; and a scrapbook (1905–1941) containing letters, clippings, programs, menus, and souvenirs collected by Munger's son, Reuben Bates Munger.

Munn, Bertha M. B. 976
Hymnal ca. 1860
1 item

Collector. A photocopy of a manuscript hymnal (ca. 1860) written in the Wyandotte (Huron) Indian language and used in mission churches before the Wyandotte removal to Oklahoma.

Murphey and Noffsinger Collection 977
Records ca. 1910–1935
.33 foot

Law firm. Legal papers (ca. 1910–1935), including court orders, appearance bonds, and arrest warrants from the law firms of Hutchings, Murphey, and German, and of Murphey and Noffsinger, in Muskogee, Oklahoma.

Murphy, William Albert Patrick (1872–1952) 978
Papers 1896–1952
.33 foot

State labor commissioner. Correspondence (1936–1947), including postcards (1907–1910) regarding family matters, Murphy's record as state commissioner of labor, and his retirement from that office; certificates (1896–1939) appointing Murphy a U.S. deputy marshal in Oklahoma Territory, incorporating the Oklahoma Association for Old Age Security, Inc., and nominating Murphy for the office of commissioner of labor; news clippings (1933–1950) regarding Murphy, and state and national labor concerns; cards (1935–1950) certifying Murphy's membership in fraternal organizations and from Murphy's re-election campaign; publications (1936–1947), including booklets regarding national labor affairs; a campaign poster (ca. 1940) printed by the Democratic Party of Oklahoma; pocket ledgers (1907) containing names and addresses, as well as a list of delegates from Oklahoma and Indian Territories attending an unidentified conference in 1907; and a funeral register (1952) signed by friends paying last respects to Murphy after his death.

Murrah, Alfred P. (1904–1975) 979
Papers 1913–1995
11 feet

Attorney and federal judge. Professional and personal correspondence (1937–1975); speeches (1948–1973); clipping files and book reviews

(1937–1975); income tax returns (1936–1976); and research files accumulated for Judge Murrah's biography. Also in the collection are speeches (1925–1975) by other political and judicial personalities.

Unpublished finding aid available.

Murray, Burbank (1911–1984)   980
Papers 1928–1974
1 foot

Engineer. Correspondence received by Murray from friends and relatives, including his mother, Alice (1931–1938), and father, William H. Murray (1932–1952). Also included is correspondence from Murray's brothers, Massena, Billy, and Johnston, and from his sister, Jean. The correspondence refers to Murray family affairs, the term of Oklahoma governor W. H. Murray, the family's participation in the Bolivia colony, and W. H. Murray's views regarding Oklahoma, politicians, World War II, the future of the United States and Mexico, and family members, including Burbank Murray.

Unpublished finding aid available.

Murray, Frankie Colbert (b. ca. 1900)   981
Papers 1924–1985
1.33 feet

Collector. Correspondence (1927–1980) regarding William Henry Murray, Sr., governor of Oklahoma, 1931–1935; Johnston Murray, governor of Oklahoma, 1951–1955; Burbank Murray; Massena Bancroft Murray; and Frankie Colbert (Mrs. Massena B. Murray); also printed material (1924–1950) regarding the Democratic Party; and clippings (1950–1985) regarding William H. Murray and Johnston Murray.

Unpublished finding aid available.

Murray, Johnston (1902–1974)   982
Papers 1950–1955
50 feet

Governor of Oklahoma. Personal papers (1950–1955), including correspondence, reports, publications, sound recordings, filmstrips, posters, and scrapbooks reflecting Murray's gubernatorial administration (1951–1955) and the affairs of state government during those years. Also included are materials from Murray's gubernatorial campaign of 1950.

Unpublished finding aid available.

Murray, Jon Kyle 983
Papers 1992–1997
.10 foot

Poet. Three poems (1992–1997) by Jon Kyle Murray, entitled "Hot Tamale Folly... Slurp & Gulp," "Comeback Encounter of the Classical Kind," and "Final Duel for a Fast-Draw Fool."

Murrow, Joseph Samuel (1835–1930) 984
Papers 1894–1928
.33 foot

Missionary. Legal documents and papers (1894–1928) relating to J. S. Murrow, his home and school for Indian orphans, and Bacone College. The collection also includes minutes and proceedings (1916–1918) of the Indian Missionary Association, and programs (1912–1921) for meetings of the Deacons and Missionaries Institute of the Cheyenne-Arapaho Baptist churches and of the Oklahoma Indian Baptist Association.

Mushulatubbee (d. 1838) 985
Speech 1835
1 item

Indian chief. A typescript of a speech (1835) by Mushulatubbee regarding peace between the Choctaw Indians and neighboring tribes to the west.

Muskogee, Oklahoma, Indian Centennial Collection 986
Printed materials 1948
.10 foot

Subject collection. Newspaper clippings describing the preliminary events, ceremonies, and special events, and historical articles relating to the commemorative celebration held in 1948 to mark one hundred years of progress by the Five Civilized Tribes.

Muzzy, W. J. 987
Ledger 1936–1937
1 item

Physician. A daybook (1936–1937) recording laboratory test results from the El Reno (Oklahoma) Sanitarium.

Myrick, E. B.   988
Printed materials 1893
1 item

Collector. One issue of *The Doctor: A Quarterly Journal of Medicine and Therapeutics*, 1893.

Nance, James Clark, Jr. (b. 1893)   989
Records 1911–1961
5.66 feet

Legislator. Transcripts of testimony (1922–1927); district court clerk reports (1911–1920); legislative committee reports (1956–1959); and legislative bills (1959) regarding prohibition in Oklahoma and calls for its repeal in 1959.

Unpublished finding aid available.

National Research Council Collection   990
Records 1933–1947
.33 foot

Scientific organization. Correspondence (1933–1947) and reports (1933–1947), produced by the National Research Council's committee on the ecology of grasslands. These materials reflect the committee's work toward establishing conservation measures for the remaining virgin grasslands in the United States.

Naval Air Technical Training Center Collection   991
Printed materials 1941–1959
.10 foot

Military base. Newspaper articles (1941–1959) and publications (1945) regarding the U.S. Naval Air Station and the U.S. Naval Air Technical Training Center, both of which were located in Norman, Oklahoma. Included in the collection are stories regarding the establishment, operation, and closing of the bases, and the condition of life there, along with information on their subsequent acquisition by the University of Oklahoma.

Neal, Henry Lee 992
Records 1895–1964
.66 foot

Postmaster. A rural mail carrier's registration book (n.d.); registers of money orders issued (1906, 1910); records of registered matter (1908–1910); and related material from the Wanette, Oklahoma, post office, plus a scrapbook (1936–1964) outlining the career of Henry Neal, Wanette, Oklahoma, postmaster from 1936 to 1964.

Neer, Charles Sumner (1879–1937) 993
Printed material 1908–1934
5 items

Physician. Five reprints (1908–1934) of articles written by Charles Sumner Neer, a Vinita, Oklahoma, physician, on ectopic pregnancies, childbirth complications, and malaria.

Nelson, George (1870–1944) 994
Papers 1908–1944
1 foot

Interpreter. Personal correspondence (1912–1943); land records (1908–1929) for allotments in the Choctaw and Chickasaw nations; lists (1939–1940) of allotments available for coal leases; files (1933) on government aid given to destitute Indians; and a catechism (n.d.) written in the Choctaw Indian language.

Unpublished finding aid available.

Nesbitt, Pleasant P. 995
Papers n.d.
5 items

Physician. Typescripts of articles (n.d.) on medical subjects by Pleasant P. Nesbitt, a Tulsa, Oklahoma, physician.

New York Mutual Life Insurance Company Collection 996
Radio scripts ca. 1953
.10 foot

Insurance company. A series of fourteen radio scripts (ca. 1953) by Gretta Baker, on public health problems, published and distributed by the New York Mutual Life Insurance Company as an educational health service.

Newby, Errett Rains (b. 1885) 997
Printed materials 1905–1973
.66 foot

University registrar. Four University of Oklahoma catalogs (1914–1918) with Errett R. Newby's notes as university registrar (1911–1920), including maps of the campus (1916) and of Norman, Oklahoma (1915); a catalog (1905) for the University of Oklahoma's School of Fine Arts; a copy (1910) of the president's report to the University of Oklahoma's Board of Regents; a copy (1914) of the University of Oklahoma's biennial report; the constitution and bylaws (1914) of the University of Oklahoma's athletic association; a proposal (n.d.) for a charter for self-government by the students; the constitution and bylaws (n.d.) of the University of Oklahoma's student senate; a typescript of an editorial (n.d.), "Do the People Rule—In Oklahoma?" by Lyman Abbott; a copy (1906) of the "Voluntary Organizations Illustrations" issue of the *Bulletin* of the University of Oklahoma; and reminiscences (1973) by Newby about the university's early history.

[239]

Newkirk First National Bank Collection 998
Records 1893–1931
22 feet

Bank. Financial records (1893–1931) of the First National Bank of Newkirk, Oklahoma, prior to its merging with the Eastman National Bank of Newkirk, Oklahoma, including ledgers, draft registers, remittance registers, journals, depositors balance ledgers, discount registers, collection registers, old and new balance books, along with a ledger (1893) from the Bank of Santa Fe, also in Newkirk, Oklahoma, before it became Eastman National Bank.

Newkirk, Oklahoma, Municipal Records Collection 999
Records 1910–1947
.66 foot

Municipal government. City improvement bonds (1919–1947); bond stubs (1910–1947); paving tax receipts (1929); and a paving collection and distribution record (n.d.) from the city of Newkirk, Oklahoma.

Newland, John Lynn (1874–1941) 1000
Manuscript n.d.
1 item

Newspaper editor. A manuscript (n.d.) of "The Editor's Story" by John Newland.

Newman, Coley   1001
Papers 1906–1910
2 items

Collector. Two deeds (1906 and 1910) for land in Harmon County, Oklahoma.

Newman, Oscar Clarence (1876–1953)   1002
Printed materials 1937–1949
5 items

Physician. Four clippings (1937–1949) regarding Oscar Clarence Newman, his medical practice, and the history of Ellis County (formerly Day County), Oklahoma; and a copy of *The Bulletin* (1943) of the Oklahoma County Medical Society, containing an article by Newman.

Nice, Margaret Morse (b. 1883)   1003
Papers 1905–1952
1.66 feet

Ornithologist. Correspondence (1920–1945) with other ornithologists; notebooks (1914–1929) of bird sightings in Oklahoma; note cards (1905–1929); and research notes (1920–1930) of Margaret Nice; a typescript copy (n.d.) of "Wildlife of Tulsa County (Oklahoma)," by Edith R. Force; a manuscript, "Economic Value of Oklahoma Birds," by E. D. Crabb; and reprints (1930–1952) of articles about birds.

Unpublished finding aid available.

Nichols, James Thomas   1004
Diploma 1903
1 item

Physician. Diploma (1903) from the Denver and Gross College of Medicine, University of Denver, awarding James Thomas Nichols the degree of doctor of medicine.

Nichols, Lea Murray (b. 1878)   1005
Papers 1865–1957
1 foot

Journalist. Correspondence (1903–1951) regarding personal affairs, politicians and political events, and the National Editorial Association;

speeches (n.d.) of Nichols; and publications (1917–1944) by pacifist organizations and government agencies regarding America's involvement in World War II, and Nazi Germany's relations with Poland, the Soviet Union, and other European nations.

Unpublished finding aid available.

Niebell, Paul M.   1006
Papers 1815–1989
23 feet

Attorney. Case files (1815–1989) of attorney Paul M. Niebell. Files are arranged by type and docket number. Cases involve lawsuits filed by Indian tribes and were tried before the Indian Claims Commission, the U.S. Court of Claims, and the U.S. Supreme Court. Niebell represented the Creek, Cherokee, Chickasaw, Choctaw, Osage, Seminole, Wichita, Caddo, Cheyenne-Arapaho, and other Indian tribes. The case files include briefs, petitions, exhibits, motions, opinions, and proceedings, as well as minutes (1952–1971) of the Creek Tribal Council.

Nieberding, Velma   1007
Papers 1891–1959
.10 foot

Historian. Typescripts of interviews (1956–1959) conducted by members of the Ottawa County (Oklahoma) Semi-Centennial Committee with pioneers of Ottawa County, in which they described settlement of the area, early businesses, social activities, and interaction with the Indians of the area.

Noble First State Bank Collection   1008
Records 1910–1933
6 feet

Bank. Financial records (1910–1933), including general ledgers, daily balance ledgers, daily statement ledgers, and note registers, from the First State Bank in Noble, Oklahoma.

Noble, Joseph Glass   1009
Printed materials 1919–1952
.10 foot

Physician. Noble's commissions as a captain (1919) and a major (1930) in the U.S. Army Medical Corps; a paper (1931) by Noble, entitled

"Examination of the Chest"; and advertisements (1940–1952) for medical products.

Norman, Oklahoma, Lions Club Collection 1010
Records 1917–1955
1 foot

Civic organization. Correspondence (1917–1955); minutes (1920); and a secretary's record (1926–1930), including club rosters, dues, cash receipts and disbursements, general accounts, and attendance records of the Norman, Oklahoma, Lions Club; and printed material such as programs, brochures, and newsletters.

Unpublished finding aid available.

Norman, Oklahoma, Woden Club Collection 1011
Printed materials 1953
2 items

Social organization. A history and membership list (1953) of the Woden Club of Norman, Oklahoma, plus a newspaper clipping (1953) marking the club's fortieth anniversary.

Norris, Clare E. 1012
Diploma 1898
1 item

Student. Diploma (1898) from the Pharmaceutical Department of the University of Oklahoma, awarding Norris the degree of pharmaceutical chemist.

Norris, Thomas T. 1013
Records 1900–1938
.10 foot

Physician. Birth records (1923–1938) and prescription slips (1936–1937) from Norris's medical practice in Krebs, Oklahoma; and a commencement announcement (1900) from the University of Nashville medical school.

Norton, Spencer Hilton (1909–1978) 1014
Papers ca. 1930–1970
1 foot

Professor and composer. Musical scores (ca. 1930–1970) of compositions by Norton, a music professor, at the University of Oklahoma in Norman, Oklahoma.

Nothstein, (Mrs.) Charles Anderson   1015
Printed materials 1902–1913
.10 foot

Collector. Publications (1902–1913) reflecting social life in territorial and early statehood periods of Hennessey, Oklahoma, including programs of the town's junior and senior high school commencements, concert programs, news clippings from a local newspaper, one regarding a tornado which struck the town, and one souvenir booklet from Hennessey, Oklahoma Territory.

Nowata County Records Collection   1016
Records 1909–1939
50 feet

County government. Judicial dockets (1909–1939) of the Nowata County, Oklahoma, civil and criminal courts; applications for homesteaders exemption taxes (1937); and tax assessment lists (1909–1939) for Nowata County, Oklahoma.

Unpublished finding aid available.

Nowata, Oklahoma, La Kee Kon Garden Club Collection   1017
Printed material 1952
1 item

Social organization. A copy of the forty-ninth annual calendar (1952) of the La Kee Kon Garden Club of Nowata, Oklahoma, containing the club history, a membership roster, and the club's constitution and bylaws.

Office of Price Administration Collection   1018
Printed materials 1942–1944
.10 foot

Federal agency. Copies of orders and regulations (1944) issued for Oklahoma by the Office of Price Administration (OPA) in regard to prices of commodities; publications (1942–1944) by the OPA, including a manual of procedures, bulletins, and newsletters; and posters (1943) listing grocery prices in Oklahoma.

Ogden, Florence 1019
Manuscript 1868–1961
1 item

Homemaker. A brief typewritten memoir (n.d.) by Ogden recounting her childhood experiences and emphasizing her contact with local Cheyenne Indians near Thomas, Custer County, Oklahoma.

Oglesby, Carson L. (b. 1906) 1020
Papers 1927–1940
4 items

Physician. Correspondence (1927) from Oklahoma City University regarding funding opportunities for new students; news clippings regarding medical care in Muskogee; and a University of Oklahoma commencement program (1937).

O'Hornett, Carl J. 1021
Papers 1946
.10 foot

Attorney. Correspondence (1946), mostly from Carl J. O'Hornett, offering oil companies oil and gas leases on 1,250 royalty acres in the North Burbank area of Kay and Osage counties (Oklahoma). Maps of the North Burbank area and a plat in Washita County, Oklahoma, are included in the collection.

Ohoyohoma Club Collection 1022
Records 1925–1959
3.75 feet

Social organization. Scrapbooks (1925–1959) containing photographs, news clippings, programs, and mementos of the Ohoyohoma Club, a McAlester, Oklahoma, women's club that limited its membership to women of Indian descent.

Unpublished finding aid available.

Oklahoma Academy of Science Collection 1023
Records 1910–1986
25.50 feet

Professional organization. Correspondence (1926–1986) regarding the academy's operation and special projects, including specialized files concerning its executive council, membership, finances, and its subsidiary organization, the Oklahoma Junior Academy of Science; and publications (1910–1985), including *The Bulletin* and *Proceedings* of the Academy, as well as the *Transactions* of the Junior Academy.

Unpublished finding aid available.

Oklahoma Association of College History Professors Collection 1024
Records 1949
4 items

Professional organization. A program, sign-up sheets, and membership lists (1949) from the first annual meeting of the Oklahoma Association of College History Professors.

Oklahoma Association for Teachers Retirement Collection 1025
Records 1936–1938
2 feet

Teachers organization. Correspondence (1936–1938) with professional and business organizations, school superintendents, political candidates, and others favoring legislation establishing teachers retirement provisions; and minutes (1936–1938) of the association's meetings.

Unpublished finding aid available.

Oklahoma Chapter of the Society of the Sigma Xi Collection 1026
Records 1930–1988
.10 foot

Scientific research society. Initiation ceremony programs (1930–1988), and the constitution and bylaws as amended and published in 1965.

Oklahoma City Boy Scout Collection 1027
Papers 1918–1920
.20 foot

Subject collection. This collection is comprised of 106 letters, dated 1918–1920, written to Thomas Rowe, an Oklahoma City Scoutmaster, by former Boy Scouts, while Rowe was in the U.S. Army during World War I.

Oklahoma City First National Bank Collection   1028
Records 1901–1926
6 feet

Bank. Daily statement ledgers (1905–1926); general ledgers (1901–1904); personal account ledgers (1910–1911); and a Liberty Bond ledger (1918) from the American National Bank of Oklahoma City, Oklahoma, which merged with the First National Bank of Oklahoma City in 1927. The collection also contains the general ledgers (1907–1909); draft ledgers (1907–1912); and statement books (1914–1917) from the Western National Bank of Oklahoma City, which merged with the American National Bank in 1917.

Unpublished finding aid available.

Oklahoma City Junior Symphony Orchestra Collection   1029
Scrapbook 1961–1963
1 item

Youth orchestra. A scrapbook (1961–1963) of clippings, programs, promotional literature, and correspondence, relating to the Oklahoma City (Oklahoma) Junior Symphony Orchestra.

Oklahoma City Tradesmens National Bank Collection   1030
Records 1919–1937
5 feet

Bank. Financial records (1919–1937) of the Tradesmens National Bank of Oklahoma City, Oklahoma, including resources and liabilities ledgers (1919–1921) and daily statements of account ledgers (1925– 1937).

Oklahoma Corporation Commission Collection   1031
Printed materials 1934–1948
.33 foot

State regulatory agency. Copies of monthly reports from the Oklahoma Corporation Commission, including Oklahoma allocated pools allotment reports (1945–1948), daily allocation reports (1946–1947), pipe lines run (1946–1947), notifications of intentions to drill (1946–1947), and abandoned oil and gas wells (1946–1947); and copies of monthly reports (1934–1937) on the Oklahoma labor market, from the Oklahoma Department of Labor.

Oklahoma Democratic Party Collection   1032
Printed materials 1916–1958
.33 foot

Political party. Campaign brochures (1930–1958) for Democratic candidates; press releases (1949–1953) of speeches and statements given by Democratic officials; a scrapbook (1958) regarding the inaugurations of Oklahoma governors E. W. Marland, Johnston Murray, Roy J. Turner, and Raymond D. Gary; a speakers manual (1936) for the Democratic campaign in Oklahoma; official proceedings (1944) of the Democratic convention; and the Democratic campaign textbook (1916) for Oklahoma.

Oklahoma Department of Public Safety Collection   1033
Printed materials 1957–1961
3 feet

State office. Scrapbooks of clippings (1957–1961) from Oklahoma newspapers on the activities of the Oklahoma Highway Patrol.

Oklahoma Farm Bureau Collection   1034
Printed materials 1937–1954
.10 foot

State agricultural organization. Typescripts (1948–1954) of a history of the Oklahoma Farm Bureau, of proposed legislation pertaining to agricultural matters, of a letter sent to the county Farm Bureau offices by the state office regarding the state of agriculture in Oklahoma, and of an analysis (ca. 1954) of the Oklahoma State Department of Agriculture.

Oklahoma Genealogical Society Collection   1035
Papers 1958
2 items

State genealogical association. Typescript (1958) regarding recommended readings on heraldry; and a speech (1958) about genealogy by R. A. Brant of the Oklahoma Genealogical Society.

Oklahoma Geological Survey Collection   1036
Records 1908–1982
44 feet

State geological survey. Records of the Oklahoma Geological Survey, including correspondence (1908–1982); area geological reports (1915–1948); field notes (1908) taken during geological expeditions; reports of the governing board (1974–1979); and book manuscripts and galley proofs (n.d.) about geology in Oklahoma. Correspondence from the University of Oklahoma Departments of Geology and Geography is also present in this collection.

Unpublished finding aid available.

Oklahoma Indian Rights Association Collection 1037
Records 1966–1980
11.50 feet

Indian advocacy organization. Records of the association (1966–1980), including correspondence, reports, financial records, and publications of the Oklahoma Indian Rights Association, regarding its involvement in the cause of American Indian civil rights, economic betterment, and the organization's relations with Oklahoma Indian tribes and nations.

Unpublished finding aid available.

Oklahoma Labor Studies Collection 1038
Printed materials 1934
1 item

Subject collection. Pamphlet (1934) entitled "Agreement Between Local 231, International Association of Oil Field, Gas Well and Refinery Workers of America, and Empire Oil and Refining Co."

Oklahoma Museum Project Collection 1039
Teaching aids 1990–1992
.33 foot

Educational project. Three museum education project notebooks on the cowboy; myth and reality; the story of Oklahoma's settlement; and archeology of Plains village people.

Oklahoma Music Educators Association Collection 1040
Records 1776–1992
6 feet

Professional organization. Records of the Oklahoma Music Educators Association. Included are subject files (1960–1992) covering topics such as All-State Band, Orchestra, and Chorus, conventions, financial records, executive board files (1985–1992) including correspondence, minutes, and reports; president's files (1967–1971); and printed materials including a copy of "Isaac Days Book," a handwritten drum instruction book (ca. 1776). Also included are transcripts of oral history interviews conducted by George McDow with Oklahoma school band directors; printed materials regarding band contests and festivals; a copy of "Instrumental Handbook" (1949–1950); and a copy of "These Things I Remember—A Story of My Life," by Oakley H. Pittman.

Unpublished finding aid available.

Oklahoma Natural Mutoscene Company Collection 1041
Papers 1908
6 items

Motion picture company. Correspondence (1908) to J. R. Abernathy from L. J. Simons, general manager of Oklahoma Natural Mutoscene Company, about the availability of films, financing, and advertisements for the company.

Oklahoma Ornithological Society Collection 1042
Records 1949–2000
7 feet

Professional organization. Correspondence and reports (1949–1999) regarding the operation and status of the society, including files concerning the organization's membership, constitution, special projects, and stance regarding the official state bird of Oklahoma; and record copies of the society's publications (1951–2000), the *Oklahoma Ornithological Society Bulletin*, and *The Scissortail*.

Unpublished finding aid available.

Oklahoma Outdoor Council Collection 1043
Printed materials 1953
6 items

Conservation organization. Materials used in an exhibit for National Wildlife Week (1953) in Oklahoma, including Governor Johnston Murray's signed proclamation, a pamphlet from the National Wildlife Federation, a map showing the distribution of the prairie chicken in Oklahoma, and a copy (1953) of *Oklahoma Game and Fish News*.

Oklahoma Pioneer Physicians Oral History Collection   1044
Papers ca. 1880–1907
.33 foot

History project. Typescripts of personal anecdotes, eyewitness accounts, and first-hand narratives (1880–1907) of physicians who were practicing medicine in Oklahoma during the late nineteenth century and early twentieth century. Also included is an interview with Oklahoma governor Johnston Murray, concerning the practice of medicine.

Unpublished finding aid available.

Oklahoma Press Association Collection   1045
Printed materials 1955
3 items

Regional press association. Directories (1955) published by the Oklahoma Press Association, listing Oklahoma newspapers and their telephone numbers.

Oklahoma Republican Party Collection   1046
Records 1953–1983
128 feet

Political party. Records of the Oklahoma Republican Party, including correspondence files (1963–1981); files on the Rules Study Committee (1965–1975); minutes (1953–1980) and memoranda (1958–1983) from the State Committee; correspondence, press releases, and promotional literature (1969–1979) from the Republican National Committee; minutes and working papers (1963–1979), and budgets and reports (1963–1976) from the State Budget Committee; subject files (1964–1980) on national and state conventions; subject files (1976–1980) of the Legislative Action Committee; fundraising files (1964–1976); research files (1959–1980) by subject and by individual; county files (1968–1974); and fiscal files, including account reports (1958–1979) and payrolls (1961–1978).

Unpublished finding aid available.

Oklahoma Safety Council Collection   1047
Printed materials 1946–1960
5 feet

Public service organization. Local reports (1948) for the National Pedestrian Protection Contest; annual inventories (1948) of local traf-

In this ledger drawing, Sioux Indian White Bull depicts himself wounding a Shoshoni Indian who was fighting with the U.S. cavalry against the Sioux and Cheyenne at the Battle of the Rosebud River (Montana), June 17, 1876. Rifle smoke pours from the opposing forces on both sides, indicating the intensity of the battle. From the Walter Stanley Campbell Collection.

fic safety activities; Public Safety Education Campaign material (1952–1960), including clippings, radio and television scripts, and pamphlets, along with news releases (ca. 1950) and reports (1946–1949) from the Oklahoma Safety Council.

Unpublished finding aid available.

Oklahoma School of Religion Collection 1048
Records 1917–1966
10 feet

Center for religious education. Correspondence (1917–1950) of E. Nicholas Comfort, the director of the school, regarding its functions, programs, and status; minutes (1927–1946) of meetings of the school's governing board; and publications (1927–1946), including school newsletters, catalogs, and annual reports of the First Presbyterian Church of Norman, Oklahoma, the school's sponsor. The collection also includes biographical materials (1956–1966) on E. Nicholas Comfort and the Comfort family.

Oklahoma Semi-Centennial Exposition Collection 1049
Printed materials 1957
2.75 feet

Statehood commemorative exposition. Printed matter (1957), including leaflets, brochures, newspapers, newspaper tear sheets, and decals produced as part of the official Oklahoma Semi-Centennial Exposition in 1957.

Unpublished finding aid available.

Oklahoma Soil Conservation Service Collection 1050
Printed materials 1960–1962
.66 foot

State agency. Programs and work plans (1960–1962) of the U.S. Department of Agriculture Soil Conservation Service program in Oklahoma, organized by soil conservation districts.

Oklahoma State Federation of Labor Collection 1051
Records 1907–1958
43.33 feet

Labor union. Correspondence (1924–1958), transcripts (1923–1956), and published proceedings (1908–1952) of Oklahoma state labor conventions; transcripts (1907–1957) concerning administrative boards, hearings, and union meetings; publications (1915–1955) of the U.S. Department of Labor; and posters (1953–1955) encouraging the purchase of union-made products.

Unpublished finding aid available.

Oklahoma State Federation of Women's Clubs Collection   **1052**
Printed materials 1922–1985
16 feet

Professional organization. Published material (1922–1985) from women's clubs throughout Oklahoma, including yearbooks, programs, newsletters, histories, and directories, arranged alphabetically by town and club.

Unpublished finding aid available.

Oklahoma State Grange Collection   **1053**
Printed materials 1916–1958
.33 foot

Agricultural association. *Proceedings* (1916–1958) of the annual sessions of the Oklahoma State Grange Patrons of Husbandry.

Oklahoma State Medical Association Collection   **1054**
Papers 1953
.66 foot

Professional organization. Biographical data sheets (1953) compiled by Oklahoma physicians regarding their lives and careers in medicine and collected by the Oklahoma State Medical Association.

Oklahoma Tax Commission Collection   **1055**
Printed materials 1936–1959
1.33 feet

State agency. Daily report of taxes collected (1957–1959) and reports and bulletins (1936–1947) of the statistical division of the Oklahoma Tax Commission, including monthly and annual collection reports,

reports of tax revenues by county and by classes of business, and reports of apportionment of taxes and state government spending; and the bulletin series (n.d.) *Know Your Government.*

Oklahoma Territorial Medical Association Collection 1056
Records 1890–1904
.25 foot

Professional organization. Constitution and bylaws (1890); membership rosters (1890–1904); programs for the annual conventions (1893–1904); and minutes (1890–1904) of the meetings of the Oklahoma Territorial Medical Association.

Oklahoma Transportation Company Collection 1057
Records 1902–1972
13 feet

Railroad company. Financial reports (1908–1972); executive and operating records (1902–1948), including annual reports, corporate bylaws, and minutes of the meetings of the governing board; and employee records (1931–1949) regarding the labor unions representing the Oklahoma Transportation Company work force, and wages paid.

Unpublished finding aid available.

Oklahoma Wheat Growers Association Collection 1058
Records 1921–1933
.66 foot

Agricultural advocacy organization. Minutes (1921–1927) of the meetings of the Oklahoma Wheat Growers Association; audit reports (1931–1932); the association's articles of incorporation and bylaws (1921); and one copy of the *Wheat Grower's Advocate* (1933).

Oklahomans For The Right To Work, Inc., Collection 1059
Printed materials 1954–1962
.25 foot

Political lobby. Organizational material (1954–1962) for county chairmen; photocopies of the articles of incorporation (1960); pamphlets (1954–1962) arguing both for and against right-to-work legislation; legislative histories (1954–1962) of state and national labor legislation; and an annotated bibliography (n.d.) from the Library of Congress Legislative Reference Service on the right-to-work controversy.

Okmulgee Abstract and Title Company Collection   1060
Records 1905–1922
.10 foot

County abstract firm. Abstracts of title (1905–1922) for property in Okmulgee County, Oklahoma.

Okmulgee Civic Improvement Club Collection   1061
Minutes 1906–1908
1 item

Civic club. A minute book (1906–1908) of the Okmulgee (Oklahoma) Civic Improvement Club.

Okmulgee County Medical Society Collection   1062
Records 1932–1947
.33 foot

Professional organization. Correspondence (1939–1947); minutes (1940–1941); membership and dues lists (1940–1947); and membership applications (1932–1946) from the Okmulgee County (Oklahoma) Medical Society; and printed material (1940–1947) from the Oklahoma State Medical Association and the American Medical Association.

Olds, Leland   1063
Papers 1951–1962
.75 foot

Collector. Business and personal correspondence (1955–1962) of Leland Olds; newspaper clippings (1951–1962) regarding politics; and statements and news releases (1957, 1962) of Robert S. Kerr.

Olinger, Paul T.   1064
Papers 1797–1917
.50 foot

Collector. Lecture notes (1859–1866) and theological books (1797–1866) of H. R. Schermerhorn, seminary student and, later, Indian Territory missionary; personal land records (1908–1917), including land deeds from the Choctaw and Chickasaw Nations and unallotted land deeds signed by Chickasaw governor Douglas H. Johnston and Choctaw principal chief Victor M. Locke, Jr.

Oochalata (d. 1891) 1065
Printed materials 1875–1891
.75 foot

Indian chief. Typescripts of newspaper articles (1875–1891), including biographical items, editorials, speeches, and messages of Oochalata, also known as Charles Thompson, the principal chief of the Cherokee Nation, 1875–1878, mostly relating to education, schools, finances, Cherokee Indian lands, and tribal government in general.

Opler, Morris Edward (b. 1907) 1066
Printed materials 1930–1971
1.33 feet

Anthropologist. Copies of journal articles (1930–1971) written by Opler concerning the Indian tribes of the American Southwest, including the Apache and Apache sub-groups, the Creek, and the Tonkawa.

Unpublished finding aid available.

Opothleyaholo (ca. 1798–1862) 1067
Manuscript 1928
1 item

Indian chief. A biographical typescript (1928) commenting on Opothleyaholo's mistrust of white men.

Order of the Eastern Star Collection 1068
Printed materials 1934–1935
2 items

Women's organization. *Proceedings* (1934–1935) of the twenty-sixth and twenty-seventh annual sessions of the Oklahoma chapter of the Order of the Eastern Star.

Ortenburger, Arthur Irving (b. 1898) 1069
Papers 1892–1943
.25 foot

Zoologist. Consumer rationing books (1943) issued during World War II to the Ortenburger family; and journals (1892–1898) maintained by Charles C. Dean, Ortenburger's father-in-law, of visits to Florida, Mexico, and Guatemala, for zoological research and vacations. Also included in this collection is a letter (1921) from Raymond L. Ditmars, whom Ortenburger considered one of the better herpetologists of his day.

Osage Indian Papers 1070
Papers 1806–1957
.25 foot

Indian tribe. Photocopies of translated letters (1805–1806) from James B. Wilkinson, Pierre Chouteau, and Francisco Caso y Luenge to Osage Indian chiefs, advising them of the need to comply with white authority; monthly returns (1863–1865) of ration issues to Osage Indians; an Osage tribal council statement (1953) contending that the U.S. government should supervise tribal affairs as long as there are mineral-producing properties held by the tribe; and publications (1957) of the Osage Indians' semi-centennial celebration of the closing of the Osage tribal roll and allotment of Osage Indian lands in severalty.

[257]

Osborne, Lyle 1071
Diary 1864
1 item

Collector. A diary (1864) of E. B. Osborne, a Union soldier, in which he relates his experiences in Tennessee near the end of the Civil War, with detailed descriptions of his company's participation in the Battle of Centerville of 1864; a trip to Georgia on the Chattahoochee, Macon, and Columbus Railroad; and a review of troops in Atlanta, Georgia, by Gen. William T. Sherman. Also included in the diary is a roster of men comprising Company I of the Thirty-first Ohio Infantry, with whom Osborne served.

Oskison, John Milton (1874–1947) 1072
Papers ca. 1917–1947
.10 foot

Author. A photo identification pass (1917) issued by the American Commission to Negotiate Peace of World War I, along with two unpublished manuscripts (n.d.), one entitled "The Singing Bird," and the other an unfinished autobiography which chronicles Oskison's life in the Cherokee Nation and elsewhere.

Other Film Club Collection 1073
Printed materials 1981–1989
1 foot

University film club. Printed flyers, newsletters, and calendars (1981–1989) of the Other Film Club at the University of Oklahoma. These materials list the titles of films shown by the Other Film Club on the campus of the University of Oklahoma, Norman, Oklahoma.

Unpublished finding aid available.

Ottawa County Medical Society Collection 1074
Records 1927–1949
2 items

Professional organization. Minutes and individual accounts of dues (1927–1930), and an account book (1936–1949), from the Ottawa County (Oklahoma) Medical Society.

Our Monthly Collection 1075
Printed materials 1873–1874
3 items

Newspaper. Original issues (1873–1874) of *Our Monthly*, published in Tulahassee, Creek Nation, Indian Territory.

Ourada, Patricia K. 1076
Manuscript n. d.
1 item

Historian. An annotated manuscript (n.d.) of Ourada's book *The Menominee Indians: A History*.

Overholser, Henry (1846–1915) 1077
Printed materials 1912
1 item

Land developer. An issue of *The Oklahoma Magazine* (1912), featuring an article about Henry Overholser.

Overton, Benjamin F. (1838–1884) 1078
Printed materials 1874–1906
.33 foot

Indian chief. Typescripts of newspaper articles (1874–1906) concerning Overton, governor of the Chickasaw Nation, and the Permit Law of 1876.

Owings, Donnell MacClure (1912–1966) 1079
Papers 1961–1965
.66 foot

Professor. Bibliographies (1962–1965); correspondence with students (1961–1963); and syllabi, lecture outlines, and schedules for Owings's University of Oklahoma history courses entitled "The American

Colonies, 1492–1789," "Historical Methods," and "Social and Cultural History of the United States 1607–1860."

Owl, Della Irene Brunsteter   1080
Papers ca. 1924–1975
.33 foot

Linguist. Research notes (1924–1975) collected by Owl regarding the Cherokee Indian language and syllabary.

Paine, Mary Graham Giles   1081
Printed materials 1921–1951
.10 foot

Editor. A personal account book (1935–1938); cards, programs, and directories, including the yearbook (1948–1949) for the Elliot Lee chapter (Pauls Valley, Oklahoma) of the Daughters of the American Revolution; and directories (1949–1951) for Oklahoma State Writers Inc., all belonging to Mary Giles Paine.

Palmer, Benn G.   1082
Printed materials 1929–1955
.10 foot

Collector. Publications (1929–1955) by and regarding the Lions Club of Bartlesville, Oklahoma, including the weekly chapter newspaper, *The Lion's Roar* (1954–1955); a souvenir edition (1953) of a Bartlesville newspaper; and a list (n.d.) of regional secretaries of Lions clubs throughout Oklahoma.

Palmer, Don L.   1083
Printed materials 1919
2 items

Collector. Playbill and magazine theatre program (1919) for a Ziegfield Follies production at the New Amsterdam Theatre in New York.

Pantoja, Father   1084
Letter ca. 1700
1 item

Priest. An unsigned three-page draft, in Spanish, of a petition from one Father Pantoja to the king of Spain, asking for the establishment of a Jesuit college in Coquimbro, Chile.

Parker, Everett C. (b. ca. 1893)   1085
Manuscript n.d.
1 item

Petroleum geologist. An autobiography (n.d.) of Parker, who recounts his activities as a student at the University of Oklahoma and as a petroleum geologist for the Marland Oil Company.

Parker, Franklin (b. 1921)   1086
Papers 1949–1989
.25 foot

Professor. Correspondence (1964–1966); newspaper and journal clippings (1964–1987); a press release (1966); and one newsletter (1967), all regarding the career and achievements of Parker during his years as professor of education at the University of Oklahoma and other institutions. Also included is a copy of Parker's resume (1989).

Parker, Harry (b. 1876)   1087
Papers 1876–1937
.10 foot

Cattleman. The autobiography (1876–1937) of Harry Parker, an Oklahoma cattleman, in which he relates his family's migration to No Man's Land (the Oklahoma panhandle area) in 1887, describing the towns, people, and the style and standard of living in that region before it became a part of Oklahoma Territory. Included in the autobiography is an account of an immigrant family who killed several people before being caught.

Parker, Robert   1088
Papers ca. 1975
11 items

Minister. Photocopies of eleven poems (ca. 1975) by Parker about God.

Parker, Thomas (1775–1890)   1089
Printed materials ca. 1872, 1928
2 items

Indian chief. A biographical sketch (1928) of Parker, and his farewell message as governor (1872) to the Chickasaw Nation legislature.

Parks, Lucile Snider (b. ca. 1894) 1090
Manuscript 1897–1903
1 item

Journalist. A photostatic copy of a typescript (n.d.) by Parks, entitled "Prairie Prelude: 1897–1903," in which she describes her childhood and life in Pawnee, Indian Territory.

[261]

Parman, James Franklin (d. 1958) 1091
Manuscript 1868–1904
1 item

Collector. An account (n.d.) by Will Brown of a white settlement in the Chickasaw Nation, (ca. 1868–1904) and attempts by the Chickasaw Indians to halt it.

Parnell, Charles 1092
Papers 1899–1935
.10 foot

Collector. Correspondence (1899–1923); notes (n.d.) for Bible lessons; a copy of a speech (1914) by William H. Murray; two issues (1935) of the *Student's Echo* from Commercial Extension, a correspondence school in Omaha, Nebraska; and an issue (1917) of *Patton's Magazine*, all belonging to Charles Parnell.

Parrington, Vernon Louis, Sr. (1871–1929) 1093
Papers 1893–1941
.10 foot

Professor. Correspondence (1908–1941); reports (ca. 1941); and a map (1931) regarding Parrington and his contributions to the University of Oklahoma, as well as efforts to name a university building for him. The collection also contains a roster of University of Oklahoma graduates from 1897–1908; a history (n.d.) of the University of Oklahoma Department of English; and a report (1908) submitted by Parrington to the Board of Regents, urging them to select a new campus plan and design for the University of Oklahoma. Also included is a map of the University of Washington at Seattle, Washington, showing the location of the Parrington Building there.

Patchell, O. W. (b. 1863)   1094
Land patent 1850
1 item

Lawyer. A patent (1850) from the United States to Mary W. Hancock, a Choctaw Indian from Mississippi, for land granted in accordance with the 1830 Treaty of Dancing Rabbit Creek.

Pate, J. D.   1095
Records 1904–1912
.25 foot

Physician. Ledgers (1904–1912) in which Pate recorded patients treated, services rendered, fees charged, and prescriptions recommended.

Patent Medicine Collection   1096
Printed materials 1884–1918
.33 foot

Subject collection. Advertisements for mad stones and medicines that offer cures for snake bite, dropsy, earache, diseases of the eye, and rupture.

Patrick, William (1831–1909)   1097
Papers 1831–1909
.10 foot

Pioneer immigrant. Photocopies of papers regarding the life of Irish immigrant William Patrick, including Patrick's diary (1857–1859) detailing his trip to California and Colorado; his Civil War service records (1864–1865); and his marriage certificate (1860).

Paul, Haskell   1098
Papers 1812–1951
.10 foot

Collector. Typewritten copies of letters (1930–1951) between the Paul family of Pauls Valley, Oklahoma, and relatives in the East, regarding the activities and genealogy of Smith Paul, founder of Pauls Valley, Oklahoma, before his immigration to Indian Territory.

Pauls Valley Chamber of Commerce Collection   1099
Printed materials 1890–1950
.10 foot

Municipal business organization. Typescripts (n.d.) regarding the history of Pauls Valley, Oklahoma; and publications (1940–1950), including a Pauls Valley promotional pamphlet and telephone directory.

Pauls Valley First National Bank Collection   1100
Records 1894–1925
11.50 feet

Bank. Financial records, including liability ledgers (1904–1910); depositor ledgers (1894–1911); discount registers (1902–1921); collection registers (1907–1924); cashier checks and drafts registers (1906–1925); stocks and securities registers (1910–1917); general journals (1916–1921); daily balance statements (1902–1921); capital stock share books (1903–1906); Liberty Loan ledgers (1917–1923); a minute book (1903–1921); and a treasurer's settlement report (1915–1920).

Unpublished finding aid available.

Pauls Valley State Training School for Boys Collection   1101
Records 1910–1939
28 feet

State reformatory. General correspondence (1924–1932); annual reports (1910–1936); storekeeper daily reports (1936–1939); commitment and parole records (1924–1929); registers of inmates (1924–1929); grade books (1924–1929); requisitions (1927–1938); remittance books (1931–1933); and related financial records (1924–1933), all reflecting the operation of Oklahoma's state reformatory for boys at Pauls Valley, Oklahoma.

Unpublished finding aid available.

Payne, David Lewis (1836–1884)   1102
Printed materials 1879–1939
1.33 feet

Colonist. Typescripts of news articles (1879–1939) from Kansas, Missouri, and Indian Territory newspapers, and also from historical journals, regarding the life of David L. Payne, his leadership of the Boomer Movement, and his attempts to colonize Indian Territory before the opening of the area to white settlement.

Unpublished finding aid available.

Payne, Okemah   1103
Papers 1902–1923
.10 foot

Collector. Correspondence (1908–1923) and business papers (1902–1917) of Tom Payne, a cowboy and businessman, reflecting his real estate and business interests in Indian Territory and early-day Oklahoma.

Pearson, John Cannon, Sr. (1862–1950)   1104
Papers 1879–1949
5.25 feet

Merchant and mayor. Correspondence (1892–1931) regarding the administration of the cities of Pierson, Iowa, and Marshall, Oklahoma; the business ventures in which Pearson was involved, including grain elevators and trade companies, coal bins, cattle herds, real estate, and ranches; and also regarding the Methodist Episcopal Church of Marshall, Oklahoma, the Masonic Order in Oklahoma, and the two hundredth anniversary celebrations of George Washington's birth; minutes of meetings (1906–1912) of the Capital Grain and Elevator Company, Marshall, Oklahoma; certificates (1906–1946) of incorporation of the Capital Grain and Elevator Company, of membership in the Methodist Episcopal Church of Marshall, and others issued to Pearson by the Oklahoma State Council of Defense; legal papers (1896–1930) from the businesses with which Pearson was associated, including leases, bills of sale, insurance documents, and deeds; programs (1909–1937) from convocations, annual gatherings, and reunions of the Masonic Order in Oklahoma; and publications (1879–1948), including books, periodicals, catalogs, newsletters, government documents, pamphlets, and brochures, regarding agriculture, the stock exchange system, the George Washington Monument, the coal and grain industries, and the Masonic Order in the United States and Oklahoma. This collection also includes membership rosters (1895–1946) for lodges and divisions of the Masonic Order in Oklahoma and Iowa, as well as the constitution, governing codes, and bylaws of the Oklahoma lodges, and the Grand Master decisions for Oklahoma and Indian territories, and the state of Oklahoma.

Unpublished finding aid available.

Pearson, Lola Clark (1871–1951)   1105
Papers 1888–1950
23 feet

Editor and clubwoman. Correspondence (1888–1950) regarding the personal affairs of Pearson, the General Federation of Women's Clubs, the *Oklahoma Farmer-Stockman* magazine, and the state and national Republican parties, including letters from notables such as Eleanor Roosevelt and Patrick Hurley; speeches (n.d.) delivered by Pearson regarding communism and other matters of national concern; scrapbooks (1920–1937) containing news clippings of a general nature; certificates (1915–1948) issued to Pearson by organizations; newspaper clippings (1919–1945) regarding women's clubs, politics, and Theodore Roosevelt; propaganda posters (1929) published by the Soviet Union; pins, ribbons, and medallions (1920) worn by Pearson as a delegate to the National Republican Convention of 1920; event programs (1918– 1948) published by women's clubs and other organizations, mostly relating to their annual conventions; minutes of meetings (1909– 1937) of General Federation of Women's Clubs committees, along with constitutions and governing bylaws (1909–1937). Also included in this collection are newspapers, magazines, pamphlets, and booklets, including *The Clubwoman, General Federation Bulletin*, and *General Federation News*.

Unpublished finding aid available.

Pearson, Ralph 1106
Ledger 1905–1912
1 item

Mortician. Register of funerals (1905–1912) from the Pearson Funeral Home in Walters, Oklahoma, with an inscription on the flyleaf, reading "D. L. Hannifin (Emb) Randlett, OK."

Pearson, Robert Shelton, Sr. (1874–1955) 1107
Papers 1923–1952
.33 foot

Artist. A scrapbook containing items reflecting Pearson's career, including correspondence (1923–1947), newspaper clippings and articles (1936–1952), ribbons (1933) awarded at a Latin American art exhibit in Florida, photographs of Pearson posing with his works, and a program (1947) of events celebrating the fortieth anniversary of Oklahoma statehood. Also included in this collection is a small landscape painting by Pearson.

Peck, Herbert Massey (b. 1890) 1108
Papers 1838–1961
.66 foot

Attorney. Correspondence (1838–1961) to Peck regarding his contributions to the development of Oklahoma and Oklahoma City, and regarding Mrs. Peck's ancestors; certificates and diplomas (1907–1958) awarded Peck by universities and by President Woodrow Wilson, and appointing him district attorney for the western district of Oklahoma. Also in this collection are presidential invitations to Peck from Herbert Hoover and Franklin D. Roosevelt. Other correspondents include Adm. William Halsey, Frank Buttram, Edward K. Gaylord, Robert S. Kerr, Elmer Thomas, Thomas P. Gore, and Robert A. Hefner.

Peeler, Paul   1109
Records 1905–1919
2 items

Collector. A financial journal (1907–1919) and a ledger (1905–1919) from the Rodger Mills Company Cooperative Association of Elk City, Oklahoma, containing a list of the association's stockholders and recording its financial transactions.

Pender, Winnfield Russell (b. 1888)   1110
Manuscript 1959
1 item

Author. An unpublished novel (1959) by Pender, entitled "The Treasures of Montezuma," which recounts an adventure-filled search for the fabled Aztec treasures.

Pendleton, Robert Henry (b. 1865)   1111
Records 1897–1949
1.33 feet

Dentist. Ledgers in which Pendleton recorded patient accounts, dental services rendered, and fees charged (1899–1907); income records (1897–1934); and appointment books (1924–1949).

Unpublished finding aid available.

Penney, Grace S. Jackson   1112
Papers 1908–1958
.50 foot

University employee. Subject files (1908–1958) regarding the history and function of the Extension Division of the University of Oklahoma. The files include materials relating to the office of the director of the Extension Division (1926–1951), interscholastic meets (1929–1952), the High School Science Service (1947–1952), WNAD radio (1946–1952), the Family Life Institute (1937–1951), Interschool Speech Service (1927–1952), and other education programs (1908–1958) of the Extension Division.

Perren, Donna Lea (b. ca. 1912)   1113
Records 1916–1924
.75 foot

Collector. Cash books (1920–1921) and individual account books (1916–1924) from the Perren Garage in Pond Creek, Oklahoma.

Perry, Adolphus Edward (1867–1939)   1114
Papers 1907–1939
.66 foot

Politician. Correspondence (1907–1936) regarding the Republican and Progressive Parties in national elections and in Oklahoma; typed lists (1908–1920) of Republican Party officers and leaders in Oklahoma; *Proceedings* of the Republican Party Convention in the state's Fourth Congressional District in 1908; and newspaper articles (1908–1939) regarding the career and death of Perry.

Perry, John C. (b. 1894)   1115
Printed materials 1909–1953
.10 foot

Physician. Publications (1936–1953) containing information about John C. Perry and his father, M. L. Perry, and a typed list of cancer patients attended by H. D. Murdock, a partner of Perry. The publications include the *Bulletin* of the Tulsa County Medical Society (1936–1944) and *The Roar* (1938–1953) of the Tulsa Lions Club.

Perryman, Joseph M. (1833–1896)   1116
Papers 1883–1901
.10 foot

Indian chief. Typescripts of newspaper articles (1883–1901), including editorials, proclamations, and reports relating to Perryman, principal chief of the Creek Nation, his term of office, 1884–1888, and his service as a delegate from the Creek Nation to the Indian International Council.

Perryman, Legus Chouteau (1838–1922) 1117
Papers 1887–1907
.33 foot

Indian chief. Typescripts of newspaper articles (1887–1907) relating to Perryman as a principal chief of the Creek Nation, the Dawes Commission, Perryman's ouster from office in 1895, and his involvement with a plan for Creek Indians to emigrate to Mexico in 1905.

Peters, Kay (b. 1885) 1118
Papers 1893–1935
.10 foot

Photographer. An account (n.d.) by Peters of his participation in the settlement of the Cherokee Strip during the land run of 1893; correspondence (1904) regarding settlement of the estate of a deceased relative of Peters; one warranty deed (1900) issued in Garfield County, Oklahoma Territory; and a Garfield County, Oklahoma, tax assessment list (1927), indicating the rates of taxation for farm and household items.

Peterson, Horace Cornelius (1902–1952) 1119
Papers 1918–1951
9 feet

Professor. Correspondence (1918–1920) regarding his books, *Propaganda For War* and *Opponents of War*, from readers and notables, including Norman Thomas, George Creek, J. Edgar Hoover, and Roger Baldwin; manuscripts and galley proofs of the two books; scrapbooks (1918–1920) containing reviews and news items regarding his books; Peterson's research notes (n.d.) on the loyalty oath in Oklahoma, including that of the University of Oklahoma; typescripts of a journal (1918–1919) kept by Ike Hoover, a member of President Woodrow Wilson's party in Paris, France, after World War I, and a report on the negotiations for peace and an eventual peace treaty; and publications (1917–1951) regarding propaganda and World War I. Also included in this collection is a typescript account (1952) of Peterson's accidental death in a University of Oklahoma classroom building, written by Alfred B. Sears and including Sears's recommendations for removing the hazards which contributed to the death.

Unpublished finding aid available.

Peterson, Robert V. (1904–1985)   1120
Printed materials 1975–1984
.66 foot

Journalist. Clippings of newspaper articles by Peterson and others regarding Oklahoma cities and towns, the economy, the standard of living, and Robert V. Peterson's travels abroad.

Pettyjohn, (Mrs.) John   1121
Papers 1910–1911
4 items

Collector. An undated letter from Will Rogers to his father, Clement Vann Rogers; and three letters (1910–1911) from Betty (Mrs. Will) Rogers to Clement Vann Rogers concerning Will Rogers's horse act.

Phi Beta Kappa Collection   1122
Records 1970–1999
.66 foot

Academic honor society. Correspondence (1971–1993); annual reports (1988–1992); agendas and meeting minutes (1979–1999); printed materials (1970–1998); scholarship application essays (1986–1993); and membership lists (1970–1999) of the Alpha of Oklahoma Chapter of Phi Beta Kappa. Other materials include the constitution and bylaws, and records on alumni members, scholarships, and annual banquets of the Alpha of Oklahoma Chapter of Phi Beta Kappa. Also included are papers (1989) regarding the Beta of Oklahoma Chapter of Phi Beta Kappa at the University of Tulsa, Oklahoma.

Phi Delta Theta Collection   1123
Certificate 1918
1 item

Fraternity. Initiation certificate (1918) issued to J. William Cordell by Phi Delta Theta fraternity at the University of Oklahoma.

Phillips Pamphlet Collection   1124
Printed materials 1820–1978
8 feet

Pamphlet collection. Pamphlets (1820–1978) containing information on U.S. government-tribal relations, and U.S. government Indian policy. Materials include memorials from Indian delegations concerning allotment, land transfer, and per capita payments; tribal agreements with the Dawes Commission; annual messages of Indian nations; legal cases argued before the Oklahoma Supreme Court and the U.S. Supreme Court; and annual reports of the Board of Indian Commissioners. Other pamphlets concern Oklahoma statehood, mining and oil and gas rights on Indian lands, railroads in Indian Territory, and claims of Old Settler Cherokees.

Unpublished finding aid available.

Phillips, George Wendel (d. ca. 1950)   1125
Records 1901–1943
.50 foot

Physician. Patient account books (1911–1943) in which Phillips recorded fees charged; and certificates and diplomas (1901–1919) awarded Phillips by schools of medicine and by the states of Kentucky and Oklahoma, granting him the privilege of practicing medicine.

Phillips, Leon Chase (1890–1958)   1126
Papers 1933–1951
10 feet

Governor. Correspondence (1934–1951) regarding Phillips's gubernatorial, legislative, and political affairs; scrapbooks (1936–1941) containing loose news clippings on his political career; publications (1933–1941) about political conventions, along with event programs from numerous organizations; trial transcripts (1943–1944) from cases involving the state of Oklahoma; speeches (1936–1944) delivered by Phillips; government documents (1940); cartoons (n.d.) regarding Phillips and his political career, as well as politics and state government; and certificates (1932–1951) awarded Phillips by businesses, civic organizations, and state government. Also included in this collection is a leather-bound copy of Phillips's 1939 inaugural address.

Unpublished finding aid available.

Pi Kappa Alpha Collection   1127
Records 1933–1943
6 feet

Fraternity. Records (1933–1943) of district fourteen of Pi Kappa Alpha fraternity, encompassing Oklahoma, Texas, and Arkansas, of which Ted W. Beaird and Herbert Scott were district presidents. The records consist of chapter files (1933–1943), including correspondence, reports, minutes, and financial statements from individual chapters; correspondence (1933–1938) with alumni and the Supreme Council; correspondence (1934–1940) concerning petitions, installations, and conventions; convention reports and publicity (1937–1941); and the constitution and bylaws (1933–1941).

Unpublished finding aid available.

Piburn, Anne Ross 1128
Papers 1883–1958
.25 foot

Collector. Programs (1937–1958) of the yearly reunions of Cherokee Seminary graduates; a report (1955) regarding the old Murrell home in Tahlequah, Indian Territory; a report (1953) regarding New Echota, Cherokee Nation; a publication (1954) of the Cherokee Foundation, Inc., entitled *Tsa La Gi' Ga Nah Se Da*'; an undated list of freedmen granted Cherokee citizenship; and memorials (1883–1899) of the Cherokee Nation and its delegation to the U.S. Congress.

Pickard, Clyde C. 1129
Papers 1893–1952
8 feet

Real estate agent. Personal correspondence (1918–1952); business correspondence (1920–1947); financial records, including bank notes (1912–1946), deeds and leases (1914–1946), daily and individual account ledgers; and certificates, including a homestead certificate (1893), all from Pickard's real estate business in Norman, Oklahoma.

Unpublished finding aid available.

Pierce, Thomas Franklin, Sr. (b. 1867) 1130
Papers 1867–1957
.10 foot

Professor. An autobiographical manuscript (n.d.) that includes Pierce's experiences as an educator in Indian Territory and Oklahoma; poetry (n.d.) by Pierce regarding the virtues of Oklahoma; and a manuscript account (ca. 1930) of Pierce's visit to the Grand Canyon.

Pitchlynn, Peter Perkins (1806–1881)   1131
Papers 1815–1888
2.75 feet

Indian chief. Correspondence (1824–1881) of Pitchlynn with prominent citizens and family members in the Choctaw Nation regarding events and troubles within the nation; Pitchlynn's personal journals (1815); Pitchlynn's diary (1828–1832); official reports (1825–1841) of the Choctaw Academy and Missionary Station in Kentucky; and Pitchlynn family records (1806–1867). The collection also includes a signed copy of the articles of surrender and peace negotiated between the Choctaw Nation and the United States at the close of the Civil War, and extensive correspondence reflecting the state of the Choctaw Nation just prior to and during the Civil War years, with special regard to slavery.

Unpublished finding aid available.

Pittman, F. D.   1132
Letter 1930
1 item

Teacher. A letter (1930) written by F. D. Pittman, a teacher from McAlester, Oklahoma, to Louis Dakil, in which Pittman describes his coming to Indian Territory in 1895 to teach, and the growth of and changes in the town of McAlester between 1903 and 1930.

Pittsburg County Medical Society Collection   1133
Ledger 1917–1936
1 item

Professional organization. A ledger (1917–1936) containing the minutes and proceedings of the Pittsburg County (Oklahoma) Medical Society, including membership rosters and physicians' obituaries.

Planned Parenthood Association Collection   1134
Papers ca. 1935–1958
1.66 feet

Nonprofit organization. Correspondence (1937–1947); reprints (1939–1955) of articles from newspapers, periodicals, and professional journals, and pamphlets relating to birth control; an unbound copy (1938) of *Season of Birth*, by Ellsworth Huntington; and a bibliography (1939) of publications on birth control and related topics.

Unpublished finding aid available.

Plummer, William A. 1135
Papers 1870–1895
.10 foot

Homesteader. Letters (1870–1895) from William A. Plummer to relatives in Pennsylvania, concerning homesteading, agriculture, real estate, the local economy, politics, religion, Indians, and the weather in the Wichita, Kansas, area. Several letters between other Plummer family members are also included.

[273]

Pollard, Tildue H. (b. 1877) 1136
Certificates 1903–1908
5 items

Physician. Certificates (1903–1904) issued to Pollard by Arkansas, Oklahoma, Indian Territory, and the Choctaw Nation, granting him the privilege of practicing medicine and pharmacy within their borders.

Pomeroy, Henry Martyn (1830–1916) 1137
Papers 1859–1860
.10 foot

Bookseller. A photocopy and typescript of a portion of the diary (1859–1860) of Henry M. Pomeroy, in which he recorded his overland journey to California, with colorful descriptions of the gold fields and the cities of Los Angeles and San Francisco, California. Also included are the minutes of a vigilante committee near Omaha, Nebraska, as well as an account of a massacre in Oregon Territory.

Pond, Nina Louise Phillipi (b. ca. 1905) 1138
Papers 1893–1968
.33 foot

Homemaker. Typescripts (1893–1950) relating to the history of the Methodist Episcopal Church of Medford, Oklahoma Territory and Oklahoma, the history of the Grant County (Oklahoma) Historical Society, and the statement of intent of the Grant County (Oklahoma) Film Library; reports (1965–1967) of services rendered by the United Methodist Church's Oklahoma Conference Ministry to the Deaf, as well as the minutes (1966–1968) of its governing board; programs (1950–1953, 1967) of the worship services of the Methodist church of Medford, and of women's civic groups in Medford, including the Mother's Club, Business and Professional Women's Club, and the Women's Society of Christian Science; and publications (1952–1968) such as *The Broadcaster*, published by the Methodist church in Medford, and *The Lamplighter*, published by the Methodist Church's Oklahoma Conference Ministry to the Deaf. Also included in this collection is a cartoon history of Oklahoma, 1541–1939, published by the *Daily Oklahoman* in 1939.

Porter First National Bank Collection   1139
Records 1900–1933
12 feet

Bank. Correspondence (1910–1916) and financial records (1900–1933) from the First National Bank of Porter, Oklahoma, including daybooks, tellers' cash books, discount registers, distribution of expenses registers, draft registers, note registers, reconciliation of accounts books, and loan registers, along with minutes of a predecessor bank, the American Bank of Porter, Oklahoma.

Porter, Joseph L. (b. 1874)   1140
Papers 1899–1938
.25 foot

Banker. The diaries (1899–1938) of Joseph L. Porter of Lawton, Oklahoma, regarding life there and his experiences as a banker and as longtime treasurer of the local board of education.

Porter, Pleasant (1840–1907)   1141
Papers 1871–1902
1.66 feet

Indian chief. Typescripts of correspondence (1894–1901); speeches (1893–1907); and newspaper articles (1871–1902) relating to Porter as a principal chief of the Creek Nation and president of the Sequoyah Convention, the allotment of lands by the Dawes Commission, the termination of tribal government, and the movement for separate statehood for Indian Territory.

Unpublished finding aid available.

Posey, Irving   1142
Diploma 1916
1 item

Student. A diploma (1916) issued to Irving Posey by Phoenix Union High School of Phoenix, Arizona.

Poster Collection 1143
Printed materials 1884–2001
800 items

Graphic arts collection. Posters (1884–2001), full color and black and white, published in the United States and Europe, publicizing wild west shows, traveling medicine shows, vaudeville acts, theatrical events, political elections, and the military services of the United States. Also included are governmental propaganda posters, published in the United States, France, and Italy, during World Wars I and II, and regarding conservation of essential materials, patriotism, liberty loans, military recruitment, and other wartime themes.

Unpublished finding aid available.

Postmasters of Oklahoma Collection 1144
Records 1890–1915
7 items

Subject collection. Ledgers (1890–1915) containing equipment inventories and listings of domestic money orders issued by U.S. post offices in five towns and settlements in the territory and state of Oklahoma.

Pottawatomie County Medical Society Collection 1145
Records 1907–1946
2 items

Professional organization. A publication (1946) of the Pottawatomie County (Oklahoma) Medical Society, entitled *The Bulletin*, along with a scrapbook belonging to the women's auxiliary of the society and containing the history of the auxiliary, which claimed to be the first women's auxiliary of a county medical society in the United States. The scrapbook also contains a copy of the first book of minutes and proceedings (1907) of the auxiliary, reflecting its preparations to host the first convention of the Oklahoma State Medical Association in 1907.

Potts, Harry Walton 1146
Printed materials 1955
3 items

Collector. "Charter Night" event programs (1955) of the newly established Madill and Mannsville, Oklahoma Lions Clubs, and a newspaper article (1955) regarding the establishment of a Lions Club in Lexington, Oklahoma.

Powell, Peter J. (b. 1928) 1147
Manuscript 1930–1966
1 item

Priest. An unedited version of Powell's book *Sweet Medicine*, published by the University of Oklahoma Press (1969), which discusses the Cheyenne Indian sun dance and other religious ceremonies.

Prague National Bank Collection 1148
Records 1902–1945
10 feet

Bank. Financial records (1906–1945) from the Prague (Oklahoma) National Bank, including balance ledgers (1906–1929); daily statement ledgers (1929–1939); daybooks (1932–1941); discount registers (1933–1945); liability registers (1929–1938); a bond register (1929–1937); certificates of deposit registers (1920–1928); and a general ledger (1928–1941). The collection also includes a liability ledger (1923–1936) from the Paden National Bank; balance ledgers (1902–1906); a tellers' cash book (1902–1903); and a journal (1902–1903) from the Lincoln County Bank, predecessor of the Prague National Bank.

Unpublished finding aid available.

Pratt, Horace 1149
Printed materials 1864
2 items

Indian chief. Typescripts of two conscription acts (1864) by the Chickasaw Nation legislature, organizing Chickasaw Indian troops for service in the Confederate States Army.

Pray, Joseph (1911–1990) 1150
Printed materials 1930
1 item

Professor. A booklet (1930) entitled "An Appreciation of James Shannon Buchanan by William Bennett Bizzell and Others," published upon Buchanan's death.

Prevost, Charles Albert 1151
Papers 1918–1919
.10 foot

Investor. Correspondence, advertisements, and stock certificates (1918–

1919) from the Okmulgee-Youngstown Oil Company and the Indian Chief Oil and Gas Company, along with an advertisement (1919) regarding the productivity of the Okmulgee (Oklahoma) oil field.

Price, Charles Gary (1882–1950)   1152
Papers 1903–1918
.33 foot

Physician. A notebook (1917–1918) containing transcripts of lectures given at Camp Greenleaf, Georgia, to military physicians, and poetry (1918), presumedly, by Price; a book (1903) entitled *Pocket Cyclopedia of Medicine and Surgery*, along with certificates and diplomas (1904–1914) awarded Price by medical associations and schools, including licenses to practice medicine in Oklahoma, Texas, and Georgia.

Price, Walter   1153
Playbills 1935
.10 foot

Vaudevillian. Playbills (1935) advertising vaudeville and theatre productions in which Price participated.

Prickett, Theodocia Cralle   1154
Papers 1902–1995
.33 foot

Collector. Correspondence (1902–1978); biographical data and memoirs (1903–1980); newspaper clippings, photocopies, and publications (1913–1995); and photographs regarding the life and career of University of Oklahoma president emeritus Stratton D. Brooks and family.

Prisoner of War Camps Collection   1155
Papers 1943–1983
.10 foot

Subject collection. Correspondence (1945–1946); publications (1945–1946); and newspaper articles (1943–1983) regarding the German prisoners of war interned in Oklahoma during World War II, and the prisoner of war camps in which they lived. Also included in this collection are the handwritten notes (1945–1946) University of Oklahoma history professor Morris L. Wardell used for his lectures to the prisoners regarding American democracy. Wardell's notes and the correspondence in this collection reflect the University of Oklahoma's efforts to educate the Germans concerning U.S. civics and government.

Proclamation Collection 1156
Papers 1868–1887
1 foot

Subject collection. Proclamations issued by governors and Indian chiefs recognizing special days and events in several states and territories of the United States. Included are days of thanksgiving, fasting, prayer and humiliation, Arbor Day, and mourning for the death of President James A. Garfield.

Unpublished finding aid available.

Proctor, C. L. 1157
Printed material 1918
1 item

Collector. A copy of the Saint Patrick's Day issue of *The Oklahoma Daily* for 1918. Printed in green ink, this issue of the University of Oklahoma student newspaper is dedicated to the engineering students of the university and their adopted saint. It bears the banner headline "St. Pat Ran the Snakes Out of Ireland and the Engineers Will Run the Kaiser Out of Germany."

Propaganda Collection 1158
Printed materials 1939–1954
.25 foot

Subject collection. Brochures, flyers, and leaflets (1939–1954) published in the United States, Great Britain, North Korea, and Australia during World War II and the Korean War. These include British publications (1943–1944) regarding World War II, as well as a typescript (n.d.) on U.S. culture and customs, given to British airmen en route to America for training; leaflets (n.d.) dropped on U.S. troops in Korea by the Chinese, advising them of the benefits of immediate surrender, as well as the procedures for doing so; and a U.S. government list (1950) of all political and social groups in this country considered subversive.

Pruitt Gin Company Collection 1159
Records 1940–1946
5 feet

Cotton gin. Daily gin reports (1940–1946); weight records (1941–1945); customer account ledgers (1940–1945); and financial records (1941–1946) of the Pruitt Gin Company of Lindsay, Oklahoma. These records reflect the trends which affected cotton gins throughout Oklahoma during this period, including the limitations and prosperity brought about by wartime conditions.

Unpublished finding aid available.

Pryor, William W. (1882–1946)   **1160**
Printed materials ca. 1920–1938
6.66 feet

Attorney. Briefs (1920–1946) of cases reviewed before the supreme court of Oklahoma, along with related correspondence (1927–1934) and a newspaper obituary (1946) of Pryor, who served as counsel to the court.

Unpublished finding aid available.

Pugmire, Donald Ross (d. 1958)   **1161**
Printed materials 1935–1958
.66 foot

Professor. Reports (1950–1958) issued by government and private agencies regarding education and schooling in Oklahoma, and authored, in many cases, by Pugmire; and Pugmire's doctoral dissertation (1936), entitled "The Administration of Personnel in Correctional Institutions in New York State."

Pumpkin, Thomas (Tah Sa Co Fah Ahwee) (1865–1899)   **1162**
Enrollment card 1902–1909
1 item

Indian allottee. The enrollment record of Thomas Pumpkin (Tah Sa Co Fah Ahwee), a Euchee Creek Indian, as created by the Dawes Commission in 1902. Subsequent notes on the record, dated 1904–1909, establish that Pumpkin died in 1899, three years before being enrolled by the government, and ten years before the Commissioner to the Five Civilized Tribes approved his enrollment.

Purdum, Helen   **1163**
Printed materials 1905–1907
5 items

Collector. Leather postcards (1905) sent from Ardmore, Indian Territory; and leaflets (1907) published by the Oklahoma Anti-Saloon League and addressed to the voters of Durant, Indian Territory, petitioning them to approve prohibition when Oklahoma is admitted to the Union.

Quapaw, Oklahoma, Town Records Collection   1164
Records 1917–1945
1 foot

Municipality. Minutes (1931–1938) of the town board of trustees; occupational licenses (1925–1941) granted to Quapaw merchants; correspondence (1945) received by the town mayor regarding the possibility of Federal Works Agency work and planning; and municipal contracts (1919–1920) for water, along with receipts of payment (1939–1941) for the same. Also included in this collection is one ledger (1917) containing the town treasurer's records.

Quigley, Michael   1165
Papers 1857
1 item

Immigrant. Naturalization papers of Ireland native, Michael Quigley, given at Mayesville, Kentucky, in 1857.

Quong, Jennie Lou Grey   1166
Papers 1923–1953
2 items

Artist. Photocopies of manuscripts (1923–1953) regarding the Korean War and the death of Quong's husband in that conflict, and the internment of Japanese-Americans in this country during World War II.

Rachlin, Carol   1167
Papers 1818–1966
2.25 feet

Anthropologist. Correspondence (1954–1974); interviews (1958–1976); research notes (n.d.); manuscripts (n.d.); and publications (1818–1958) relating to Rachlin's research on the Sac and Fox and the Shawnee Indians. Also included are field notes (1954) from her archaeological research on the weaving of the mound-builders.

Unpublished finding aid available.

Rader, Jesse Lee (b. 1883)   1168
Papers 1901–1952
.75 foot

University librarian. Correspondence (1906–1953) from friends and library associates, regarding the Oklahoma Library Commission and Oklahoma Library Association, including a letter from University of Oklahoma president David Ross Boyd, regarding Boyd's dismissal and the dismissal of numerous faculty at the university, including Rader, by Governor C. N. Haskell; postcards (1907) of Virginia scenes; a speech (1952) delivered by Rader at a dinner in his honor; minutes (1952) of meetings of the Oklahoma Library Association; student grade reports (1905–1906) issued to Rader by the University of Oklahoma; consumer rationing books (1942–1943) used by Rader and family during World War II; publications (1901–1952), including a newspaper, the front page of which is devoted to news of the first oil well in the Oklahoma City oil field; an original book jacket for Adolph Hitler's *Mein Kampf*; a University of Oklahoma student handbook (1904–1905); a magazine, *The Delta*, published by Sigma Nu; newspaper articles regarding the presidency of Theodore Roosevelt; certificates (1905–1951) issued to Rader; programs (1909–1910) of ceremonies and events conducted by University of Oklahoma fraternities and the Oklahoma Library Association; and constitutions and bylaws (1905–1907) of the Oklahoma Library Association and of University of Oklahoma student clubs and societies, including the Websterian Literary Society and Kanuntaklage Dramatic Club. Also included in this collection is an anthropometrical table (1902) used by the University of Oklahoma to measure and chart student physiques.

Rader, Katherine   1169
Papers 1908–1973
.66 foot

Collector. Correspondence (1908–1971) and newspaper clippings (1973); one scrapbook (1909–1973) and five photographs (n.d.) documenting the career of Jesse L. Rader, librarian at the University of Oklahoma (1909–1952); and one scrapbook (1909–1957) by Fanny Rader, documenting the history of Theta Gamma chapter of Delta Delta Delta sorority.

Rainey, George (b. 1866)   1170
Papers 1880–1968
3 feet

Author. Rainey's correspondence files (1902–1954); newspaper clippings (1910–1954), including reviews of Rainey's books and other articles relating to the Rainey family and Oklahoma history; diaries and notebooks (1880–1940); pamphlets and booklets (1903–1968); and manuscripts by Rainey and others relating to Oklahoma and U.S. history; certificates (1905–1937) issued to Rainey; a copy of a patent (1904) for an adding machine; and a billfold (ca. 1890) carried by Rainey during the Oklahoma land run of 1893.

Unpublished finding aid available.

Ralls, Joseph G., Sr. (1864–1933)   1171
Papers 1870–1924
9.33 feet

Attorney. Correspondence (1870–1924) and legal case files (1890–1924) from Ralls's law practice, including those concerning his representation of Choctaw Indians during the allotment of Choctaw lands and townsite payments.

Ramsay, J. J.   1172
Records 1895–1934
.10 foot

Collector. Tax receipts (1895–1934) issued to Ramsay by Kay County, Oklahoma Territory and Oklahoma, listing the annual taxes levied by the county for those years.

Ramsay, James Ross (1821–ca. 1890)   1173
Manuscript ca. 1890
1 item

Missionary. A typescript of Ramsay's autobiography (ca. 1890), in which he relates his education and experiences as a Presbyterian missionary among the Seminoles, hardships during the Civil War, and accounts of medical treatment.

Ramsey, Flora Belle Simmons (b. 1866)   1174
Papers 1889–1897
.10 foot

Pioneer. Manuscripts (n.d.) by Ramsey recording her impressions and experiences (1889–1897) as a participant in the land run of 1889 and as a homemaker in Payne County, Oklahoma Territory.

The November 1841 issue of *Siwinowe Kesibwi* (*The Shawnee Sun*) is one of two known surviving copies of this rare newspaper. Published from 1835 to 1844 at the Shawnee Baptist Mission in Kansas, it was the first exclusively Indian-language periodical printed in the United States. The paper was begun by Jotham Meeker of the Shawnee Baptist Mission, who also created orthographies for the languages of the Indians he served. From the Alan Farley Collection.

Randall, William B. (b. 1882)   1175
Papers 1905–1929
.10 foot

Oil field contractor. A time book (1905–1906) kept by Randall while an oil rig contractor; a life insurance policy (1919) issued to Randall; a certificate (1919) of his election as a trustee of Ramona, Oklahoma; and numerous novelty postcards (1907–1913). Also in this collection are a high school diploma (1914) issued by Ramona High School; a map (1904) of Oklahoma and Indian Territories; and a blueprint (1934) for an oil field apparatus.

Ransom, Will Hewitt (1878–1955)   1176
Papers 1847–1955
.33 foot

Typographer. Correspondence (1847–1869) regarding general news and a packet boat trip in 1847; a diary (1877) of an unidentified woman regarding her experiences as a teacher and her life in general; scrapbooks (1877–1882) containing calling cards, news clippings, and correspondence; and publications (1882–1955) including a premium list from the New England Agricultural Society, a teachers' memorandum, and a catalog of publications by the Philip C. Duschnes Company. Also in this collection are diplomas (1876–1878) issued to Ransom's relatives by Olivet College in Michigan and by Michigan State Normal School.

Rawlinson, Sally   1177
Poster ca. 1926
1 item

Collector. A 14" x 21" black on white poster (ca. 1926) advertising a football game to be played at the University of Oklahoma's Owen Field, Norman, Oklahoma.

Ray, Dee Ann   1178
Printed materials 1981–1985
1 foot

Librarian. Newspaper articles (1981–1985) by Dee Ann Ray regarding the history of Clinton and Cordell, Oklahoma; a copy of the "Pioneer Edition" (1984) of the *Cordell Beacon*; and a copy of the "Anadarko Oil and Gas Appreciation Edition" (1982) of the *Clinton Daily News*.

Unpublished finding aid available.

Ray, Grace Ernestine   1179
Papers 1939–1982
26 feet

Professor. Manuscripts (1947–1980) of articles and books by journalism professor Grace Ernestine Ray; journals and newspapers (1939–1968) containing her articles; printed materials (ca. 1940–1970) and other papers used for research; and Ray's professional correspondence (1939–1982).

[285]

Ray, Jessie Dimple Newby (b. ca. 1888)   1180
Papers 1909–1928
.10 foot

Collector. Ledgers (1919–1928) recording the daily business of the H. Warner Newby Rooming House in Oklahoma City, Oklahoma; and event programs (1909–1910) of the University of Oklahoma Class of 1910, including its graduation and senior banquet programs, along with event programs for the Senate Literary Society and the Zetaletheans. Also included is the commencement program (1905) for the Logan County High School in Guthrie, Oklahoma Territory.

Reagles, James, Jr.   1181
Papers 1864–1868
.10 foot

Army surgeon. Correspondence (1866–1868) to and from Reagles regarding personal matters, his assignment at Fort Arbuckle, Indian Territory, and some Indians with whom he had contact. The collection also contains Reagles's diary (1864–1867), in which he recorded his experiences as a U.S. Army surgeon in Virginia during the Civil War, and his post-war experiences with the U.S. Tenth Cavalry at Fort Arbuckle, including English translations of Chickasaw, Choctaw, and Comanche words, impressions of Indian tribes, and a sketch of a Caddo village.

Ream, Ruth K.   1182
Papers 1909–1915
.33 foot

Collector. Ream's invitations to parties, weddings, and high school commencements (1910–1915), along with a report card (1909) from a Canadian County, Oklahoma, school and a souvenir (1915) from Union City Public School, Union Township, Oklahoma.

Reaves, Samuel Watson 1183
Papers 1897–1914
.33 foot

Student. Lecture notes (1897–1914) taken by Reaves while a math and physics student at Cornell University and the University of Chicago.

Records, Ralph Hayden 1184
Papers 1871–1968
2 feet

Professor. Magazine and journal articles (1946–1968) regarding historiography, along with a typewritten manuscript (1871–1899) by L. S. Records, entitled "The Recollections of a Cowboy of the Seventies and Eighties," regarding the lives of cowboys and ranchers in frontier-era Kansas and in the Cherokee Strip of Oklahoma Territory, including a detailed account of Records's participation in the land run of 1893.

Unpublished finding aid available.

Rector, Newton (1839–1935) 1185
Printed materials 1913–1935
10 items

Physician. Newspaper clippings (1917–1935) regarding the careers and deaths of Dr. and Mrs. Newton Rector; medallions (1913–1932) issued by the Oklahoma State Medical Association; and Rector's student admittance card issued by the University of Nashville, Tennessee, for observance of anatomy and surgery sessions in its medical school.

Red Rabbit Oil Company Collection 1186
Ledger 1919
1 item

Petroleum company. A ledger (1919) containing the articles of incorporation, certificate of incorporation, and minutes of the stockholders' meetings of the Red Rabbit Oil Company of Oklahoma City, Oklahoma.

Redwine Trading Company Collection 1187
Records 1896–1925
21 feet

Mercantile firm. Ledgers (1896–1922) in which the daily commerce of this Spiro, Oklahoma, general store and cotton-ginning operation were recorded. Among these are day books (1898–1918); cash books and notary records (1904–1906); funeral records (1901–1911); ginners' cotton books (1908–1918); and books (1903–1925) recording cotton bought and sold. Also included in this collection are a petition (n.d.) of Spiro, Indian Territory, regarding the relocation of the U.S. District Court, and the treasurer's records (1907) from a Spiro-area school district. The records of this collection span thirty years and reflect the economic conditions of the Choctaw Nation, of Indian Territory, and of the state of Oklahoma, including periods of depression and prosperity.

Unpublished finding aid available.

Redwine, Wilburn Nash (b. 1862)   **1188**
Papers 1898–1943
16 feet

Attorney. Correspondence (1898–1943) regarding Redwine's legal practice in Spiro, Oklahoma; files on legal cases (1898–1943) in which Redwine was involved; published legal briefs (n.d.); expense ledgers (1904–1917), in which Redwine recorded the nature of cases and the fees charged; and political posters and leaflets (1910, 1924) published during Redwine's campaigns for election to the state senate and supreme court. The expense ledgers prior to November 1907 reflect legal services provided for a number of Choctaw Indian families experiencing difficulty receiving or claiming allotments.

Unpublished finding aid available.

Reed, Gertrude Clark   **1189**
Printed materials 1907
2 items

Collector. Photocopies of an article and a photograph (1907) from the *Globe Dispatch and Democrat* of Guthrie, Oklahoma, regarding Oklahoma statehood.

Reed, Horace   **1190**
Papers 1901–1951
.10 foot

Physician. Typescripts (n.d.) of five articles by Reed regarding the treatment of appendicitis and ulcers and the art of surgery; along with certificates and diplomas (1901–1951) awarded Reed by medical schools and boards.

Reed, Milo T.   1191
Papers 1936–1938
2 items

Collector. A petition (n.d.) signed by approximately eighty citizens of Seminole County, Oklahoma, declaring their intent to capture the murderer of a fellow citizen and listing the rewards pledged by each for the capture of the criminal; and copies of letters (1936–1938) to Reed from Isaiah and Mary Rutherford regarding family affairs.

Reeds, Chester Albert (b. 1882)   1192
Printed materials 1907–1937
.33 foot

Geologist and museum curator. Reprints (1907–1937) of articles on geology by Chester Albert Reeds, an alumnus of the University of Oklahoma class of 1906, and curator of the American Museum of Natural History.

Reeds, Clarence   1193
Papers 1895–1928
.75 foot

Collector. A script for the play, "Our American Cousin," produced by the students of the University of Oklahoma in 1905; and publications (1905–1928) of the University of Oklahoma, including *The Sooner, The Umpire, The University Umpire, The University Newsletter, The University Oklahoman, The Sooner Alumnus,* and the program for the 1928 football season. Also in this collection are a number of books (ca. 1895) in German and artifacts (1905), including a beret and a football sweater marked "05."

Reese, Jim E.   1194
Printed materials 1943
1 item

Collector. A photocopy of a magazine feature (1943) by Dr. J. Frank Dobie, entitled, "Old Bill, Confederate Ally," a fiction piece regarding a beloved dog during the Civil War.

Reeve, Lelia Hudson   1195
Papers 1880–1922
.10 foot

Pioneer. Typewritten manuscripts (ca. 1922) by Reeve, entitled "Early Days in Western Kansas," "Santa Fe Trail," and "Early Days in Oklahoma."

Religious Denominations of Oklahoma Collection   1196
Printed materials 1895–1950
2.33 feet

Subject collection. Publications (1895–1950) of several religious denominations and individual churches in Oklahoma, including Baptists, Catholics, Congregationalists, Episcopalians, Lutherans, Mennonites, Methodists, and Presbyterians. These printed materials include church bulletins, directories, conference proceedings, and church pamphlets.

Unpublished finding aid available.

Renner, John W.   1197
Papers 1949–1991
9 feet

Professor. Manuscripts and personal papers relating to the life of John W. Renner, Professor of Science Education at the University of Oklahoma. The collection includes articles and notes (1949–1960); and manuscripts, publications and textbooks (1951–1979) by Renner and others on physics and science education.

Unpublished finding aid available.

Rennie, Albert (1863–1948)   1198
Papers 1900–1951
14.50 feet

Attorney. Family and business correspondence (1900–1951); legal documents (1900–1939); and printed material (1900–1951) belonging to Rennie, a Pauls Valley, Oklahoma, attorney. Much of the material relates to real estate transactions, including land allotted to Choctaw and Chickasaw Indians.

Unpublished finding aid available.

Renze, Dolores C.   1199
Printed materials 1892–1898
5 items

Collector. Proclamations (1892–1898) issued by the governors of Oklahoma Territory regarding the official observance of Columbus Day and Thanksgiving Day in the territory.

Reynolds, Norman E., Jr.   1200
Papers 1951–1965
4 feet

Legislator and attorney. Briefs and other legal documents, correspondence, research files, maps, and printed materials relating to reapportionment in Oklahoma (1951–1965) and to the Oklahoma Turnpike Authority (1960–1961).

Unpublished finding aid available.

Rhoads, Earl Roaine   1201
Papers 1936–1949
.33 foot

U.S. Marine. Correspondence (1936–1944) from Rhoads to his brother Sherman, his sister-in-law Ruth, and his nieces Shirley and Gaytha, from military posts in the United States, Iceland, and Guam. The collection also includes correspondence between family members including Rhoads's parents, Shirley and Lettie Rhoads, and his sister Della. The collection contains a diary (1942) kept by Rhoads while in Iceland; funeral register pages and a funeral announcement (1949) when his body was returned to the United States along with the U.S. flag covering his coffin; Rhoads's military identification card; six medals, including the Purple Heart; and war ration books used by the Rhoads family during the war.

Rhodes, Charles B. (1862–1949)   1202
Papers 1864–1950
.75 foot

U.S. marshal. Correspondence (1895–1946) regarding the Indian Territory Day celebration of 1939 and regarding Thomas Rhodes's experiences in the military during World War I; certificates (1864–1912) appointing Charles B. Rhodes as a teacher in Arkansas and in the Cherokee Nation and as a U.S. deputy marshal, and exempting a relative of Rhodes from military service during the Civil War; news clippings (1905–1950) regarding lawmen, outlaws, judges, and Rhodes; postcards (1929–1949) of Colorado's Royal Gorge bridge and of the Southern Belle Railroad; a score (1894) of a patriotic hymn composed by a youth from Indian Territory; a poster (1900) advertising a reunion of the Old Settlers Band of the Cherokee Indians; poetry and short stories (1894–1942) regarding Oklahoma, Belle Starr, and the Creek National Council House at Okmulgee, Indian Territory; political ribbons (1907–1912) advertising the first Muskogee County (Oklahoma) Republican Party convention, the Muskogee County delegation to the first state Republican Party convention, and the delegation's support of William H. Taft for president in 1909; and publications (1908–1938), including programs of the reunion of former U.S. marshals in 1908, and of the forty-fifth anniversary of the First National Bank of Vinita, Oklahoma. Also in this collection is an original manuscript (1875–1907), presumably by Rhodes, regarding the U.S. District Court at Fort Smith, Arkansas, its judge, Isaac C. Parker, and the cases tried there, with commentary regarding the crimes and criminals of Indian Territory.

Rice, Clyde Vernon   1203
Papers 1908–1937
16 items

Physician. Reprints of medical articles (1918–1936) by Clyde Vernon Rice, including an issue of the *Journal of the Oklahoma State Medical Association* (1918) and an issue of *Archives of Pediatrics* (1936); certificates and diplomas (1908–1937) awarded to Rice by medical schools and civic groups, as well as licenses to practice medicine in the states of Oklahoma and Missouri.

Richards, Aute (b. 1885)   1204
Papers 1895–1950
4 feet

Professor. General correspondence (1939–1947); correspondence (1934–1950) relating to the Lions Club and to the University of Oklahoma biology department; printed material (1916–1941), including university publications and copies of zoology professor Aute Richards's published articles; scrapbooks (1931–1950) of newspaper clippings on Oklahoma history and World War II; newspaper clippings on Norman, Oklahoma, history; books (1895–1926) on music and on prose and poetry readings; reviews (1941–1948) of scientific books; and postcards, road maps, and travel brochures (ca. 1910–1950) collected by Richards.

Unpublished finding aid available.

Richardson, David Phillip (b. 1869)   1205
Papers 1890–1954
.25 foot

Banker and physician. Correspondence (1947–1948) and news clippings (1938–1939) regarding Richardson's medical career and his service as an Oklahoma banking official; publications (1906–1939), including telephone directories (1906–1907) for Union City, Oklahoma Territory, and magazines and journals such as *Harlow's Weekly* (1928) and *The Oklahoma Banker* (1928–1938), which contain articles about Richardson as a banking commissioner.

Riedt, G. A.   1206
Records 1907–1936
.33 foot

Collector. Ledgers (1907–1936) of the minutes and proceedings of the Twentieth-Century Club of McAlester, Indian Territory and Oklahoma.

Riggs, Rollie Lynn (1899–1954)   1207
Papers 1926–1966
.66 foot

Poet and playwright. Correspondence (1921–1936), with some poetry enclosed; newspaper and magazine clippings (1926–1966); and manuscripts (1924–1932) by or about Riggs and his plays and poetry, as well as his relations with the artist communities of the University of Oklahoma, Taos and Santa Fe, New Mexico, Hollywood, California, and New York City. Correspondents include Betty Kirk Boyer and Willard Spud Johnson. The collection also includes playbills for a number of his plays.

Riley, Rob   1208
Printed materials 1931–1998
.66 foot

Collector. Typescripts (1931–1954) of plays by Oklahoma playwright Lynn Riggs, and articles (1988–1993) regarding the works of Lynn Riggs, collected by Robert Shawn Riley, a Riggs fan. The collection also includes a finding aid to the Lynn Riggs Papers at the Beinecke Library, Yale University, and correspondence (1995–1998) of Rob Riley regarding research materials on Lynn Riggs.

Rinsland, Henry Daniel (b. 1889)   1209
Papers 1918–1953
8.66 feet

Professor. Correspondence (1941–1953) of Rinsland with colleagues regarding his work and research in the field of education, educational testing and measurement, the study and teaching of spelling and vocabulary, and the standardization and methodology of testing, both for personnel selection and educational purposes, as well as other uses; unpublished reports (1945) of research conducted by the Works Progress Administration regarding the vocabulary and word use frequency of children; and publications (1929), including copies of *A Brief on the Rinsland Spelling Book* and guide books for *The Alice and Jerry Basic Readers* series.

Unpublished finding aid available.

Rister, Carl Coke (1889–1955)   1210
Papers 1868–1951
.75 foot

Historian. Student grade books (1929–1951) from history courses taught by Rister at the University of Oklahoma; manuscripts (1889–1920) regarding the settlement of Oklahoma, written by early settlers about their experiences and observations; and typescripts of the official reports (1868–1871) of generals William T. Sherman and Philip H. Sheridan regarding the actions and experiences of their units against Indians, with detailed descriptions of armed engagements and of negotiations with chiefs and tribes. The Sherman and Sheridan reports are copies of the originals in the Library of Congress, Washington, D.C.

Rittenhouse, Frank A.   1211
Records 1848–1949
.33 foot

Freemason. Financial reports (1945–1949) and bylaws (1906–1944) of the Guthrie (Oklahoma) Lodge of Freemasons; typescripts (n.d.) of speeches and presentations made by Rittenhouse to Oklahoma freemasonry groups regarding the seventy-fifth anniversary of Indian Territory freemasonry, the fifty-sixth anniversary of Oklahoma Territory freemasonry, and the fortieth anniversary of freemasonry in the state of Oklahoma; and publications (1890–1949), including *Joseph Samuel Murrow's Masonic Monitor* (1903) and a program (1949) marking the fiftieth anniversary of freemasonry in Oklahoma.

Rittenhouse, George B. 1212
Certificate 1905
1 item

Attorney. Certificate issued to George B. Rittenhouse to practice law in Oklahoma Territory, 1905.

Ritzenthaler, Robert E. 1213
Dissertation 1949
1 item

Anthropologist. A dissertation (1949) by Robert E. Ritzenthaler, entitled *Chippewa Preoccupation with Health: Change in a Traditional Attitude Resulting from Modern Health Problems.*

Robertson, James Brooks Ayers (1871–1938) 1214
Papers 1903–1938
4 feet

Governor. Correspondence (1906–1938) regarding the Oklahoma Constitutional Convention of 1906, the condition and governance of the state after World War I, and the Okmulgee County (Oklahoma) trial incident; publications (1906–1925), including *Referendum News* and the *Oklahoma Odd Fellow*, published by the International Order of Odd Fellows, of which Robertson was a member; newspaper clippings (1914–1938) regarding Robertson; scrapbooks and notebooks (ca. 1938) regarding Robertson's career and influence in politics; speeches (n.d.) by Robertson regarding his positions on prohibition, the eighteenth amendment to the federal constitution, the Oklahoma Department of Pardon and Parole, and his inauguration; along with condolence cards (1938) received by Robertson's widow and family upon his death. The collection also includes gubernatorial Special Order No. 11 (1922) regarding the membership of Oklahoma National Guard officers in the Ku Klux Klan.

Unpublished finding aid available.

Robertson, Samuel W. (b. 1860) 1215
Papers 1876–1939
.33 foot

Teacher. Correspondence (1876–1931) between Robertson and his parents, mostly regarding family life and mission activities; and an autobiography of Samuel W. Robertson, with biographical information on Robertson's parents, William S. and Ann W. Robertson, who were Presbyterian missionaries to the Creek Indians.

Robey, Roberta (b. ca. 1891)   1216
Diary 1833–1835
1 item

Missionary. A diary (1833–1835) of Cassandra Sawyer Lockwood describing her journey to the Cherokee Nation, Indian Territory, and life at Dwight Mission. The diary also describes efforts by the mission staff to free slaves held by local white settlers.

[295]

Robinson, Jim Lee   1217
Records 1922–1932
6 items

Collector. Chattel mortgages (1929–1932) issued in Beckham County, Oklahoma; and receipts (1922–1929) for payment of Beckham County taxes, on the reverse of which are listed tax schedules for county, city, township, and school districts for the year.

Rock Island, Illinois Collection   1218
Printed materials ca. 1880
.33 foot

Subject collection. A souvenir booklet (ca. 1880) from the Tri-cities, Moline and Rock Island, Illinois, and Davenport, Iowa.

Rock Island Technical Society Collection   1219
Records 1879–1987
160 feet

Historical society. Records of the Chicago, Rock Island, and Pacific Railroad Company, including dismantling files (1981–1987); contract and easement listings (1981–1987); inventory records by subdivision (1980– 1985); highway crossings by state and county (1973–1987); tract estimates (1972–1985); review committee reports of land sales by city (1981–1984); motor vehicle reports (1972–1987); purchasing and sales files (1971–1986); engineering files (1930–1986); law department files (1906–1984); VPO contracts (1879–1984); tax and stock reports to states (1910–1984); card files containing information on locations of gas, water, and sewer pipe lines (1914–1984); daily reports concerning the thirty-five day strike by the clerks' union (1979); inspection trip reports concerning the southern division of the railroad (1969–1976); files concerning railroad operations at El Reno, Oklahoma (1977– 1979); and company general orders for the southern division (1972– 1977).

Unpublished finding aid available.

Rogers County Medical Society Collection   1220
Records 1915–1952
1.33 feet

Professional organization. Correspondence (1915–1916, 1936–1952); minutes (1943–1951); and printed material from the records of the secretary-treasurer of the Rogers County (Oklahoma) Medical Society, which became the Rogers-Mayes County Medical Society in 1950.

Rogers, Henry Collins   1221
Papers 1902–ca. 1945
.10 foot

Physician. A letter (1902) to Rogers praising his services as a physician; a resolution (ca. 1945) by the Muskogee, Oklahoma, chapter of Woodmen of the World noting Rogers's death; and a diploma (1914) issued to Rogers, along with medical instruments he used in his practice.

Rogers, John Powell (b. 1892)   1222
Papers 1924–1941
1.33 feet

University regent. Correspondence (1924–1941); minutes (1924–1927) of the University of Oklahoma Board of Regents; and annual reports, building reports, and financial statements (1930–1933) of the office of the president, all regarding the operation and maintenance of the University of Oklahoma. Also included in this collection are publications of the Association of Governing Boards of State Universities and Allied Institutions.

Rogers, William Charles   1223
Printed materials 1893–1907
.66 foot

Indian chief. Typescripts of editorials and newspaper articles (1893–1907) concerning Rogers, the last principal chief of the Cherokees prior to statehood; a court case in 1900; the 1903 campaign for chief of the Cherokees; the closing of tribal government; and the Sequoyah Movement.

Rogers-Neill Collection   1224
Papers 1871–1943
1 foot

Collectors. Business correspondence and papers (1871–1935) of Fritz Sittell relating to the Choctaw Coal and Railway Company, the Choctaw Trading Company, Sittell's other business interests, and the development of the town of McAlester, Oklahoma; personal correspondence (1871–1943) including letters from Tams Bixby, Peter Pitchlynn, the Pitchlynn family, Green McCurtain, Robert L. Owen, Moritz Lippman, and others; and certificates (1890–1900) of Sittell's appointment as U.S. marshal and special deputy sheriff of Tobucksy County, Choctaw Nation, along with clippings, business cards, a sketch of house floor plans, government documents, and biographical materials relating to Sittell's family.

Unpublished finding aid available.

Roodhouse, Frank S. 1225
Printed materials 1929–1930
2 items

Collector. Copies of "Proposed Amendments to the City Charter of Shawnee, Oklahoma" (1929) and "City Charter of Shawnee, Oklahoma: Proposed Amendments of 1930."

Rose, Noah Hamilton (d. 1952) 1226
Papers 1925–1952
6.33 feet

Professional photographer. Biographies (ca. 1925) of Texans and other southwesterners; publications (1929–1933) by national councils and committees regarding cosmopolitanism, disarmament, and the League of Nations, as well as by the Nanking government of the Republic of China concerning the Sino-Japanese War; posters and placards (1931) regarding disarmament; and a newspaper (1932) published in Osaka, Japan, bearing the banner headline, "The Republic of Manchuria— Birth of a New Nation," the topic to which the entire issue is devoted.

Unpublished finding aid available.

Rosenthal, Elizabeth Clark 1227
Papers 1876–1989
60 feet

Anthropologist. Professional correspondence (1936–1977) of Elizabeth "Betty" Clark Rosenthal, and printed research materials (1876–1989) on Indians of the Southwest, collected during Rosenthal's career as an anthropologist and Indian advocate. Rosenthal served as program director of Intercultural Studies Group in New York City, New York, a regional association concerned with the interrelationships between Indians and non-Indians with respect to education, the arts, and community services. Rosenthal was associated with Episcopal Church missions to Indians and was the founder of United Scholarship Service, Inc., which brought American Indian students to study at New England schools and colleges.

Ross, John (1790–1866) 1228
Printed materials 1829–1874
.50 foot

Indian chief. Typescripts of newspaper articles (1829–1874) regarding Ross, the history of the Cherokee Indians, and political and social conditions within the Cherokee Nation.

Ross, Leslie P., Sr. (1863–1944) 1229
Papers 1892–1944
.50 foot

Territorial politician and jurist. Correspondence (1892–1916) received by Ross regarding party politics and politicians in Oklahoma Territory and requests for appointment to political offices; a newspaper obituary (1944) of Ross; and a homestead certificate (1902) issued by President Theodore Roosevelt to a pioneer in Oklahoma Territory. A principal correspondent of Ross was William C. Renfrow, and Renfrow's letters comment on his activities before and during his term as governor of Oklahoma Territory.

Ross, Samuel Price (b. 1862) 1230
Papers 1867–1936
.33 foot

Physician. Ledgers (1912–1922) in which Ross recorded patients attended and fees charged; certificates and diplomas (1889–1922) awarded Ross by medical schools, brotherhoods, and the medical board of the Choctaw Nation; and a typescript (1867–1936) of an account by Mrs. Ross of her experiences as the wife of a physician in Indian Territory, describing with detail the social conditions of the area, the state and practice of medicine there, and the lives and customs of its inhabitants.

Ross, William Potter (1820–1891)   1231
Printed materials 1866–1891
.75 foot

Indian chief. Typescripts of newspaper articles (1866–1891) of Ross's messages and instructions to the Cherokee Nation, the Cherokee council, and the Cherokee delegation to Washington, D.C., regarding reconstruction, tribal government, financial matters, organization of Oklahoma Territory, education, Sequoyah, and the use of lands, along with biographical information on Ross.

Rotary International of Oklahoma Collection   1232
Printed materials 1914–1985
11.50 feet

Service organization. Programs (1935–1985); minutes and club records (1952–1985); club publications (1914–1985); and histories (1914–1985) of the clubs throughout Oklahoma, all accumulated in 1985–1986 by the Rotary International of Oklahoma, under the direction of Doane Farr.

Unpublished finding aid available.

Ruggiers, (Mrs.) Paul Eddleman   1233
Notebook 1920
1 item

Collector. A notebook (1920) in which Ruggiers's father, Morgan W. Eddleman, recorded engineering field notes and related information, while an engineering student at the University of Oklahoma.

Ruggiers, Paul George (b. 1918)   1234
Records 1956
.66 foot

Professor. Records (1956), including correspondence, reports, speeches, financial records, and guides produced by the Great Plains Conference on Higher Education, which convened at the University of Oklahoma in 1956 to address the question, "What distinctive cultural services, both traditional and newly conceived, may our universities and colleges render to the Great Plains?"

Russell, Campbell (1863–1937) 1235
Papers 1904–1937
1.33 feet

State official and politician. Correspondence (1905–1937) to and from Russell regarding the Oklahoma Corporation Commission, of which he was a commissioner, and regarding Oklahoma politics in general; political posters (ca. 1920–1930) printed by Russell to support his campaigns for election to the Oklahoma Corporation Commission and to Congress and also regarding various political issues of the day; speeches (ca. 1920–1930) delivered by Russell; bylaws and the certificate of incorporation (1933) for the Self Help Exchange, a Depression-era unemployed persons' league; publications including newspapers (1919–1925) printed by Russell; periodicals (1925–1936) such as *The Cactus Hornet* and *The Oklahoma Banker*; a booklet (1919) proposing federal ownership of the railroad system; and transcripts (n.d.) of the proceedings of the Oklahoma Supreme Court.

Unpublished finding aid available.

Russell, Earl C. 1236
Records 1939–1953
4 feet

Collector. Correspondence (1949–1953); membership reports and rosters (1949–1952); financial and expense records (1952–1953); and publications (1949–1953) received or generated by the office of the district governor of the Oklahoma Regional Lions Clubs International, and accumulated by Russell while serving as regional district governor of the Lions from the late 1940s through the early 1950s.

Unpublished finding aid available.

Nancy Russell Trust Collection 1237
Records 1914–1997
6 feet

Estate trust. Records of the Nancy Russell Trust, which acted as executor of the Charles M. Russell Estate. Records include the last will and testament of Charles M. Russell; the court records of the Russell estate; a list of Charles M. Russell bronzes; correspondence regarding issues of ownership, claims, and assessments related to the estate; various court orders and petitions; tax documents; correspondence regarding movies and television films about Russell; correspondence regarding the Russell estate and the National Cowboy Hall of Fame; court pleadings; correspondence with legal firms; museum catalog materials; and biographical materials about Charles M. Russell.

Unpublished finding aid available.

Russell, (Mrs.) U. S.   **1238**
Printed materials 1872–1949
1 item

Homemaker. A newspaper article (1949) by Mrs. U. S. Russell regarding the history of Atoka, Oklahoma, and the origin of the town's name.

Russo, Peter E.   **1239**
Printed materials 1946–1952
2 items

Physician. A reprint of a journal article (1952), entitled "Pioneering in the Use of X-Ray and Radium in Oklahoma," by Everett S. Lain; and a reprint of a speech (1946) by Russo, entitled "Pioneer Users of X-Rays in Oklahoma."

Ruth, Charles P.   **1240**
Papers 1953
.10 foot

Collector. Typescript (1953) by George Coffey, entitled, "Ten Days in a Hunting Camp with Charley Russell," describing a hunting trip Coffey made with Charles M. Russell in the Sun River, Montana, area in 1922.

Ruth, Kent (1916–1990)   **1241**
Papers 1920–1990
46 feet

Writer. The original manuscript (1959), first proof, and plate proof of Ruth's book *Colorado Vacations*, published by the Alfred A. Knopf Company in 1959; personal and professional correspondence (1920s–1980s); research files (1961–1987) for a travel series Ruth wrote for Oklahoma newspapers; research files (1965–1988), primarily on Oklahoma and southwestern topics; research files (1956–1977) exclusively on Oklahoma places and points of interest; drafts, story lines, ideas, and manuscripts, including published items, (1928–1965) for articles and books; travel columns (1971–1985); manuscripts and published items for filler pieces (1953–1986); trip notes (1950–1985); and general research notes (1962–1990).

Unpublished finding aid available.

Rutherford, L. Morton, II   1242
Papers 1940
2 items

Attorney. A report (1940) of the Oklahoma state senate Committee on Oil Investigation, of which Rutherford was a member; and a letter (1940) to his son regarding the same.

Ryan, Jesse Willis   1243
Papers 1888–1974
.75 foot

Collector. Correspondence (1888–1915) between family members regarding Ryan family affairs and the move to El Reno, Oklahoma Territory, in 1902; and newspapers (1939–1974) regarding declarations of war in 1939 and 1941, the American landings on the moon, and the resignation of President Richard M. Nixon.

Sac and Fox Indian Agency Collection   1244
Records 1840–1888
.33 foot

Indian tribal agency. Ledgers (1876–1888) recording receipt of and payment for supplies, expenditures for freight costs, the police force, employee salaries, cash payments to Indians, and names of Indians eligible for payment; copies of correspondence (1840–1872) from agent John Beach to the governor of Iowa and other officials regarding land distribution, employment, depredations, trade, education, and problems among the Sac and Fox; and one letter (1872) from the governor of Kansas to Gen. John Pope regarding Indian depredations in western Kansas and the capture of Mary Jordan by raiding Indians.

Saint John's Protestant Episcopal Church Collection   1245
Records 1938–1942
.25 foot

Christian church. Six roll books (ca. 1938–1942) from the Sunday school; reports (1940) of the rector, wardens, and vestrymen; a report

(1940) of the secretary of the Protestant Episcopal Cathedral Foundation of the Diocese of Oklahoma; a report (1935–1941) of property added and improvements made; a report (1942) on construction; two bulletins (April–May 1942); and the constitution and canons (1939) of the Diocese of Oklahoma, all from Saint John's Protestant Episcopal Church in Oklahoma City, Oklahoma.

Salasovic, Robert J.   1246
Papers 1956
.10 foot

Airman. Correspondence (1956) from Robert J. Salasovic to his relatives regarding his experiences as an enlisted airman at the Naval Air Technical Training Center in Norman, Oklahoma.

Salter, Lewis Spencer (d. ca. 1987)   1247
Papers 1893–1933
.25 foot

Collector. Typescript of a diary (n.d.) by Anna K. Wood recounting her trip from Denver, Colorado, to the border of the Cherokee Outlet in preparation for the 1893 land run; minutes (1912–1921) of the Arthur Foote Music Club at the University of Oklahoma; a roster (1898) of soldiers in Company "M" of the First Volunteer Infantry Regiment of Indian Territory; and a published history (1933) of the Men's Dinner Club in Oklahoma City, Oklahoma.

Sanders, Stella E.   1248
Manuscript 1815–1964
1 item

Professor. A dissertation (1964), bound but unpublished, written by Sanders in French for the Sorbonne University in Paris, France, and entitled "Le Theatre de Henri-René Lenormand." Bound-in are letters (1952–1964) from Paul Blanchart, Gabriel Marcel, and Jean-Jacques Bernard, as well as an edict (1815) authorizing Pierre-Henri-René Lenormand to collect taxes in his district of Paris.

Sapulpa (1824–1887)   1249
Papers 1864–1972
.25 foot

Indian chief. Papers regarding Creek chief Sapulpa, including a transcript of Sapulpa's discharge from the Confederate States Army (1864); a certificate of Confederate States of America bonds (1864); a letter from the superintendent of the Five Civilized Tribes to James Sapulpa (1920); a bill of sale for a mule (1927); and a biographical sketch of Sapulpa by Jean Brown (1972).

**Sapulpa (Oklahoma) Euchee Boarding School Collection   1250
Records 1915–1918
.25 foot**

U.S. Indian Service school. Ledgers (1915–1918) recording supplies used by the school, along with the number of teachers and students in attendance.

**Sapulpa (Oklahoma) Frankoma Pottery Company Collection 1251
Printed materials 1952
.10 foot**

Manufacturer. A brochure (1952) and picture postcards (1952) regarding the operations and products of the Frankoma Pottery Company of Sapulpa, Oklahoma, a nationally and internationally recognized pottery manufacturer.

**Sattler, Helen R.   1252
Papers 1922–1992
25 feet**

Author. Correspondence, galley proofs and manuscripts, research materials, and publishing contracts relating to Helen R. Sattler's career as an author of children's books such as *Brain Busters, Dinosaurs of North America*, and *Fish Facts and Bird Brains*.

**Savage, William Woodrow, Jr.   1253
Papers 1973–1982
2.66 foot**

Professor. Original manuscripts and galley proofs (1973–1977) for Savage's books, including *The Cowboy Hero..., Cowboy Life, The Frontier, The Cherokee Strip Livestock Association: The Impact of Federal Regulations...*, and *Indian Life Transforming: An American Myth*, along with correspondence and papers (1981–1982) relating to comparative frontier studies at the University of Oklahoma.

Unpublished finding aid available.

Saxon, Mary Esther 1254
Records 1951–1980
.66 foot

Librarian. Records of the University of Oklahoma Libraries including annual reports (1951–1980); administrative reports and memoranda (1970–1977); policies and rules (1968–1979); minutes (1970–1980); bulletins and newsletters (1970–1979); and a new building program statement (1979–1980).

Schaefer, Hedwig 1255
Papers ca. 1914
2 items

Collector. A mimeographed Christmas letter (1914) from Hiram H. Clouse, pastor of the Rainy Mountain Baptist Mission, to supporters and friends of the mission describing the year's activities, trials, and accomplishments, along with a brochure entitled "Rainy Mountain," which gives a brief history of the mission with biographical information on the Kiowa deacons and interpreters.

Schaper, William August (1869–1955) 1256
Papers 1909–1957
1.25 feet

Professor. Correspondence (1909–1957) regarding the administration of the political science department at the University of Minnesota, Schaper's dismissal from the university faculty in 1917 due to his stance on the war with Germany, and the state of the Progressive Party in the presidential election of 1912; and typescripts (ca. 1922) of a speech by Professor Frederick Hindekoper regarding military policy and history. Also in this collection are publications (1913–1917), including a booklet urging citizens of Minneapolis, Minnesota, to vote for a new charter for that city, and the proceedings of the Board of Regents of the University of Minnesota regarding Schaper's dismissal.

Unpublished finding aid available.

Schmidt, Robert W. 1257
Papers 1864–1889
5 items

Collector. Correspondence (1864–1889) received by the Schmidt family, immigrants to this country, from family members remaining in Germany. The letters are written in German.

Schmitt, Karl, and Iva Schmitt   1258
Papers 1947–1965
4.50 feet

Anthropologists. Field notes (1947–1951); articles (1947–1965); and other research notes (n.d.) concerning the Schmitts' work among the Wichita Indians, the Caddo, the Pawnee, and other southern plains tribes.

Unpublished finding aid available.

Schonwald, Fred P.   1259
Papers 1875–1977
.33 foot

Oil producer. Business and personal correspondence (1934–1966); catalogs (1953–1958) of art exhibits and collections; publications relating to the oil industry; a copy of a map of the U.S. northwestern territories (ca. 1875); and minutes and correspondence (1962–1977) of the Indian Territory Posse of Oklahoma Westerners.

Schuster-Barbour Collection   1260
Papers 1892–1952
1 foot

Collectors. This collection contains manuscripts (1938–1949) by James Henry Shears, also known as "Oklahoma Jim," regarding his life and experiences; newspaper clippings regarding Shears and Charles Dunn, also known as the "Oklahoma Kid"; and a scrapbook (1941–1949) of newspaper clippings about Shears.

Unpublished finding aid available.

Schwegler, Caroline   1261
Papers 1871, 1958
2 items

Collector. Copy of a poem (1871) by an unidentified Cherokee Indian, and correspondence (1958) to Caroline Schwegler from Westminster College, Fulton, Missouri, regarding an attempt to identify the poem's author.

Scott, George W. (b. 1872)   1262
Papers 1904–1909
.75 foot

Indian statesman. Correspondence (1904–1909) regarding Choctaw Nation affairs and issues, including the movement for separate statehood for Indian Territory, statehood for Oklahoma, Choctaw politics, and Green McCurtain.

Scott, Howell A.   1263
Speech 1953
1 item

Physician. A typescript of a speech (ca. 1953) by Scott regarding the history of hospitals in Muskogee, Oklahoma, and the roles played by area physicians in their establishment.

Searcy, Emmett Coldwell (1865–1945)   1264
Papers 1832–1934
1 foot

Collector. Correspondence (1902) and a manuscript (ca. 1890) regarding the Red Moon Indian Boarding School for Cheyenne-Arapaho Indians; musical scores (n.d.) by Kate Searcy; publications (1892–1903) of temperance societies; items from the world fairs of 1893 and 1904; correspondence (1933–1934) from a veteran of the 1868 Battle of the Washita describing the role of George Armstrong Custer and the conflict in general; and nineteenth-century textbooks published between 1832 and 1866.

Sears, Alfred Byron (1906–1954)   1265
Papers 1917–1973
5.33 feet

Professor. Personal correspondence (1917–1973) of Sears and his wife, Helen Sears; professional correspondence (1946–1959) of Sears; research materials (1906–1954) on the history of aviation, including publications and reports of the Oklahoma Aviation Commission, magazine articles and clippings, and bibliography cards.

Unpublished finding aid available.

Seay, Abraham Jefferson (1832–1915)   1266
Papers 1832–1923
.75 foot

Territorial governor. An autobiography (1832–1893) of Governor Seay describing his childhood, his terms as an associate justice of the Oklahoma Territorial Supreme Court and later as governor of the territory; a biography (1915) of Seay, including a history of his family, written by Clark Brown; typescripts of Seay's diaries (1862–1864, 1892–1893), in which he recorded his experiences as a Union soldier in the Civil War, and his actions as governor of Oklahoma Territory. Also included in this collection are typescripts of letters (1905–1909) sent and received by Seay, regarding the events of his life after his retirement from government, and his pivotal role in early territorial politics.

Seay, Edgar W., Jr.   1267
Papers 1915–1950
2 feet

Collector. Nineteen engineering drawings, primarily by the Chicago, Rock Island, and Pacific Railroad Company, showing rights-of-way for areas in Arkansas, Louisiana, Oklahoma, and Texas.

Unpublished finding aid available.

Selby, (Mrs.) Bruce (b. ca. 1902)   1268
Papers 1917–1968
.10 foot

Collector. Correspondence (1917–1919) from American soldiers in Europe during World War I, along with World War II ration books (1942–1945).

Seminole Nation Papers   1269
Papers 1840–1979
.10 foot

Indian tribe. Typescripts of correspondence (1840–1939) and newspaper articles (1906–1933) regarding John Jumper and Seminole land disputes, along with resolutions and ordinances (1969–1979) of the Seminole General Council.

Seneca Nation Papers   1270
Papers 1892–1916
.10 foot

Indian tribe. Acts (1892) of the Seneca Nation, along with correspondence (1892–1916) regarding the allotment of tribal lands in northeastern Oklahoma and claims of the Cayuga Indians against the Seneca Nation.

Seneker, George Washington   1271
Records 1894–1913
.10 foot

Collector. Records of School District No. 11, in Kingfisher County, Oklahoma Territory, including registers of pupils (1894–1906); a receipt book (1894–1908) indicating payments for supplies purchased and wages paid; and a school district clerk's financial ledger (1894–1913), in which the names of the school district officials are also recorded.

Seran, A. M.   1272
Printed materials 1904–1908
.10 foot

Merchant. Booklet (ca. 1904) entitled "We-wo-ka," describing the benefits of life and industry in Wewoka, Oklahoma; and an issue of *Sturm's Oklahoma Magazine* (1908) containing articles regarding the personalities and history of the new state.

Serviss, Irma Porter   1273
Records 1894–1934
.75 foot

Collector. Territorial- and early statehood-era school records from districts in Noble and Grant Counties, Oklahoma, including teachers' record books (1907–1938); school district clerks' records (1915–1934); pupil rosters (1907–1917); listings of teachers and district officials (1894–1941); records of annual meetings (1915–1934); and school warrants issued (1915–1934).

Shackelford, F. P.   1274
Papers 1897
1 item

Collector. Correspondence regarding a visit by F. P. Shackelford to old mines in Stonewall County, Texas.

Shackelford, Marshall, Jr. (b. ca. 1928)   1275
Papers 1862–1921
.10 foot

Collector. Typescripts of letters (1862–1863) written by Robert L. Shackelford, a Confederate soldier, to his parents in Georgia, describing his experiences in the Civil War. Also included is a letter (1921) from the United Daughters of the Confederacy regarding Shackelford's service record.

Shadid, Michael Abraham (1882–1966)   1276
Printed materials 1912–1984
1 foot

Physician. Newspaper and journal articles (1912–1984) and publications (1924–1947) regarding the life and career of Michael A. Shadid and his contributions to cooperative medicine, especially the Cooperative Community Hospital that he established in Elk City, Oklahoma, with information regarding its history, status, cost, and the unsuccessful attempt by the Beckham County (Oklahoma) Medical Association to close the hospital. The collection includes the *Community Hospital Bulletin* (1945–1953) and the cornerstone (1934) of the original hospital building.

Unpublished finding aid available.

Sharp, Paul F. (1918–)   1277
Papers 1964–1989
8 feet

Professor and university president. Papers (1964–1989) including correspondence, speeches, book contracts, and research materials relating to Paul Sharp's presidency at Drake University, Des Moines, Iowa, and the University of Oklahoma, Norman, Oklahoma, his publications, and his attendance at conferences, commencement exercises, and inaugurations of other university presidents. Also included is information about his career in higher education and correspondence with history professor Gilbert Fite.

Unpublished finding aid available.

Sherrill, Rufus Hansen (1883–1952)   1278
Papers 1926–1930
10 items

Physician. Correspondence (1926–1930) from Indians to Sherrill, a general practitioner in Broken Bow, Oklahoma, asking for medical treatment and medicines.

Shilling, Marvin   1279
Papers 1931–1932
.33 foot

Attorney. Correspondence (1931–1932); legal documents (1931–1932); and newspaper clippings (1931–1932), all regarding the trial of two Carter County, Oklahoma, deputies charged with killing the children of two prominent Mexican families, including a relative of the Mexican president, Pascual Ortiz Rubio. The collection also contains a transcript of the preliminary hearing of the deputies, as well as telegrams and correspondence from Oklahoma governor William H. Murray, concerning the delicacy of the situation and the dangers of an unjust trial.

Shippey, E. E.   1280
Records 1912–1928
.10 foot

Physician. Account books (1912–1928) in which Shippey recorded insurance policies sold to clients in the town of Wister, Oklahoma.

Shook, William Vance (b. 1871)   1281
Papers 1871–1954
.10 foot

Minister. A typewritten autobiography (1871–1953) of W. Vance Shook regarding his life as a rural circuit-riding minister in Oklahoma Territory and Oklahoma, with descriptions of the communities in which he lived, and of the churches he founded and served as pastor; newspaper clippings (1938–1957) regarding the death of Shook's wife, Lottie Lee, and the establishment of the Methodist Episcopal churches in Putnam City, Oklahoma, and at Eighth and Lee streets in Oklahoma City, Oklahoma; and publications (1918–1935), including the programs of the annual conferences of the Methodist Episcopal Church of Oklahoma, a booklet regarding the history of Methodism in Logan County, Oklahoma, and event programs issued by the Putnam City Methodist Church and the Methodist church at Eighth and Lee streets in Oklahoma City, Oklahoma.

Shorbe, Howard B.   1282
Printed materials 1938–1953
7 items

Physician. Reprints (1938–1953) of articles by Howard B. Shorbe regarding medical maladies.

Short, George F.   1283
Letter 1962
1 item

Attorney. A letter (1962) from Lacey Mullen to Short regarding the friendship of Mullen's father with Short, and praising Short's admirable qualities.

Short, Julia A. "Julee"   1284
Papers 1832–1970
.25 foot

Author. A copy of the final issue (1968) of *The Oklahoma Advertizer*; student term papers (n.d.) and journal articles regarding the surrender of Stand Watie, the lives of Walter Campbell and Roger Williams, and Washington Irving's tour of the Oklahoma area in 1832. The collection also contains some correspondence (1967–1970) from scholars regarding the above topics.

Shull, Russell Johnson (1878–1954)   1285
Papers 1918–1954
3 items

Physician. Certificate (1918) awarded to Russell Johnson Shull by the American Legion for service during World War I; a typescript of United States Army special orders (1954) regarding Shull; and an obituary (1954) for Shull.

Shumard, Evelyn Hughes   1286
Papers 1898–1939
2 feet

Collector. Minutes (1898–1902) of the city council of Sapulpa, Indian Territory; diaries (1915) of Evelyn Shumard; short manuscripts (n.d.) by Shumard, entitled "Outlaws," "The Parade," The Spirit of Tulsa," "My Life," and "Oklahoma"; scrapbooks (n.d.) by Marion, Alice, and

Gordon Shumard on various topics, including "An Early History of Sapulpa"; and memorabilia (n.d.) from schools attended by the Shumards.

Unpublished finding aid available.

Shumate and Sons Collection   1287
Records 1932–1935
1.33 feet

Mercantile company. Ledgers (1932–1935) recording the items sold and prices paid by customers in the Shumate Department Store in Pauls Valley, Oklahoma, during the Great Depression.

Shumate, Enola   1288
Ledger ca. 1897
1 item

Collector. A ledger (ca. 1897) containing census cards recording members of the Seminole tribe in Indian Territory.

Sigler, Earle Marion (b. 1916)   1289
Diary 1860–1861
1 item

Collector. A photocopy of Thomas Harrison's travel diary which he kept aboard the U.S.S. *Susquehanna* while on a cruise in the Mediterranean Sea in 1860–1861. Harrison describes his impressions of ports of call and provides a complete listing of expenses, compiled item by item and city by city.

Sigma Alpha Epsilon Collection   1290
Printed materials 1906–1954
4 feet

College social fraternity. Publications relating to the Sigma Alpha Epsilon (S.A.E.) fraternity, including a yearbook (1909–1910), a history of S.A.E. (1911), copies of *The Record* (1910–1920), *Pi Alpha* (1914–1934), and *Songs of S.A.E.*; scrapbooks (1916–1978); minute books (1906–1909, 1949–1954); and a biographical record (1909–1921) relating to the University of Oklahoma chapter of S.A.E.

Unpublished finding aid available.

Sigma Delta Chi Collection   1291
Records 1948–1958
1 foot

Honorary fraternity. Correspondence (1952–1958); reports (1948–1958); memoranda; and publications regarding the University of Oklahoma's chapter of Sigma Delta Chi, a national journalism fraternity.

Unpublished finding aid available.

Sigma Nu Collection   1292
Printed materials 1917–1953
1 foot

College social fraternity. Printed materials, including chapter manuals (1946–1950); a yearbook (1949); a program (1939); copies of journals (1941–1948); and reports relating to the Sigma Nu fraternity, along with autograph books (1917–1927) and receipt books (1947) from the University of Oklahoma chapter of Sigma Nu.

Simon, Earle Marvin (1895–1974)   1293
Papers 1900–1960
7.33 feet

City clerk and civic leader. Papers (1900–1960), including pamphlets, books, newspaper clippings, and other printed materials, plus correspondence relating to the American Legion, Oklahoma City, Oklahoma, and Simon's teaching career; certificates and awards presented to Simon; and a scrapbook concerning Simon's life.

Unpublished finding aid available.

Simpson, John Andrew (1871–1934)   1294
Papers. 1889–1938
2.75 feet

Farm leader. Correspondence (1917–1934) with Simpson regarding Oklahoma Farmers Union and National Farmers Union policies, issues, stances, and activities, including financial papers and meeting minutes of the Farmers Union; Simpson's nomination for the position of U.S. secretary of agriculture in Franklin D. Roosevelt's first cabinet; Simpson's opposition to President Herbert Hoover and his support of Al Smith's candidacy for president; Simpson's opinions regarding bimetallism, the National Farm Board, compulsory military service, and allegiance to the state; and condolences received by Simpson's widow upon his death. Principal correspondents include Franklin D. Roosevelt, Huey P. Long, Henry Morgenthau, James A. Farley, and Elmer Thomas. Also in this collection are Simpson's diaries (1924–1934); transcripts of radio and other speeches (1919–1933) delivered by Simpson; news clippings (n.d.); and newspapers (1917–1934), all relating to farm topics; and orders (1934) for Simpson's book *The Militant Voice of Agriculture*.

Unpublished finding aid available.

Simpson, (Mrs.) Morris S.   1295
Papers 1909–1925
.10 foot

Collector. Certificates of stock ownership (1909–1918) issued by the University Improvement Association in Lawton, Oklahoma, and by the Crescent Mining, Milling and Oil Company, also of Lawton, Oklahoma; news clippings (n.d.) regarding Lawton citizens; a letterhead (ca. 1930) from the Lawton Mercantile Company; and a handwritten resolution (1925) composed by dinner guests of the Simpsons regarding their hosts' hospitality and kindness, and signed by all present, including Senator Elmer Thomas and several army generals stationed at Fort Sill, Oklahoma.

Skelly, William Grove (b. 1878)   1296
Speech 1954
1 item

Oilman. A typescript of a speech given by Skelly in 1954 at the University of Oklahoma Association's annual "Achievement Day."

Skinner, Esthmer H.   1297
Papers 1944–1969
.33 foot

Collector. A booklet (1969) published by Orange County, California, in tribute to President Richard Nixon; certificates (1933) issued to Skinner by the Republican Party of California and by the University of Oklahoma Foundation; and propaganda (1944–1945) printed by the Nazis and air-dropped to American troops fighting the Battle of the Bulge near Bastogne, Belgium, advising them of their certain defeat and death, and of the post-war demise of the United States. Also included are sheets of postage stamps (1948–1957) commemorating the fiftieth anniversary of Oklahoma statehood and the centennials of the petroleum industry and the Five Civilized Tribes of Oklahoma.

Slick, Thomas Baker (1883–1929)   1298
Papers 1914–1973
4 feet

Oilman. Correspondence (1920–1939); reports (1930–1939); leases and deeds (1914–1973); and tax records (1926–1933) from the estate of Tom Slick, all regarding his petroleum and real estate business interests in Oklahoma.

Unpublished finding aid available.

Slover, James Anderson, Sr. (b. 1824)   1299
Manuscript 1826–1907
1 item

Missionary. A photocopy of the autobiography (ca. 1907) of James Slover, a missionary to the Cherokee Nation during the Civil War. The typewritten manuscript contains his observations of Cherokee attitudes toward slavery, and their support of the Civil War and the Confederacy, with specific reference to the Cherokee regiment organized and led by Stand Watie, and to Slover's duties as regimental chaplain. Also included are accounts of post-Civil War difficulties in Arkansas, due to the depressed economy, race relations, and the Reconstruction government, and Slover's subsequent decision to move to California.

Smalley, Joseph A. (d. 1953)   1300
Records 1955
1 item

State legislator. A resolution (1955) of the Oklahoma Senate memorializing Joseph A. Smalley.

Smalley, Marjorie Beard   1301
Papers 1890–1987
.25 foot

Collector. The collection consists of photocopies and typescripts (1890–1987) regarding the life of Marjorie Beard Smalley; Beard family history; Depression-era Sapulpa, Oklahoma; her father Lyman F. Beard, who was a Rough Rider; and her mother Buda McCormick Beard, who was the first schoolteacher in Shawnee, Oklahoma. The collection also includes typescripts of newspaper articles and personal letters related to these and other family members, some of whom were prominent in Oklahoma history.

Smallwood, Ben F. (1829–1891)   1302
Printed materials 1889–1891
5 items

Indian chief. Typescripts of Smallwood's messages (1889–1890) to the Choctaw Nation on the affairs of government, especially in the area of education; and articles (1891) commenting on his death and containing biographical information.

Smiser, (Mrs.) Butler Stonestreet (b. 1865)   1303
Papers 1915–1950
.10 foot

Publisher. Newspaper clippings (1935–1950) regarding the Smisers, their publishing activities, and their early years in Atoka, Indian Territory; a memorial (1915) to Katrina Ellett Murrow, wife of Joseph Samuel Murrow and a Baptist missionary to the Choctaw Indians; and an unpublished paper (n.d.) by John E. Dodd, entitled "The Life of J. S. Murrow."

Smith, (Mrs.) E. P.   1304
Scrapbook 1832–1948
1 item

Collector. A scrapbook containing news clippings regarding the history (1832–1948) of the Hughes County, Oklahoma, region. Also included is a hand-drawn map of Hughes County, showing the route of the Texas Road and the locations of Camp Holmes, Oak Ridge Seminary, and Edwards Trading Post.

Smith, Franklin Campbell (b. 1874)   1305
Papers 1836–1946
.33 foot

Minister. A typescript of Smith's autobiography (1874–1946), which relates his experiences in Oklahoma Territory and the origins of Oklahoma place names, as well as stories concerning religion, settlers, cowboys, marshals, weather, opinions about the Spanish-American War, and the Crazy Snake Rebellion in Indian Territory. The collection also includes a typescript of Smith's biography (1836–1877) of Maj. James Patrick, C.S.A., who held important commands in the Southwest during the Civil War.

Smith, H. P. 1306
Diary 1901–1902
1 item

Collector. A diary (1901–1902) kept on a tour of Spain and the Middle East. The author was a Mr. Covey, who traveled with his wife. The diary includes a poem written by the Coveys, regarding their travels and dedicated to their fellow passengers aboard the SS *Ramses the Great*.

Smith, Isabel Foster 1307
Papers 1887–1925
.10 foot

Collector. A diary (1887) kept by nineteen-year-old Lula Hulett until her death later in the same year; a letter (1887) regarding Miss Hulett's death; an obituary (1896) written for the Huletts' dog; and newspaper articles (1925) regarding the death of Capt. A. W. Hulett.

Smith, James Morton 1308
Papers 1946
.10 foot

Graduate student. A master's thesis (1946) by James Morton Smith, completed at the University of Oklahoma, entitled *Criminal Syndicalism in Oklahoma*.

Smith, Jedediah Strong (1799–1831) 1309
Printed materials 1958
.10 foot

Explorer. A newspaper clipping (n.d.) regarding the life of Jedediah Smith, and a printed pamphlet (1958) entitled *He Opened the West: Jedediah Strong Smith*. The pamphlet reproduces diary entries of Smith and Harrison Rogers, recorded during their travels through the Humboldt and Del Norte regions of California Territory in 1828.

Smith, Joseph G. (b. 1870) 1310
Records 1888–1955
.10 foot

Physician. Records (1906–1955) kept by Smith regarding the obstetrical cases he attended in Washington County, Oklahoma; publications (1924–1946) regarding the history and future of the Methodist Episcopal Church in Bartlesville, Oklahoma; medical articles (1924–1928) published by Smith; a newsletter (1946) of the Bartlesville Rotary Club;

an article (1944) regarding the Bartlesville YMCA; and certificates and diplomas (1888–1952) awarded Smith by medical schools and societies, including a license to practice (1903) in Oklahoma Territory. Also included in the collection is a letter of reference (1888) written for Smith.

Smith, Maggie Aldridge   1311
Papers 1929–1992
.25 foot

Author and poet. Correspondence from Maggie Aldridge to William D. Daniel (1929–1930); a poem by Smith, entitled "An Indian's First Deer Shot," (n.d.); Oklahoma High School Honor Society certificates (1930–1932) issued to Smith; and a booklet of letters from Aldridge to Daniel, published in 1992.

Smith, Merle G.   1312
Papers 1913–1982
10.15 feet

Attorney and University of Oklahoma alumnus. Legal case files (1913–1982) for litigation handled by Merle G. Smith, and Merle G. Smith, Jr., attorneys at law in Guthrie, Oklahoma. The case files include correspondence between the Smiths and their clients, as well as related legal documents. The collection also contains memorabilia from Merle G. Smith's student days at the University of Oklahoma, including two felt University of Oklahoma beanie caps (n.d.), one felt armband bearing the letters "S A T C" (n.d.), and one dance card for the Freshman Christmas Dance (1919). Also includes twenty-seven reproduction photographs of University of Oklahoma buildings and events, and one piece of correspondence (1919) from Smith regarding freshman activities.

Unpublished finding aid available.

Smith, Micah Pearce   1313
Papers 1930–1936
.10 foot

Historian. Manuscripts (n.d.) written by Smith and entitled "The Seminole Presbyterian Mission," "Dr. Emmet Starr," and "Daniel Collins Home"; research notes (1930–1936) on the Oklahoma towns of Fred, Ninnekah, Chickasha, and Bloomfield, along with a biographical questionnaire relating to Rhoda Gunn Colbert Potts, Daniel Collins, and the Colbert family.

Smith, Samuel Walter (b. 1877) 1314
Printed materials 1877–1949
.10 foot

Pioneer and banker. The memoirs (1877–1949) of Sam Smith, in which he recorded his and the Smith family's adventures in frontier Kansas and Colorado, and their participation in the land run of 1893 into the Cherokee Strip. Of note are his accounts of life and social conditions in a number of Kansas and Colorado towns, and also his mother's reaction to moving into the family's first sod house.

Smith, Stewart K. 1315
Papers 1896–1920
.50 foot

Mining engineer. Smith's correspondence (1902–1907), reports (1896–1920), and appraisals (1896–1920) relating to his career as a civil engineer and mining consultant. Included in the collection are blueprints of mines (1905–1918). Most of Smith's work was with coal mines in Oklahoma, Indian Territory, Iowa, Missouri, Montana, and West Virginia.

Smith, Woodrow W. 1316
Papers 1933–1939
2 items

Sailor. Scrapbooks (1933–1939) kept by Woodrow W. Smith while serving in the U.S. Navy aboard the U.S.S. *Oklahoma*. The scrapbooks include invitations, newspaper clippings, photographs, autographs, addresses of friends, certificates, and a diary.

Smithe, P. A. 1317
Records 1907–1923
.10 foot

Surgeon. Patient account records (1907–1923) of the fees charged, but not services rendered, by Smithe; and medical artifacts used by Smithe in the Red Cross, including two hypodermic kits.

Snider, Denton Jacques (1841–1925) 1318
Manuscript ca. 1921
1 item

Author. A manuscript of Snider's book *A Biography of Ralph Waldo Emerson*, published by the William Harvey Miner Company of Saint Louis, Missouri, in 1921.

The diary of Samuel Murray Stover, a physician who recorded his experiences during an overland trail journey from eastern Tennessee to the Davis settlement of California in 1849. Stover and his traveling companions hoped to enter California's mining industry. Stover recounts in detail his experiences on the journey, including physical descriptions of the lands through which his company passed, a description of Stover's killing a buffalo for sport, and his impressions of the Indian tribes the company encountered along the trail. From the Samuel Murray Stover Collection.

Snider, Nell Achsah Smith (1873–1955)   1319
Papers 1897–1955
2 items

Collector. Typescripts (n.d.) regarding pioneer life in early Kansas and Oklahoma Territory, and the lives of Lucile Snider Parks and Nell Achsah Smith, and their experiences in Pawnee, Oklahoma Territory.

Snodgrass, Bill (b. ca. 1937)   1320
Manuscript 1959
1 item

College student. A term paper (1959) entitled "Early Development of Labor Unions in Oklahoma," in which the author details the rise of labor guilds, brotherhoods, and unions in Indian Territory and Oklahoma Territory.

Snow, Jerry Whistler   1321
Papers 1893–1915
2 feet

Collector. Correspondence (1893–1915) to and from members of the Whistler family regarding life in Oklahoma Territory, and describing a first ride in an automobile, sicknesses and quarantines, floods, Sac and Fox Indian dances and customs, the Sac and Fox Indian Agency and its agent, Lee Patrick, the Chilocco Indian School, wild west shows, Christmas traditions, and Independence Day celebrations. Correspondents include Maude Mayes Whistler, Pearl Mayes Whistler, and Gertrude Nadan.

Unpublished finding aid available.

Snyder, Lawrence H.   1322
Papers 1833–1958
.10 foot

Geneticist. Sketchbooks (1833–1862) in which Snyder's mother wrote poems and drew leaves and cross-sections of flowers; and articles (1947–1958) by Snyder regarding genetics.

Society of Friends Collection   1323
Printed materials 1952–1973
.25 foot

Religious denomination. Published reports (1953–1956) of annual meetings of the Society of Friends (Quaker) Committee on Indian Affairs; a report (1952) entitled "American Indian Development," by the National Congress of American Indians; annual reports (1972–1973) of Friends Centers in Oklahoma; a checklist (n.d.) of repositories holding Society of Friends records; and related publications by the Society of Friends concerning the church's support of Indian affairs.

Sohlberg, George Gustar (b. 1863)   1324
Papers 1857–1942
7 feet

Miller. Financial papers (1883–1929) detailing Sohlberg's association with business interests in early Oklahoma City, Oklahoma, especially the milling industry; and publications (1882–1939), including books, pamphlets, brochures, and flyers on art, music, travel, and motion pictures, along with event programs from the 1914 season of the Overholser Theatre in Oklahoma City, and from the seven hundredth anniversary of the city of Berlin, Germany, an automobile construction and care manual published in 1919 by the Cole Motor Car Company, and numerous works regarding major cities and countries throughout the world as they were before World War I; paper money (1857) issued by a bank in Nebraska; and certificates (1909–1934) issued to Sohlberg and others, including one appointing him a member of the Oklahoma City reception committee for President Woodrow Wilson. Also in this collection are booklets detailing the status of aviation (ca. 1920) in the Kingdom of Siam.

Unpublished finding aid available.

Southeastern Oklahoma Medical Association Collection   1325
Records 1921–1942
.33 foot

Medical society. Minutes (1921–1939); correspondence (1930–1942); and the constitution (1922) of the association. The collection also includes papers (n.d.) read before the association, which consists of members from eleven southeastern Oklahoma counties.

Southern Plains Indian Agencies Collection   1326
Records 1804–1899
4.25 feet

Governmental agency. Photocopies of correspondence (1804–1899) between U.S. Indian agents throughout the southern Great Plains region and government officials, regarding the Arapaho, Cheyenne,

Kiowa, Osage, Pawnee, Sac and Fox, Wichita, and other Indian tribes. Correspondents include John Beach, Lawrie Tatum, and generals E. D. Townsend, Philip H. Sheridan, and William T. Sherman.

Unpublished finding aid available.

[324] **Southwestern Association of Naturalists Collection**   1327
Records 1953–1988
3 feet

Professional organization. Correspondence (1953–1981) and general files (1953–1988) regarding the operation, function, and activities of the Southwestern Association of Naturalists. Included in the collection are the minutes of the board of governors, the organization's constitution, and files regarding the history of the association.

Unpublished finding aid available.

Southwestern Oklahoma Survival Association Collection   1328
Records 1869–1959
6 feet

Citizens' organization. Records (1957–1959), including correspondence, news releases, news clippings, and municipal, organizational, and legislative resolutions regarding the U.S. Army's intention in 1957 to greatly expand the land area of Fort Sill, Oklahoma, for purposes of creating a missile firing range, and the formation of a regional citizens' coalition, the Southwestern Oklahoma Survival Association, which eventually thwarted those plans. Also included in this collection is information regarding prior expansions of Fort Sill, Oklahoma, 1869–1957.

Unpublished finding aid available.

Southwick, (Mrs.) Harl F.   1329
Manuscript 1898–1949
1 item

Collector. A manuscript (ca. 1949) relating the origin and history of the Garber Christian Church in Garber, Oklahoma.

Spencer, Maude Clinkenbeard   1330
Printed materials ca. 1962
4 items

Genealogist. Genealogies (1962) of the Clinkenbeard and Willford families, compiled by Maude Spencer, including an entry regarding the captivity and rescue of relatives kidnapped by Delaware Indians in 1757; and a history of the Winchester store in Winchester, Woods County, Oklahoma.

Spinden, Herbert Joseph 1331
Papers 1932
1 item

Anthropologist. A paper read at the 1932 meeting of the American Association for the Advance of Science, entitled "Manuscripts of Southern Mexico." The manuscripts referred to are the Selden and Bodley codices, held in the Bodleian Library at the University of Oxford.

Spring, Otto F. 1332
Papers 1923–1964
.33 foot

Archaeologist. Correspondence (1923–1964) received by Spring regarding archaeological projects in Oklahoma, including excavations or explorations of mounds, earthworks, settlements, and caverns. The collection includes many items of correspondence from Joseph Thoburn of the Oklahoma Historical Society, expressing that organization's interest in Spring's work.

Springstead, Clarence S., Jr. (b. ca. 1936) 1333
Papers 1882–1946
.10 foot

Collector. Correspondence (1911–1945); postcards (1934); newspaper clippings (1893); naturalization certificates (1882–1894); military records (1884–1933); and a last will and testament (1946), all regarding the immigration to the United States of Haus Kjennernd, a Norwegian, and his subsequent service in, and retirement from, the U.S. Army. Also included in this collection are maps (1881–1890) of Washington, D.C., and of Oslo, Norway.

Stafford, B. S. (b. 1853) 1334
Papers 1853–1932
.10 foot

Businessman. A manuscript (1932) of B. S. Stafford's memoirs, entitled "Incidents and Recollections of My Life," in which he describes the Civil War in South Carolina and slavery on his father's plantation. Also included are accounts of land speculation and bank failures in Oklahoma and Texas.

Staggs, Carrie Edna   1335
Diplomas 1909–1913
2 items

Musician. Two diplomas (1909–1913) issued to Carrie Edna Staggs by Stephens College in Missouri and by the University School of Music in Michigan.

Stalker, Harry   1336
Papers 1892–1954
4 feet

Physician. General correspondence (1904–1950); a diploma (1896) and medical licenses (1896–1909); notebooks and correspondence relating to his education; and correspondence (1936–1948); printed material (ca. 1910–1950); ledgers (1894–1914); daybooks (1896–1951); and other financial records, all relating to his medical practice and farm in Pond Creek, Oklahoma.

Unpublished finding aid available.

Standifer, John E. (1867–1934)   1337
Records 1900–1908
3 items

Physician. Ledgers (1900–1907) in which Standifer recorded patient accounts; and certificates (1900–1908) authorizing him to practice medicine in Oklahoma. Included in the back of one ledger is a speech written by Standifer regarding an unidentified medical topic.

Standifer, Orion C. (b. 1896)   1338
Printed materials 1900–1903
3 items

Physician. Issues of medical magazines entitled *The Medical Council* (1900) and *Medical Talk* (1903).

Stephens, Margaret Clark (b. ca. 1920)   1339
Papers 1847–1969
.10 foot

Collector. Newspaper and magazine articles (1847–1969) regarding James Kirker (also referred to as Santiago Querque and Santiago Kirker); and a photocopy of a manuscript (1907) regarding frontier life and conditions near Arkansas City, Kansas, during the opening of the Cherokee Strip and subsequent settlement in Oklahoma Territory.

Stevens, Robert S.   1340
Papers 1870–1875
.25 foot

Railroad manager. Typescripts of letters to and from Robert S. Stevens regarding Stevens's management of the Missouri, Kansas, and Texas Railroad, of which he was general manager. Included in the collection is a letter to Stevens from President U. S. Grant regarding a trip Grant made from St. Louis, Missouri, to Springfield, Missouri, and Indian Territory. The Western History Collections also holds a more complete set of the Stevens papers on microfilm. The original Stevens Family Papers are in the Division of Rare Books and Manuscripts, Cornell University Library, Ithaca, New York.

Stewart, Elijah King   1341
Papers 1950
.10 foot

Politician. Correspondence (1950) from Victor Wickersham, Oklahoma congressman, and from Elijah King Stewart regarding their contest for Wickersham's congressional seat in 1950; and one of Stewart's political posters used during the campaign. In the correspondence are allegations of wrongdoing brought by Stewart against Wickersham, as well as Wickersham's response to the charges.

Stewart, Roy Pittard (1905–1989)   1342
Papers 1980–1982
1.33 feet

Journalist. Manuscripts and galley proofs of books (1980–1982) by Stewart, including *The Turner Ranch* and *One of a Kind: The Life of C. R. Anthony*; and one unpublished manuscript, "Ambassador on Horseback," regarding the life and career of Oklahoma-born jockey Everett Haynes. The manuscript regarding Haynes details his experiences as a jockey in Oklahoma, California, Mexico, France, and Germany, and describes with clarity the history of Germany as observed by Haynes from the mid-1920s through World War II, including accounts of his visit with President Paul von Hindenburg, the burning of the Reichstag in Berlin in 1933, and Haynes's flight from the Nazis in 1939.

Unpublished finding aid available.

Stigler First National Bank Collection 1343
Records 1903–1940
35 feet

Bank. Financial records of the First National Bank of Stigler, Oklahoma, including general ledgers (1905–1939); tellers' cash books (1903–1940); journals (1908–1940); discount registers (1918–1938); warrant registers (1914–1932); transfer ledgers (1906–1918); bank remittance ledgers (1915–1930); drafts registers (1909–1924); reconciliation of accounts books (1909–1937); individual loans registers (1920–1927); liability ledgers (1906–1927); distribution of expenses ledgers (1907–1935); bills receivable ledgers (1916–1918); certificate of deposit registers (1903–1922); and an insurance policy ledger (n.d.).

Unpublished finding aid available.

Stigler Masonic Lodge No. 121 Collection 1344
Ledger 1920–1922
1 item

Local Masonic chapter. A ledger containing the minutes (1920–1922) of the A. F. & A. M. Lodge No. 121, a Masonic order chapter in Stigler, Oklahoma.

Stigler, Oren 1345
Papers n.d.
.10 foot

Student. Two copies of a paper (n.d.) written by Oren Stigler as a student at the University of Oklahoma, entitled "The Early Explorations of the Columbia River."

Stith, Ruth Brewer 1346
Papers 1863–1931
.10 foot

Collector. Correspondence (1911, 1931) relating to the works of Theodore F. Brewer, and short manuscripts by Brewer concerning Methodism in Indian Territory, entitled "The Indians of Oklahoma," "Muskogee Ministerial Association," "Work Among the Indians," "A Historical Sketch of our Work in Oklahoma," "Meeting of the General Board of Education," and "Spaulding Female College." Also included is a manuscript poem (1863) entitled "Red Shiloh," attributed to Brewer, and purportedly written after his participation in the Battle of Shiloh.

Stone, DeWitt (1874–1937)   1347
Ledger 1926
1 item

Physician. A ledger (1926) in which DeWitt Stone recorded patient accounts, including services rendered and fees charged.

Stone, Lucile Oliver   1348
Publications 1917–1943
.10 foot

Collector. Publications and programs (1917–1943) of P.E.O. chapter and state meetings; the Alternate Saturday Club of Pauls Valley (1917–1925); and the Music Club of Pauls Valley, Oklahoma (1917).

Stough, D. F., Sr. (d. 1950)   1349
Printed material 1943
1 item

Physician. A yearbook (1945) published by the Oklahoma State Medical Association containing all state laws and regulations pertaining to the practice of medicine in Oklahoma as of 1945.

Stovall Museum Collection   1350
Papers 1634–1721
7 items

Natural history museum. Handprinted and painted antiphonaries, psalmody manuscripts, and a Roman missal (1634–1721) from a colonial-era church in San Lucas Camotlán, Oaxaca, Mexico.

Stovall, John Willis (1891–1953)   1351
Papers 1925–1952
3.50 feet

Paleontologist. Correspondence (1935–1952) and ledgers (1935–1938) regarding archaeological excavations in Oklahoma, sponsored by the Works Progress Administration and by the Stovall Museum of the University of Oklahoma, including site reports, findings, and operation reports and requests; and publications (1925–1950) by Stovall and others regarding zoology, evolution, and paleontology, as well as operations and procedural manuals of the Works Progress Administration. The correspondence series of this collection reflects the University of Oklahoma's involvement with the Works Progress Administration.

Unpublished finding aid available.

Stover, Samuel Murray   1352
Diary 1849
2 items

Physician. A diary kept by Stover recording his trek from Missouri to California in 1849, along with a privately printed edition of the diary, published by Stover's descendants.

Stromstad, Ralph J.   1353
Papers and printed materials 1932–1996
2.15 feet

Author. Correspondence (1932–1992); manuscripts (1945–1996); poetry (n.d.); and published works (1980–1994) by Ralph J. Stromstad. Includes text and illustrations for Stromstad's books, such as *The Little People of Castle Mountain* (1980–1981), *There Goes the Neighborhood* (1994), and *The Saga of G.I. Joe* (1990).

Stroud State Bank Collection   1354
Records 1893–1943
38.50 feet

Bank. Financial records (1893–1943) from the Stroud (Oklahoma) State Bank and its predecessors, the Sac and Fox Bank and the Milfay State Bank, including general ledgers, cash journals, stock certificate ledgers, tellers' cash books, draft registers, discount registers, insurance registers, distribution of expense ledgers, bills receivable ledgers, reconcilement ledgers, note and discount registers, and remittance registers; also, correspondence (1900–1918) from the Stroud State Bank; a bank examiner's report (1941) on the Stroud State Bank; and minutes (1919–1924) of the Milfay State Bank's board of directors.

Unpublished finding aid available.

Struble, (Mrs.) Howard   1355
Papers 1885–1923
.10 foot

Collector. Profit-sharing certificates (1906) issued by Sears, Roebuck, and Company, and a souvenir program (1922) from the seventieth-anniversary celebration of the Chicago, Rock Island, and Pacific Railroad Company, held in McAlester, Oklahoma. Though brief, the program contains the early railroad history of the area, as well as information regarding the settlement and subsequent growth of the towns of North McAlester and South McAlester, Oklahoma.

Sturgis, James Wellings 1356
Papers 1931–1949
3 items

Professor. A letter (1932) from David R. Boyd congratulating Mr. and Mrs. Sturgis on receiving the "Most Useful Citizens" award from the city of Norman, Oklahoma, along with a news magazine (1949) and news clippings (n.d.) regarding the career and death of Mrs. Sturgis's brother, George Burton Parker, a nationally known journalist and former Oklahoman.

Sullivan, (Mrs.) Jim L. 1357
Records 1893–1901
2 items

Collector. A certificate (1893) appointing James Wilks as the first postmaster of Rathbone, Oklahoma Territory; and a land patent (1901) issued to the Wilkses for property in Rathbone, located in County "G," Oklahoma Territory.

Summer Institute of Linguistics Collection 1358
Printed materials 1949–1966
.10 foot

University language center. Reprints of articles by authors affiliated with the Summer Institute of Linguistics at the University of Oklahoma. The collection also includes copies (1962) of *Proceedings of the Ninth International Congress of Linguists*.

Sutton, George Miksch (1898–1982) 1359
Papers ca. 1914–1967
31 feet

Ornithologist. Correspondence (1943–1982); manuscripts (ca. 1920–1967); diaries and field notes (1914–1920); artifacts relating to ornithology in Oklahoma and Mexico; and copies of dissertations (n.d.) by his students. Correspondents include George Lynn Cross, Jean and Richard Graber, John Kirkpatrick, and Olin Sewell Pettingill.

Unpublished finding aid available.

Swank, David (1931–) 1360
Papers ca. 1965–1975
5 feet

Professor. Correspondence and legal papers (1965–1975) of Swank, along with printed materials relating to his legal research at the University of Oklahoma.

Unpublished finding aid available.

Swearingen, Martha T. (b. ca. 1873) 1361
Records 1895–1909
.10 foot

Pioneer homemaker. Appraisals (1905) issued by the Townsite Commission of the Cherokee Nation for lots in Ramona, Indian Territory; a lease (1909) for land in Washington County, Oklahoma; and a work permit (1895) issued by the Cherokee Nation to one of its citizens, Whiteturkey, granting him the privilege of hiring a white non-citizen to farm his land. This collection also includes a patent (1907) for land in Ramona, Indian Territory.

T-Bone Ranch Collection 1362
Papers 1914, 1931–1932
3 items

Cattle ranch. Reprint of an article by Walter Harrison from the *Tiny Times*; a pen and ink drawing by Amber Davis; and a poem entitled "Dreams at the T-Bone Ranch," by Clarence Douglas.

Tait, J. H. 1363
Papers ca. 1920–1925
1 foot

Engineer. Correspondence (1920–1925) and reports (1920–1925) of J. H. Tait, district engineer in Muskogee, Oklahoma, for the Oklahoma Highway Commission. These materials reflect the state of highway construction in Oklahoma in the early 1920s.

Tanghe, Jerry 1364
Printed materials 1882–1962
.10 foot

Collector. Newspaper clippings and three typescript accounts by survivors of the 1862 Lake Shetek massacre in Minnesota, and a Lyon County, Minnesota, road map.

Tantlinger, Edith, and D. Vernon Tantlinger (b. 1864) 1365
Printed materials 1903–1936
.50 foot

Performers. Scrapbooks (1905–1936) and diaries (1903–1912) regarding the Tantlingers' performances in wild west shows, including Buckskin Bill's Historical Wild West Show and the Miller Brothers 101 Ranch Wild West Show.

[333]

Tarpley, Bloyce 1366
Papers 1862–1863
3 items

Collector. Photocopies of correspondence (1862–1863) between Jacob Moss, a Union soldier, and his family in Missouri, who sympathized with the Confederates, regarding Moss's experiences and the issues that divided his family.

Taylor, Guy William 1367
Papers 1893–1940
5 feet

Physician. General correspondence (1893–1940); financial records (1902–1937) and personal writings of Taylor; two scrapbooks (n.d.), one of his school days, and one containing postcards; biographical materials; minutes and programs (1895–1935) of the Athenaeum Club of El Reno, Oklahoma; and personal artifacts including locks of hair, pins, beadwork, and a cloth napkin.

Unpublished finding aid available.

Taylor, John C. (d. 1935) 1368
Records 1920–1930
.10 foot

Physician. Medical case histories (1920–1924); correspondence (1920–1930) concerning cases; and notes (1920–1930) on testing and treatment procedures, all from Taylor's medical practice in Chelsea, Oklahoma.

Taylor, Joseph Richard (1907–2000) 1369
Papers 1932–1997
.66 foot

Professor and sculptor. Correspondence (1997) by Joseph R. Taylor; newspaper articles (1947–1995) regarding Taylor's work; exhibition programs (1959–1984) featuring Taylor's work; newspaper articles (1969–

1979) regarding Taylor's wife, Elsie Taylor; and a scrapbook (1932–1969) containing photographs of the Taylor family, friends, and works, along with newspaper clippings and brochures regarding Taylor's career as a sculptor and professor of art at the University of Oklahoma.

Taylor, William Merritt 1370
Papers 1881–1892
3 items

Soldier. Items regarding Taylor's service in the U.S. Army's Eighth Infantry Battalion, including his copy of the *Soldier's Handbook* (1881) and certificates (1889–1892) of promotion to the ranks of corporal and sergeant, respectively.

Teeter, Mary Bachelor 1371
Papers 1885–1910
.10 foot

Collector. A children's book (1885); and newspaper clippings (1905–1910) from the Mangum, Oklahoma, area.

Temple First State Bank Collection 1372
Records 1909–1925
8 feet

Bank. Correspondence (1909–1923) from the First State Bank, Temple, Oklahoma, regarding the daily commerce of the bank; and general ledgers (1909–1925) in which daily financial transactions were recorded.

Territorial Oklahoma Manuscripts Collection 1373
Papers 1881–1907
.33 foot

Subject collection. Typescript and original manuscript accounts (1881–1907) by pioneers and frontiersmen, regarding the settlement of Oklahoma and Indian territories.

Territory of Kansas Collection 1374
Printed materials 1856–1880
.25 foot

Subject collection. Documents (1856–1880) regarding territorial and early statehood-era Kansas, including settlement leaflets and brochures; U.S. centennial celebration event programs (1876); Civil War–era government proclamations and patriotic event programs (1863–

1873); a leaflet (1888) published by the Plainsville (Kansas) School Board denying the accusation that they ordered history texts sympathetic to the Confederate cause; and one leaflet (1879) regarding the influx of African-American settlers to Kansas from southern states.

Thompson, Alfred M., Sr. (1859–1948)   **1375**
Papers 1885–1948
.50 foot

Merchant. Correspondence (1902–1948) concerning the death of Thompson's son in France during World War I, and the controversy over a new townsite for Walters, Oklahoma Territory; publications (1913–1919) regarding the Allies' victory in World War I and Oklahoma's contributions to the cause; a program (1936) of the Wichita Mountains Easter Pageant; and certificates (1885–1920) appointing Thompson postmaster of a small city in Texas, a member of the official reception committee in Oklahoma City for President Woodrow Wilson, and chairman of the Democratic Party Precinct Committee. Also in this collection are a scrapbook and a typescript (n.d.) of a speech by Thompson regarding the origin and early years of Walters, Oklahoma Territory.

Thompson, Harry Edgar (1865–1964)   **1376**
Papers n.d.
1 item

Professor. A photocopy of a membership certificate (n.d.) issued to Harry Edgar Thompson by the 89ers Association of Oklahoma.

Thornton, Agatha R.   **1377**
Papers 1919–1931
.10 foot

Teacher. Collection includes printed materials (1919–1931) on educational activities at the University of Oklahoma and Lahoma High School, Lahoma, Oklahoma; four grade books (1926); and correspondence (1926) from students.

Thornton, Hurschel Vern (b. ca. 1900)   **1378**
Papers 1940–1951
1.66 feet

Professor. Correspondence (1940–1951) regarding the annual Boys State of Oklahoma, as well as a proposed revision of the constitution of Oklahoma. Included in this collection are budgets and procedural manuals (1940–1951) of the Boys State of Oklahoma conventions.

Three Forks Ranch Collection 1379
Papers 1835–1986
.10 foot

Ranch. Correspondence (1985–1986) with accompanying information submitted in an effort to place the ranch on the National Register of Historic Places, including maps of the ranch and environs, a history of the ranch from 1835 to 1986; and news clippings regarding the history of the town of Okay (formerly North Muskogee) in Wagoner County, Oklahoma, near where the Three Forks Ranch is located.

Tibbs, Burrell 1380
Printed materials 1898–1918
1.50 foot

Collector. Scrapbooks containing newspaper stories and clippings (1898–1918) detailing the early history of aviation in Oklahoma.

Tiger, Moty (b. 1840) 1381
Printed materials 1899–1931
.25 foot

Indian chief. Typescripts of newspaper articles (1899–1931) relating to the change in status of the Creek Nation, and the role of Tiger, its first principal chief after the amalgamation of Indian Territory into Oklahoma.

Tilghman, William Matthew (1854–1925) 1382
Papers 1843–1960
2 feet

Lawman. Correspondence (1901–1960) regarding the Tilghmans, as well as gangsters and outlaws, Communist infiltration of the Works Progress Administration in Oklahoma, and poets and writers of Oklahoma; Tilghman's personal financial records (n.d.); manuscripts and typescripts (n.d.), including the memoirs of Bill Tilghman and writings by Zoe Tilghman regarding the first Christmas in Oklahoma City, Oklahoma Territory; publications (1843–1949) by the Poetry Society of Oklahoma, the Oklahoma Authors Club, and the Women of '89 Club, including a mid-nineteenth century book on feminine etiquette; programs (1903–1934) of academic, social, charitable, and religious institutions and organizations; newspaper clippings regarding outlaws; and showbills (n.d.) for western-oriented motion pictures.

Unpublished finding aid available.

Timmons, Alice, and Boyce Timmons (1911–1996)   **1383**
Papers 1892–1982
.33 foot

University employees. Correspondence (1972–1976) and printed materials (1966–1982) relating to American Indian projects in which the Timmonses were interested, such as the Alaska Native Law Project, the North Slope Legal Assistance Project, the American Indian Institute, and the Alaska Legal Services Corporation.

[337]

Tittle, Leon H. (b. ca. 1895)   **1384**
Papers 1891–1903
.10 foot

Attorney. Legal documents (1891–1900), including tax and pay receipts; and judicial documents (1894–1899), including injunction bonds, writs of injunctions, and transcripts of court judgments, all from Greer County, Texas, and, after 1896, Greer County, Oklahoma Territory. Also included in this collection are sheriff deputization certificates (1895–1899); citizen announcements of cattle brands claimed (1894); one homestead certificate (1903); and one teacher certificate (1899), also from Greer County, Oklahoma Territory. The homestead certificate bears the signature of President Theodore Roosevelt, and a number of earlier documents bear the official stamp of Greer County, Texas. The teacher certificate is among the first issued in Greer County, Oklahoma Territory.

Tobias, Henry Jack (b. 1925)   **1385**
Printed materials 1913–1980
1.50 feet

Professor. A typescript (n.d.) regarding Martin I. Zofness and the history of Poles in Bartlesville, Oklahoma; a photocopy of a thesis (1946) by Randall Falk regarding Jewry in Oklahoma; and a photocopy of a report entitled "The Story of Oklahoma Jewry," along with photocopies and original issues of Jewish newspapers (1913–1980) published in Oklahoma. The collection also includes photocopies of published biographies of prominent Oklahoma Jews, and a letter (1975) by Lt. Gov. George Nigh to Zofness regarding Zofness's suggestion for promoting tourism in Oklahoma.

Unpublished finding aid available.

Tolbert, James Randolph (1862–1942) 1386
Papers 1909–1941
20 feet

Attorney. Correspondence (1909–1941) regarding Tolbert's participation in Oklahoma politics, including his election to office, terms served as a state legislator, and the Al Smith for President campaign in Oklahoma, of which he was head; reports (1923) and accompanying documentation for the impeachment proceedings and investigation of Governor Jack Walton by a special committee of the legislature, of which Tolbert was vice chair; and posters (1942) by Norman Rockwell, produced during World War II and entitled "The Four Freedoms."

Tolbert, Raymond A. 1387
Papers 1909–1951
3 feet

University regent. Correspondence (1922–1951) regarding the planning, construction, and operation of the University of Oklahoma's student union building and football stadium, and regarding the School of Law, the Alumni Association, and the university hospital, along with the articles of incorporation (1923–1928) for the Oklahoma Memorial Union board of governors.

Unpublished finding aid available.

Tolleson, William Alfred (1869–1953) 1388
Records 1873–1953
16 feet

Physician. Tolleson's personal and professional correspondence (1896–1953) on matters including his employment as a physician for the Missouri, Kansas, and Texas Railroad; financial papers (1877–1949) of the Tolleson family; lecture notes (1894–1895) taken by Tolleson while in medical school; newspaper clippings (1925–1942) regarding medicine; and materials from Tolleson's medical practice in Eufaula, Indian Territory, and Oklahoma, including medical equipment and supply catalogs (1928), registers of medical prescriptions given (1929–1937), and patient account and appointment registers (1873–1942). Also in this collection are posters (1895–1898) depicting seventeenth- and eighteenth-century medical practices, and certificates (1948–1949) marking Tolleson's long service to the practice of medicine in Oklahoma.

Tompkins, Stuart Ramsay (b. 1886)   **1389**
Papers 1917–1956
4.75 feet

Historian. Personal and professional correspondence (1932–1956); Tompkins's book manuscripts (n.d.) on the Soviet Union; lecture notes (n.d.) used by Tompkins in his classes on Russian history; student grade registers (1932–1955) from Tompkins's courses at the University of Oklahoma; and Tompkins's diary (1917) detailing his experiences with the Sixth Canadian Trench Mortar Battery in France during World War I.

Tonkawa Public Library Collection   **1390**
Papers 1834–1938
.10 foot

Subject collection. Typescripts (1938) of interviews with pioneers and army officers associated with the Tonkawa, Oklahoma, area regarding U.S. Army operations, Indians, the establishment of churches, schools, forts, communities, trails and roads, and the general settlement of that area from 1834 forward. Also in this collection are several typescripts (1938) of news articles regarding settlement in Oklahoma and Oklahoma Territory.

Tonkawa Sunny Side Club Collection   **1391**
Minutes 1917–1918
1 item

Social club. A minute book (1917–1918) recording the proceedings, attendance, and activities of the Tonkawa (Oklahoma) Sunny Side Club, a literary and patriotic society formed during World War I.

Torrey, John Paine (b. 1870)   **1392**
Papers 1892–1928
5 items

Physician. Diplomas and certificates (1892–1928) issued to John Paine Torrey by medical schools, hospitals, and the armed services, licensing him to practice medicine.

Totco, Incorporated Collection   **1393**
Printed materials 1984
3 items

Petroleum company. Full-color posters (1984) honoring the oil field worker and oil drilling profession, 1920–1930.

Tracy, Fred
Papers 1889–1911
.10 foot

1394

Writer. Three manuscripts (n.d.) by Fred Tracy entitled "Acts of Violence in No Man's Land," "Reminiscences of No Man's Land," and "B. M. and E.," all regarding the history of the Oklahoma panhandle region and the efforts to obtain railroad service in Beaver, Oklahoma.

Treat, Guy Bradford (d. 1980)
Records 1903–1955
4 feet

1395

Railroad official. Correspondence (1925–1947); reports (1906–1955); minutes (1945); financial records (1918–1946); maps (1904–1955); and publications (1909–1955) regarding the operations, financial status, and policies of railway companies in central and southeastern Oklahoma. The companies included are the Oklahoma Railway, the Oklahoma City Railway, the Metropolitan Railway, and the El Reno Interurban and the Norman Interurban railroads. The collection also contains correspondence (1947) regarding the liquidation of the Oklahoma City streetcar system, and the development of the Diamond Dishwasher Company (1925).

Unpublished finding aid available.

Trimble, Vance H. (1913–)
Papers 1899–1997
10.5 feet

1396

Journalist and author. Correspondence (1937–1995); research files (1986–1990); manuscripts (1953–1990); newspaper clippings, magazines, and scrapbooks (1899–1997) from the life and career of journalist and 1960 Pulitzer Prize winner Vance H. Trimble. In 1960, Trimble was awarded a journalism "triple crown": the Pulitzer Prize for national reporting, the Sigma Delta Chi award for distinguished Washington correspondence, and the Raymond Clapper Award for the year's best Washington reporting, for an investigation of nepotism and payroll abuses in Congress. The collection also includes publicity and book reviews for Trimble's biographies of Happy Chandler, E. W. Scripps, and Sam Walton.

Unpublished finding aid available.

Truss, Sam M. 1397
Manuscript 1913
1 item

Collector. A manuscript entitled "History of the Truss Family From 1786 to 1912," by C. C. Truss.

Tucker, Amelia A. (d. 1956) 1398
Papers 1913
1 item

Collector. A certificate (1913) appointing Marshall Tucker as a delegate to the Southern Commercial Congress of 1913, held in Mobile, Alabama.

Tucker, Barren E., and Wanda Tucker 1399
Printed materials 1935–1980
.10 foot

Collectors. Printed materials (1935–1980) regarding Spiro, Oklahoma, and vicinity. Included are histories of New Hope Cemetery and the Spiro Baptist Church, and an article entitled "Our Choctaw Heritage."

Tucker, Fred V. (b. ca. 1895) 1400
Manuscript ca. 1890–1940
1 item

Rancher. A photocopy of an unpublished, untitled manuscript (n.d.) by Tucker, regarding life and times (1890–1940) in Kenton, Oklahoma Territory, and the surrounding region, of which Tucker was an early resident.

Tucker, Hampton (b. 1870) 1401
Papers 1895–1945
15 feet

Lawyer. Legal case files (1895–1945); correspondence (1895–1945); coal mining reports (1899–1916); and related papers concerning Tucker's service as mining trustee for the Choctaw Nation, 1912–1918, as national attorney for the Choctaw Nation, 1924–1929, and as mining trustee for the Choctaw and Chickasaw Nations, 1929–1949.

Unpublished finding aid available.

Tucker, Marshall A. (1871–1939)   1402
Papers 1896–1939
3 items

Pharmacist. A poem (1936) by Tucker regarding his deceased mother; a biographical sketch (1939) of Tucker; and a diploma (1896) awarded Tucker by the University of Oklahoma Territory. It was the second degree awarded by the university.

Tucker, R. Truman (b. ca. 1910)   1403
Papers 1930–1979
.66 foot

Rancher. A scrapbook (1930–1975) of news clippings and mementos regarding early days in Kenton, Oklahoma, and vicinity; correspondence (1975–1979) and news clippings (1975–1979) regarding the discovery of prehistoric footprints, known as the "Black Mesa footprints," on Tucker's ranch.

Tuggle, C. E.   1404
Papers 1901–1921
7 items

Grocer. Letters of reference (1901) written by Texas bankers regarding Tuggle; a printed letter (n.d.) in President Woodrow Wilson's handwriting urging Americans to support the country's war effort during World War I; picture postcards (ca. 1907) of Siloam Springs, Arkansas, and the University of California at Berkeley; along with a stock certificate (1921) issued by the Grady County Park in Chickasha, Oklahoma.

Tulsa County Medical Society Collection   1405
Printed materials 1908–1945
1 item

Professional society. A booklet (1945) published by the Tulsa County (Oklahoma) Medical Society regarding its history from its establishment through World War II.

Tulsa Public Schools Collection   1406
Report 1907–1957
1 item

Public school system. A report (1957) by the Tulsa, Oklahoma, superintendent of schools, entitled "Fifty Years of Progress in the Tulsa Public Schools 1907–1957." Also included in the document is the superintendent's annual report for the 1956–1957 school year.

Turbyfill, Harper Subert (b. ca. 1900)   **1407**
Papers 1916–1923
.50 foot

Teacher. High school yearbooks (1916–1923) from the towns of Norman, Moore, and Seminole, Oklahoma; and a scrapbook (1918–1923) containing photographs, news clippings, drama, and other event programs from Turbyfill's student days at the University of Oklahoma.

Turley, Louis Alvin   **1408**
Manuscript 1947
1 item

Professor. An unpublished manuscript (1947) by Turley, entitled "Nephron: A Critical Study of the Data from the Structure, Pathology, and Experimentation on the Function of the Several Parts of the Kidney."

Turlington, Marcellus Martin (1868–1949)   **1409**
Records 1891–1937
4 feet

Physician. Ledgers (1906–1937) in which Turlington recorded medical services rendered and the fees charged. Two of these ledgers record accident and disability cases of workers from the nearby Seminole oil field, and the others document changing social and health-care conditions in Indian Territory and Oklahoma during this period. Also in this collection are certificates (1891–1906) awarded Turlington during his career.

Unpublished finding aid available.

Turnbo, Silas C. (b. ca. 1844)   **1410**
Manuscript 1861–1865
1 item

Confederate soldier. A bound typescript (n.d.) of Turnbo's journal, in which he records his personal observations regarding the actions and views of the citizens of Indian Territory and the states of Arkansas, Missouri, and Kansas during the Civil War.

Turner, Martin Luther (1863–1921)   1411
Papers 1888–1921
.50 foot

Financier. Correspondence (1888–1921); news clippings (1896–1921); scrapbooks (1896–1917); and broadsides, regarding Turner's life, his campaign for election as U.S. senator from Oklahoma, his involvement in the world of finance, both in Oklahoma Territory and elsewhere, and his death. A number of the clippings pertain to the economic climate, politics, and living conditions in Oklahoma Territory. Of special note are letters (1916–1920) addressed to Turner from Brig. Gen. John J. Pershing requesting Turner's assistance and influence in obtaining a promotion to major general. One letter is addressed from the headquarters of the U.S. Army Punitive Expedition in Mexico, and others are from Europe, sent by Pershing while commander-in-chief of the American Expeditionary Forces during World War I.

Turpin, Carl J. (d. 1942)   1412
Papers 1888–1941
3 feet

Railroad developer. Correspondence (1888–1941) to the Turpins regarding family and personal affairs; reports (1934–1938) of the Oklahoma State Federation of Women's Clubs; newspaper clippings (1916–1941); cancelled checks (1913–1918); and event programs (1909–1938) from organizations and clubs, including the Oklahoma Symphony Orchestra, the Oklahoma State Federation of Women's Clubs, and the New Century Club, along with the Edelweiss Club and Literary Club, both of Clinton, Oklahoma.

Unpublished finding aid available.

Turtle, Willie   1413
Papers 1901–1911, 1944
.33 foot

Collector. Land allotment documents (1901–1911) signed by William McKinley, allocating land to four Kiowa Indians. The collection also includes weekly ration coupons (ca. 1944) for the Geimansaddle family.

U.S. Army Collection: Tenth Infantry Regiment   1414
Records 1855–1903
6 feet

Military unit. Correspondence (1865–1866); reports (1855–1902); muster rolls (1865–1869); and casualty returns (1856–1868), reflecting the service of the regiment in Minnesota, Kansas, Utah, and the Dakota territories, as well as Cuba and the Philippine Islands. Included in these registers are casualty statistics and brief action reports, several of which document engagements with Sioux and Cheyenne Indians. Those registers from the Spanish-American War forward include many enlistees from Fort Reno, Oklahoma Territory.

Unpublished finding aid available.

U.S. District Court Collection: Central District of Indian Territory 1415
Ledger 1903
1 item

Federal court. A ledger (1903) of the court, entitled "Abstract of Mortgages, Liens and Deeds of Trust," in which entries regarding these documents were recorded.

U.S. District Court Collection: Northern District of Indian Territory 1416
Ledger 1897–1900
1 item

Federal court. A prisoner docket book kept by the U.S. marshal, Leo E. Bennett, of the Northern District of Indian Territory, Muskogee, Indian Territory, for the years 1897–1900. The book records prisoners' names, race, age, criminal charge, date received, arresting officer, committing judge, sentence, and dates released.

U.S. District Court Collection: Western District of Arkansas 1417
Records 1872–1903
.25 foot

Federal court. Correspondence (1872–1903) regarding U.S. District Court business and the administration of justice in Indian Territory. The collection includes a legal opinion by Isaac Parker regarding the case of *Ex-Parte James E. Reynolds*.

U.S. District Court Collection: Western District of Oklahoma 1418
Records 1890–1935
156 feet

Federal court. Stenographers' notebooks (1893–1910); books of statutes (1873–1912); cases and rules of procedure; U.S. marshals' records (1890–1912); and court clerks' records (1892–1921) concerning witness, juror, prisoner, and court staff expenses; ledgers (1898–1935); and correspondence (1894–1926) of the court clerk and the marshal with the attorney general, the U.S. attorney, and others.

Unpublished finding aid available.

USS *Oklahoma* Collection 1419
Printed materials 1917–1939
.10 foot

U.S. Navy battleship. Newsletters published by the crew of the USS *Oklahoma*, including *Oklahoma's* (1917–1918); *The Sea Bag of the USS Oklahoma* (1933–1935); and *The Oklahoma Powwow* (1938–1939).

Unger, Marion Draughon Murray 1420
Papers 1924–1936
1.25 feet

Oklahoma colonist in Bolivia. Correspondence (1924–1928) from Marion Murray, the wife of Johnston Murray, to family members in Oklahoma regarding the experiences of the Murray family in Bolivia, including accounts of their travel to Bolivia, the establishment of Murray's colony, and of its daily operation. A number of letters contain diagrams of the colony's layout. Also included in this collection are miscellaneous items such as Bolivian travel permits, newspapers, artifacts, and newspaper articles (1932–1936) regarding William H. Murray.

Unpublished finding aid available.

Union Equity Coop Exchange Collection 1421
Printed materials 1926–1948
.33 foot

Agricultural coop. Brochures (1926–1948) regarding the Union Equity Coop Exchange, including the history and bylaws, and a directory of its members.

United Auto Workers Collection 1422
Printed materials 1945–1957
.10 foot

Labor union. Brochures and booklets (1945–1957) published by the

United Auto Workers regarding its stance on such issues as civil rights, automation, strikes, and time study, and regarding programs offered by the union, including employment plans, training programs, and guaranteed payment programs. The collection also includes copies of a journal (1956–1957) published by the union and entitled *UAW Ammunition*.

University of Oklahoma Association Collection 1423
Papers 1910–1912
.10 foot

Alumni organization. Letters (1910–1912) from each member of the university's Class of 1910, describing his or her experiences after graduation.

University of Oklahoma College of Pharmacy Collection 1424
Printed materials 1934–1948
1 foot

University college. Constitution and bylaws (1938); programs (1934–1948) of the annual conventions; programs of the annual banquets (1939–1943); and a placard (1944) of the Oklahoma University Pharmaceutical Association. The placard is for the association's War Conference and bears the inscription "Pill-Rolling for Victory." The collection also contains correspondence (1939) regarding the possible appointment of Everett E. Duncan to the Federal Trade Commission.

University of Oklahoma Press Collection 1425
Records 1928–1962
195 feet

Scholarly press. Correspondence (1928–1956) between directors of the press and University of Oklahoma officials and department heads, and with authors and prospective authors, regarding the daily operation of the press, its publishing procedures and standards, and books published. Correspondents include William Bennett Bizzell, Joseph A. Brandt, Bernard Devoto, J. Frank Dobie, and Archibald MacLeish. Also included in this collection are readers' reports (1930–1956) submitted to the press, critiquing authors' works; book manuscripts (1934–1956) rejected by the press, and book manuscripts (n.d.) accepted, filed by author; and minutes and proceedings (1944–1961) of various working committees of the American Association of University Presses, and of the University of Oklahoma, including the Semi-Centennial Committee (1956–1957); the DeGolyer Committee (1949–1955), charged with forming what is now the University of Oklahoma's History of Science Collection; the Distinguished Service Citation Committee (1947–1955); the Committee on University and Town (1944–1945); and the Division of Manuscripts, Archives, and Rockefeller Foundation Committee (1946–1948), charged with establishing what is now the manuscript division of the Western History Collections.

Unpublished finding aid available.

University Women's Association Collection   1426
Records 1949–2000
3 feet

University association. Official records of the University Women's Association, including minutes (1949–1999), directories (1960–2000), newsletters (1970–1998), scrapbooks (1949–1982), and the bylaws and constitution.

Updegraff, Ruth   1427
Papers 1843–1909
3 Items

Collector. Copies of two declarations of sale (1832, 1853) of slaves in the Cherokee Nation, and a declaration of land allotment (1909).

Utterback, Bert R. (1891–1926)   1428
Papers 1895–1945
.10 foot

Author. Short story manuscripts (n.d.) by Utterback, written around his reminiscences (1895–1945) of territorial and early statehood-era New Mexico, with descriptions of the roles cowboys, ranches, cattle, horses, and influenza epidemics played in the social fabric and progress of the region.

Van Ausdal, Harvey G.   1429
Printed material 1898–1950
1 item

Pharmacist. A newsletter (1950) entitled *Dr. Hess Dealer News*, containing an article regarding the history of the Van Ausdal Drug Store of Centralia, Indian Territory, and, later, Welch, Oklahoma.

Van Cleave, William E. (b. 1877) 1430
Papers 1926–1940
.25 foot

Physician. Correspondence (1926–1940); manuscripts entitled "Indian Medicine" and "Important Points in the Early Diagnosis of Tuberculosis," by Van Cleave; a biographical sketch of Van Cleave; annual reports (1926–1934) of medical activity at the Choctaw-Chickasaw Sanitorium; issues of the *TB Tom Tom* newsletter (1933); and newspaper clippings about Van Cleave, the sanitorium, and his work with the Indians at the sanitorium.

Van Dorn, Fred 1431
Papers 1969
.33 foot

Military officer. An invitation to the presidential inauguration of Richard M. Nixon and Spiro T. Agnew, along with a list of inaugural activities, a calendar, and an order form for inauguration souvenirs.

Van Dyke, Gerald Mason (1895–1959) 1432
Papers 1912–1961
.10 foot

Soldier and musician. Poetry and music manuscripts (ca. 1912–1961) composed by Van Dyke about his philosophies on life and death, the Japanese attack on Pearl Harbor, and life in Cordell, Oklahoma. Also included in this collection is a biographical sketch of Van Dyke.

Vance, Leon Robert, Jr. (1916–1944) 1433
Papers 1933–1953
.50 foot

Soldier. Correspondence (1946–1953); newspaper clippings (1944–1953); and published materials, including magazines and event programs regarding Vance's death, his posthumous receipt of the Congressional Medal of Honor, the renaming of the Enid, Oklahoma, Army Air Field in his honor, and the dedication of a dormitory at the University of Oklahoma in his name, all in recognition of his wartime achievements. The collection also includes correspondence (1933–1945) regarding his father's death, as well as letters of praise he received from his parents while he was a student at the University of Oklahoma.

Vaughan, Floyd Lamar (b. 1891)   1434
Papers 1951
1 item

Professor. Reprint (1951) of an article by Floyd Lamar Vaughan entitled, "Important Differences in U.S. and U.K. Patent Systems."

Vaught, Edgar Sullins, Sr. (1873–1959)   1435
Printed materials ca. 1907–1955
1 foot

Judge. Typescripts of instructions (1907–1955) to juries regarding civil and criminal cases, some given by Judge Vaught while presiding over the U.S. District Court, Western District of Oklahoma. Types of cases include prostitution, negligence, personal injury, mail fraud, civil rights, breach of contract, bankruptcy, conspiracy to defraud, murder, pornography, embezzlement, price fixing, and drug trafficking.

Unpublished finding aid available.

Vinita Lions Club Collection   1436
Records 1943–1955
.66 foot

Civic club. Records (1932–1955), including correspondence, reports, and membership rosters of the Vinita, Oklahoma, Lions Club.

Virden, John M. (1908–1968)   1437
Papers 1951–1968
4 feet

U.S. Air Force officer. Correspondence (1953–1968) regarding Virden's writings and other subjects; newspaper and magazine articles (1951–1968) by and about Virden; and one book-length manuscript (ca. 1965) entitled "Andrew J. Byrne," written by U.S. ambassador to France, James M. Gavin, with Virden's assistance. Principal correspondents in this collection include James M. Gavin, Carl Albert, Neill Bohlinger, Walker D. Grisso, and Arthur McAnally.

Unpublished finding aid available.

Vliet, Richard M.   1438
Papers 1934–1965
4 feet

Pharmacist. Personal correspondence (ca. 1934–1948) of Vliet and his wife, Gertrude M. Vliet; diaries (1937–1952) kept by Gertrude M. Vliet; financial records (ca. 1935–1965); and correspondence (1934–1948) relating to the Fox-Vliet Drug Store in Oklahoma City, Oklahoma.

Unpublished finding aid available.

Von Keller, Frederick Philander P.   1439
Papers 1888–1935
.10 foot

Physician. An expense book (1888–1889); student lecture notes (1895) from Von Keller's electro-therapy class; and certificates and diplomas (1888–1935) issued to him by medical schools and by the Chickasaw Nation.

Wagner, J. E.   1440
Manuscript 1874–1896
1 item

Farmer. Memoirs entitled "Memories of Oklahoma," in which Wagner relates his experiences in Texas and Oklahoma Territory.

Walker, Andrew Beattie   1441
Papers 1903–1972
.10 foot

Dentist. Manuscripts (n.d.) regarding the history of the Bank of Fairview, Oklahoma, and the arrival of the railroad in that city, along with a savings account record book (1903) from the bank; a letter (1903) regarding the Oklahoma (Territory) Dental Association and the Board of Dental Examiners; a certificate of practice (1903) issued to Walker; and news clippings (1961–1972) regarding the history of the *Fairview Republican* newspaper and of the town of Quapaw, Oklahoma.

Walker, Charles F. (b. 1875)   1442
Letter 1898–1956
1 item

Physician. A letter by Walker (1956) regarding his life and career in Grove, Indian Territory and Oklahoma.

Walker, Christopher Columbus (1874–1952) 1443
Printed materials 1927–1952
7 items

Banker. Newspaper clippings (1927–1952) regarding the death and burial of C. C. Walker, and his contribution to the city of Okemah, Oklahoma.

Walker, John Riley (b. 1880) 1444
Papers 1904–1944
.33 foot

Physician. Papers (ca. 1930–1940) presented by Walker before the Oklahoma State Medical Association; and a college yearbook (1904) from Keokuk College in Keokuk, Iowa, along with a booklet (1907) also published by the college.

Walker, Tandy C. (1814–1877) 1445
Printed materials 1877–1929
5 items

Indian statesman. Typescripts of news articles (1877–1929) on the career and death of Col. Tandy C. Walker, the organizer of the first Choctaw-Chickasaw regiment for Confederate army service.

Walker, Thelma Brown 1446
Manuscript 1889–1907
1 item

History student. A typewritten paper (ca. 1970) by Walker regarding the history of Oklahoma Territory, the Cherokee Strip, and Fairview, Oklahoma Territory.

Wallace, Cecile Boone 1447
Scrapbook 1957
1 item

Teacher. An ethnobotanical pressbook (1957) compiled by Wallace containing wild plant specimens along with descriptions of their use by Indian tribes.

Wallace, Jesse E. (1880–1955)   1448
Printed materials 1955
2 items

Physician. Obituaries (1955) of Tulsa physician Jesse E. Wallace.

Walton, John Calloway (1881–1949)   1449
Papers 1903–1948
3 feet

Governor of Oklahoma. Personal and official correspondence (1916–1948) regarding Walton's governorship, his removal from office, electioneering, and his campaign to rid Oklahoma of the Ku Klux Klan; election campaign literature and materials (1919–1938) generated during Walton's bids for public office; speeches (1922–1938) delivered by Walton as governor; newspaper clippings (1919–1943) regarding Oklahoma politics; transcripts (1923) of testimony given at trials concerning racist and Klan-sponsored incidents in Oklahoma, and at Walton's impeachment; and publications (1923–1924) regarding the Klan, politics, and government.

Unpublished finding aid available.

Ward, D. C.   1450
Printed material 1889–1939
1 item

Missionary. A typescript of an article (1939) regarding the history of the Cache Creek Indian Mission in southwestern Oklahoma, which ministered to Plains Indian tribes.

Wardell, Morris L. (1889–1957)   1451
Papers 1921–1956
34 feet

Professor and historian. Correspondence (1921–1956) relating to Wardell's service as a professor of history and an assistant to the president of the University of Oklahoma, and concerning student affairs, foreign students, curriculum, academic department administration, military training, housing, the University of Oklahoma during World War II, post-war planning, and legislative matters, as well as Wardell's involvement in civic organizations, his teaching, and his publishing activities; reports (1929–1945) from the deans, personnel department, registrar's office, and academic departments of the University of Oklahoma; and lecture notes, research materials, and manuscripts relating to the Cherokee Indians, and specifically to Wardell's book *Political History of the Cherokee Nation* (University of Oklahoma Press, 1938), to the Osage Indians, to historic sites in Oklahoma, and to the history of the West in general.

Unpublished finding aid available.

Warne, Rhoda Foster   1452
Printed materials 1938
2 items

Collector. Newspaper clippings (1938) regarding the history of Helena Township, Oklahoma Territory, and of a pioneer who participated in the 1893 land run into the Cherokee Outlet.

Warner, Carolyn Rexroat   1453
Papers 1947–1995
.10 foot

Television personality and politician. Photographs and newspaper clippings which document the life and career of Carolyn Rexroat Warner as a student at Classen High School in Oklahoma City, Oklahoma, as a student at the University of Oklahoma, as a television personality at WKY-TV in Oklahoma City, as a contestant in the Miss Oklahoma City contest, as the Arizona Superintendent of Public Instruction, as the 1984 Arizona Democratic Gubernatorial nominee, and as the author of *The Last Word*. Also includes newspaper clippings and a photograph of actress Susan Peters, and an interview with Warner regarding her role in early radio talk shows and television in the Oklahoma City area.

Watson, Archer Hunter, Sr.   1454
Papers 1910
.10 foot

State official. Correspondence (1910) from Watson to his fiancée regarding the controversial decision to move the capitol of Oklahoma from Guthrie to Oklahoma City. Watson was a member of the State Corporation Commission and these letters reflect an inside knowledge of the conflict. Also included in this collection is a news clipping regarding the hostility of citizens in Shawnee, Oklahoma, to Watson's support for the Oklahoma City site.

Watts, Charles Gordon, Sr. (1875–1964)   1455
Papers 1907–1944
113 feet

Judge. Correspondence (1907–1944) regarding Watts's personal affairs, politics and government at the state and local levels, and the progress and resolution of legal cases in which he was involved; and publications (1914–1944), also regarding politics and government at the local, state, and national levels. The correspondence series of this collection reflects Watts's interest in the welfare of the Democratic Party in all state and national elections from 1910 to 1944, with many letters and telegrams regarding the character and suitability of candidates for office.

Unpublished finding aid available.

Waynoka Commercial Bank Collection   1456
Records 1909–1940
8 feet

Bank. Financial records (1909–1940), including cash books, journals, Liberty Bond registers, treasurer's warrant registers, insurance policy registers, trial balance ledgers, and general ledgers, all from the Waynoka (Oklahoma) Commercial Bank.

Wear, John B.   1457
Records 1885–1900
.10 foot

Physician. A ledger (1898–1900) in which Wear recorded services rendered to patients, as well as fees charged in his Poteau, Indian Territory, medical practice, along with admission cards (1885–1887) for lectures at an Arkansas college.

Weaver, Carlton (1881–1947)   1458
Papers 1906–1924
.10 foot

Newspaper editor. Correspondence (1906–1947) to and from Weaver regarding the prospects for, and operation of, a newspaper in Ada, Indian Territory, and in the proposed state of Oklahoma, along with information regarding Ku Klux Klan activities in Oklahoma, especially the Klan's involvement in party politics and its effect upon local politicians.

Weaver, Claude Dickens, Sr. (b. 1867)   1459
Papers 1885–1934
.25 foot

Attorney. Diplomas (1885–1887) from Gainesville (Texas) High School and from the University of Texas, along with certificates (1904–1934) authorizing Weaver to practice law in Texas and before the supreme courts of the United States and Oklahoma Territory, appointing Weaver secretary to the governor, a district judge, a delegate to the National Conference on the Interstate Liquor Question in Washington, D.C., and postmaster of Oklahoma City, Oklahoma.

Webbers Falls, Indian Territory Collection   1460
Records 1889–1894
.10 foot

Municipality. A journal (1889–1894) listing account names and amounts forwarded, and recording information about the cost of a house built in Vinita, Oklahoma.

Weber, S. G. (d. 1952)   1461
Records 1931–1937
.33 foot

Physician. Ledgers (1931–1937) in which Weber recorded patient accounts and fees charged at his Bartlesville, Oklahoma, medical practice, including accounts with the Indian Territory Illuminating Oil Company and Phillips Petroleum Company.

Websterian Literary Society Collection   1462
Records 1907–1931
.25 foot

Social club. Minutes (1907–1920) of meetings; membership rosters (1907–1931); event programs (1928); and the constitution and bylaws (1907) of the Websterian Literary Society of the University of Oklahoma.

Weese, Asa Orrin (1885–1955)   1463
Papers 1921–1956
3.66 feet

Professor. Correspondence (1948–1955) regarding personal matters;

articles (1921–1943) published by zoology professor Asa Orrin Weese; reports and publications (1947–1953) of the Oklahoma Academy of Science and the Oklahoma Fish and Game Council; and minutes (1942–1956) of the meetings of the University of Oklahoma Department of Zoology faculty, and of the University of Oklahoma Faculty Senate. Also included in this collection are meteorological and climatological reports (1933–1947) compiled for the Oklahoma City, Oklahoma, area.

Unpublished finding aid available.

Welch, Oklahoma, Town Records Collection 1464
Records 1899–1926
.66 foot

Municipality. A criminal docket (1899–1909) for the municipal court of Welch, and the minutes (1911–1926) of the town council. Welch, originally located in the Delaware District of the Cherokee Nation, Indian Territory, is now in Craig County, Oklahoma.

Welsh, Jack D. 1465
Papers 1861–1865
2 feet

Collector. Photocopies of the service records of ninety-seven Confederate States Army generals.

Unpublished finding aid available.

Weltfish, Gene 1466
Papers 1935–1954
.50 foot

Anthropologist. Analysis worksheets (1954) for Pawnee prehistoric weaving samples, and microfilmed field notes (1935) relating to Weltfish's work among the Pawnee Indians.

Wenner, Fred Lincoln (1865–1950) 1467
Papers 1887–1956
3.33 foot

Journalist. Typescripts and manuscripts (1889–1939), and newspaper clippings (n.d.) regarding the settlement and history of the territory and state of Oklahoma, with information concerning schools, cities and towns, justice, government, and religion; and correspondence (1904–1950) between Wenner and the Territorial Board for the Leasing of School Lands, of which Wenner was secretary, regarding board business, and from governors and other notable personalities of Oklahoma Territory regarding politics and government, social conditions, and early territorial history. This collection also includes a warrant issued by the city of East Guthrie, Indian Territory, (later Guthrie, Oklahoma Territory) and dated June, 1889.

Unpublished finding aid available.

West, Beth 1468
Papers 1913–1983
2.66 feet

Teacher. Subject files (1913–1983) containing correspondence, diaries, family history, and school yearbooks relating to Beth West's career as a schoolteacher, her student activities at Alva High School and Northwestern State Teachers College, Alva, Oklahoma, and her participation in organizations such as the Oklahoma Heritage Association and the Daughters of the American Revolution.

Unpublished finding aid available.

Westfall, Chester Harold (b. ca. 1898) 1469
Printed materials 1917–1919
.10 foot

Oilman. One copy of *Sooners in the War*, the official report of the Oklahoma State Council of Defense, of which Westfall was secretary, and seventy-five, four-color propaganda posters published by the U.S. government during World War I, including those of the U.S. School Garden Army, Red Cross, and Victory Loans series.

Wheatley, Thomas W. 1470
Papers 1905–1939
.50 foot

Coal mine operator. Correspondence (1928–1937); labor contracts (1933–1939); wage notices (1917–1936); machine contracts (1921–1939); advertising brochures (1926–1936); and orders (1937–1939) issued by the National Bituminous Coal Commission of the U.S. Department of the Interior, all in regard to the coal mining industry in southeastern Oklahoma. Included is information regarding wages, mine safety and accidents, organized labor, industry standards, coal production, mine railroads, and a 1930 mine explosion in Pittsburg County, Oklahoma, in which thirty miners were killed. This collection also contains survey reports (1905–1906) submitted to the Samples Coal Mining Company regarding the potential coal wealth of the Choctaw Nation, Indian Territory, which the Samples Company later mined.

Wheeler, J. Clyde   1471
Printed materials 1943–1955
.10 foot

Clergyman. An autographed book manuscript (1955) by Wheeler, entitled "Here Lies Our Hope," about the history of the Christian faith, 1943–1955.

Wheelock Seminary Collection   1472
Papers 1898
1 item

Orphan school. An account of expenses incurred while transporting groceries from Clarksville, Texas, to Wheelock Seminary in Garvin, Indian Territory.

Whitaker, Lovie   1473
Papers 1953–1963
.10 foot

Collector. Correspondence, newspaper clippings, and printed material (1953–1963) relating to the U.S. Army's attempt to take over a part of the Wichita Mountains Wildlife Refuge for a missile firing range.

White Shrine of Jerusalem Collection   1474
Printed materials 1940
.10 foot

Charitable organization. Publications (1940) explaining the mission and purpose of the Oklahoma chapter of this women's organization devoted to helping the sick.

White, Hal H.   1475
Manuscript 1935
1 item

Physician. A paper on ureteral calculi (1935), presented at a meeting of the North Texas Medical Association.

一九三七年十月，挺向冀西的晋察冀八路军骑兵营。

Cavalry Battalion moving towards Western Hopeh - Oct 1937

一九三七年十月，向长城内外进军之找晋察冀八路军一路主队。

8R Route Army seizing strategic points along the Great Wall - Oct 1937

This page is from a scrapbook given to Patrick J. Hurley, U.S. Ambassador to China, by the staff of General Headquarters of Chin Cha Chi Military Region, China, 1944. The photographs and text describe the military activities of the 8th Route Army near the Great Wall of China in 1937. From the Patrick J. Hurley Collection.

White, (Mrs.) J. R. 1476
Warrant 1898
1 item

Collector. A warrant (1898) for fifty dollars issued by Wilson Fisher, treasurer of Red River County, Choctaw Nation, and made payable to himself.

White, Lida 1477
Papers 1891–1952
2.50 feet

Teacher. Correspondence (1891–1952) regarding White's employment, her historical research, her investments in Montana real estate, and personal matters with family and friends; leases and contracts (1936–1947); notebooks (n.d.) containing lecture notes; unorganized research notes (n.d.) entitled "Indian Lore"; and four notebooks containing typescripts of interviews (1934–1942) that White conducted with elderly Indians in Tulsa, Oklahoma, and with early settlers of the Oklahoma City area. In addition to biographical and socio-economic information, the interviews focus on the education of Indians and the establishment of schools in Indian Territory and Oklahoma.

Unpublished finding aid available.

Whitehill, Walter Muir (b. 1905) 1478
Manuscript 1967
1 item

Author. An annotated manuscript (1967) by Whitehill, entitled "Dumbarton Oaks—The History of a Georgetown House and Garden, 1800–1966."

Whitney, Charles W. 1479
Records 1864–1865
.10 foot

Army officer. Correspondence (1864–1865) of the military commissary general, Lt. C. W. Whitney, of Port Hudson, Louisiana, during the Union Army's occupation of that city.

Wichita Indian Agency Collection 1480
Papers 1871–1876
3 items

Indian agency. A letter (1872) to agent Jonathan Richards regarding the return of two Indians to the Kiowa Agency; a photostatic copy of

[361]

a statement (1871) of funds remitted to the agency; and a photostatic copy of a report (1876) of the agency's employees.

Wilkins, Thurman 1481
Papers 1986
.33 foot

Author. A manuscript and galley proof of Wilkins's book *Cherokee Tragedy: The Ridge Family and the Decimation of a People*, published by the University of Oklahoma Press in 1986.

Wilkinson, Otha 1482
Papers 1891–1907
.10 foot

Clergyman. A letter (1896) from Wilkinson to his family in McLoud, Oklahoma, describing his journey from Oklahoma to California; diaries (1891–1907) kept by Wilkinson, detailing his evangelizing activities in Oklahoma, Kansas, and the Midwest; and news clippings (1903) about church meetings and events in several Oklahoma Territory towns.

Will Rogers Scholarship Fund Collection 1483
Records ca. 1940–1955
2 feet

College scholarship fund. Scholarship applications (1941–1949) from University of Oklahoma students, along with correspondence (ca. 1940–1955) relating to the applications.

Willard, Melissa Kate 1484
Papers 1782–1852
3 items

Collector. Land registration records (1785–1786) for land located between the Tennessee and Cumberland rivers in what would become the state of Tennessee; and receipts (1851–1852) issued by the U.S. postmaster and by a private express company, both in San Francisco, California, for a money transfer and for the shipment of gold dust to New York City.

Williams, Arthur James (1877–1954) 1485
Papers 1905–1951
7 feet

Professor. Correspondence (1913–1930) from the Oklahoma Bureau of Geology regarding its publications and operations, and the geological and mineral characteristics and potential of Oklahoma counties; geological reports (1913–1930), with accompanying maps, regarding the geological and mineral characteristics and resources of Oklahoma counties; oil well logs (1905–1925), organized by county; and registers of students grades (1915–1951) compiled by Williams while a member of the University of Oklahoma faculty.

Unpublished finding aid available.

Williams, Charles H.   1486
Papers 1937
1 item

Collector. A paper entitled "We Visit a Home Over 20,000 Years Old in the Arkansas Mountains, and Find the Master Still There," a written account of the experience of Charles Williams and Otto Spring while exploring a cave in the Boston Mountains in Arkansas, also known as the Outlaw Mountains.

Williams, John Robert (1866–1931)   1487
Papers 1906–1910
.50 foot

Political campaign manager. Correspondence (1906–1910); telegrams (1909–1910); publications (1910); news clippings (1910); and broadsides (1910) regarding the Democratic and Republican parties in Oklahoma, and the campaigns of Lee Cruce and his opponent for the governorship of Oklahoma in 1910. The collection includes correspondence (1906) from Senator Gordon Russell regarding Congress's plans for admitting Oklahoma to the Union.

Williams, Mary Clay   1488
Records 1871–1911
.33 foot

Collector. Receipts (1871–1911) of Henry Clay and Mary Jennings of Lancaster, Kentucky, for purchases of food, hardware, general merchandise, and carriage equipment. Also in this collection is a letter (1909) describing a collision between an early automobile and a horse-drawn buggy.

Williams, Meredith Newton (1904–1949)   1489
Papers 1919–1950
.33 foot

Journalist. Correspondence (1942–1950) from Governor Leon C. Phillips and from Walter M. Harrison, a newspaper editor, praising stories Williams wrote as a reporter for the *Daily Oklahoman* newspaper and regarding his transfer to a newspaper in Iowa; interdepartmental memos (1929–1930) of the *Daily Oklahoman* regarding the assignment of stories and potential stories; telegrams (1949–1950) and newspaper obituaries (1949) regarding Williams's death; an event program (1935) for an Oklahoma City Gridiron Club banquet; and copies of the Marshalltown, Iowa, *Times-Republican* newspaper (1945–1950), for which Williams worked after leaving Oklahoma. Also included in this collection is Williams's diploma (1919) from the Wentworth Military Academy of Lexington, Missouri.

Williams, Samuel   1490
Papers 1909–1949
.66 foot

Cotton farmer. Correspondence (1909–1949) to and from Williams regarding the Beckham County, Oklahoma, war relief and finance efforts during World War I, Williams's invention and eventual patenting of a cotton-cleaning machine, and Williams's views on world and national events in the post–World War II years; blueprints (ca. 1924) for the cotton-cleaning machine; a typescript (n.d.) by Williams regarding the Chisholm Trail in Beckham County; and official reports (1918–1919) regarding the progress and status of the Liberty Bond and Liberty Loan drives in Beckham County during World War I. The correspondence includes a letter (1918) from Governor Robert L. Williams regarding the war finance effort in Oklahoma.

Williams, Stephen   1491
Papers 1955
.33 foot

Professor. A photocopy of a report by Williams, entitled "The Aboriginal Location of the Kadohadacho and Related Indian Tribes." Its stated purpose is to present available data concerning the location of the Caddo Indians from the period of the first recorded contact (the 1512 DeSoto Expedition) to the Treaty of 1835.

Willibrand, William Anthony 1492
Papers 1927–1955
.25 foot

Professor. Typescripts (1952) of Willibrand's speech regarding the twenty-fifth anniversary of *Books Abroad* (now *World Literature Today*), and marking the seventieth birthday of its first editor, Roy Temple House; reprints of articles, and periodicals containing articles (1940–1955) authored by Willibrand; and copies of lectures (1946) entitled "Currents in American Thought," delivered at the Fort Reno, Oklahoma, prisoner-of-war camp by a German inmate just after the close of World War II.

Willis, Robert F. 1493
Papers 1912–1913
1 item

Inventor. A patent issued to Robert F. Willis of Gotebo, Oklahoma, for improvements in Windrower attachments for mowers. A diagram of the invention is included on the application.

Willour, J. A. 1494
Scrapbook 1904–1905
1 item

Collector. A scrapbook containing letters of reference (1904–1905) from prominent citizens in the northeastern United States for F. J. Bonesteel, a lawyer from New York who settled in Indian Territory.

Wilson, Andrew R. 1495
Ledger 1907–1908
1 item

Hosteler. A guest register (1907–1908) from the Eskridge Hotel in Wynnewood, Oklahoma, listing guests, their home addresses, and prices of rooms.

Wilson, Milbourne Otto (b. 1890) 1496
Records 1926–1952
.50 foot

Professor. Student grade books (1930–1952) kept by Wilson for his psychology classes at the University of Oklahoma, along with a program (1926) from the inauguration of William B. Bizzell as president of the University of Oklahoma. The collection also includes an annual report (1935–1936) of the public schools of Glencoe, Illinois.

Wimberly, Harrington (b. 1901)   1497
Records 1924–1948
6.33 feet

Journalist and political leader. Official stenographer's reports (1945–1946) of the eight hearings of the U.S. Federal Power Commission's investigation of the natural gas industry; and reports (1947–1948) containing the findings of the commission. Also included in this collection are supporting documents (1924–1943) used during the investigation, including maps, charts, publications, and reports. Among the publications are the annual reports (1924–1940) of the Federal Power Commission, of which Wimberly was vice chairman.

Unpublished finding aid available.

Witcher, Esther   1498
Scrapbook 1935
1 item

Librarian. A scrapbook (1935) containing newspaper clippings of Will Rogers's column and accounts of his death.

Witte, (Mrs.) Juan R.   1499
Records 1896–1921
.10 foot

Collector. Legal papers issued to Frank R. Rogers regarding the acquisition and use of lands in Georgia and Oklahoma Territory, including a mining lease (1896) for land in Georgia; a deed of conveyance (1907) for land in Gotebo, Oklahoma Territory; a homesteading certificate (1904) issued by Governor Frank Frantz and signed by President Theodore Roosevelt; and mortgage contracts (1920–1921). Also included is a grazing lease (1907) issued by Governor Frantz, which specifies the conditions under which school lands could be used.

Wolf, Jonas (d. 1900)   1500
Printed materials 1884–1900
.25 foot

Indian chief. Typescripts of messages, statements, and proclamations (1884–1900) made by Wolf as governor of the Chickasaw Nation on the issues of land use, finances, allotments, and statehood, along with typescripts of newspaper articles and editorials (1894) regarding Wolf's arrest for embezzlement.

Wolf, Leland   1501
Papers and sound recordings 1952–1974
.33 foot

Speaker of the Oklahoma House of Representatives. A transcript (ca. 1974) of an interview with Leland Wolf, in which he reminisces about former governors, legislators, and major legislation during his twenty-two years of service in the Oklahoma House of Representatives.

Wolfe, Oscar (1888–1963)   1502
Manuscript 1960
1 item

Pipeline consultant. A two-volume manuscript (1960) entitled "The Hydraulic Design of Oil and Gas Pipe Lines," written by Oscar Wolfe.

Wolfe, Reed E. (1885–1948)   1503
Records 1918–1948
1 foot

Physician. Account books (1918–1948) in which Wolfe recorded patient services rendered and fees charged; and minutes (1920) of the Choctaw County (Oklahoma) Medical Society, in which a list of county physicians is included, along with one letter regarding the Tri-County Medical Society of Choctaw, Pushmataha, and McCurtain (Oklahoma) counties.

Unpublished finding aid available.

Womack, John (1911–1987)   1504
Papers 1889–1984
11.33 feet

Postal employee and historian. Publications written by Womack, including manuscripts (1982–1984), newspaper clippings (1984), and pamphlets (1981–1983), along with correspondence (1980–1984) and research materials relating to these publications. The research materials include claims (1890–1920); saloon licensing papers (1896–1909); tax levies and assessments (1902–1912); bonds (1906–1912); reports (1902–1910); and related records of Cleveland County, Oklahoma, and its townships and cities.

Unpublished finding aid available.

Woman's Christian Temperance Union Collection   1505
Records 1918–1925
.25 foot

Civic organization. Minutes (1918–1925) of the Woman's Christian Temperance Union of Bismarck, North Dakota. The minutes include administrative details as well as financial statements. Also in the collection are four receipts for goods and services provided to the Methodist church where the organization met, and two announcements of meetings.

Women's History Project Collection   1506
Papers 1870–1900
.25 foot

History project. Typescripts of reports (1977) regarding the history of women and women's rights in Oklahoma, as well as biographies of historically prominent women, prepared by students participating in the University of Oklahoma Women's History Project.

Wood, Edwin K.   1507
Papers 1875–1892
.25 foot

Collector. An act (1875) of the Choctaw Nation, establishing burglary as a crime; acts (1889–1892) of the Cherokee Nation, appointing Elias C. Boudinot II, Thomas M. Buffington, David Rowe, and Richard M. Wolfe as Cherokee delegates to Washington, D.C., along with instructions to address land issues such as the return of Fort Gibson, Indian Territory, to the Cherokees; requests (1905–1906) for payment of salaries and expenses of the attorneys and special marshal of the Cherokee Nation; a committee report (1889) regarding payment for Cherokee lands given the Osages under the Cherokee Treaty of 1866; and a term paper (n.d.) by Wood, entitled "The Indian Treaty Maker."

Woodard, Fred Barton (b. 1871)   **1508**
Papers 1920–1953
.33 foot

Lawyer. Personal and business correspondence (1934–1953), mostly relating to Republican Party politics, with Hamilton Fish and John H. Kane the principal correspondents. Also included are government documents and other published materials (1920s–1940s) regarding American Indians, such as hearings before congressional committees on Indian affairs, relating to relief of needy Indians (1940); claims of the Shawnee and Delaware tribes (1920s–1936), the Yakima tribe (1939), the Snake or Paiute tribe (1940), and the Wichita and related tribes (1939); restrictions on the lands of the Quapaw Indians (1939); a report (1946) illustrating the reduction in size of the Fort Berthold Indian Reservation; a proposed constitution for the Brotherhood of North American Indians; a tearsheet of a biographical sketch of Charles Journeycake, a chief of the Delaware, written by Woodard in 1943; and publications on Indian lands in general.

Woodrow, Thomas W. (d. 1919)   **1509**
Papers 1880–1918
3.75 feet

Clergyman and socialist. Manuscripts (n.d.) and sermons (1880–1891) by Woodrow regarding his views on God, religion, socio-economics, and socialism; ledgers (ca. 1912) containing subscription requests for Woodrow's publication, *Woodrow's Monthly*; and publications (1913–1918) regarding the Socialist Party in Oklahoma and in the United States, the nature of God, and German war practices during World War I.

Woods, E. K.   **1510**
Papers 1876–1914
.25 foot

Collector. A bibliography (1876–1914) compiled by Woods on index cards and slips of paper, regarding the Indians of North America in Indian Territory, the U.S. agencies responsible for their administration, the clothing and dress of whites and Indians of the western United States, and the cattle brands common to the Cherokee Strip and Oklahoma Territory. The information regarding cattle brands includes a drawing of each brand, the name and location of the ranch on which it appears, and the name of the proprietor of the ranch.

Woodward, Grace 1511
Manuscript 1957
1 item

Writer. A manuscript (1957) by Woodward recounting the efforts of Edward D. Hicks, a Cherokee Indian, to establish the Cherokee Telephone Company at Tahlequah, Indian Territory, in 1885.

Woolaroc Museum Collection 1512
Printed materials 1950
4 items

Museum. Brochures (1950) published by the Woolaroc Museum in Bartlesville, Oklahoma, regarding its holdings and programs.

Wooton, Esther A. Reed 1513
Papers 1860–1941
.25 foot

Collector. An unpublished book-length manuscript (n.d.) by William E. Reed, entitled "As It Should Be," and letters (1941) by Reed describing the history of the town of Paris, Illinois, from the 1860s forward. The manuscript is a work of fiction set in Oklahoma at the close of the Civil War.

Worcester Academy Collection 1514
Printed materials 1885–1890
.25 foot

Indian school. Catalogs (1885–1890) of the academy listing trustees, officers, faculty, students, course offerings, and a general history and description of the school; a copy (1884) of "Pages from Cherokee Indian History" by Nevada Couch; and photocopies of documents relating to the founding and operation of the academy. Also included is an issue of the University of Oklahoma's *Extension Review* devoted to the life and career of Joseph W. Scroggs, the founder of Worcester Academy.

Works Progress Administration (WPA) Archaeological 1515
  Survey Project Collection
Records 1937–1942
1.25 feet

Federal project. Reports (1937–1942) submitted by the WPA Archaeological Survey Project of Oklahoma, regarding sites excavated in thirteen counties of Oklahoma and the findings therein. Included are reports entitled "Excavation of Prehistoric Indian Sites."

Unpublished finding aid available.

Works Progress Administration (WPA) Historic Sites and Federal Writers' Project Collection   **1516**
Records 1937–1941
23 feet

Federal project. Book-length manuscripts, research and project reports (1937–1941) and administrative records (1937–1941) generated by the WPA Historic Sites and Federal Writers' projects for Oklahoma during the 1930s. Arranged by county and by subject, these project files reflect the WPA research and findings regarding birthplaces and homes of prominent Oklahomans, cemeteries and burial sites, churches, missions and schools, cities, towns, and post offices, ghost towns, roads and trails, stagecoaches and stage lines, and Indians of North America in Oklahoma, including agencies and reservations, treaties, tribal government centers, councils and meetings, chiefs and leaders, judicial centers, jails and prisons, stomp grounds, ceremonial rites and dances, and settlements and villages. Also included are reports regarding geographical features and regions of Oklahoma, arranged by name, including caverns, mountains, rivers, springs and prairies, ranches, ruins and antiquities, bridges, crossings and ferries, battlefields, soil and mineral conservation, state parks, and land runs. In addition, there are reports regarding biographies of prominent Oklahomans, business enterprises and industries, judicial centers, Masonic (freemason) orders, banks and banking, trading posts and stores, military posts and camps, and transcripts of interviews conducted with oil field workers regarding the petroleum industry in Oklahoma.

Unpublished finding aid available.

Works Progress Administration (WPA) Historical   **1517**
Records Survey Collection
Printed materials ca. 1933–1942
24 feet

Federal project. Inventories (1937–1942) of church, county, state, and federal archives in thirty-three states, compiled by the Works Progress Administration Historical Records Survey. Included are inventories for church, state, and federal departments and agencies, and archives in eleven Oklahoma counties, as well as the vital statistics records for the state (1941) and a listing of church and religious organizations (1942) in Oklahoma. The collection also includes inventories of fifty-three Texas county archives and federal departments and agencies in that state.

Unpublished finding aid available.

Works Progress Administration (WPA) Statewide Projects Collection
Printed materials 1937–1942
.50 foot

1518

Federal project. Publications (1937–1942) of WPA programs in Oklahoma, including the Statewide Recreation Project; the Statewide Museum Service; and the Community Service Program. The collection also includes a radio script for the "Museum of the Air" series, sponsored by the WPA on the University of Oklahoma radio station, WNAD, in Norman, Oklahoma.

World Literature Today Collection
Papers 1926–1994
52 feet

1519

Literary journal. Correspondence (1926–1994) between *World Literature Today* editors and University of Oklahoma administrators and faculty, and with authors and prospective authors, regarding the operation of the journal, its publishing procedures and standards, and works published. Literary correspondents include Sherwood Anderson, John Dos Passos, Upton Sinclair, Thornton Wilder, and H. L. Mencken. Also included in this collection are specialized files (1926–1951) regarding the flight of authors and playwrights from Nazi Germany and Spain, and their exile in the United States and Mexico; reasons why women have not produced successful plays; and the special writing projects undertaken by prominent authors.

Unpublished finding aid available.

World Neighbors, Incorporated Collection
Records 1951–1958
.66 foot

1520

International relief organization. Correspondence (1954–1955); financial records (1951); minutes of boards and committees (1951–1954); and publications (1951–1958) of the Oklahoma-based World Neighbors, Incorporated, and its predecessor, World Assistance, Incorporated.

Woyna, Fritz Willie (1919–1965)   1521
Papers 1932–1965
11.66 feet

Television station director. Manuscripts (1941–1965) of short stories and novels by Woyna on various themes, including science fiction and westerns; research material (1933–1965) used for stories and novels; subject files (1952–1961) regarding advertising statistics, methods, and budgets; subject files (1953–1959) relating to television broadcasting, including files regarding sets, cameras, procedures, and budgets, and all reflecting the philosophy and methodology of the early days of television programming.

Unpublished finding aid available.

Wright, Albert Daniel (b. 1863)   1522
Manuscript 1881–1947
1 item

Merchant. A typescript (1947) of an account by Wright regarding his participation in the land run of 1889, settlement in the towns of Guthrie and Chandler, Oklahoma Territory, and his experiences and hardships in each.

Wright, Allen (1826–1885)   1523
Papers 1866–1930
2 feet

Indian chief and Presbyterian minister. Session minutes (1886–1900) of the Tali Hekia Presbyterian Church, Blue County, Indian Territory; Sunday school attendance records (1925–1926) of the Presbyterian church, Wapanucka, Oklahoma; typescripts of messages, proclamations, and statements (1866–1930) made to the general council of the Choctaw Nation by Wright, as principal chief; and typescripts of Wright's letters (1866–1885) to the editors of the *Vindicator* and other newspapers, all regarding governmental issues of the Choctaw Nation. Also included are books and pamphlets (1846–1900) relating to the Presbyterian church and its missionary programs, along with a typewritten biography (1930) of Allen Wright and an inventory (n.d.) of his private library.

Unpublished finding aid available.

Wright, Michael P.   1524
Printed materials 1976–1985
.10 foot

Collector. This collection includes seven issues of the *Oklahoma Socialist Movement Newsletter* (1976), and an unpublished manuscript (1985) by Maggie Gover, entitled "Will the Real Herb Hollomon Please Stand Up."

Wright, Rush L.   1525
Printed materials 1930–1942
.90 foot

Physician. Newspaper clippings (1930–1942) collected by Rush L. Wright while superintendent of the LeFlore County Health Department, LeFlore County, Oklahoma. Most clippings are in regard to health conditions in LeFlore County, although some report on social events such as births and deaths and events sponsored by community organizations.

Wyatt, Robert Lee, III (1940–)   1526
Printed materials 1907–1988
5 items

Collector. Publications (1907–1988) regarding the history of the First Presbyterian Church and the First Baptist Church of Grandfield, Oklahoma, and the First Baptist Church of Devol, Oklahoma, as well as pictorial directories of the membership of the First Baptist Church in Grandfield.

Wyatt, Rose Mary Burt (b. 1871)   1527
Papers 1886–1911
.10 foot

Collector. Printed speeches (1911) of Oklahoma senator Robert L. Owen; letters (1938–1943) from Samuel Sandheimer; and letters (1886–1889) from Mother Mary Joseph and Sister Mary Frances Bernard, Wyatt's former instructors at Sacred Heart Mission, Indian Territory. The letters were written from Saint Mary's Academy at Sacred Heart Mission, Saint Joseph's Convent in Krebs, Indian Territory, and Saint Catharine's Convent in Lehigh, Indian Territory, and are about mission work in those respective locations and throughout Indian Territory.

Yale First National Bank Collection 1528
Records 1900–1939
28 feet

Bank. Correspondence (1917–1939), and financial records (1902–1939), including general ledgers, draft registers, tellers' cash books, and daily statements, all regarding the daily business and financial status of the First National Bank of Yale, Oklahoma.

[375]

York, Bill 1529
Printed materials 1939–1949
.25 Foot

Radio station director. Songbooks (1939–1949) containing the music and words of songs by recording artists popular in Oklahoma in the 1940s and 1950s, including those of Roy Rogers, Ernest Tubb, and Merle Travis.

Young Men's Christian Association (YMCA) and Young 1530
   Women's Christian Association (YWCA) Collection
Records ca. 1920–1955
44 feet

Civic organizations. Activity, financial, and administrative records (1931–1948); and correspondence (1920–1950) of the University of Oklahoma branches of the YMCA and YWCA, along with bibliographies, scrapbooks, and clippings (1925–1950) relating to the organizations and their programs.

Unpublished finding aid available.

Young, Glen Olen (b. 1894) 1531
Papers 1950–1953
.10 foot

Politician. A typescript of a speech (1953) by Young to the National Conference to Abolish the United Nations, entitled "U.N.—Trap Door to Stalin's Jail, Baited with the Dove of Peace"; campaign literature (1950) regarding Young's candidacy for Congress; a biography (n.d.) of Young, produced for his election campaign; and publications (ca. 1953) authored by Young and produced by the Presbyterian church in Sapulpa, Oklahoma, alleging massive communist infiltration of the Presbyterian Church in the United States.

Young, Hiram 1532
Papers 1885–1921
.10 foot

Collector. Personal and family correspondence (1885–1921) between Hiram Young and other members of his family, in which they describe their lives in Indian Territory and the Neosho, Missouri, area. Correspondents include L. A. Young, Ada Jones, Mollie Davidson, and W. A. Davis.

Young, James Harvey 1533
Printed materials 1953
1 item

Physician. A reprint of an article (1953) by Young, entitled "Patent Medicines: The Early Post-Frontier Phase."

Yowell, Lillian J. 1534
Papers 1811–1849
2 items

Collector. A deed (1811) transferring ownership of two slaves, and a letter (1849) to David Elliot from Robert L. Elliott regarding his plans to settle in Texas.

Zweigel Mercantile Company Collection 1535
Records 1904–1940
51.50 feet

General store. General correspondence (1912–1930); bills of lading (1911–1921); account ledgers (1904–1928); and orders (1914–1924) of the Zweigel Mercantile Company of Atoka, Indian Territory, and Oklahoma. The collection also includes oil, gas, and mining leases (1935) to Choctaw Indian lands.

Unpublished finding aid available.

INDEX

Numbers in the index refer to entry numbers, not to page numbers. Entry numbers in boldface type refer to a collection of the same name as the index entry.

Abbott, J. H., **1**
Abbott, Lyman, 997
Abell, Okla., 648
Abernathy, J. R., 1041
Abrams, Abner W., **2**
Absentee Shawnee Indians, 1124
Abstracts of title (Okmulgee County, Okla.), 1060
Achilles, Nash, 640
Actors, 609, 1453
Ada, Indian Terr., newspapers in, 1458
Ada, Okla., history of, 895; lynching, 878
Adair, John L., 243
Adair, W. P., 243
Adair, W. T., 243
Adair family, 243; genealogy, 466
Adams, Arthur Barto, **3**
Adams, Joseph Quincy, **4**
Adams, Ramon Frederick, **5**
Adams family, 704
Aderhold, Thomas, **6**
Adkins, Art, 640
Adkins, (Mrs.) Jim, **7**
Advertisements, 291, 753, 907, 1009, 1096, 1143, 1151
Advertising cards, **8**, 673
Aeronautics (Okla.), 639
Africa, description and travel, 676
African-Americans, 347, 395, 437; admission to University of Oklahoma, 347; Cherokee Nation, 243, 446; colonization in Oklahoma, 639; education in Oklahoma, 347, 446, 963; 4-H clubs in Oklahoma, 648; religious education in Oklahoma, 963; slavery of, 1216

Agnew, Spiro T., 1431
Agricultural colleges (Okla.), 639, 753
Agricultural colonies (Bolivia), 1420
Agricultural cooperatives, 1034, 1421; Great Plains, 622; legislation, 1034; Oklahoma, 1421
Agriculture (Okla.), 567, 639; advocacy organizations, 1058, 1294; cooperatives, 399, 444, 562, 689, 710, 1034, 1053, 1109, 1421; soil conservation, 1050
Air bases (Okla.), 639, 1433
Air Force. *See* U.S. Army, Air Force
Airmail service, posters advocating, 861
Airmen, 731, 1246
Airports (Okla.), 639
Alabama Infantry Regiment, Twenty-Sixth, 820
Alaska, description and travel, 676, 973; gold rush, 321; Indians of, 364
Alaska Legal Services Corporation, 1383
Alaska Native Law Project, 1383
Albert, Carl Bert, 640, 1437
Albert Einstein College of Medicine, Yeshiva University (N.Y.), 708
Albert Pike Hospital, **9**
Alberty, Blue, 243
Alcorn, Ken, **10**
Alcorn, Steven, **10**
Aleut Indians, 364
Alexander, Ira Olyen, **11**
Alexander family, 11
Alfalfa County, Okla., 639; Ku Klux Klan membership, 787
Algonquin Indians, 1124
Allen, Clarence, **12**

Allen, Neva, **13**
Allen, Susie Keefer, **14**
Allen, Walter Bruce, **14**
Alley, Charles, **15**
Alley, John, **16**, 640
Allman, George, **17**
All Saints Hospital (McAlester, Okla.), 9
Alpha Chi Sigma, **18**
Alpha Epsilon Delta, **19**
Alpine, Tex., description of, 575
Alternate Saturday Club (Pauls Valley, Okla.), 1348
Altus, Okla., attorneys, 45, 657
Alva, Okla., colleges, 1468; health care, 28; high schools, 1468
Ambrose, Arthur, 260
American Association of University Presses, records of, 1425
American Association of University Women, **20**
American Bank (Porter, Okla.), 1139
American Cancer Society, 1451
American Civil Liberties Union, 736
American Federation of Labor, 188
American Garden Service, history of, 86
American Indian Aid Association, **21**
American Indian File Collection, **22**
American Indian Institute (University of Oklahoma), **23**, 932, 1383
American Legion, 667; certificate awarded by, 1285; posts in Oklahoma, 24, 255, 454, 1293
American Legion National American Commission, 255
American Legion Post 303: **24**
American Medical Association, 807
American National Bank (Oklahoma City, Okla.), records of, 1028
American Party (Mo.), 770
American Red Cross, 667; Beckham County, Okla., **25**; Cleveland County, Okla., **26**, 296
Ameringer, Oscar, 640
Ames, Charles Bismark, **27**
Ames, F. A., Company (Ky.), 398
Ames, H. B., **28**
Amos, French Stanton Evans, **29**
Amusements (Okla.), 639
Anadarko, Okla., 678, 1178
Anderson, R. M., **30**
Anderson, R. R., **31**
Anderson, Richard T., **32**
Anderson, Sherwood, 461, 1519

Andrus, Selden Eugene, **33**
Anglin, Tom, 640
Anthony, Charles Ross, 640
Anthony, Travis Dan, **34**
Anthony family, **34**
Anthropologists, dissertations of, 438, 1213; papers of, 102, 950, 1227, 1331, 1466; research of, 79, 102, 854, 856, 1066, 1167, 1258
Anti-Horse Thief Association, records of, **35**
Antiphonaries, 1350
Apache, Okla. Terr., postmasters of, 200
Apache Indian Mission (Fort Sill, Okla.), records of, 233
Apache Indians: bibliography, 713; culture, 1066; depredations, 1124; Fort Sill band, 713; history, 96; land transfers, 54; wars, 698
Aplington, Kate Smith, 800
Apollo space missions, promotional literature, 581
Apushmataha, **36**
Arapaho, Okla., banks and banking, 339; newspapers, 934; politics, 934
Arapaho Indians: depredations, 1124; environmental studies, 611; housing surveys, 611; legends, 55; missions, 1124; relations with U.S. government, 1326; wars, 698
Arbuckle, Matthew, 223, 386
Archaeologists, 743
Archaeology (Okla.), 639, 1403, 1515; expeditions, 79; projects, 1332; sites, 1351
Architects, 529
Architecture (Okla.), 639
Archival administration (Latin America), 827
Archivists, writings of, 47, 827
Ardrey, Helen, **37**
Arizona, gubernatorial nominees, 1453; superintendent of public instruction, 1453; wildlife, 570
Arkansas: Civil War, 307; history of, 498; mines and mining, 747; post–Civil War period, 1299; prohibition, 50; railroad development, 476, 507; state currency, 284; western boundary of, 579
Arkansas Central Railroad, 476
Arkansas City, Kans., opening of the Cherokee Outlet (Strip), 1339
Arkansas Riverbed Authority, 848

Armstrong Academy (Indian Terr.), 1131
Arne, Sigrid, 640
Arnold, Ben, **38**
Arnold, John O., **294**
Art (Okla.), 639
Art exhibits, catalogs, 1259, 1369
Arthur, Patti Joy, **39**
Arthur Foote Music Club, records of, 1247
Artists, 320, 1107; Indian, 332; Oklahoman, 707; western, 1237
Asahl, John, **40**
Ashbrook, William, **41**
Ashley, Charles, **42**
Asp, Henry E., 640
Association of Governing Boards of State Universities, 1222
Athenaeum Club (El Reno, Okla.), records of, 1367
Athletics, golf, 267
Atlanta, Ga., cotton exposition, 511
Atlantic Oil Corporation, 730
Atoka, Indian Terr., 1303; Zweigel Mercantile Company, 1535
Atoka, Okla., medical care, 494; naming of, 1238
Atoka Baptist Seminary, student notebooks, 469
Atoka County, Okla., 639; election returns, 310
Atoka County Medical Society, records of, 494
Atoka Lions Club, **43**
Atoka State Bank (Okla.), **44**
Atsidi Sani, 275
Attocknie, Albert, 640
Attorneys, 80, 92, 113, 370, 371, 911, 1108; Indian Territory, 129, 318, 331, 353, 1171, 1188, 1401, 1494; Kansas, 768; Oklahoma, 38, 45, 151, 318, 413, 423, 454, 495, 564, 657, 678, 736, 802, 934, 977, 979, 1006, 1160, 1188, 1198, 1312, 1384, 1401, 1494; Oklahoma Territory, 1212; records of, 45, 151, 318, 454, 495, 678, 736, 802, 977, 1006, 1160, 1171, 1188, 1198, 1384, 1401, 1494; Texas, 936
Austin, William Claude, **45**
Australia, description and travel, 271
Authors, 5, 34, 78, 108, 132, 149, 155, 174, 207, 277, 307, 309, 322, 380, 433, 459, 461, 486, 490, 502, 582, 605, 608, 618, 630, 635, 636, 639, 642, 664, 680, 686, 748, 752, 776, 777, 794, 800, 806, 828, 839, 859, 878, 889, 922, 927, 946, 956, 972, 1000, 1072, 1110, 1119, 1147, 1170, 1241, 1252, 1284, 1286, 1313, 1318, 1342, 1353, 1382, 1389, 1394, 1396, 1425, 1428, 1437, 1451, 1471, 1478, 1481, 1519, 1521
Autograph books, 427, 495
Automobiles, 65, 639; accidents in 1909: 1488
Automotive business: Iowa, 65; Kansas, 2; repair, 1113
Autry, Gene, 640
Avant, James Louis, 404
Avants, Thomas Warren, 640
Aviation, 143; history of, 1265; Latin America, history of, 490; Oklahoma, history of, 1380
Axton, Hoyt, 640
Aydelotte, Dora, 640
Ayer, Hugh M., **46**
Aztec Indians, fiction, 1110

Babcock, James M., **47**
Bacon, Charles W., **48**
Bacone College (Okla.), 56, 738, 984
Bacon Rind, 342
Badger, Ina, **49**
Baehl, Zelma I., **50**
Baggett family genealogy, 735
Bailey, Hurshel, **51**
Baird College (Mo.), student life, 63
Baker, Frances, **52**
Baker, Gretta, 996
Baker, Jesse Albert, **53**
Baker, Thad J., 640
Baldridge family, 243
Baldwin, Delmar H., **54**
Baldwin, Roger, correspondence, 1119
Balenti, Bill, **55**
Balenti, Lucille, **55**
Balenti family, **55**
Ball, Ralph, 640
Balyeat, Frank Allen, **56**
Bandy, Mary, **57**
Bankers, personal papers, 424, 452, 688, 721, 1140, 1205
Bank of Augusta, Georgia, currency, 284
Bank of Santa Fe (Newkirk, Okla. Terr.), 998
Bank of Udall (Okla.), **58**
Banks: Kansas, 103; Oklahoma, 44, 58, 213, 234, 263, 274, 300, 301, 339, 415, 418, 419, 440, 443, 474, 487, 557, 639,

[379]

655, 691, 750, 813, 953, 998, 1008, 1028, 1030, 1100, 1139, 1148, 1334, 1343, 1354, 1372, 1441, 1443, 1456, 1528; Oklahoma Territory, 953, 998; Switzerland, 37; Texas, 1334
Bannock Indians, depredations, 1124
Baptist Church, 639, 1196; missions, 56
Baptist churches (Okla.), history of, 1526
Baptist Missionary Training School, 712
Barbed wire, 277
Barbour, John, **59**
Barbour, Robert, **59**
Barker, N. L., **60**
Barking Water, copy of, 53
Barnard, Kate, 314, 386, 640
Barnes, Arch, **61**
Barnes, Cassius McDonald, 53, 640
Barnes, D. Elijah, **62**
Barnes, Sudie McAlester, **63**
Barnes family, 61
Barnes Medical College (Mo.), students' class notes, 362
Barnett, Jackson, 640; estate of, 224
Baroy, John Baptiste, 825
Barrett, Charles F., 640
Barrett, Hershel, **64**
Barrett, Paula Colby, **65**
Barrett, T. H., correspondence, 599
Bartell, E. C., **66**
Barthelme, Donald, 355
Bartlesville, Okla.: banks, 302; fiftieth anniversary, 615; Lions Club of, 1082; Methodist Episcopal Church in, 1310; physicians, 1461; Polish in, 1385; post office, 255; Rotary Club, 1310; YMCA in, 1310
Bartlett, Dewey, 640
Barton, Ray O., 640
Bass, Althea Leah Bierbower, **67**
Bass, Henry Benjamin, **68**, 640
Bass, Nathan, 376
Bassett, Ann, 640
Bassett, Mabel, 640
Bataafsche Petroleum Maatshappij (Netherlands), 304
Bates, S. R., **69**
Battenburg Press (Norman, Okla.), **70**
Battey, Thomas C., **71**
Battle, Bobby, 736
Battle vs. Park Anderson, 736
Baum, F. J., **72**
Baumgartner, A. Marguerite, **73**
Baumgartner, Frederick M., **73**

Beach, John, 1244, 1326
Beaird, Thomas Marion, **74**
Beale, A. J., 640
Beam, J. P., **75**
Bear, William L., 67
Beard, Buda McCormick, 1301
Beard, Lyman F., 1301
Beard family, 1301
Beauticians (Lawton, Okla.), 894
Beaver, Okla., railroad service to, 1394
Beaver County, Okla.: description of, 668; history of, 744, 882
Beck, Ethel, 76
Beck, G. W., General Merchandise Co., 76
Beck, Mabel, 76
Beck Family Collection, **76**
Beckham County, Okla., 639; American Red Cross chapters in, 25; mortgages, 1217; taxation, 1217; teachers' contracts, 349; World War I, 1490
Beckham County (Okla.) Medical Association, 1276
Beecher Island, Battle of, 1868: 472
Belcher, Page Henry, 640
Bell, Earl L., **77**
Bell, Jack, **78**
Bell, James Madison, papers of, 243
Bell, John A., 243
Bell, Lucien B., 243
Bell, Robert E., **79**
Bell, Watie, 243
Bellmon, Henry, 640
Belt, Robert V., **80**
Belvin, G. N., **81**
Belvin, Harry J. W., 640
Bender family (Kans.), 307
Benedict, John D., **82**
Benedict, Omer K., 640
Benge, George W., 243
Bennett, H. G., 640
Bennett, (Mrs.) Harold R., **83**
Bennett, Leo E., 1416
Bennington, Okla., history of, 11
Benson, Mildred June Tompkins, **84**
Benson, Oliver, **85**
Benson, Robert R., **86**
Bent, George, 93
Benton, Joseph Horace, **87**
Bentonelli, Joseph. *See* Benton, Joseph Horace
Bernard, Jean-Jacques, 1248
Bernard, Mary Frances (Sister), 1527
Berry, Everett, **88**

Berry, Jean, **88**
Berry, Josie Craig, **89**
Berry, Roger M., **90**
Berry, Virgil, **91**
Berry, William Aylor, **92**
Berthrong, Donald J., **93**
Bethany College (Topeka, Kans.), student life, 422
Bethany Nazarene College (Okla.), **94**
Bethel, Okla., 889
Betts, D. C., **95**
Betzinez, Jason, **96,** 640
Bevan, Wilbur Harrison, **97**
Beveridge, Albert J., 640
Bibliographers, 579
Bienfang, Ralph David, **98**
Big Bow, 640
Bigfoot, 447
Biggers, Helen, **99**
Biggers, Jesse, **99**
Big Sandy Valley (Ky.), residents of, 307
Billings, James F., **100**
Billings family, 100
Bingham, George, **101**; estate of, 378
Bingham Photograph Gallery, 101
Biologists, 570
Birds: Mexico, 1359; Oklahoma, 639, 1003, 1359
Birth control, 1134
Birth records: Kingfisher County, Okla., 388; Krebs, Okla., 1013; Nowata County, Okla., 428; Payne County, Okla., 643
Bismarck, N.Dak.: Women's Christian Temperance Union, 1505; women's clubs, 790
Bitter Creek, early settlement on, 49
Bittle, William E., **102**
Bituminous Coal Producers Board, reports, 292
Bixby, Tams, 640; correspondence, 1224
Bixby family, genealogy, 466
Bizzell, William Bennett, 88, **103,** 134, 1150, 1425, 1496
Bizzell family, genealogy of, 103
Blachly, Charles Dallas, **104**
Blachly, Lucile Spire, **104**
Black, Albert Hamilton, **105**
Black Beaver, 640
Black Dog, 640
Black Mesa (Okla.), 1403
Blackwell, A. J., 640
Blaine County, Okla. Terr., schools, 769

Blakely, Thomas Thurston, 640
Blakemore, Jesse Lee, **106**
Blakeney, R. Q., 640
Blanchard, James Lyon, **107**
Blanchart, Paul, correspondence, 1248
Blanding, Donald Benson, **108,** 640
Blanton, Jr., (Mrs.) James T., **109**
Blew, W. Bryan, **110**
Blinn, Richard F., **111**
Blinn family, captivity of, 111
Blomshield, John, **112**
Blood Indians, 1124
Bloomfield, Okla., 1313
Blue Eagle, Acee, 640
B'nai B'rith (Tulsa, Okla.), 915
Boatman, Andrew Nimrod (Jack), **113**
Bodine, John James, **114**
Bodley Codex, 1331
Boggs, Herbert Otho, **115**
Bohlinger, Neill, 1437
Boirun, G. D., **116**
Boke, Norman, **117**
Bolivia: description and travel, 1420; Murray Colony in, 980, 1420
Bollinger, Clyde John, **118,** 640
Bond, (Mrs.) A. L., **119**
Bond, George M., **120**
Bond, Redford, 640
Bond family, 120
Bonds, European, 506
Bone, Kathleen, **121**
Bonesteel, F. J., 1494
Bonner, Thomas N., **122**
Book collections: Adams and Henry Stevenson, 4; Bizzell Memorial Library (University of Oklahoma), 4
Books Abroad, 664, 1492. *See also World Literature Today*
Boomer Literature Collection, **123**
Boomer Movement (Indian Terr.), 1102
Boomers, 236
Boone, Charles A., **124**
Booth, G. R., **125**
Boren, David L., **126,** 640
Borglum, Gutzon, 464
Borum, Fred Sidney, 640
Bosin, Blackbear, Sr., 640
Boston Mountains, Ark., 1486
Boswell, H. D., **127**
Bosworth, Caroline M., **128**
Botanists: illustrations by, 791, 1322; writings by, 117, 791
Botany, 98, 329, 814; societies, 1327

[*381*]

Boudinot, Elias, 243
Boudinot, Elias Cornelius, II, 243, 640, 1507
Boudinot, Frank J., **129**, 243
Boudinot, William P., **130**, 243
Boudinot family, 386; papers of, 243
Boundaries (Okla.), 639
Bourland family, 11
Bowen, Myrtle Evans, **131**
Bowen family, genealogical information, 131
Bower, B. M., **132**
Bowlegs, David, 426
Bowling, Clara Ellen Merkel, **133**
Bowling, R. E., 133
Bowman, Wes, 640
Boyd, David Ross, **134**, 343, 1356; correspondence, 1168
Boyd, Mary Alice, 134
Boyd, Phleat, 640
Boyd family, genealogy of, 134, 421
Boydston, Samuel M., **135**
Boyer, Betty Kirk, 776; correspondence, 1207
Boyer, Dave, **136**
Boyer, Elizabeth Mahala Kirk *See* Boyer, Betty Kirk
Boyer, Wilfred, 136
Boyers family, 200
Boyles, Richard, 640
Boy Scouts (Okla.), 1027
Boys State (Okla.), 1378
Braden, John, **137**
Bradley, Calvin W., 165
Bradley, Joseph P., 165
Bragg, Arthur Norris, **138**
Brandt, Joseph August, 126, **139**, 625, 1425
Branen, Joseph L., **140**
Braniff, Thomas Elmer, 640
Branson, Carl Colton, **141**
Brant, R. A., 1035
Bray, John, Society, **142**
Brazell, J. H., 143
Brazell, James C., **143**
Brecht, Bertolt, 165
Breeding, (Mrs.) W. K., **144**
Breen, Dick, 640
Brennan, John, **145**
Bressie, Okla., history of, 146
Bressie, R. M., **146**
Bressie family, genealogy of, 146
Brewer, Theodore F., 1346
Brewster, Edythe Pearl, **147**

Bridges, natural, 743
Brillhart, Norman W., **148**
Brinkley, William C., **149**
Briscoe, Isaac, **150**
British Legion cavalry, 477
Brittan, Shawnee, 640
Brizzolard, James, 836
Broadcaster, The, 1138
Broaddus, Bower, **151**
Broken Bow, Okla., physicians, 1278
Broken Bow Lions Club, **152**
Bronson, Edgar S., **153**
Brooks, Stratton Duluth, **154**, 343, 1154
Broome, Bertram C., **155**
Brotherhood of North American Indians, constitution of, 1508
Brown, Benjamin H., **157**
Brown, Clark, 1266
Brown, Hugh, **158**
Brown, Jean, 1249
Brown, John, 158, 307, 591
Brown, John F., **159**
Brown, Phillip, **160**
Brown, Samuel H., **161**
Brown, W. H., **162**
Brown, Will, 1091
Brown Brothers Mercantile Store, records of, 160
Brown-Wilcox Family Collection, **156**
Bruccoli, Matthew, 355
Bruner, Joe, 640
Bryan, Frank, **163**
Bryan, J. R., **164**
Bryan, Joel M., 640
Bryan, John, **165**
Bryan, John A., **166**
Bryan, William Jennings, 188
Bryan County, Okla., 639; history of, 386, 964
Bryant, William J., **167**
Brydia, Catherine, 640
Buchanan, Carl B., 640
Buchanan, F. R., **168**
Buchanan, James Shannon, **169**, 343, 1150
Buchanan, Joseph Rodes, 46
Buchanan family, 169
Buckskin Bill's Historical Wild West Show, performers in, 1365
Buffalo, hunting of, 618
Buffalo, Okla., medical care, 198
Buffett, Richard H., **170**
Buffington, Thomas M., 243, 1507
Buggies, advertisements for, 398

Bullock family, 199
Burch, Clarence, 509
Burch, Don, **171**
Burchardt, August Gustave, **172**
Burchardt, George M., **173**
Burchardt, William, **174**
Burdine, C. A., **175**
Burditt, Mary Edna, **176**
Bureau of Government Research Collection, **177**
Bureau of Indian Affairs: correspondence, 832; publications, 22, 56
Buried treasure (Okla.), 456, 639
Burney, B. C., **178**
Burns, David A., **179**
Burns, Samuel Lee, **180**
Burton, Patricia, **181**
Busby, Orel, **182**
Busey, Ralph, 14
Bush, Barbara, 656
Bush, (Mrs.) C. S., **183**
Bush, Charles C., II, **184**
Bush, Geoffrey, **185**
Bush, George H. W., 656
Bushyhead, Dennis Wolf, **186**, 243, 544
Business and Professional Women's Club (Medford, Okla.), 1138
Butcher, Nahum Ellsworth, **187**
Butcher, W. H., **188**
Buttram, Frank A., **189**, 640; correspondence, 1108
Butts, (Mrs.) Ferrol Ellis, 640
Byington, Cyrus, 578
Byrd, Hiram, **190**
Byrd, Wallace, **190**
Byrd, William L., **191**
Byrum, Rollie E., **192**

Cable Temperance Union (Ill.), **193**
Cache Creek Indian Mission (Okla.), history of, 1450
Cactus and Succulent Society of Oklahoma City, papers of, 791
Cactus Hornet, 1235
Cactus Mining Company, 52
Caddo, Indian Terr., description and travel, 432
Caddo County, Okla., 639; land deeds, 349; medical care, 195; teachers' contracts, 349
Caddo County Education Archives, **194**
Caddo County Medical Association, **195**
Caddo Indians, 1124; attorneys for, 678,

1006; Civil War, 303; claims, 678; culture, 1258; history of, 608, 1491
Cade, Indian Terr., general stores, 732
Calendars, 99, 495
California: description and travel, 150; discovery of gold in, 10; exploration of, 1309; gold rush of 1849: 107, 150, 1137; history of, 86; shipment of gold from, 1484
Calling cards, 1176
Calloway, John R., **196**
Calvin, Okla., retail stores, 679
Camden, Ark., description of, 158
Camden, Harriet, 640
Camp, Earl F., **198**
Camp Augur, Okla., 639
Campbell, Anson, **199**
Campbell, Charles Duncan, **200**
Campbell, George W., 649
Campbell, Grace Frances, 924
Campbell, J. E., 682
Campbell, J. F., **201**
Campbell, James Robert, 640
Campbell, John McKoy, **202**
Campbell, John Sidney, Sr., **203**
Campbell, Robert Boyers, **204**
Campbell, S. W., **205**
Campbell, W. E., 204
Campbell, W. H. L., **206**
Campbell, Walter Stanley, **207**, 640, 1284
Campbell, Wilbur E., 200
Campbell family, 199
Campbell Funeral Home, records of, 203
Campbell Hardware Store, records of, 203
Camp Fire Girls, costume, 259
Camp Holmes, Okla., 1304; Treaty of, 892
Camp Mason, Indian Terr., 223
Camp Nichols, Okla., 639
Camp Radziminski, Okla., 639
Camp Supply Collection, **197**
Camp Travis, Tex., 176
Canadian, Okla., physicians, 809
Canadian County, Okla., 639
Canton, Frank M., **208**, 640
Canton, Okla., medical care, 168
Cantonment, Okla., 639
Cantonment Indian Agency, **209**
Cantonment Training School, 209
Capital Grain and Elevator Co., records of, 1104
Capital punishment (Okla.), 639
Capitol (Okla.), 639; building, 803
Capone, Al, 925

[383]

Capshaw, Madison T. J., **210**
Capshaw, Walter, 210
Carlisle Barracks Collection, **211**
Carlock, Arlie Ernest, **212**
Carmen First National Bank (Okla.), **213**
Carpenter, Dan H., correspondence of, 214
Carpenter, Everett, **214**
Carpenter, Grant, 794
Carpenter, Paul Simon, **215**
Carpenter family, genealogy of, 215
Carriker, Robert C., **216**
Carseloway, James Manford, **217**
Carson, Christopher (Kit), 653
Carson, Frank L., **218**
Carson, Lamoine S., **219**
Carter, Angeline, 649
Carter, Charles D., 640
Carter, Elizabeth, 649
Carter, Frank C., **220**, 640
Carter, M. L., **221**
Carter County, Okla., 639; murder of Mexican citizens, 1279; schools, 639
Cartoonists, 12, 282
Carver, George Washington, 498
Casey, Alvin Harold, **222**
Cashion, Okla., 648; retail stores, 663
Caskets, 361
Caso y Luenge, Francisco, correspondence, 1070
Cass, Lewis, **223**
Catalogs: art exhibits, 1259; books and publications, 1176; caskets, 361; cattle sales, 493; eyeglasses, 512; hardware, 293; household goods, 293; jewelry, 293; mail-order, 291; manufactured housing, 538; medical equipment, 838; saddlery, 293; stoves, 293; surgical supply, 512
Cate, Roscoe Simmons, **224**
Cates, P. M., **225**
Catholic Church, 639, 846, 1196; programs, 17
Catlin, George, 640
Cattle branding, 322
Cattle brands, 1384; Cherokee Outlet (Strip), 467, 1510; Indian Territory, 467; Kansas, 322, 467; Oklahoma, 322, 452, 639; Oklahoma Territory, 1510; Texas, 322, 467
Cattle Brands Collection, **226**
Cattle dipping, 939

Cattle drives, 488, 541; description of, 575; Indian Territory, 632
Cattle trade, 628, 639, 1104
Cattle trails, 86, 639; Oklahoma Territory, 566; Texas, 575
Caudron, Theophile, **227**
Cayuga Indians, claims of, 228, 1270
Cayuga Nation Papers, **228**
Celebrations: Christmas, 1321, 1382; '89ers, 279; Independence Day, 1321; semi-centennial (Okla.), 1049
Cemeteries: Deyo Mission (Lawton, Okla.), 342; Independent Order of Odd Fellows, 449; Indian Territory, 109, 1516; Kiowa Indians (Duncan, Okla.), 342; Oklahoma, 639, 1516
Census (U.S.) of 1930: 639
Centennial celebrations (Okla.), 1049
Centennial Collection, **229**
Center for Studies in Higher Education, (University of Oklahoma), **230**, 614
Central America, description and travel, 1069
Central Christian College (Bartlesville, Okla.), 183
Central Great Plains, agriculture, 622
Centralia, Indian Terr., Van Ausdal Drug Store, 1429
Central State Teachers College (Okla.), presidents, 967
Central State University (Okla.), **231**
Certificates and Diplomas Collection, **232**
Chaat, Robert P., **233**
Chaffin, W.A., 640
Chamberlin, A. N., 446
Chambers of commerce: Claremore, Okla., **262**; Norman, Okla., 688; Oklahoma state, 639
Chaminade Club (Oklahoma City, Okla.), 881
Chandler, Happy, 1396
Chandler, Okla. Terr.: banks and banking, 234; history of, 236; settlement of, 1522
Chandler, Thomas Albert, 640
Chandler National Bank (Okla. Terr.), **234**
Chaney, Lon, 640
Chaney, Warren P., **235**
Chapbooks, 256
Chapman, Amos, 640
Chapman, Berlin Basil, **236**, 369
Chapman, T. Shelby, **237**

Charleston, S.C., cotton exposition, 511
Chattahoochee, Macon, and Columbus Railroad, 1071
Chautauquas, 639
Checotah, Indian Terr., retail trade, 51
Checote, Samuel, **238**, 243, 324, 544
Chelsea, Indian Territory, Town Records Collection, **239**
Chelsea, Okla.: photography studios, 620; physicians, 1368
Cherokee, Okla., Ku Klux Klan activity, 700
Cherokee Advocate, **240**, 243; records of, 243
Cherokee Bibliography Project, **241**
Cherokee Bilingual Education Project, **242**
Cherokee Bill (Crawford Goldsby), 640
Cherokee Commission, minutes of, 1896: 386
Cherokee County, Ga., 729
Cherokee County, Okla., 639
Cherokee Foundation, Inc., publications of, 1128
Cherokee Indians: African-American, 243; allotment of land, 703, 869, 1124; authors, 1072; bibliography, 241; census, 243; chiefs, 186, 217, 243, 386, 585, 848, 868, 869, 1065, 1223, 1228, 1231; citizenship, 243, 602, 1124; Civil War, 243, 1124, 1299; claims, 243, 386; courts, 243, 1124; Dawes Commission, 243, 869, 1124; Delawares, adopted, 1124; delegates and agents, 217, 243; Eastern (North Carolina) band, 243, 827, 1124; elections, 243; freedmen, 243, 1128; genealogy, 386, 848; health, 243, 848; history of, 1481; hymnals, 446; Keetoowah Society, 129; land transfers, 130, 1507; language, 242, 523, 542, 836, 1080; laws, 243; legends, 55; medicine and medical care, 243, 612; missionaries to, 446, 578, 1299; newspapers, 240, 243, 244; Old Settlers, 243, 386, 1124; orphan asylum, 130, 243; per capita payments, 243; poets, 1261; politics, 129, 585, 868; removal, 243, 386; schools, 243, 848, 940, 1065, 1514; seminary graduates, 1128; slavery, 1427; smallpox, 243; syllabaries, 56, 242, 1080; telephone companies, 1511; tribal factionalism, 740; tribal government, 186, 243; tribal rolls, 869; wars, 243; westward migration, 771; women, 627, 848; writings about, 1451
Cherokee Nation: allotment of land, 243, 585, 622; Arkansas lands, 243; asylum for the blind, 612; Bell project, 848; bibliography, 241; Bingo Outpost, 848; boundaries, 1124; boundary surveys, 243; capital, 836; capitol building, 243; cattle, 243; census, 243; Cherokee Gardens, 848; Cherokee Housing Authority, 848; Cherokee National Council, 243, 353; Cherokee National Historical Society, 848; Cherokee Nation Industries, 848; Cherokee Land Office, 703; Cherokee Outlet, dissolution of, 651, 868; Cherokee Strip Livestock Association, 186; Civil War, 243, 386; community development, 848; Community Loan Fund, 848; courts, 243, 629; crime, 243, 1124; delegations to Washington, D.C., 243, 386; description of, 466, 1072; description of life in, 1861–1865: 471; disputes with the federal government, 243; districts, 243, 836; divorces, 243; economy, 466, 848; education, 243, 848, 940, 1065, 1231; elections, 243, 848; environmental programs, 848; financial affairs, 243, 848, 1065, 1231; geographical studies of, 622; Head Start program, 848; health issues, 848; history of, 466, 782, 1228, 1451; Home Improvement Program, 848; housing, 848; insane asylum, 243; intermarriage, 243; intruders, 243; Job Training Partnership Act, 848; land, 1124; land transfers, 585, 629, 1065; law enforcement, 243; laws, 243; leases, 243; legal affairs, 243; licenses, 243; liquor, 1124; memorials and resolutions, 1128; missionaries, 430, 446, 471, 1216, 1299; missions, 446, 940; money, 836; New Echota Church, 430; Oaks Mission School, 848; officials, 243; oil wells in, 217; Old Settlers, 243, 386, 1124; orphans, 243, 1124; Park Hill Mission, 446; pensions, 612; permits and fees, 243; politics, 243, 466, 612, 1228; Presbyterian Church,

[*385*]

430, 446; prisons, 243; railroads, 130, 243, 1124; reconstruction in, 1124, 1231; records of, 243, 848; rivers, 836; roads, 940; schools, 243, 848, 940, 1065, 1514; Sequoyah High School, 848; Shawnees, adopted, 1124; slavery in, 1216, 1427; smallpox, 243; social conditions in, 1228; statehood, 1231; Talking Leaves Job Corps, 848; Texas, 1124; timber cutting, 243; town lots, 243; township maps, 622; trade and traders, 243; treaties, 243, 386; tribal government, 585, 1065, 1223, 1231; Vann murder case, 243
Cherokee National Party, 612
Cherokee Nation Papers, 243
Cherokee Outlet (Strip), 243, 1124; cattle brands used in, 1510; cowboy life in, 1184; dissolution of Indian title to, 868; history of, 1446; land run of 1893: 53, 408, 524, 599, 1118, 1184, 1314, 1339, 1452; maps, 387, 599; social history, 674
Cherokee Phoenix, 244
Cherokee Strip Livestock Association, 186; history of, 1253
Cherokee Telephone Company, 1511
Cherokee Treaty Fund, claims, 243
Cheyenne and Arapaho Indian Baptist Mission, 712
Cheyenne-Arapaho Indian Agency, 321, 779
Cheyenne-Arapaho Indians: allotments, 950; attorneys of, 1006; bands, 950; census, 950; ceremonies, 950; child care, 950; farming, 779; genealogy, 950; history, 121; kinship, 950; missions to, 712; religion and mythology, 105; schools, 1264; social customs, 950; societies, 950; wars, 197
Cheyenne Indians: captives of, 111; depredations, 1124; environmental studies, 611; housing surveys, 611; legends, 55; matrifocality, 438; probate records, 950; relations with U.S. government, 1326; relations with whites, 1019; religion and mythology, 1147; rites and ceremonies, 1147; Sand Creek band, 950; Sand Creek, Battle of, 639; Sappa Creek, Battle of, 642; sun dance, 386, 1147; wars, 472, 698, 1414; women, 438

Chiang Kai Shek, (Madame), 844; correspondence of, 685
Chicago, Rock Island, and Pacific Railroad, 247; health and pension plans, 500; history of, 1355; physicians, 463; records of, 634, 1219, 1267
Chicago, Texas, and Mexican Central Railway Company, 579
Chi Delta Phi Collection, 245
Chickasaw Indians: allotment of land, 121, 331, 879, 964, 968, 1064, 1198; attorneys, 900; banks and banking, 721; business interests, 721; cemeteries, 109; chiefs, 178, 556, 586, 727, 827, 879, 968, 1078, 1089, 1500; citizenship claims, 318, 331; Civil War, 964, 1131, 1149; conscription, 1149; Dawes Commission, 879; education, 1124; freedmen, 1124; health care, 1430; land transfers, 121, 401, 1064, 1198; language, 1181; litigation, 318, 900; mineral resources of, 1401; relations with U.S. government, 1401; relations with whites, 1091; slaves, ownership of, 727; taxation, 900; tribal factionalism, 586; tribal government, 178, 191; tribal politics, 964
Chickasaw Nation: allotment of land, 586, 994, 1124, 1500; attorneys of, 1006; boundaries, 1124; chiefs, 589; claims, 727; description and travel, 235; education, 727; elections, 556, 586; finances, 727, 1500; history of, 827; land, 1124; land transfer, 235, 248; land use, 1500; laws, 248; legislation, 589; mineral resources, 727; mining trustee for, 1401; Oklahoma statehood, 1500; orphans, 1124; per capita payments, 1124; Permit Law of 1876: 1078; railroads, 1124; schools, 586; tribal factionalism, 586; tribal government, 248, 727; tribal legislation, 556; white settlement in, 1091
Chickasaw Nation Collection, 248
Chickasha, Okla., 1313; clubs and societies, 49; Grady County Park, 1404; milling companies, 249
Chickasha Milling Company Collection, 249
Child labor (Okla.), 351
Children, research on vocabulary of, 1209

Children's literature, 680, 752, 806, 859, 1252, 1353, 1371
Childs, (Mrs.) William Oscar, **250**
Chile, Jesuits in, 1084
Chilocco Indian School: Indian Terr., 366; Okla., 1321
China, foreign relations, 1939–1946: 685
Chippewa Indians, 1124, 1213
Chisholm, Jesse, 640
Chisholm Trail, 639; in Oklahoma, 566, 1490
Chisum family, 11
Chi Upsilon Collection, **246**
Choate, May Treadwell, **251**
Choctaw Academy and Missionary Station (Ky.), 1131
Choctaw-Chickasaw Sanitorium, 1430
Choctaw Coal and Railway Company, 1224
Choctaw County, Okla., 639; medical care, 221; Medical Society, records of, 1503
Choctaw Indians: alcohol use, 1131; allotment of land, 252, 334, 593, 737, 964, 1064, 1171, 1188, 1198; attorneys, 900; chiefs, 16, 167, 289, 334, 402, 489, 593, 662, 705, 737, 805, 816, 829, 885, 886, 887, 897, 985, 1131, 1302, 1523; citizenship, 318, 386; Civil War, 774, 964; culture, 674; education, 297, 1124, 1131, 1302; freedmen, 1124; funds, 1124; genealogy, 1399; general stores, 732; health care, 1430; history, 305, 386, 452; hymnal, 469; land transfer, 235, 401, 1064, 1094, 1198; language examples, 81, 469, 492, 732, 898, 994, 1181; law enforcement, 836; libraries, private, 1523; lighthorse, 836; litigation, 318, 900, 1188; mineral resources of, 1401, 1470, 1535; mineral rights, 737; missionaries to, 578, 774; Mississippi band, 685; poets, 898; relations with other Indians, 985; relations with U.S. government, 1401; relations with white settlers, 711; religious texts, 469, 492; removal of, 115, 774, 1131; slavery, 503, 774, 1131; social history, 674; taxation, 900; textbooks, 492; townsite payments, 1171; tribal council proceedings, 289; tribal government, 16, 252, 289, 1302; tribal politics, 115, 737, 964

Choctaw (Okla.) Medical Society, 929
Choctaw Nation: allotment of land, 252, 401, 503, 685, 829, 994, 1124; attorneys of, 685, 844, 1006 1401; boundaries, 1124; businesses in, 1187; citizenship, 885, 1124; Civil War, treaty of peace, 1131; claims, 685; coal lands royalties, 289; coal mining, 508, 1470; courts, 289, 318, 508; crime and criminals, 1507; description and travel, 235; elections, 252; financial affairs, 503; general council records, 252, 469; general council, speeches to, 732; history of, 827; intruders, 289; land, 1124; land transfers, 252, 685; law enforcement, 836; laws, 252, 469; legislation, 508; mineral rights, 886; mining trustee, papers of, 1401; per capita payments, 1124; politics, 252, 402, 886, 1262; railroads, 885, 886, 1124; schools, 402, 508, 884, 1131; slavery, 503, 774, 1131; statehood, 886, 1262; stock raising, 402; timber lands, 508; townsites, 886; treasurers of, 1476; treaties, 1131; tribal citizenship, 289; tribal factionalism, 503; tribal government, 252, 402, 829, 884, 885, 886, 887, 897, 1131
Choctaw Nation Papers, **252**
Choctaw Trading Company, 1224
Chodos, Israel, 640
Choska Trading Company Collection, **253**
Chouteau, Auguste, 254
Chouteau, Edward L., 342
Chouteau, Indian Terr., medical care, 91
Chouteau, Jean Pierre, 223, 254, 640
Chouteau, Myra Yvonne, **254**, 640
Chouteau, Pierre, correspondence, 1070
Chouteau, Rosalie Capitaine, 342
Christian Church, history of in Oklahoma, 1329
Christianity, history of, 1471
Christie, Ned, 640
Christmas traditions, 1321, 1382
Christopher, Ernest Randell, **255**
Christopher, Joe R., **256**
Christopher, Thomas W., 640
Chupco, John, **257**
Churches: Baptist, 639; Catholic, 639; Christian, history of, 1329; Disciples of Christ, 639; Episcopal, 1227, 1245; Mennonite, 639; Methodist, 639; Presbyterian, 82, 446, 639

[*387*]

Churchill, Winston, 461; correspondence, 685
Church of Jesus Christ of Latter-Day Saints, currency issued by, 284
Ciba Pharmaceutical Collection, **258**
Ciereszko, Leon, **259**
Cigar bands, 495
Cimarron City, Okla., 648
Cimarron County, Okla., 639
Cimarron Rose (Rose Dunn), 640
Circuses, 925
Cities Service Oil and Gas Corporation, **260**, 316, 479
Civil Rights Commission (Okla.), **261**
Civil War, 1861–1865: Arkansas, 1410; battles and battlefields, 369, 386; border states, 498; Caving Banks, Battle of, 369; Centerville, Battle of, in 1864: 1071; Cherokee Indians, 243, 386; Choctaw Indians, 1131; Confederate veterans, 563, 577; correspondence about, 297, 431, 481, 820; CSA Indian policy, 303; damage claims, 371; discharge papers, 165; historical fiction, 752, 1194; history of, 68, 902; Indian involvement in, 119; Indian Territory, 514, 774, 1299, 1410; Indian troops, 1149, 1299, 1444; Kansas, 307, 442, 1410; maps of battlefield maneuvers, 550; military service records, 1097; Missouri, 1410; naval engagements, 344; oath of allegiance to the U.S., 766; officers, 171; pensions, 165; personal narratives, 15, 143, 145, 325, 344, 371, 431, 516, 547, 550, 770, 874, 883, 1071, 1181, 1266, 1275, 1366, 1410; poetry about, 1346; Shiloh, Battle of, 1346; South Carolina, 1334; Tennessee Theater, 1071; trans-Mississippi West, 431, 498; U.S. occupation of Louisiana, 1479; veterans, 563, 577
Civil War Centennial Commission, 592; records of (Okla.), 68
Clapper, Raymond, award, 1396
Claremore, Okla.: Chamber of Commerce, **262**; index to records of, 42; mayors of, 42; utility rates, 650
Clarita Farmers State Bank (Okla.), **263**
Clark, B. C., 640
Clark, Ben, **264**
Clark, Carter Blue, **265**
Clark, Glenn C., 88
Clark, Joseph J., **266**, 640
Clark, Shirley R., 1201
Clark, Stanley A., 940
Clarke, Georgia Lee, 267
Clarke, (Mrs.) Hulbert S., **267**
Clarke, John R., **268**
Clarkson, Addie W., **269**
Classen, Anton H., **270**
Classen High School (Oklahoma City, Okla.), 888, 1453
Clay, Henry, 1488
Clay Center, Kans., 100
Cleckler, Frank Stuart, **271**
Clemens, Samuel Langhorne, **272**
Clements, Frank B., **273**
Cleo Springs, Okla., banks and banking, 274
Cleo State Bank (Okla.), **274**
Clergymen, 548, 1088, 1281, 1299, 1305, 1346, 1471, 1482; papers of, 1509, 1523
Cleveland, Arlyss, **275**
Cleveland, Paula, **275**
Cleveland County, Okla., 639; American Red Cross chapters in, 26; history of, 1504; IOOF cemetery, 449; medical care, 276; records of, 1504
Cleveland County (Okla.) Children's Clinic, **276**
Clifton, Robert T., **277**
Climatology, 639
Cline, (Mrs.) B. F., **278**
Clinkenbeard family, genealogy of, 1330
Clinton, Okla., 156; Edelweiss Club, 1412; family histories, 904, 905; history of, 1178; Literary Club, 1412; physicians, 793
Clouse, Hiram H., 1255
Clubb, Laura, 640
Clubs: civic, 971, 1011, 1348, 1391, 1436; garden, 1017; Lions Club and Lions International, 43, 110, 140, 152, 172, 222, 273, 346, 741, 823, 824, 1010, 1082, 1115, 1146, 1204, 1236, 1436, 1451; men's, 861, 1232, 1247; music, 638, 645, 945, 1247; Oklahoma, 639, 1061, 1105, 1206, 1232; political, 629; professional, 1382; Rotary International, 1232; social, 1462; women's, 49, 296, 352, 497, 783, 787, 881, 906, 1022, 1052, 1068, 1081, 1105, 1138, 1412
Coaches, football, 840

Coachman, Ward, **280**, 324
Coal County, Okla., 639
Coal mining: Arkansas, 747; Indian Territory, 747, 1315; Iowa, 1315; Missouri, 1315; Montana, 1315; Oklahoma, 292, 639, 747, 941, 974, 1315, 1470; West Virginia, 1315
Cobb, Isabel, **281**
Cobb, William, murder case of, 243
Cobblers, 391
Cobean, Samuel E., **282**
Cocke family, records of, 51
Cody, William F. (Buffalo Bill), 207, 459, 640
Coffey, George, 1240
Coffey, John L., **283**
Coins, Tokens and Money Collection, **284**
Colbert, Winchester, **285**
Colbert family, 1313
Colby, John, **286**
Colby Motor Company, Iowa, 65
Colcord, Charles Francis, **287**, 640; memoirs of, 582
Colcord, Harriet Scoresby, 287, 640
Colcord, Ray, 287
Colcord, Sidney, 287
Colcord, Will C., 287
Colcord family, genealogy, 287
Coldiron, Daisy Lemon, **288**, 640
Cole, Coleman, **289**
Cole, Redmond S., **290**
Coleman, Emma Alberta White, **291**
Cole Motor Car Company, 1324
Colleges and universities: course outlines, 561, 1079; deans, 647; diplomas, 1176; faculty attitude toward World War I, 1256; faculty lecture notes, 103, 184, 218, 435, 482, 771, 827, 858, 954, 967, 1079, 1155, 1389, 1451; fraternities, records of, 1127, 1290, 1291, 1292; libraries, 308; loyalty oaths, 236; medical students, 19, 212, 485, 643, 659, 681, 826, 857, 880, 1439; Oklahoma, 16, 94, 177, 231, 639; presidents, 967, 1222, 1277; presidents (Okla.), 88, 103, 126, 134, 139, 154, 169, 343, 430, 464, 997, 1150, 1154, 1168, 1222, 1277, 1496, 1524; presidents (Tex.), 103, 256; professors, 4, 16, 29, 85, 87, 93, 98, 102, 118, 184, 207, 215, 256, 314, 328, 343, 348, 355, 365, 395, 396, 416, 435, 448, 482, 526, 561, 607, 619, 633, 647, 664, 771, 799, 827, 828, 832, 836, 846, 850, 858, 902, 954, 955, 961, 967, 972, 1014, 1079, 1086, 1093, 1130, 1168, 1179, 1204, 1209, 1248, 1253, 1256, 1265, 1277, 1360, 1369, 1389, 1451, 1463, 1485, 1492, 1496; publications, 1444; school songs, 519; student class notes, 103, 362, 468, 469, 485, 573, 578, 643, 659, 681, 826, 880, 911, 913, 931, 1064, 1183, 1233; student grade reports, 1168, 1389, 1485, 1496; student life, 34, 39, 63, 67, 215, 422, 526, 881; student writings, 343, 858, 954, 1320. *See also* University of Oklahoma
Collins, Arza Bailey, **294**
Collins, Daniel, 1313
Collins Coal Company, 292
Collins Hardware Store, **293**
Collums, D. B., **295**
Collums, Garner G., **295**
Collums, (Mrs.) Garner G., **296**
Collyer, Vincent, 445
Colonial Dames Collection, **297**
Colony, Okla., medical care, 350
Colony Mercantile Company (Okla.), 772
Colorado, mines and mining, 747
Columbia River, exploration, 1345
Columbus Day, proclamation of (Okla. Terr.), 1199
Comanche, Okla., buried treasure, 456
Comanche County, Okla., 639; history of, 621; school boards, 621
Comanche County Historical Society, **298**
Comanche Indian Mission (Fort Sill, Okla.), 233
Comanche Indians: Civil War, 303; census, 928; constitution, 928; customs, 377; dictionaries, 377; encounters with whites, 837; land transfers, 54; language, 377, 1181; wars, 698, 735
Combest, George Marion, **299**
Comfort, E. Nicholas, 1048
Comfort family, 1048
Commerce, Okla., municipal records, 300
Commerce First State Bank (Okla.), **300**
Commercial National Bank (Muskogee, Okla.), **301**
Committee on Oil Investigation, 1242
Commonplace books, Elizabethan, 4
Communism, attitudes toward, 1105, 1531

[*389*]

Community Hospital Bulletin, 1276
Composers, 654, 762, 777, 903, 1014
Condit, (Mrs.) J. A, **302**
Condit, W. A., **302**
Confederate States Army: conscription of Indian troops, 1149; Dublin Provost Guard, 766; general officers, 171, 1465; Indian troops, 243, 386, 1149, 1249, 1444; soldiers' personal narratives, 145, 820, 874, 883, 1275, 1410; Twenty-sixth Alabama Infantry, 820; veterans, 563, 577
Confederate States of America: bonds certificate, 1249; currency, 284, 861; Indian policy, 303, 386, 1299; Missouri, Confederate Legislature of, 171
Confederate States of America Indian Affairs Collection, **303**
Congregationalist Church, 1196
Conklin, Richard A., **304**
Conlan, Madeline Czarina Colbert, **305**
Conn, J. L., **306**
Connelley, William Elsey, **307**
Conner, Bart, 640
Connors State Agricultural College, **308**
Conservation: advocacy organization, 1328; grasslands, 990
Conservationists, 542, 1473
Conservatoire National (France), 215
Constant, Alberta Anne Wilson, **309**
Constant, Edwin, correspondence, 309
Constitutional Convention (Okla.), 53, 598, 706, 1214; history of, 686, 914; records of, 177
Consumer cooperatives, 464
Continental Asphalt and Petroleum Company, 170
Continental Investment Corporation, records of, 730
Coocoochee, 815
Cook, Benjamin R., **310**
Cook, F. L., **311**
Cookbooks, 99, 495, 627, 931. *See also* Recipes
Cooksey, Harold S., **312**
Cooper, Ann Mayer, **313**
Cooper, Leroy (Gordon), 640
Cooperative Community Hospital (Elk City, Okla.), 1276
Co-operative Publishing Company, **279**
Copeland, Edith, 314, 640, 724
Copeland, Fayette, Jr., **314**, 640
Coppadge, Ethel, **315**

Coquimbro, Chile, Jesuit college of, 1084
Cordell, J. William, 1123
Cordell, Okla.: description, 1432; history of, 1178; physicians, 761
Cornell, Doris, **316**
Cornell, Kearns Bryon, **317**
Cornish, Alice, 441
Cornish, Cecil, 640
Cornish, Melven, **318**
Cornish family, 441
Correspondence schools, 1092
Cosgrove Fire Protection, Inc., 316
Costumes, 639
Cotteral, John W., 640
Cotton: cleaning machines, invention of, 1490; gins and ginning, 560, 1159, 1187; trade expositions, 511. *See also* Cotton trade
Cotton County, Okla., 639
Cotton trade: Indian Territory, 1187; Oklahoma, 160, 1159, 1187
Couch, Nev., 1514
Coulter, Okla., 648
County government (Okla.), court records, 1016; financial records, 474, 1016
Court, Nathan Altshiller, **319**
Courts: Arkansas, 404, 1202; district court clerk reports, 989; Indian Territory, records of, 1415, 1416, 1417; Oklahoma, 639, 718, 948; Oklahoma, records of, 151, 1016, 1418, 1435; Oklahoma Territory, records of, 1418
Covert, Alice Lend, 640
Covey, Arthur S., **320**
Covington, J. A., **321**
Cowboys, 1, 147, 207, 322, 568, 575, 604, 639, 668, 744, 1039, 1103, 1184, 1253, 1305, 1428
Cowles, Fred G., 849
Coyle, Okla., 648; retail stores, 663
Crabb, E. D., 1003
Crable, A. Lawrence, 640
Crawford, L. E., **322**
Crazy Snake Rebellion, 16, 1305
Creek, George, correspondence, 1119
Creek County, Okla., 639
Creek Indian Museum Collection, **323**
Creek Indians: allotment of land, 544, 938, 1124; census, 386; chiefs, 238, 280, 544, 580, 702, 892, 893, 1067, 1116, 1117, 1141, 1249, 1381; Civil War participation, 1249; constitution

of 1867: 280; crime, 1124; culture, 1066; education, 1124; guardians, 1124; history, 323, 386, 544; immigration to Mexico, 1117; land, 1124; lands in Alabama, 544; language of, 81; legends, 323; McIntosh family, 789, 893; McIntosh family coat of arms, 893; missionaries to, 1215; newspapers of, 1075; Oklahoma statehood, opposition to, 938; poets, 938; relations with whites, 1067; removal, 544; Snake Clan, 938; speeches, 892; towns in Alabama, 224; towns in Oklahoma, 224; tribal factionalism, 280, 544, 702, 815; tribal government, 238; tribal politics, 544

Creek Nation: allotment of land, 544, 1141; attorneys of, 1006; boundaries of, 837; courts, 324; Dawes Commission, 1117; finances, 702; general stores, 253; Green Peach War, 544; judicial system, 789; land titles, 324, 702; land transfers, 544; politics, 544, 789, 1117; politics and the McIntosh family, 789, 893; records of, 324; statehood for Indian Territory, 1141; tribal government, 324, 580, 702, 892, 1006, 1116, 1141

Creek Nation Collection, **324**
Crescent, Okla., 648
Crescent Mining, Milling, and Oil Company (Lawton, Okla.), 1295
Cress, Sherry Marie, **325**
Crime and criminals: Carter County, Okla., 1279; Cobb, William, murder case of, 243; criminals conferences on, 68; Fountain, Albert Jennings, murder case, 58; Indian Territory, 866, 1202, 1416, 1417, 1464; Kelly, George (Machine Gun), 802; No Man's Land (Okla. panhandle), 1087; Nowata County, Okla., 1016; Oklahoma, 639, 775, 1418, 1435, 1464; Oklahoma Territory, 1418; Seminole County, Okla., 1191; Urschel kidnapping case, 287
Crittendon, William Dial, **326**
Cronkhite, Kitty, **327**
Crook, Kenneth E., **328**
Cross, George Lynn, **329**, 1359
Cross, John M., 640
Crouch, Aziel Henry, **330**
Cruce, Cruce, and Bleakmore Collection, **331**

Cruce, Lee, 331, 640, 861; campaign for governor of Oklahoma, 1487
Crumbo, Woody, **332**
Cuadra, José de la, 664
Cuba, 916
Cuddeback, Frank J., **333**
Cullison, James B., 640
Culwell, Frankie, **334**
Cummins, Jim, 640
Cunningham, Robert O'Darrell, **335**
Curry, Arthur R., **336**
Curtis, Charles, 640
Cushing Refining and Gasoline Company, **337**
Cushman, Pauline, 640
Custer, (Mrs.) C. C., 316
Custer, George Armstrong, 148, 207, 1264
Custer County, Okla., 156, 639; banks and banking, 339; family histories, 904, 905; medical care, 338
Custer County, Okla. Terr., frontier and pioneer life, 1019
Custer County Medical Society, **338**
Custer County State Bank (Okla.), **339**
Cutler, Violona, **340**
Cutlip, C. Guy, **341**
Czechoslovakians in Oklahoma, 616

Dahlberg, Sophie Little Bear, **342**
Dairy farmers league, creation of (Okla.), 710
Dakota Territory: Sisseton Indian reservation, 599; Wahpeton Indian reservation, 599
Dale, Edward Everett, 134, **343**, 625
Dale, F. Hiner, 640
Dalton brothers, 459, 640
Dalton family, 16
Dams and reservoirs (Okla.), 217, 639
Danforth, Thatcher O., **344**
Dangerfield, Royden James, **345**
Daniel, Harley A., **346**
Daniel, William D., 1311
Daniels, Opherita Eugenia, **347**
Dannelly, Paul Edward, **348**
Danner, Clyde, **349**
Darlington, Brinton, 422
Darnell, Bill, 640
Darnell, E. E., **350**
Darrow, Clarence, 461
Daugherty, Charles L., **351**
Daughters of the American Revolution, **352**, 1468; Elliot Lee chapter, 1081

[*391*]

Davenport, Iowa, 1218
Davenport, James S., **353**
Davidson, Frank. *See* McCurdy, Elmer
Davidson, Mollie, 1532
Davis, Alice Brown, **354**, 640
Davis, Amber, 1362
Davis, Jefferson, correspondence, 671
Davis, Robert Murray, **355**
Davis, W. A., 1532
Davison, Oscar William, **356**
Dawes Commission, 63, 159, 175, 186, 235, 243, 252, 503, 585, 938, 968, 1124, 1162
Dawkins, (Mrs.) Ernest, **357**
Dawson, Herron Victor, **358**
Dawson, Winnie M., **359**
Day, John Lewis, **360**
Day County, Okla. Terr., 639, 1002
Deacons and Missionaries Institute, 984
Deadwood, S.Dak., description of, 877
Deal [Photography] Studio (Chelsea, Okla.), records of, 620
Dean, Charles C., 1069
Dean, Samuel C., **362**
DeBarr, Edwin C., **363**
DeBarr family, 363
Debo, Angie Elbertha, **364**, 640, 801; publication of *And Still the Waters Run*, 625
De Camp Consolidated Glass Casket Company Collection, **361**
Decker, Charles Elijah, **365**
DeGolyer, Everette Lee, 640; correspondence, 573
DeKnight, Emma H., **366**
Delaware Indian Agency, **367**
Delaware Indians, 1124; captives of, 1330; chiefs, 1508; claims against U.S. government, 1508; land transfers, 367; removal, 367
Del Norte County, Calif., 1309
Delta Kappa Gamma, publications of, 169
Delta Sigma Rho, membership certificate, 74
Delta Tau Delta Collection, **368**
Deming, Samuel A., 800
Democratic Club (Vinita, Indian Terr.), records of, 629
Democratic Party (Okla.), 755; campaigns, 92, 182, 755, 876, 1032, 1455, 1487; elections, 1455; labor legislation, 351; publications of, 981
Democratic Party Convention of 1900, admission ticket to, 629; Oklahoma convention of 1944 proceedings, 1032
DeMoss, Robert, **369**
Dennis, Frank Landt, Sr., **370**
Dentists (Okla.), records of, 1111
Denton, B. E. (Cyclone), 640
Denver, James William, **371**
Denver and Salt Lake Railroad, **372**
Denver family, 371
Department of the West, **373**
Department stores (Okla.), records of, 278, 1287
DeRosier, Arthur H., **374**
Des Champs, John Lefeber, **375**
Des Champs family, 375
DeStwolinski, Louis C., **376**
Detrick, C. H., **377**
DeVilliers, Myrtle, **378**
Devoe, Cavnelos, 379
Devoe Family Collection, **379**
Devol, Okla., First Baptist Church, 1526
Devoto, Bernard, 1425
Dewey, Frederick Stanley, 857
Dewey, George H., 857
Dewey, Okla., hotels, 13
Dewey County, Okla., 639
Dewlen, Al, **380**
D'Hanis, Tex., history of, 501
Diamond Dishwasher Co., history of, 1395
Diamond Jubilee Commission, **381**
Diaries, 15, 63, 68, 71, 149, 205, 207, 224, 271, 294, 299, 307, 321, 325, 341, 366, 386, 392, 441, 422, 430, 454, 464, 466, 501, 516, 527, 547, 549, 553, 550, 561, 573, 578, 595, 621, 718, 738, 768, 815, 816, 926, 1071, 1097, 1131, 1137, 1140, 1170, 1176, 1181, 1201, 1216, 1247, 1266, 1286, 1289, 1306, 1307, 1316, 1352, 1359, 1389, 1438, 1482. *See also* Journals
Dill, C. A., **382**
Dillon, Bob, 231
Dinkler, Frank A., **383**
Diplomas. *See* Certificates and Diplomas Collection
Diplomats (United States), personal papers, 513, 685
Dirkson, Everett, 78
Disarmament, 104; posters about, 1226; publications about, 1226
Disciples of Christ Church, 639

Disney, Dorothy Cameron, 640
Disney, Richard Lester, **384**
Ditmars, Raymond L., correspondence, 1069
Ditzler, Walter Linginfelter, **385**
Division of Manuscripts Collection, **386**
Division of Manuscripts Map Collection, **387**
Dixon, A., **388**
Doan, Jonathan, 640
Doan's Crossing (Okla.), 639
Dobie, J. Frank, 1194, 1425
Dodd, John E., 1303
Dodge, Arthur J., 640
Dodge, Henry Chee, 275
Dodge City, Kans., description of, 207, 575, 668
Doggett, E. J., 4
Doherty, Henry, 260
Dolman, Lewis Samuel, **389**
Donahoe, Keating, 640
Donnelley, Herndon Ford, **390**
Donnelley family, 390
Doody, Maurice, **391**
Doolin, Bill, 718
Doolin, Edith, 718
Doran, Lowry A., **392**
Dorchester, May Miner, 936
Dorrance, Lemuel, **393**
Dos Passos, John, 1519
Dott, Robert Henry, **394**
Doubleday, R. R., 640
Douglas, Clarence, 1362
Dowd, Jerome H., **395**
Downing, Lewis, 243
Doyle, Thomas Henchion, 640
Drake, Noah Fields, **396**
Drake University (Des Moines, Iowa), presidents, 1277
Drug stores: Indian Territory, 1429; Oklahoma, 59, 300, 739, 778, 816, 1429, 1438; Oklahoma Territory, 383, 778, 816. *See also* Pharmacies, records of
Drumm, Andrew, 640
Drury College (Mo.), 103
Dry goods stores, records of, 912
DuBois family, **397**
Duff, H. R., **398**
Duffy, Homer, **399**
Duke Indian Oral History Collection, **400**
Duke, James Monroe, **401**
Dukes, Gilbert W., **402**
Dumbarton Oaks, history of, 1478

Dunbar, Diana, 374
Dunbar, William, 374
Duncan, Everett E., 1424
Duncan, Hank, **403**
Duncum, Floy, **404**
Dungan, Eva Ellsworth, **405**
Dunlap, S. T., **406**
Dunn, Charles (Oklahoma Kid), 1260
Dunn, Jesse J., 640
Dunn, Rose (Cimarron Rose), 640
Durant, William A., **407**
Durham, Walter W., 723
Dust storms (Okla.), 600
Dutch Reformed Church (Indian Terr.), 233
Duvall, Preston Van Buren, **408**
Dwamish Indians, 699
Dwight, Ben, 640
Dwight Mission, **409**, 532; description of, 1216

Eagle-Picher Mining and Smelting Company, 127, **410**
Eagleson, Alexander Lloyd, 640
Earlsboro, Okla. Terr., 64
Eason Oil Company, 730
Eastern Oklahoma A&M College (Wilburton, Okla.), 926
East Guthrie, Indian Terr., 1467
Eastman, Francis B., **411**
Eaton, Frank, 640
Economics, manuscripts on, 3, 641
Economists, 641
Eddie, B. D., 640
Eddleman, Morgan W., 1233
Edelweiss Club (Clinton, Okla.), 1412
Editors, 130, 1000
Edmondson, James Howard, 640
Education, 590; higher, 584, 1234, 1277; intercultural, 1227; museum education, 1039; Oklahoma, 639, 1161; research, 1209, 1234; testing and measurement, 1209; textbooks, 54, 176, 492, 548, 1064, 1264; trends (United States), 391
Educators: correspondence of, 100; writings of, 1086, 1209
Edwards, Archibald Cason, **412**
Edwards, John N., correspondence, 959
Edwards, R. J., Inc., records of, 412
Edwards, Thomas Allison, **413**
Edwards, Va., **414**
Edwards family, correspondence of, 412

[393]

Edwards Trading Post (Hughes County, Okla.), 1304
Eggan, Fred, field notes of, 950
Eisenhower, Dwight David, 78
Ela, George, 307
Elder, Frederick Stanton, **416**
Eldridge, J. W. (Buck), 640, 939
Election returns, Atoka County, Okla., 310
Elections: Oklahoma, 268, 351, 639, 1114; United States, 1114
Elk City, Okla., 483; agricultural cooperatives, 1109; banks and banking, 418, 419; hospitals, 1276; medical care, 417
Elk City Community Hospital, **417**
Elk City Farmers National Bank (Okla.), **418**
Elk City First National Bank (Okla.), **419**
Elkins, Harrison M., **420**
Elliott, J. Ross, **421**
Elliott, Robert L., 1534
Ellis, Newal A., 640
Ellis County, Okla., history of, 1002. *See also* Day County, Okla. Terr.
Ellison, (Mrs.) C. D., **422**
Ellison, Ralph, 89
El Meta Bond College (Okla.), 56
El Reno, Okla., banks and banking, 415; clubs, 1367; railroad operations at, 1219
El Reno Citizens National Bank (Okla.), **415**
El Reno Interurban Railway Co., (Okla.), records of, 1395
El Reno Sanitarium (Okla.), 6, 987
Emblems, state (Okla.), 639
Embry, John, **423**
Emerson, Caro, 422
Emerson, Ralph Waldo, 1318
English, Frank Miller, **424**
English, William M., **425**
Enid, Okla.: physicians, 767; training school for nurses, 767
Enid, Okla. Terr., settlement of, 524
Enid (Okla.) Army Air Field, naming of, 1433
Epidemics, influenza, 210
Episcopal Church, 1196; missions to Indians, 1227
Epton, Hicks Byers, **426**
Epworth College of Medicine (Oklahoma City, Okla.), 955
Epworth Spotlight, The, 792
Equal Rights Amendment (Okla.), 626

Erdmann, E. M., **427**
Erwin, A. M., **428**
Eskridge Hotel (Wynnewood, Okla.), records of, 1495
Eta Kappa Nu Collection, **429**
Ethnobotany, 1447
Ethnology (Okla.), 639
Ethiopian/Amharic language, manuscripts in, 211
Etiquette, book of, 1382
Euchee Boarding School (Sapulpa, Okla.), records of, 1250
Euchee Indians, 161; schools, 1250. *See also* Yuchi Indians
Eufaula, Indian Terr., physicians, 1388
Eufaula, Okla., general stores, 160; physicians, 1388
Eureka Springs, Ark., development of railroads, 507
Europe, description and travel, 676, 1289
Evans, Arthur Grant, 430
Evans, Arthur W., **430**
Evans, Charles, **431**
Evans, Elisha, 432
Evans, Luther H., 47
Evans, Melissa, **432**
Evans, Oren F., **433**
Evergood, Philip, 112
Ewing, Amos Alexander, **434**; correspondence, 306
Ewing, Cortez Arthur Milton, 84, **435**
Ewing, Finis W., **436**
Exchange National Bank (Tulsa, Okla.), correspondence, 452
Exline, George, 762
Expeditions, southwestern United States, 501
Explorers, in California, 1309
Ezell, John Samuel, **437**

Fagin, Kay K., **438**
Fairland, Indian Terr., retail trade, 203
Fairland, Okla.: banks, 440; grain businesses, records of, 921; municipal government, records of, 439; retail trade, 203
Fairland Municipal Records Collection, **439**
Fairland National Bank Collection, **440**
Fairview, Okla.: banks, 1441; newspapers, 1441; physicians, 716; railroads, 1441
Fairview, Okla. Terr., history of, 1446

Falconer, Ray, **441**
Falconer, Velma, **441**
Family Life Institute (University of Oklahoma), 1112
Fanciers organizations (Okla.), 753
Farley, Alan W., **442**
Farley, James A., 1294
Farm Credit Administration, publications of, 562
Farmers, 116
Farmers Cotton Gin Company, records of, 560
Farmers National Bank (Hydro, Okla.), records of, 691
Farmers National Grain Corporation, records of, 562
Farmers State Bank (Okla.), **443**
Farmers Union Cooperative Gin Company, **444**
Farm relief programs, 464
Farms and farming, 632; Indian Territory, 116; Kansas, 307, 1135; mortgages, 220; Oklahoma, 689, 710; Oklahoma Territory, 1440; Texas, 116, 1440
Farr, Doane, 1232
Farris, Okla., public schools, 176
Farwell, John V., Jr., **445**
Faulk, Odie B., 640
Fauna (Tulsa County, Okla.), 1003
Faux, Kathleen, **446**
Fay, Helen S., **447**
Fay, Robert O., **447**
Feaver, John Clayton, **448**
Federal district courts, records of, 151
Federal Home Loan Bank (Topeka, Kans.), records of, 103
Federal Power Commission, annual reports of, 1497; investigation of natural gas industry, 1497
Feed stores (Okla.), records of, 520
Felger, (Mrs.) J. H., **449**
Ferguson, Lucia Loomis, correspondence, 452
Ferguson, Milton James, **450**
Ferguson, Thompson Benton, **451**, 452
Ferguson, Walter Scott, **452**, 640
Ferrell, Sally, **453**
Feuquay, Courtland Matson, **454**
Feuquay, J. W., 454
Field, J. Walker, **455**
Fields, John, 534
Fillman, Irvin, **456**
Financial firms (Okla.), records of, 412

Findlay, James Franklin, **457**
Fine arts organizations, 842
Fink, John Berlin, **458**
Finley, Ira M., 265
Finney, Frank Florer, **459**
Finney, Thomas McKean, **459**
Finney family, 459
First, Francis Ray, Sr., **460**
First National Bank (Carmen, Okla.), 213
First National Bank (Oklahoma City, Okla.), records of, 1028
First State Bank (Noble, Okla.), 1008
Fish, Hamilton, 1508
Fisher, Clyde, publications of, 462
Fisher, Daniel G., **461**
Fisher, Te Ata, **462**
Fisk, Charles W., **463**
Fite, Gilbert C., **464**
Fitzpatrick, H. L., **465**
Five Civilized Tribes, 1124; Civil War, participation in, 303, 386; commemorative celebrations, 986; principal chiefs of, 16, 386. *See also* individual tribes
Flags: poems about, 537; state (Okla.), 639; United States, 126, 1201
Flathead Indians, 1124
Flenner, John W., 624
Fletcher, Margaret Catherine, **466**
Fletcher family genealogy, 466
Flint, Indian Terr., retail stores, 671
Flint District, Cherokee Nation, description of, 466
Flipper, Henry O., 640
Flitch, Sylvester, **467**
Floods and flood control (Okla.), 639
Flora, Snowden Dwight, **468**
Flora (southwestern United States), 791
Florida, description and travel, 1069
Floyd, Charles (Pretty Boy), 640
Floyd, Gilbert, 163
Fluke, Louise, 640
Folk songs, 947
Folsom, David, 578
Folsom, Israel, 578, 1131
Folsom, Lee W., **469**
Folsom, Nathaniel, 578
Folsom, Sampson, 1131
Folsom family, correspondence, 469, 1131
Folsom Reunion Association, records of, 470
Folsom Training School, **470**

[395]

Football, play diagrams, 840
Force, Edith R., 1003
Ford, Okla., history of, 146
Foreign policy, United States, 392
Foreman, Carolyn Thomas, 640
Foreman, Grant, 640
Foreman, James, death of, 740
Foreman, Stephen, **471**
Foreman family, 386, 471
Forests and forestry (Okla.), 639
Forsyth, George Alexander, **472**
Fort Arbuckle, Indian Terr., 639, 1181
Fort Berthold Indian Reservation, 1508
Fort Clark, Tex., **473**
Fort Cobb, Okla., 639
Fort Coffee, Indian Terr., 639
Fort Davis, Indian Terr., 639
Fortescue, John W., **477**
Fort George Wright, Wash., 411
Fort Gibson, Indian Terr., 1507; cemetery, 771; establishment of, 771
Fort Gibson, Okla., 639; banks and banking, 474; financial records, 474
Fort Gibson First National Bank (Okla.), **474**
Fort Gibson Quartermaster Collection, **475**
Fort Griffin, Tex., description of, 575
Fort McCulloch, Indian Terr., 639
Fort Marion, Fla., 639
Fort Reno, Okla. Terr., 639, 1414; description of, 575, 618
Forts. *See individual forts and camps*
Fort Sill, Okla., missile firing range at, 1328
Fort Sill, Okla. Terr., 639; description of, 618
Fort Smith, Ark., 639; description of, 466; history of, 514; U.S. district court at, 1202
Fort Smith, Subiaco, and Eastern Railway Company, **476**
Fort Supply, Indian Terr., 639; description of, 575; history of, 216
Fort Towson, Indian Terr., 639
Fort Union, N.Mex., records from, 501
Fort Washita, Indian Terr., 639
Fort Washita, Okla., 148
Fort Wayne, Indian Terr., 639
Foster, Del Oneita, **478**
Foster, Henry, 479
Foster, Henry Vernon, **479**
Foster Petroleum, 479

Fountain, Albert Jennings, murder case, 58
Fourche family, estate of, 283
4-H clubs (Okla.), 648
Four Mothers Society, 81
Fowler, David, **480**
Fowler, Ezra, **481**
Fowler, Nathaniel M., 640
Fowler, Richard Gildart, **482**
Fox-Vliet Drug Store, (Oklahoma City, Okla.) records of, 1438
France: political affairs, 533; theatrical history, 1248; transfer of real property, 326
Francis, (Mrs.) William, **483**
Franklin, William Monroe, **484**
Frankoma pottery, 1251
Frantz, Frank, 640
Fraternal Order of Eagles, correspondence relating to, 631; receipt from, 939
Fraternal organizations, 631, 939; proceedings of, 780; publications, 863; ribbons and buttons, 559
Fraternities, records of, 18, 368, 429, 1123, 1127, 1290, 1291, 1292
Frayser, E. B., **485**
Fred, Okla., 1313
Frederick, Okla.: mortgages, 966, realtors, 966; telephone directory of 1926: 173
Frederickson, Mary Brownlee, **486**
Freedom State Bank (Okla.), **487**
Freeman, Margaret, **488**
Freeman family, 488
Freemasonry, 665. *See also* Masonry
Freeny, Ellis, **489**
Fremont, J. C., 373
Freudenthal, Elsbeth Estelle, **490**
Frick, Charles D., 362
Friedman, Milton, 641
Frieman, Robinson, 729
Friends Hillside Mission (Indian Terr.), records of, 548
Fritts, Mary, **491**
Frontier and pioneer life: Colorado, 1314; Indian Territory, 131, 175, 446, 696, 711, 805, 815, 1007, 1090, 860, 1230, 1373, 1532; Kansas, 100, 668, 1314, 1319, 1339, 1374; New Mexico, 1428; Oklahoma, 64, 131, 524, 668, 1015, 1305, 1321; Oklahoma Territory, 524, 543, 599, 621, 656, 696, 711, 744, 924, 1015, 1174, 1195, 1210,

1247, 1305, 1319, 1339, 1373, 1390, 1400, 1411, 1440, 1452, 1467, 1522; Texas, 488, 1440
Frontiers, comparative studies of, 1253
Fuller, Agnes, **492**
Fullerton, Samuel Clyde, 493
Fullerton, Samuel Clyde, Jr., **493**
Fulton, J. S., **494**
Fulton Bow Plane, 933
Fulton Flotsam, 933
Funeral homes: Indian Territory, 203, 1187; Oklahoma, 203, 1106, 1187; records of, 671, 975, 1106
Funk, John, 495
Funk, Rose, **495**
Funk, Russell Milton, 640
Funk family, 495
Funnell, Roberta Ann Paris, **496**
Furniture stores, records of, 975

Gaillardia Garden Club, **497**
Gainer, Ina, 601
Gaither, Edna, **498**
Galbraith, James, 641
Galen Society, **499**
Gallaher, William M., **500**
Gamble, Richard Dalzell, **501**
Gambling (Kans.), 437
Ganado Mucho, 275
Gantt, Ernest S., 875
Garber, Okla., Christian Church at, 1329
Gardner, Florence Guild Bruce, **502**
Gardner, Jefferson, **503**
Gardner, Oscar, **504**
Garfield, James A., 544; death of, 1156
Garfield County, Okla., 639; taxes, 1118
Garland, Hamlin, 461
Garner, James, 640
Garretson, Anna Kate, **505**
Garretson, Henry David, **506**
Garrett, Buck, 640
Garrett, Lyle, correspondence, 431
Garrett, Patrick, 640
Garrity, Richard T., **507**
Garton, John William, 640
Garvin, Isaac L., **508**
Garvin County, Okla., 639; teachers in, 176
Gary, Raymond Dancel, **509**, 640; inauguration of, 1032
Gassaway, Percy Lee, **510**
Gatchell, Theodore Dodge, **511**
Gavin, James M., 1437

Gaylord, Edward King, 640; correspondence, 1108
Gee, Robert L., **512**
Geissler, Arthur H., **513**
General Federation of Women's Clubs (Okla.), 1105
General stores: Indian Territory, 253, 310, 671, 732, 871, 1187; Oklahoma, 160, 663, 679, 1187
Genetics, 1322
Geographers: research of, 118, 622; writings of, 961
Geography: Cherokee Nation, Indian Terr., 622; Great Plains, 622
Geologists, 163, 304, 365, 396, 433, 536, 539, 573, 669, 687, 1085, 1192
Geology (Okla.), 639, 1036, 1485
George, David Lloyd, 461
Georgia: land records, 1499; state currency, 284
Gerlach, Robert, 946
German State Bank (Elk City, Okla.), records of, 418
Germany: bonds of, 506; description of, 1933–1939: 1342; foreign relations with Europe, 1005; German prisoners of war in Oklahoma, 1492; immigration of authors from, 1519
Geronimo, 364, 640, 1516
Getty, J. Paul, 640
Ghost towns: Indian Territory, 1516; Oklahoma, 1516
Gibson, Arrell Morgan, **514**, 640
Gibson, Iva Thomas, **515**
Gibson, Rosemary, 640
Giessmann, Gary, **516**
Giffin, LaDonna, **517**
Giffin family, 517
Gilcrease, Thomas, 640
Gildart, Francis, 477
Gildart, J. B., 518
Gildart, W. B., **518**
Gildart family, 518
Giles, Albert S., 265
Gilkey, Jessie Lone Clarkson, **519**
Gilkey, John E., **520**
Gill, (Mrs.) B. Franklin, **521**
Gilles, Albert S., 640
Gillespie, F. E., **522**
Gillespie, John D., **523**
Gilliland, J. W., **524**
Girl Scouts of America, 296
Gist, Chris, **525**

[397]

Gittinger, Roy, **526**
Gladney, Essa, **527**
Glasstone, Samuel, **528**
Glencoe, Ill., public school system, 1496
Glickman, Mendel, **529**
Goddard, Eunice May Stewart, **530**
Gold, discovery of in California, 10
Gold miners, personal narratives, 107, 150
Goldsby, Crawford (Cherokee Bill), 640
Goldwater, Barry, 78
Golf, 267
Golobie, John, **531**, 720
Gomes, Pat, **532**
Gone With The Wind, 165
Gooch, Brison, **533**
Good, Nancye, **534**
Gooding, Henry Leavenworth, 640
Goodland Indian Mission (Okla.), 746
Goodland Indian Orphanage and School (Okla.), 504
Goodland Indian School, 504, **535**
Goodnight, Charles, 86
Goodnight, Okla., retail stores, 663
Goodnight Pasture, 1
Goodrich, Harold Beach, **536**
Gordon, Charles Ulysses, **537**
Gordon-Van Tine Company, **538**
Gore, Jonathan, 768
Gore, Thomas Pryor, 640, 718; correspondence, 1108
Gould, Charles Newton, **539**
Gover, Maggie, 1524
Governors: Oklahoma, impeachment of, 1449; Oklahoma, personal papers of, 567, 598, 728, 980, 982, 1126, 1214, 1449; Oklahoma Territory, 1229, 1266
Governor's Interstate Indian Council, **540**
Graber, Jean, 1359
Graber, Richard, 1359
Graber, Stan L., **541**
Grady County, Okla., 639
Grady County Park (Chickasha, Okla.), 1404
Graham, Gideon Wesley, **542**
Graham, Griff, 640
Graham, Martha, 165
Grain trade (Okla.), 249, 921, 1104
Grand Army of the Republic, encampment programs, 547
Grand Canyon (Ariz.), description of, 1130
Grandfield, Okla.: First Baptist Church, 1526; First Presbyterian Church, 1526

Grand River Dam (Okla.), history of, 217
Granite, Okla., physicians, 796
Grant, Ulysses S., 1340
Grant County, Okla., school district records, 1273
Grant County (Okla.) Film Library, 1138
Grant County (Okla.) Historical Society, history of, 1138
Grass, Frank, **543**
Grass, Patty, **543**
Grasslands (United States), conservation of, 990
Gray Horse, Okla. Terr., 459
Gray Horse Trading Post, 459
Grayson, Ambrose T., **545**
Grayson, George W., 238, 544
Grayson, Washington, 544
Grayson Family Papers, **544**
Great Britain, foreign relations, 1939–1946: 685
Great Depression (Okla.), 708; recipes from, 627
Great Plains: agriculture, 622; geography of, 622; Indian tribes of, 93; village people of, 1039
Great Plains Conference on Higher Education, records of, 1234
Green Peach War, 544
Greer County: Okla., 639; description, 711; education in, 192; Oklahoma Territory, 1384; Texas, 1384
Greeting cards, 99, 495, 816, 894, 916
Gregory, A. R., 659
Gregory, Arthur Leslie, **546**
Grey, Lucy, 2
Griffin, D. W., 640
Griffin, Victor, 640
Griffith, Alfred, **547**
Griffitts, James Addison, **548**
Grimes, Mary E., **549**
Grisso, D. Horton, **550**
Grisso, Walker D., **551**, 1437
Gritts, Levi D., 640
Grocery stores (Okla.), records of, 520
Grove, Indian Terr., physicians, 1442
Guaranty Bank (Oklahoma City, Okla.), 813
Guardian Funeral Home (Okla.), 822
Guam, U.S. marines in, 1201
Guatemala: description and travel, 114, 1069; U.S. ambassador to, 513
Guess, George. *See* Sequoyah
Gulledge, George Washington, **552**

Gulliford, Andrew, **553**
Gunning, Boyd, **554**
Guthrie, Okla.: attorneys, 1312; banks and banking, 939; cemeteries, 648; churches, 648; drugstores, 816; '89er celebration, 279; historic homes, 648; history of, 279, 648, 816; Lions Club, 222; newspapers, 1189; retail stores, 663; schools, 648; state capitol, movement of, 1454
Guthrie, Okla. Terr., settlement of, 1522
Guthrie, Woody, 640
Guthrie District Medical Association Collection, **555**
Guthrie family genealogy, 466
Guthrie Lodge of Freemasons (Guthrie, Okla.), records of, 1211
Guy, William M., **556**
Guymon, Okla.: banks and banking, 557; newspapers, 867
Guymon First National Bank (Okla.), **557**
Gypsy Oil Company, 925

Haas, Mary R., **558**
Hackett, Helen, **559**
Haddix, J. F., **560**
Hadjo, Milly Francis, 640
Hadley, Theodore Johnson, 640
Hadsell, Sardis Roy, **561**
Hague, Lyle L., **562**
Hailey, Daniel Morris, **563**
Hainer, Bayard Taylor, **564**
Haines, Sarah Deborah, **565**
Hair, Fannie M. Townsend, **566**
Hall, David, **567**, 640
Hall, Horace Mark, **568**
Hall, Joseph S., 568
Hallinen, Andrew, estate of, 569
Hallinen, John A., Jr., 569
Hallinen, Joseph E., **569**
Halloran, Arthur F., **570**
Halsell, Harold Hallet, **571**
Halsell, Oscar D., 571
Halsey, William, correspondence, 1108
Hamilton, (Mrs.) C. P., **572**
Hamilton, Charles W., **573**
Hamilton, Robert, 712
Hamilton Hardware Store (Hollis, Okla.), records of, 572
Hammonds, O. O., 640
Hamon, Earl, **574**
Hanby, Benjamin R., 654
Hancock, Mary W., 1094

Hancock, William Box, **575**
Handbook of Oklahoma Writers, 850
Handy family, correspondence of, 412
Hannifin, D. L., 1106
Harbison, Robert B., 45, **576**
Hardin, Joe, **577**
Hardman, P. V., 382
Hardware stores: Indian Territory, 40, 203; Oklahoma, 203, 293, 572; records of, 572, 975
Hardy, Summers, 53
Hargett, Jay L., **578**
Hargrett, Lester, **579**
Harjo, Lochar, **580**
Harkey, Ben, 640
Harkins, George, 115
Harlow, James Gindling, **581**
Harlow, Victor E., **582**, 640
Harmon County, Okla., land deeds, 1001
Harper, Robert Henry, **583**
Harrall, Stewart, **584**
Harreld, John W., correspondence, 957
Harrell, (Mrs.) J. B., 521
Harriman, Averell, correspondence, 685
Harris, Colonel Johnson, 243, **585**
Harris, Cyrus H., **586**, 640
Harris, Fred, 640
Harris, Giles Edward, **587**
Harris, Harvey, 588
Harris, James A., **588**
Harris, Robert M., **589**
Harris, William Torrey, **590**
Harris family, genealogy, 588
Harrison, Jacob, **591**
Harrison, Walter, 1362
Harrison, Walter M., 403, **592**, 1489
Harrison, William H., **593**
Harrod, Neva Belle, **594**
Harrold, Jack, **595**
Hart, (Mrs.) Hugh, **596**
Hartman, Jacob, 640
Hartshorne, Okla., hospitals, 212
Hartshorne, William O., Jr., 406
Harvard University (Mass.), faculty, 343
Haskell, Charles Nathaniel, **598**, 640, 1168
Haskell and LeFlore Counties Medical Society, **597**
Haskell County, Okla., medical societies, 597
Hassler, Jasper O., 640
Hastings, William Wirt, 401, 640
Hatfield, Edna Greer Porter, **599**

[399]

Hathaway, A. H., **600**
Havemeyers-Seamans Oil Company, 170
Hawks, Rex B., **640**
Hawley, Fred, 640
Hayes, James H., **601**
Haynes, Everett, 1342
Haynes, Micajah P., **602**
Hayt, E. A., **603**
Heagy family, 704
Healdton Petroleum Company, 170
Health care industry, legislative reform, 496
Healy, Frank Dale, Jr., **604**
Healy, George Henry, 604
Healy, William D., 386
Healy family, history of, 604
Heck, Bessie Holland, **605**
Heffner, Edna Swenson, **606**
Heffner, Roy E., **607**
Heflin, Cleo Eugene, **608**
Heflin, Van, **609**
Hefner, Robert Alexander, **610**, 640; correspondence, 1108
Hefner family, genealogy, 610
Helena Township, Okla. Terr., 1452
Helpenstein family, correspondence, 543
Henderson, Arnold G., **611**
Hendricks, James R., **612**
Hendrickson, Gwen, **613**
Hendrickson, Samuel Harvey, 613
Hengst, Herbert Randall, Sr., 230, **614**
Henkle, George, **615**
Hennessey, Okla.: history of, 616, 1015; medical care, 388; tornadoes, 1015
Hennessey, Okla. Terr.: drug stores, 383; settlement of, 524
Hennessey High School (Okla.), **616**
Hennings, A. E., **617**
Henryetta, Okla., 127, 227
Hensley, Claude, **618**
Herbert, Harold Harvey, **619**
Herpetologists, 1069
Herring, Alvin J., **620**
Hertzog, Anna Laura Brisky, **621**
Hester Mercantile Store (Boggy Depot, Indian Terr.), 310
Heston, J. Edgar, 260
Hewes, Leslie, **622**
Hewitt, Robert C., **623**
Hewitt family, 623
Heydrick, L. C., **624**
Hickok, James Butler (Wild Bill), 307
Hicks, Edward D., 1511
Hicks, Jimmie, **625**

Higher education, 584, 1234, 1277. *See also* Colleges and universities; Education
High School Science Service, 1112
Higley, Brewster, 640
Hi Koller Ranch, 1
Hilbert-Price, Shirley, **626**
Hildebrand, Trudie Flanagan, **627**
Hill, Anita, 640
Hill, Francis M., **628**
Hill, George Washington, **629**
Hill, Weldon, **630**
Hindekoper, Frederick, 1256
Hine, L. T., **631**
Hines, M. D., **632**
Hinkel, John W., **633**
Hinkhouse, Steven, **634**
Hinsdale, Harriet, **635**
Hinton, S. E., **636**
Hipes, Jessie James, **637**
Hirsch, Leon, 265
Hisel, (Mrs.) O. R., **638**
Historians, 1313; papers of, 648, 1389, 1451; research notes, 207, 501, 648, 514, 902, 964, 1265; writings of, 46, 86, 93, 184, 207, 216, 217, 236, 305, 343, 364, 437, 464, 638, 674, 686, 771, 801, 902, 910, 954, 1076, 1210, 1241, 1253, 1277
Historic buildings (Okla.), 639
Historic homes (Okla.), 648
Historic Oklahoma Biographies Collection, **640**
Historic Oklahoma Collection, **639**
Historic sites: Indian Territory, 1516; Oklahoma, 639, 648, 1516
Hitch, James Kerrick, 640
Hixson, William F., **641**
Hobart, Okla., crime and criminals, 775
Hoffman, Roy V., 16, 640
Hogarth, Andrew, **642**
Hoig, Stan, 231
Holbrook, Mabel Jackson, correspondence, 644
Holbrook, Ralph Winfrey, **643**
Holbrook, Richard Burkey, **644**
Holdenville, Okla., 914; clubs, 645
Holdenville Schubert Music Club, **645**
Holidays: Indian Territory, proclamations of, 1156; Oklahoma Territory, proclamations of, 1199; United States, proclamations of, 1156
Holland, W. B., 454

Hollem, Anna Iverson, **646**
Hollem, Charles L., 646
Hollis, Okla., hardware stores, 572
Holloman, John Herbert, 1524
Holloway, William Judson, 640
Holmberg, Gustaf Fredrik, **647**
Holmes, Helen F., **648**
Holt, James Doepel, **649**
Holt, Smith Lewis, **649**
Holt Adoption Program, 962
Holtzendorff, Crichton Brooks, **650**
Homestead certificates, 406, 1229
Homesteading, 605; Texas, 488, 867
Honey Creek Ranch (Grove, Okla.), 628
Hood, Darla, 640
Hood, F. Redding, **651**
Hooper's Printing (Norman, Okla.), **652**
Hoops, Mary Griffith, **653**
Hoover, Earl R., **654**
Hoover, Herbert, 82, 459, 844; correspondence, 685, 1108
Hoover, Ike, 1119
Hoover, J. Edgar, 68, 78; correspondence, 1119
Hopeton State Bank (Okla.), **655**
Hopi Indians, 275, 1124
Hopkins, Harry, correspondence, 685
Hopson, Etta Roberts, **656**
Horses (Okla.), 639
Horton, Guy K., **657**
Horton, T. D., correspondence, 874
Horton family, 657
Hoskinson, Thomas Bowman, 658
Hoskinson, William Earl, **658**
Hoskinson family, history, 658
Hospitals: cooperative, 417, 1276; mental, 722; Muskogee, Okla., 1263; Oklahoma, 6, 157, 212, 417, 639; Oklahoma, records of, 9, 276
Hoss, Henry Sessler, **659**
Hosterman, Jacob, **660**
Hotchkiss and Cronkhite Loan & Investment Company, **661**
Hotels (Okla.), 13, 639, 1180, 1495
Hotema, Solomon E., **662**
Houghton, Fred Ernest, **663**
House, Roy Temple, **664**, 1492
Houses, floor plans of (Indian Terr.), 1224
Housh, Earl C., **665**
Houston, Andrew Jackson, 640
Houston, Sam, 640
Houston, Temple, **666**
Howard, Walter Alonzo, **667**

Howdy Folks, 935
Howe, A. N., **668**
Howell, Jesse V., **669**
Howell, O. E., **670**
Hoxie, Jack, 640
Hudson, Waddie, **671**
Hudson family, 671
Huff, Thomas J., **672**
Huffman, Jacob C., 673
Huffman, John, **673**
Huggard, Christopher James, **674**
Hughes, Jim, **675**
Hughes, John Elmer, **676**
Hughes, Josephine S., **677**
Hughes, Okla., medical care, 125
Hughes County, Okla., 639; county seat, 914; history of, 1304
Hugo, Okla.: medical care, 512; physicians, 719
Hulett, A. W., 1307
Hulett, Lula, 1307
Hull, Cordell, correspondence, 685
Humboldt County, Calif., 1309
Hume, Annette Ross, 640, 678
Hume, Carlton Ross, **678**
Humphrey, Hubert H., interview with, 78
Hundley, John, **679**
Hungary, bonds of, 506
Hunt, Blanche Seale, **680**
Hunt, J. O., **681**
Hunt County, Tex., 723
Hunter, H. A., **682**
Hunter, Thomas W., **683**
Hunting Horse, 640
Huntley, A. A., **684**
Hurley, Alice, 844
Hurley, Patrick Jay, **685**; correspondence, 844, 1105
Huron Indians, 1124
Hurst, Irvin, **686**
Hurst, Sylvester, 640
Hutchings, Murphey, and German law firm, records of, 977
Hutchings, Nannie, 640
Hutchison, L. L., **687**
Hutto, Robert W., **688**
Hyde, Clayton H., **689**
Hyde, Sadie M., **690**
Hydro, Okla.: banks and banking, 691; hardware stores, 293
Hydro First National Bank (Okla.), **691**
Hymnals, 658; Cherokee, 446; Choctaw, 469; Protestant, 359; Wyandotte, 976

[401]

Ice, Rodney D., **692**
Ice family genealogy, 692
Iceland, U.S. marines in, 1201
Illustrators, 806, 1322
Immigrants: German, family correspondence, 1257; in the U.S., 1333; naturalization records, 1165; personal narratives, 531
Imperial Council of the Ancient Order of the Nobles of the Mystic Shrine, 665
Impson, Hiram, **693**
Independent Oil and Gas Company, 730
Independent Order of Odd Fellows, 449, **694**
Indiana, Eleventh Volunteer Infantry, 325
Indian agencies, records of, 1326, 1480
Indian Chief Oil and Gas Company, 1151
Indian Claims Commission, **695**, 1006
Indian International Council, Creek Indian delegates to, 1116
Indian Missionary Association, records of, 984
Indian-Pioneer Papers, **696**
Indians of Mexico, 954; fiction, 1110
Indians of North America, 639; advocacy organizations, 21, 23, 848, 1037, 1383; agencies, 209; alcohol use, 102, 726; allotment of land, 102, 334, 593, 703, 737, 860, 964, 1064, 829, 869, 879, 968, 1070, 1124, 1141; annual messages of Indian nations, 1124; anthropological field notes on, 102; antiquities, 1167; archaeological sites (Okla.), 1515; art, 102, 207, 332, 639; authors, 1072; banks, 1354; baskets, 275; bibliography, 1510; bingo, 848; block grants, 848; buffalo hunting, 553; captives of, 111; cemeteries, 109; censuses, 1288; chiefs, 16, 36, 159, 161, 167, 178, 186, 207, 217, 238, 243, 257, 280, 289, 334, 354, 386, 402, 407, 489, 503, 508, 544, 556, 580, 586, 589, 591, 593, 661, 662, 702, 705, 727, 732, 737, 742, 745, 805, 827, 829, 848, 868, 869, 879, 885, 886, 887, 892, 893, 897, 919, 968, 985, 1067, 1078, 1089, 1116, 1117, 1131, 1141, 1156, 1223, 1228, 1231, 1249, 1302, 1381, 1500, 1508, 1523; citizenship, 1124; civil rights, 23, 932, 1037; Civil War, 119, 303, 774, 964, 1124; claims, 331, 354, 386, 678, 727, 1006, 1124, 1508; colleges, 738; commemorative celebrations, 986; community development, 848; constitutions, 639, 1124; conversion to Christianity, 233; costume and dress, 102, 1510; courts, 508; courtship and marriage, 102; culture, 102, 207, 275, 400, 768, 854, 856, 1066, 1258; dances, 102, 1147, 1516; Dawes Commission agreements, 1124; depredations, 1244; descriptions of, 1181; diseases of the skin, 792; education, 23, 56, 71, 243, 386, 727, 848, 932, 1124, 1131, 1227, 1244, 1302, 1516; employment, 848, 1244; environmental studies, 611; ethnobotany, 102, 275, 1447; ethnophysiology, 102; ethnozoology, 102; farming, 779; fiction, 155; folklore, 55, 102, 462, 854, 1167, 1477; funds, 1124; games, 102; government relations, 93, 257, 386, 832, 848; health and health care, 243, 386, 848, 1124, 1213, 1430; historic sites (Okla.), 1516; history, 207, 243, 305, 400, 409; housing, 611, 243, 848; hymnals, 446, 469, 976; industries, 848; inheritance and guardians, 1124; intertribal relations, 985, 1227; kinship, 102; land, 1124; land fraud, 423; land quality, 781; land titles, 702; land transfers, 54, 121, 275, 397, 503, 544, 585, 1064, 1065, 1124, 1244, 1508; languages, 102, 243, 307, 553, 558, 1124; leases of agricultural lands, 378; legends, 55, 102; libraries, private, 1523; liquor, 102, 1124; litigation by, 695, 1006; living conditions, 781; medical research, 955; medical treatment, 102, 1278; mineral resources, 508, 727, 994, 1124, 1470, 1535; mineral rights, 737; missionaries to, 56, 386, 446, 578, 745, 774, 815; missions to, 1124, 1227, 1450, 1516; musical instruments, 275; oil production, 479, 1124; oral history, 102, 275, 400, 1477; organizations, 540, 848; orphanages, 243, 504, 535; Pacific northwestern tribes, 699; Peace Council of 1874: 745; per capita payments, 1124, 1244; performers, 462; peyotism, 102, 459, 639, 856; physicians, 944; poets, 938; police forces, 1244; pottery, 275; poverty among, 1508; prayer sticks, 275; railroads on lands of, 1124; relations with

Spain, 701; relations with the U.S. government, 1070, 1124, 1326; relations with whites, 307, 1019, 1067, 1070; religion and mythology, 105, 307, 856, 1147; removal, 386, 774; reproduction, 102; reservations, 599, 952, 1508; rites and ceremonies, 102, 400, 1147; rugs, 275; schools, 209, 243, 378, 402, 404, 470, 504, 508, 535, 586, 774, 848, 884, 1065, 1321, 1477, 1514, 1516; slaves, ownership of, 727; social conditions, 1037; social life and customs, 102, 1466; social welfare, 848, 994; speeches, 892; storytellers, 462; suffrage, 1124; taxation of lands, 900; territorial government (Okla.), 1124; timber resources, 508; tipis, 207; trade, 1124; traders with, 459, 772; trading license renewal, 209; trading posts (Okla.), 1516; treaties, 93, 257, 695, 699; tribal council proceedings, 23; tribal factionalism, 243, 586, 815; tribal government, 191, 243, 289, 324, 378, 402, 503, 585, 702, 727, 829, 848, 884, 886, 1065, 1141; tribal politics, 243, 544, 737, 848, 868, 964; wagon train attacks, 970; wars, 16, 102, 207, 544, 698, 835, 1210, 1414; weaving, 1167, 1466; white captives, 397, 1244, 1330; women, 102, 848, 1167; youth programs, 23

Indians of the Northwest Collection, **699**

Indian Territory: attitude toward Oklahoma Territory, 1231; attorneys, 1494; banks and banking, 1100; businessmen, 1103; business permits, 814; capital punishment, 836; cattle industry, 1516; cemeteries, 1516; Civil War, 514, 860; clubs, 1206; coal mining, 508, 1470; court records of, 318, 1415, 1416, 1417; courts, 866; crime and criminals, 866, 1416, 1417, 1464; description of, 175, 235, 466, 516, 693, 805, 815, 837, 860; education, 798; elections, 629; fiction about, 1513; First Volunteer Infantry Regiment, 1247; forts, 216, 475, 575, 639, 771, 1181, 1507, 1516; fraternal organizations in, 694; frontier and pioneer life, 131, 175, 446, 696, 711, 805, 815, 1007, 1090, 860, 1230, 1373, 1532; funeral homes, records of, 1187; general stores, 871, 1187; ghost towns, 1516; history of, 343; holiday proclamations, 1156; Indian Meridian, 363; intruders, 243, 920; judges, 866, 1416, 1417; labor unions in, 1320; land surveys, 374; law enforcement, 836; legality of marriages performed in, 758; letterheads, 808; libraries, private, 1523; maps of, 387; masonry (Scottish Rite) in, 1211; medical care, 91, 237; medical societies, records of, 697; Methodism in, 1346; military posts, 475, 1516; mineral resources, 508; mines and mining, 747; missionaries, 446, 984, 1216. (*see also* missions and missionaries); missions, 446, 940, 1450, 1527 (*see also* missions and missionaries); municipal government, 239; newspapers in, 1458; oil wells in, 217, 479; patriotic hymns, 1202; physicians, 965, 1230, 1442; physicians' personal narratives, 949; physicians' records, 1457; place names, 1516; political organizations, 629; publishers, 1303; ranches, 1516; realtors, 1103; retail stores, 1535; roads, 940; schools, 297, 366, 378, 402, 430, 446, 508, 746, 798, 884, 940, 1346, 1472, 1477, 1514; Seminole Nation, description of, 693; settlement of, 696; statehood, 402, 430, 860, 886, 938, 1130, 1141, 1223, 1262, 1381, 1500; telephone service in, 618, 1511; timber resources, 508; townsites, 374; trading posts, 1516; white settlement in, 1102; women in, 466, 1230; work permits, 1361

Indian Territory Illuminating Oil Company, 479; publications, 459

Indian Territory Medical Association, **697**; history of, 237; proceedings, 463

Indian Union, 289

Indian University (Okla.), 123

Indian War Veterans Collection, **698**

Individual Opportunity Achievement Ranch (Perkins, Okla.), 390

Indochina, description and travel, 676

Industry (Okla.), 639

Infantry: Eleventh Indiana Volunteer, 325; Twenty-third Iowa, 431

Ingram, Edwin L., **700**

Inskip, Diana, 390

Insurance, fire, 822

Intercultural Studies Group (N.Y.), 1227

[403]

Internal Provinces of New Spain, **701**
International relations, 345
Interschool Speech Service (University of Okla.), 1112
Intertribal Council of the Five Civilized Tribes, 848
Inventors, 1493
Investment firms (Okla.), records of, 412, 414
Investment opportunities, U.S., 700
Invitations, 916; commencement, 772; social events, 908, 1182; weddings, 772, 1182
Ionie Indians, 1124
Iowa: Fifth Volunteer Cavalry, 15; Keokuk College, 1444; newspapers, 1489; shoemakers, 660; Twenty-third Infantry, 431
Iowa Indians, 1124; agriculture, 294; land leases, 294; lands, 313
Irelan, Singer B., 260
Irrigation, Great Plains, 622
Iroquois Indians, 1124
Irving, Washington, 640; in Oklahoma in 1832: 1284
Isparhecher, 243, 324, **702**
Ittner, Benjamin, 165
Ivask, Ivar, 640

Jack, Timmie, 640
Jackson, C. C., **703**
Jackson, Hedy Steincamp, **704**
Jackson, Jacob Battiest, **705**
Jackson, Robert Edward, Jr., **706**
Jackson, Samuel D., 649
Jackson County, Okla., 639; state senators, 576
Jacobson, Oscar Brousse, 640, **707**
Jaffe, Eli, **708**
James, Jesse, 640
James, Marquis, 640
James, Will, 461
Jameson, John, **709**
Jameson family, 709
Jamestown, Va., cotton exposition, 511
Jamieson, W. C., **710**
Jansky, Carl, 640
Japan, World War, 1939–1945, battle scenes, 896
Jarboe, (Mrs.) W. C., **711**
Jayne, Mary Prosser, **712**
Jayroe, Jayne, 640
Jazhe, Benedict, **713**

Jennings, Al J., 640
Jennings, Mary, 1488
Jessup, Thomas S., 224
Jesuits (Chile), 1084
Jet, Okla., 639
Jewel Drug Store (Hennessey, Okla. Terr.), 383
Jewish residents of Oklahoma, 1385
Joblin, Walter Ridgway, **714**
Jockeys, 1342
John, Walter N., **715**
Johnson, B. F., **716**
Johnson, Ben, 640
Johnson, Bob, **717**
Johnson, Dorothy, **718**
Johnson, Edgar Allen, **719**
Johnson, Edith Cherry, **720**
Johnson, Edward Bryant, **721**
Johnson, Henry Lee, **722**
Johnson, Henry S., 640
Johnson, Hugh S., 640
Johnson, James T., **723**
Johnson, Jed, 640
Johnson, Lyndon B., interview with, 78
Johnson, Martha Sherwood Finch, **724**
Johnson, N. B., 640
Johnson, Oscar Warren, **725**
Johnson, S. D., 640
Johnson, Willard Spud, correspondence, 1207
Johnson, William E., **726**
Johnson County, Okla., 639
Johnston, Douglas H., 640, **727**, 827
Johnston, Henry Simpson, **728**
Johnston, Marshall, **729**
Johnston, Paul Imbrie, **730**
Jones, Ada, 1532
Jonesboro, Ark., 904
Jones, Cecilia, 731
Jones, Daniel C., **731**
Jones, Dovie, **732**
Jones, Gomer, **733**
Jones, John Paul, **734**
Jones, Lydia Caroline Baggett, **735**
Jones, Robert M., 640
Jones, Stephen, **736**
Jones, Tom, 372
Jones, Wilson N., 732, **737**
Jones family, genealogy, 735
Jordan, Glenn, **738**
Jordan, J. F., **739**
Jordan, John D., **740**
Jordan, Mary, 1244

Jordan, Omar L., **741**
Jordan Drug Store, 739
Journalism, history of, 314
Journalists, 78, 149, 153, 288, 314, 370, 452, 453, 461, 592, 619, 644, 720, 748, 776, 875, 1000, 1005, 1120, 1179, 1241, 1342, 1396, 1458; papers of, 951, 1241, 1396, 1467, 1489
Journals, 97, 116, 158, 371, 382, 386, 471, 612, 837, 857, 973, 1069, 1119, 1131. *See also* Diaries
Journeycake, Charles, **742**, 1508
Judd, Neil Merton, **743**
Judges: Indian Territory, 341, 612, 836, 866; Oklahoma, 38, 120, 151, 182, 202, 290, 341, 384, 510, 654, 979; Oklahoma Territory, 53, 290, 564; papers of, 1435, 1455
Judy, Thomas J., **744**
Jumper, John, **745**, 1269
Juvenile delinquency (Okla.), 395

Kabotie, Fred, 640
Kagey, Joseph Newton, **746**
Kali-Inla Coal Company, **747**
Kamp, Fred W., 640
Kane, John H., 1508
Kansa (Kaw) Indians, 1124; allotments, 749; agriculture, 749; financial affairs, 749; history, 599; land transfers, 749
Kansas: agriculture, 1135; Civil War, 307; crime and criminals, Bender family, 307; description and travel, 66, 445, 717; farm life, 307; fire insurance, 822; frontier and pioneer life, 517, 653, 1135, 1195, 1339; gambling, 437; history of, 307, 442, 498; homesteading, 1135; Indians in, 695, 1135; Indian wars, 442, 1244; mines and mining, 333; politics, 1135; preachers, 1482; prohibition, 50; ranches and ranching, 1184; real estate, 1135; religion, 1135; settlement of, 442
Kansas, Oklahoma, and Gulf Railway Company, 375
Kansas Territory, **1374**; frontier and pioneer life, 1374
Kanuntaklage Dramatic Club (University of Oklahoma), 1168
Kaufman, Kenneth Carlyle, **748**; poetry of, 951
Kaw Indian Agency, 553, **749**; history of, 459

Kaw Indians, 553. *See also* Kansa Indians
Kay County, Okla.: banks and banking, 750; oil and gas leases, 925, 1021; taxation, 1172; wild west show in, 925
Kay County, Okla. Terr., taxation, 1172
Kay County Oil and Gas Company, 925
Kay County State Bank (Okla.), **750**
Keechi Indians, 1124
Keefer, Ann, 14
Keefer, Lewis, 14
Keel, Howard, 640
Keeler, William A., 640
Keetoowah Society, 129
Keezer, William Stillman, 859
Keiger, Charles Guy, **751**
Keith, Harold, **752**
Keller, Helen, 461; correspondence, 685
Keller-Clarke Seed Store, **753**
Kelley, Francis Clement, 640
Kelly, George (Machine Gun), 802
Kelly, James S., 640
Kendall, George Wilkins, 314
Kennedy, John, **754**
Kennedy, John C., **755**
Kennedy, John Fitzgerald, **756**, 902; assassination of, 756; interview with, 78
Kennedy, Kay Don, **757**
Kennedy, L. P., **758**
Kennedy, Robert F., correspondence from, 690; interview with, 78
Kennedy, W. S., **754**
Kennerly, Caleb Burwell Rowan, 501
Kenton, John, 759
Kenton, Okla., description of, 1403
Kenton, Okla. Terr., description of, 1400
Kenton, Simon, **759**
Kentucky, currency of, 759
Keokuk College (Iowa), publications of, 1444
Keown, William H., **760**
Kerley, J. W., **761**
Kerr, Harrison, **762**
Kerr, Jeanne, 762
Kerr, Robert Samuel, 640, 763; correspondence, 1108; news releases, 1063
Kerr-McGee Corporation, **763**
Kessler, Edwin, III, **764**
Keyserling, Leon, 641
Kibbey, W. Beckford, **765**
Kibler, Nell, **766**
Kickapoo Indians, lands, 313, 423, 695
Kidd, Robert L., 260
Kiebler, W. G., **767**

[405]

Kiel, Okla., medical care, 388
Kimble, Lawrence, 946
Kincaid, John W., 768
Kinder, George, 769
King, (Mrs.) A. J., 770
King, Charles Francis Xavier, 771
King, Donald, 772
Kingfisher College (Okla.), 16, 773, 881; history of, 960; publications of, 773; records of, 773, 960
Kingfisher County, Okla., 639; land deeds, 57; school district records, 1271
Kingsbury, Cyrus, 578, 640, 774
Kiowa-Apache Indians, 102
Kiowa County, Okla., 639; history of, 522; schools, 56
Kiowa County Historical Society, 775
Kiowa Indians: allotment of land, 1413; cemeteries, 342; census, 928; depredations, 1124; land transfers, 54; missions, 1255; relations with the U.S. government, 1326; relations with white settlers, 711; schools, 404; wars, 698
Kirk, Betty (Betty Kirk Boyer), 776; correspondence, 1207
Kirkendall, Willie Inex, 334
Kirker, James (Santiago), 1339
Kirkpatrick, Albert J., 777
Kirkpatrick, Jeanne, 640
Kirkpatrick, John, 1359
Kjennernd, Haus, 1333
Klah, Hosteen, 275
Klamath Indians, 1124
Klapp's Drug Store, 778
Kliewer, Heinrich, 779
Klikitat Indians, 1124
Knights of Labor, 188
Knights Templar of Oklahoma, 780, 853
Know Your Government, 1055
Knox, John J., 781
Knox, William W., 781
Kobel, Raleigh, 782
Korean language materials, 962
Korean War, 1950–1953: 924, 1166; propaganda, 1158
Korn, Anna Lee Brosius, 783
Kowetah Manual Labor Boarding School, 639
Kraettli, Emil Rudolph, 88, 784
Krebs, Indian Terr., missions at, 1527
Krebs, Okla.: coal mining, 292; physicians, 1013

Kroff, Charles, 325
Krohn Oil Review, 389
Krugers, Albert, 785
Kruis, Roland, 786
Ku Klux Klan: activities of, 700; anti-Klan activism, 700; in Oklahoma, 265, 639, 700, 787, 1449, 1458; political candidates, 700; publications, 265
Ku Klux Klan Women Collection, 787
Kuyrkendall, Louis C., 788
Kvaloy, Kare, 789

Labor legislation (Okla.), 351, 675, 1059
Labor litigation, 747
Labor market (Okla.), 1031
Labor organizers, 708
Labor relations: petroleum industry, 1038; railroads, 1219; strikes, 1219
Labor unions, 188, 480, 747, 1422, 1470; Oklahoma, 135, 227, 356, 675, 1051, 1057, 1320
Lacey, Okla., medical care, 388
Lacy, A. J., 386
Ladies' Aid Society, 790
Lafferty, John F., 550
Lahman, Marion Sherwood, 791
Lahoma High School (Okla.), 1377
Lain, Everett S., 792
La Kee Kon Garden Club, records of, 1017
Lake Shetek, Minn., survivors of 1862 attack, 1364
Lake Texoma (Okla.), 665
Lake Thunderbird (Okla.), 312
Lakes (Okla.), 312, 639, 665
Lamar, L. Q. C., correspondence, 671
Lamb, Ellis, 793
L'Amour, Louis, 640
Lamplighter, The, 1138
Land deeds: Georgia, 629; Illinois, 327; Indian Territory, 629, 821; Missouri, 41; Oklahoma, 57, 785, 1001, 1129; Oklahoma Territory, 298, 821, 1001, 1118; Texas, 723; Vermont, 785; Wisconsin, 376
Land fencing, 622
Land grants, certificates of, 729; Maxwell, 551
Landon, Alfred M., 710
Land speculation: Oklahoma, 1334; Texas, 1334
Lane, Rose Wilder, 794
Lang, John D., 445
Langsford, William, 795

Langston, Okla., 648
Lansden, J. B., **796**
Larch-Miller, Aloysius, 640
Lardner, Ring, 461
Las Dos Americas, **797**
Latimer County, Okla., 639
Latin America: archival administration, 827; history of, 954; librarianship, 827
Latting, Patience, 640
Latty, James Monroe, **798**
Law enforcement (Okla.), 639, 1033, 1382
Law enforcement officers: Alaska, 208; Indian Territory, 1202, 1224; Oklahoma, 208, 927, 1382; reminiscences, 404; Texas, 208; Wyoming, 208
Lawn mowing equipment, 1493
Lawson, E. B., 682
Lawton, Okla., 298, 894; banks and banking, 424, 1140; cotton mills, 957; description of life in, 1140; fiftieth anniversary celebration, 851; history of, 1295; lumberyards, 646; real estate businesses, 957; retail stores, records of, 928
Lawton, Sherman Paxton, **799**
Lawton Pioneer Club (Lawton, Okla.), yearbook, 851
Layton, Helen Elizabeth Blackert, **800**
Lead, S.Dak., description of, 877
League of Nations, 1226
League of Women Voters, publications of, 84
Leatherwork, 391
Leckie, Shirley A., **801**
Ledbetter, Eugene P., **802**
Ledbetter, Walter A., **803**
Lee, Ottie, **804**
Lee, R. C. (Crockett), 804
Lee Vining Creek, Calif., history of, 86
Lefeber family, 375
LeFlore, Basil L., 640, 805
LeFlore, Carrie, **805**
LeFlore, Greenwood, 640
LeFlore County, Okla., 639; medical care, 1525; medical societies, 597
Legal industry, legislative reform, 496
Legends (Okla.), 639
Legislature (Okla.), 639, 989, 1126; legislative reforms, 496
Lehigh, Indian Terr., missions at, 1527
Leidesdorff, William A., 10
Leiper, Fanny, 446
Leiper, Joseph, 446

Leiper, Joseph McCarrell, 446
Lenormand, Henri-René, 1248
Lens, Sidney, 641
Lenski, Lois, **806**
Leslie, Samuel B., **807**
Letterhead Collection, **808**
Lewallen, Wesley P., **809**
Lewis, Anna, 640
Lewis, Powell K., **810**
Lewis, W. M., 649
Lewis, Walter E., **811**
Lewis, William, 176
Lewis and Clark Centennial Exposition, **812**
Lexington, Okla., Lions Club, 1146
Liberty National Bank (Okla.), **813**
Librarians, 336, 450, 527, 636, 846, 850, 1168
Librarianship (Latin America), 827
Libraries: Oklahoma, 639; private, 569, 1523
Ligon, Mary Louise, **814**
Lilley, (Mrs.) John B., **815**
Lillie, Foress B., **816**
Lillie, Gordon William (Pawnee Bill), **817**, 925
Lillie's Drug Store (Guthrie, Okla.), 816
Lincoln, Abraham, 68, 846
Lincoln County, Okla., 453, 639; history of, 313; medical care, 818
Lincoln County, Okla. Terr., history of, 236
Lincoln County Bank (Prague, Okla.),records of, 1148
Lincoln County Medical Society, **818**
Lindbergh, Charles A., 461, 594
Lindsay, Okla.: cotton gins, 1159; history of, 199
Lindsey, Newton Harvey, **819**
Lindsey, Ray H., **820**
Lindsey, Thomas G., correspondence, 820
Linguistics, 1358
Lininger, Herbert K., **821**
Lininger, W. H., **822**
Linzee, E. H., 618
Lions Club, **823**; 1451; Atoka, Okla., 43; Broken Bow, Okla., 152; Lexington, Okla., 1146; Madill, Okla., 1146; Mannsville, Okla., 1146
Lions International (Okla.): club reports, 346, 1451; conventions, 273, 1451; correspondence about, 1204, 1451; directories, 824; history of district 3-

[407]

A, 741; publications, 172, 273, 346, 741, 1010, 1082, 1115, 1451; records of, 110, 140, 172, 222, 273, 741, 823, 1010, 1236, 1436, 1451
Lions International Collection, **824**
Lipe, DeWitt, 243
Lisa, Manuel, **825**
Lisbon, Portugal, description of, 547
Literary Club (Clinton, Okla.), 1412
Literary criticism, 355
Literary societies, 245, 1462
Little, Jesse Samuel, **826**
Little Bear, Haynes, 342
Little Bear family, genealogy, 342
Little Bighorn River, Battle of, 1876: 845
Little Jim, 640
Little River Reservoir (Okla.), 312
Litton, Gaston, **827**
Liverpool Quarterly Magazine, 394
Livezey, William Edmund, **828**
Lloyd, W. J. B., 640
Lobbyists, 496
Locke, Newt, 524
Locke, Victor M., Jr., 16, **829**
Lockwood, Cassandra Sawyer, 1216
Logan, Bill, **830**
Logan, Leonard M., **832**
Logan County, Okla., 639; cemeteries, 648; churches, 648; 4-H clubs, 648; historic homes, 648; history of, 279, 648; records of, 831; roads, 831; schools, 648
Logan County High School, 1905 commencement program, 1180
Logan County Road Record Collection, **831**
Long, Charles Alexander, 640, **833**
Long, Huey P., 1294
Longhorn, Helen Reid, 640
Longstreet, James, **834**
Lookout, Fred, 640
Lorca, Garcia, 640
Lord family, 704
Los Angeles, Calif., description of, 1137
Lottinville, Savoie, **835**
Love County, Okla., 639
Love, Tom J., **836**
Lovelace, Bryan W., **837**
Loving, Lydia, 867
Loyalty oaths (Okla.), 1119
Loy-McDonald Clinic, **838**
Luce, Henry, 844
Luce, John Bleecker, 553

Lucka, Emil, 664, **839**
Ludlow, Edwin, correspondence, 578
Lumber companies, 917; records of, 300
Lumberyards (Okla.), 646
Luster, Dewey William (Snorter), **840**
Lutheran Church, 1196
Lyles, Harold L., **841**
Lynching (Ada, Okla.), 878
Lyon County, Minn., 1364

McAlester, Indian Terr.: clubs, 1206; description, 1132
McAlester, James Jackson, 63, 640, **871**
McAlester, Okla.: clubs, 1206; development of, 1224; fiftieth anniversary celebration, 870; medical care, 237; Ohoyohoma Club, 1022; physicians, 788
McAlester Anniversary Incorporated Collection, **870**
McAlester (Okla.) General Hospital, 9
McAlester Mercantile Company, records of, 871
McAlester News-Capital, history of, 849
McAnally, Arthur, 1437; correspondence, 551
MacArthur, Douglas, 78, 502; correspondence, 685
McBride, Earl D., **872**
McBride, Marguerite, **873**
McBride family, 640
McCall, William, **874**
McCammon, J. D., **875**
McCarrell, Margaret, 446
McCarthy, Thomas Joseph, **877**
McCarthy (Eugene) Campaign Collection, **876**
McCarville, Mike, **878**
McClain County, Okla., 639
McClure, Tecumseh A., **879**
McClure, William C., **880**
McClure, William L., **880**
McCombs, Solomon, 640
McCormick, Ada P., correspondence, 664
McCornack, Ruth, **881**
McCoy, A. M., **882**
McCoy, James Stacy, **883**
McCoy, Thomas, 883
McCurdy, Dave, 640
McCurdy, Elmer (Frank Davidson), 640
McCurtain, D. C., **884**
McCurtain, Edmond, **885**
McCurtain, Green, **886**; correspondence, 1224

McCurtain, Jackson E., 640
McCurtain, Jackson Frazier, **887**
McCurtain, James Austin, 640
McCurtain County, Okla., 639
McDonald, James, 946
McDonald, Louis, 640
McDonald, William, 759
McDow, George, 1040
MacDowell Club (Norman, Okla.), **842**
McEldowney, James, **888**
McFarlin, Lecy, 640
McGee, C. R., **889**
McGee, Dean A., 763
McGhee, George, **890**
McGhee Production Company (Tex.), 890
McGuffey's Eclectic Reader, 176
McGuire, Bird S., 451, 452, 640
McIntosh, Roley Cub, **892**
McIntosh, William, **893**
McIntosh County, Okla., 639; medical societies, 891
McIntosh County Medical Society, **891**
McIntosh family, 640
McKennon, Paul, 693
Mackenzie, Ranald Slidell, **843**
McKenzie, W. H., **894**
McKeown, Roy J., **895**
Mackey, (Mrs.) Clifton Marion, **844**
McKinley, William, assassination of, 594
McKinney, Raymond, **896**
McKinney, Thompson, **897**
McKinney, William H., **898**
McLain, Raymond Stallings, 640, **899**
MacLeish, Archibald, 1425
McMurray, John Frank, **900**
McPhaul, Thomas C., **901**
McReynolds, Edwin C., 566, **902**
McReynolds, S. A., 777, **903**
McSpadden, Sallie Rogers, 640
Madill, Okla., Lions Clubs, 1146; oil fields, 389
Madsen, Christian C., 54, 640, 718, **845**
Magee, Carl, 640
Maguire, Grace Adeline King, **846**
Maguire, James D., 640, 846
Majestic Cookbook, 495
Major County, Okla., 639
Makah Indians, 699
Maledon, George, 640
Malone, E. L., **847**
Mangum, Okla., 1371; medical care, 201
Mankiller, Wilma Pearl, 640, **848**
Mankiller family, 848

Mankin, Peter, 640
Mannsville, Okla., Lions Clubs, 1146
Manos, Grace C., **849**
Mantle, Mickey, 640
Manuelito, 275
Mao Tse-tung, correspondence, 685
Maps, 387; Indian Territory in 1904: 1175; military posts, 458; northwestern territories (United States), 1259; Oklahoma, 639; Oklahoma Territory in 1904: 1175; road maps, 1204
Marable, Mary Hays, **850**
Marcel, Gabriel, correspondence, 1248
March, (Mrs.) Abe, **851**
Marcy, Randolph B., 640
Marion, Kans., description of, 653
Marland, Ernest Whitworth, 179, 640, **852**; inauguration of, 1032
Marland, Okla., 925
Marland Oil Company, 1085
Marlow, Okla., telephone service, 861
Marquart, Vida, **853**
Marriott, Alice, 640, **854**, 856
Marriott, Sydney C., **855**
Marriott-Rachlin Collection, **856**
Marrs, Frederica S. Dewey, **857**
Marrs, James Wyatt, 640, **858**
Mars (planet), 528
Marshall, Okla.: Christian Church, 140; government of, 1104; granaries, 1104; Methodist Episcopal Church, 1104
Marshals, United States, 639
Martin, Cy, **859**
Martin, Richard L., **860**
Martin, Thomas Pugh, Jr., **861**
Martinez, Julian, 275
Martin Mill and Elevator Company, articles of incorporation, 861
Mary Joseph (Mother), 1527
Mason, Viola, **862**
Masonic Lodge of Oklahoma, **863**
Masonry (Scottish Rite), 188, 250, 1104, 1211; publications of, 863, 1211; records of, 341, 1344
Massad, Ernest L., **864**
Matador Land and Cattle Company, 541
Mathematicians, publications of, 319
Matheney, James Curtis, **865**
Mathews, John Joseph, 640
Matthews, A. D., 866
Matthews, Sam P., **866**
Maupin, Mary B., **867**
Maxwell, Lucien B., 640

[409]

Maxwell land grant, 551
Mayes, Joel Bryan, 243, 386, **868**
Mayes, Samuel Houston, 243, **869**
Mayes County, Okla., 639
Maysville, Okla.: cotton gins, 560; general stores, 225
Meacham, Ed, **904**
Meacham, George A., III, **905**
Meacham family, 904, 905
Meason, Sam, 640
Mechling, Wallace B., 640
Medals of honor, 639
Medawakanton Indians, 1124
Medford, Okla.: churches, 1138; clubs, 906; department stores, 278; women's clubs, 1138
Medford, Okla. Terr., churches, 1138
Medford Progress Club, **906**
Medical associations and societies: Oklahoma, 494, 555, 597, 667, 697, 807, 818, 891, 1062, 1074, 1115, 1133, 1145, 1220, 1276, 1325, 1405, 1503; Oklahoma Territory, 1056, 1441
Medical care: Oklahoma, 6, 9, 28, 69, 72, 75, 106, 195, 311, 338; Texas, 60, 62
Medical clinics, records of, 838
Medical education, 6, 19, 30, 164, 362, 1439
Medical equipment, 1388
Medical instruments, 880, 1221
Medical literature, 72, 500, 667, 872
Medical research, 1408, 1444, 1475
Medical schools, 552
Medicine (Okla.), 639, 1349
Medicine, patented, 907, 1096, 1533
Medicine shows, **907**; posters, 1143
Mediterranean area, description and travel, 1860–1861: 1289
Meigs, Return J., 386, 544
Mein Kampf, original book jacket of, 1168
Memminger, Charles B., **908**
Mencken, H. L., 1519
Mennonite Church, 639, 1196
Menominee Indians, history of, 1076; timber, 1124
Men's Dinner Club (Oklahoma City, Okla.), history of, 1247; program from, 861
Mental hospitals, 722
Menton, John William, **909**
Menus, 545

Meridian, Okla., retail stores, 663
Merrick, Henry Spencer, **910**
Merrill, Maurice, **911**
Merrill, Orpha, 911
Merriott, C. L., **912**
Merriott's Dry Goods Company (Walters, Okla.), records of, 912
Mertes, John E., **913**
Mescalero Apache Indians, 1124
Messenger, Eugene Fields, **914**
Mesta, Perle Skirvin, 640
Metcalf, Augusta, 640
Meteorology, 468
Methodism: Logan County, Okla., 1281; Oklahoma, 1281
Methodist Church, 639, 1196; Indian Territory, 1346; mission schools, 470
Methodist Episcopal Church: Bartlesville, Okla., 1310; Marshall, Okla., 1104; Medford, Okla., 1138; Norman, Okla., 365
Methodist Episcopal Church of Oklahoma, 1281
Metropolitan Railway Co., (Oklahoma), records of, 1395
Mexican Coal and Coke Company (Mexico), 578
Mexican Gulf Oil Company, correspondence, 573
Mexican Revolution, 1910–1921, description of, 573, 765
Mexico: Confederate Army émigrés, 959; currency, examples of, 861; description and travel, 114, 959, 1069; history of, 776, 954; international relations, 776; manuscripts in, 1331; revolutionary activities in Sonora in 1929: 765; Seminole land claims, 354; Spanish colonial institutions, 954
Meyer, Apelona, **916**
Meyer, Leo, **915**
Meyer, William, **916**
Miami, Oklahoma: history of, 76; lumber companies, 917; municipal government, records of, **918**; stores, 76, 300
Miami Indians, litigation by, 695
Miami Lumber Company Collection, **917**
Micco, Hulbutta, **919**
Michigan, Indians in, 695
Michigan Territory, frontier and pioneer life, 766

Mid-Continent Farmers Cooperative, records of, 399
Mid-Continent Petroleum Corporation, 730
Middle East: description and travel in 1901–1902: 1306; foreign relations in 1939–1946: 685
Midkiff, Charles F., **920**
Midland Valley Railroad Company, 375
Midway Mirror, 933
Milbourn, Dolly, **921**
Milbourn, George F., **921**
Milburn, George, 835, **922**
Miles, Charles, **923**
Miles, Nelson A., 264
Miley, William Halliburton, 924
Miley (Mary Clarke) Foundation, **924**
Milfay State Bank (Stroud, Okla.), records of, 1354
Military posts: Indian Territory, 197, 475, 1516; New Mexico, 501; Oklahoma Territory, 458, 1516. *See also individual forts and camps*
Miller, Florence Graves, **926**
Miller, Floyd C., **927**
Miller, Freeman E., correspondence, 633
Miller, G. R., **928**
Miller, George L., 925
Miller, George W., 925
Miller, Joe, 640, 925
Miller, John Sinclaire, **929**
Miller, LaVerle, **930**
Miller, Lena Rivers Been, 930
Miller, Lillie Kate, **931**
Miller, Robert L., **932**
Miller, Stephen, **933**
Miller, Zack T, 640, 925
Miller Brothers 101 Ranch, **925**
Miller Brothers 101 Ranch Wild West Show, performers in, 925, 1365
Miller County, Okla., 639
Milling companies, 249, 1324
Millington, Okla., medical care, 269
Mills, Walter Scott, **934**
Milsten, David Randolph, **935**
Minco, Okla., physicians, 826
Miner, Frederick William, **936**
Mineral Point, Wisc., land deeds, 376
Mines and mining: Chickasaw Nation, 1401; Choctaw Nation, 1401, 1535; Choctaw Nation, coal, 508; Indian Territory, coal, 508, 1315; Iowa, coal, 1315; labor unions, 480, 1470; mine safety, 1470; Kansas, lead and zinc, 333; Missouri, coal, 1315; Missouri, lead and zinc, 333; Montana, coal, 1315; Oklahoma, 410, 639, 1485; Oklahoma, coal, 292, 941, 974, 1315, 1470; Oklahoma, equipment sales, 95; Oklahoma, lead and zinc, 2, 447, 333; Oklahoma, private investment, 33; Oklahoma, Wichita Mountains area, 621; Texas, 1274; western U.S., 700; West Virginia, 1315
Mining companies, records of, 410
Mining engineers, personal papers of, 1315
Mining equipment suppliers, records of, 95
Minion, John A., correspondence, 845
Ministers: circuit riding, 1281; Oklahoma, 1281; Oklahoma Territory, 1281, 1305
Minneapolis, Minn., city charter of, 1256
Minniear family, 704
Missals, 1350
Missionary Federation of Muskogee, Oklahoma, history of, 638
Missions and missionaries, 471, 607, 738, 1064, 1299; Baptist, 56, 712; Brazil, 833; Indian Territory, 446 984, 1216, 1527; Methodist, 833, 1346; Muskogee, Oklahoma, 638; Nebraska, 297; Nigeria, 606; Oklahoma, 639, 1450; Peru, 606; Presbyterian, 430, 446, 638, 774, 815, 1173, 1215, 1313, 1523; Society of Friends (Quaker), 71, 422, 548, 1323
Missouri: Confederate Legislature of, 171; history of, 498, 783, 902; mines and mining, 333; political parties, 770; prohibition, 50
Missouri, Kansas, and Texas Railroad Company, 788, 1340, 1388; officials of, 804
Missouria Indians, 1124
Missouri Medical College (Mo.), 212
Missouri River, description and travel in 1803: 386
Mitchell, (Mrs.) Alfred, **938**
Mitchell, Irene Eldridge, **939**
Mitchell, Robert Thurston, **940**
Mitchell, Sam W., **941**
Mitchell-Benham Collection, **937**

[411]

Mitchell family, genealogy, 940
Mix, Tom, 640, 925
Mixon, A. M., **942**
Model Railroad Interest Group, newsletters of, 507
Modoc Indians, 1124
Mohawk Indians, 1124
Molesworth, Charles, 355
Moline, Ill., 1218
Momaday, N. Scott, 640
Monnet, Julien Charles, **943**
Monroney, Mike (Almer Stillwell), 640
Montague County, Tex., frontier and pioneer life, 735
Montezuma, Carlos, 275, 640, **944**
Montgomery, Merle Aline, **945**
Monuments (Okla.), 639
Moore, Chauncey O., **947**
Moore, Ercelle O'Brien Davis, **946**
Moore, Ethel, **947**
Moore, Jessie Elizabeth Randolph, **948**
Moore, John D., **949**
Moore, John H., **950**
Moore, Louise Beard, **951**
Moore, Robb, **952**
Moore (Okla.) High School, yearbooks, 1407
Mooreland, Okla., banks and banking, 953
Mooreland Security State Bank (Okla.), **953**
Moorhead, Max Leon, **954**
Moorman, Lewis Jefferson, 640, **955**
Mootz, Grace V., 956
Mootz, Herman Edwin, **956**
Morford, Robert Boyd, **957**
Morgan, Clyde, **958**
Morgan, (Mrs.) Lawrence Nelson, **959**
Morgan, Robert J., **960**
Morgenthau, Henry, 1294
Mormonism, 970
Morris, Carl, 640
Morris, Joe, 640
Morris, John Wesley, **961**
Morrison, Cammie, **962**
Morrison, G. A., **963**
Morrison, James, **964**
Morrison, Robin Leroy, **963**
Morrison, W. D., **964**
Morrow, John A., **965**
Mortgages (Okla.), 966
Mosby, George Waldo, **966**
Moseley, John Ohleyer, **967**

Mosely, Palmer S., **968**
Moss, Jacob, 1366
Mother's Club (Medford, Okla.), 1138
Motion pictures, advertising, 670, 1041, 1073, 1382
Moulton, Herbert, **969**
Mountbatten, Louis, correspondence, 685
Mount Holyoke Female Seminary (Mass.), student essays, 67
Mount Pleasant School (Blaine County, Okla. Terr.), 769
Mount Rushmore national monument, 464
Mountain Meadows Massacre, **970**
Mountain View, Okla.: clubs, 971; history of, 971
Mountain View, Okla. Terr., history of, 236
Mountain View Twentieth-Century Club, **971**
Movies. *See* Motion pictures
Mower, George, 717
Mueller, Gustave Emil, **972**
Muldrow, Annie Oliver, correspondence, 973
Muldrow, Henry Lowndes, Jr., **973**
Muldrow, Henry Lowndes, Sr., **973**
Muldrow, Robert, correspondence, 973
Mulhall, Okla., 648
Mulhall, Zack, 925
Mulhall family, 640
Mullen, Lacey, 1283
Mullen Coal Company Collection, **974**
Munger, Reuben Bates, 975
Munger, William Houston, **975**
Munger Hardware, Furniture and Undertaking Store, records of, 975
Municipal government (Okla.), 84, 439; financial records, 474, 999, 1164; records of, 1164
Munn, Bertha M. B., **976**
Murdock, H. D., 1115
Murphey and Noffsinger Collection, **977**
Murphy, William Albert Patrick, **978**
Murrah, Alfred P., 640, **979**
Murrah, Alfred P., Federal Building, 126, 639
Murray, Alice Hearrell, 640; correspondence, 980
Murray, Billy, correspondence, 980
Murray, Burbank, **980**, 981
Murray, Cicero J., 640

Murray, Frankie Colbert, **981**
Murray, Johnston, 640, 981, **982**, 1044, 1420; correspondence, 980; inauguration of, 1032; political campaign of 1950: 584; proclamations, 1043
Murray, Jon Kyle, **983**
Murray, Massena Bancroft, 981; correspondence, 980
Murray, William Henry (Alfalfa Bill), 53, 640, 784, 980, 981, 1092, 1279, 1420
Murray County, Okla., 639
Murray family, 1420
Murrell, George Michael, 640
Murrell home (Tahlequah, Indian Terr.), 1128
Murrow, Joseph Samuel, 56, 640, 738, **984**, 1303
Murrow, Katrina Ellett, 1303
Museum of the Air, radio program script, 1518
Museums (Okla.), 639
Mushulatubbee, **985**, 1131
Music: All State Band (Okla.), 1040; band directors, 1040; classical, 762, 777, 903; country and western, 627, 1529; education, 1040; folk songs, 947; Japanese, 87; manuscripts, 762, 777, 1350, 1432; Oklahoma, 639, 762; performance, 595, 777; professional organizations, 945; publications on, 762; published, 549, 762; sacred, 1350; teachers, 595, 549, 762, 1040
Musical compositions, 478, 762, 855, 903
Musical productions and performances: programs of, 87, 215, 405, 412, 672, 762; reviews of, 87
Musical scores, 87, 144, 215, 358, 502, 519, 762, 903, 1014, 1264
Music Club (Pauls Valley, Okla.), 1348
Musicians, 762, 945, 1335
Muskogean languages, 558
Muskogee, Okla.: attorneys, 151; banks and banking, 301; churches, 82; hospitals, 157; law firms, 977; medical care, 106, 659, 1020; physicians, 901
Muskogee, Oklahoma, Indian Centennial Collection, **986**
Muskogee County, Okla., 639; financial records, 474
Muskogee Ministerial Association (Okla.), 1346
Muzzy, W. J., **987**
Myrick, E. B., **988**

Nadan, Gertrude, 1321
Nagle, Patrick Sarsfield, 640
Nance, James Clark, Jr., 640, **989**
Napoleonic wars, 374
Nash, Frank, 640, 775
Nashville, Tenn., cotton exposition, 511
National Aid Life Association, 855
National Bituminous Coal Commission, 1470
National Board of Farm Organizations, 710
National Conference of Commissioners of Uniform State Law, 911
National Conference on Higher Education, Sixth Annual, 584
National Congress of American Indians, 848
National Cowboy Hall of Fame, 592, 1237
National Editorial Association, 1005
National Farmers Union, 399, 1294
National Federation of Music Clubs, 945
National Indian Health Board, 848
National Play Bureau of the Federal Theater Project, 165
National Research Council, **990**
National Security Training Commission, 899
National Wildlife Federation, 1043
Native American Rights Fund, 848
Natural gas industry: corporate records, 730; investigation of, 1497; leases, 802. *See also* Petroleum industry
Naturalists, 569; societies, 1327
Navajo Indians, 275, 1227
Naval Air Technical Training Center, **991**, 1246
Neal, Henry Lee, **992**
Nebraska Territory, description and travel in 1849: 717
Neer, Charles Sumner, **993**
Nelson, George, **994**
Nelson, Indian Terr., postal service, 166
Neosho, Mo., description of, 1532
Nesbitt, Pleasant P., **995**
New Amsterdam Theater (N.Y.), 1083
Newby, Errett Rains, 640, **997**
Newby Rooming House (Oklahoma City, Okla.), records of, 1180
New Century Club (Okla.), 1412
New Echota, Cherokee Nation, 1128
New Echota Church (Cherokee Nation), records of, 430
New Helvetia, Calif., 10

[413]

New Hope Cemetery (Okla.), 1399
New Hope Seminary (Indian Terr.), 547
Newkirk, Okla.: banks and banking, 998; high school, 574; municipal records, **999**
Newkirk First National Bank (Okla.), **998**
Newland, John Lynn, **1000**
Newman, Coley, **1001**
Newman, Oscar Clarence, **1002**
New Mexico: frontier and pioneer life, 1428; Spanish colonial records of, 701; wildlife, 570
New Orleans, La.: carnival ball invitation, 357; cotton exposition, 511; description, 374
New Spain, Spanish colonial records of, 701
Newspapers: Japanese, 1226; military, in 1939–1945: 933
New York Mutual Life Insurance Company, **996**
New Zealand, description of, 873
Nez Percé Indians, 1124
Nice, Margaret Morse, **1003**; correspondence, 811
Nichols, James Thomas, **1004**
Nichols, Lea Murray, **1005**
Niebell, Paul M., **1006**
Nieberding, Velma, **1007**
Nigeria, missionaries in, 606
Nigh, George, 640
Ninety-six ("96") Ballard Oil and Gas Company, records of, 263
Ninnekah, Okla., 1313
Nisqualli Indians, 699
Nix, Evett Dumas, 640
Nixon, Richard M., 78, 1297; inauguration as president, 1431; resignation as president, 348, 1243
Noble, Ed, 640
Noble, Joseph Glass, **1009**
Noble, Lloyd, 640
Noble, Okla., banks and banking, 1008
Noble County, Okla., school district records, 1273
Noble First State Bank (Okla.), **1008**
Noble High School (Noble, Okla.), 652
No Man's Land (Okla. Terr.), 639; crime and criminals, 1087; history of, 744, 1087; ranching in, 1087; settlement of, 1
Norbeck, Peter, 464
Norman, Okla.: banks and banking, 721;

chamber of commerce, 688; city government, 84; clubs and societies, 296; DAR, Black Beaver Chapter, records of, 352; drug stores, 59; First Presbyterian Church, 1048; Gaillardia Garden Club, records of, 497; grocery stores, 520; high school, yearbook, 1407; history of, 1204; Lions Club, records of, **1010**; MacDowell Club, 842; mayors, 84; Methodist Episcopal Church, 365; Oklahoma School of Religion, 1048; printers, 70; radio station WNAD, 827, 1112; realtors, 1129; records of, 84, 90; retail stores, 846; schools, 187; U.S. Naval Air Station, history of, 530, 991; U.S. Naval Air Technical Training Center, 530, 991, 1246; utility companies in, 169; Woden Club, **1011**
Norman, Okla. Terr., medical care, 210
Norman Interurban Railway Co., (Okla.), records of, 1395
Norris, Clare E., **1012**
Norris, Thomas T., **1013**
North America, description and travel, 18th century, 386
North Burbank (Okla.) area, map of, 1021
North Carolina, state currency, 284
North Dakota, women's societies and clubs, 790, 1505
Northern Pacific Railroad Company, land sales, 77
North McAlester, Okla., settlement of, 1355
North Muskogee, Okla., history of, 1379
North Slope Legal Assistant Project, 1383
Northwestern State Teachers College (Alva, Okla.), 666, 1468
Norton, Spencer Hilton, **1014**
Notary records (Tahlequah, Indian Terr.), 671
Nothstein, (Mrs.) Charles Anderson, **1015**
Nowata, Okla.: La Kee Kon Garden Club, **1017**
Nowata County, Okla.: courts, 1016; medical care, 428; records of, **1016**; taxation, 1016
Nuclear power, legislative reform, 496
Nuclear weapons (United States), 104
Numismatics, 284
Nunn, Sam, 126
Nurseries (plants), 632

Oak Ridge Seminary (Hughes County, Okla.), 1304
O'Brien, Bob, 873
Ocean travel, descriptions of in 1860–1861: 1289; descriptions of in 1901–1902: 1306
O'Donnell, Cathie, 640
Odum, Dock, 640
Office of Price Administration, **1018**
Ogden, Florence, **1019**
Oge ranch (San Antonio, Tex.), 575
Oglesby, Carson L., **1020**
Ohio, Thirty-first Infantry, 1071
O'Hornett, Carl J., 386, **1021**
Ohoyohoma Club, **1022**
Oil production. *See* Petroleum industry
Okay, Okla., history of, 1379
Okemah, Okla., 1396; banks and banking, 1443
Okfuskee County, Okla., 639
Oklahoma (play), programs, 923. *See also* Riggs, Rollie Lynn
Oklahoma: agricultural advocacy organizations, 1058; agricultural legislation, 1034; agriculture, 567, 639, 689, 1034; agriculture cooperatives, 399, 444, 562, 710, 1034, 1053, 1109; archaeological sites, 1515; art and artists, 639, 707, 1369; associations and institutions, 639; auditors, 915; automobile travel in 1930: 710; aviation, 1380; banks and banking, 44, 58, 339, 415, 418, 419, 443, 557, 639, 655, 688, 691, 750, 813, 953, 998, 1008, 1028, 1030, 1100, 1139, 1205; bibliography, 639; birds of, 639, 811, 1003, 1042; boundaries, 639; budget, 509; buildings, 639; buildings, state capitol, 803, 1454; buried treasure, 639; business and industry, 1516; capital punishment, 639; capitol, 639, 1454; cartoon history of, 1138; cattle industry, 1516; cemeteries, 1516; census of 1930: 639; chamber of commerce (state), 639; chautauquas, 357, 639; child labor, 351; churches, 1196; cities and towns, 639, 1120, 1516; climatology, 639; clubs, 639; commerce, 639; commissioner of labor, personal papers, 978; communication, 639; Confederate Veterans Association, 563; congressmen, 1341; conservation of soil, 1050, 1516; conservation of wildlife,

312, 542, 639, 1043, 1516; constitution, 639, 706, 1378; Constitutional Convention of 1906: 53, 169, 177, 686, 706, 914, 915, 1214; costumes, 639; county histories, 1516; courts, 290, 639, 718, 948, 989, 1016; courts, records of, 1418, 1435; crime and criminals, 54, 287, 639, 775, 802, 1016, 1308, 1418, 1435, 1464; dams, 639; Democratic Party in, 1032; Depression era, 708; description of, 710, 717, 1241; disaster relief, 567; dust storms, 639, 600; economic conditions, 639, 1120; education, 356, 639, 1040, 1161; elections, 351, 534, 639, 1114; emblems, 639; ethnology, 639; farm markets, 710; flags, state, 639; floods and flood control, 639; folk songs, 947; forests and forestry, 639; forts and camps, 639, 1516; fraternal organizations in, 694, 780; frontier and pioneer life, 64, 131, 524, 668, 1015, 1305, 1321; general stores, 1187; geology of, 141, 539, 639, 1036, 1485; ghost towns, 1516; government, 345, 509, 1126; governors, 1501; governors' inaugurations, 861, 1032, 1214; governors' personal papers, 509, 567, 598, 728, 980, 982, 1126, 1214, 1449; health care, 48, 832 (*see also* medical care); highway construction, 1363; historical fiction, 309; historic personalities, 1516; historic sites, 639 1241, 1451, 1516; history of, 86, 119, 207, 343, 386, 422, 498, 539, 639, 902, 948, 1170, 1204, 1241, 1272, 1516; horses, 639; hospitals, 417, 639; hotels, 639; House of Representatives rules, 915; immigration, Czechoslovakian, 616; industry, 639; jails, 708; Jewish people in, 1385; juvenile delinquency, 395; Ku Klux Klan, 639, 700, 1449, 1458; labor, 639; labor legislation, 399, 675; labor market in, 1031; labor organizers, 708; lakes, 639; land run of 1889: 279, 345, 639, 1174, 1522; land run of 1893: 53, 64, 408, 524, 599, 639, 1118, 1184, 1247, 1339; land runs, 123, 313, 613, 639; law enforcement, 639, 1033; legends, 639; legislation, 509, 626, 639, 989, 1034, 1126, 1501; legislators, 657, 830, 1300, 1501; legislators' papers, 454, 484, 576, 989, 1386; letterheads,

[415]

808; librarians, 1178; libraries, 639, 1254; literature, 639; lobbyists, 496; loyalty oaths, 1119; maps of, 387; Masonry (Scottish Rite) in, 1211; medical care, 6, 9, 28, 31, 91, 417, 555, 587 639 (*see also* health care industry); medical laws, 500; military posts, 639; mines and mining, 333, 621, 639, 747, 941, 974; monuments, 639; motion picture industry, 1041; mountains, 639; movie theaters, 639; museums, 639; music, 639, 947, 1040; newspapers, 639, 1489, 1516; oil investigations, 1242; opening of the Cheyenne and Arapaho lands, 613; organizations, 639; organized labor, 11, 135, 351, 356, 639, 675, 747, 978, 1051, 1057; outlaws, 639; panhandle area, description of, 604; panhandle area, history of, 744, 882, 1087, 1394; parking meters, 639; parks, 639, 1516; petroleum industry, 536, 551; pharmacists, 48; pharmacy laws, 816; photographs, 639; place names, 539, 639, 1241, 1305, 1516; poetry about, 1202; political appointments, 351; politics, 12, 27, 113, 136, 182, 220, 268, 317, 331, 345, 534, 639, 657, 728, 755, 804, 948, 982, 1046, 1114, 1126, 1214, 1235, 1294, 1386, 1411, 1449, 1455, 1487, 1508; post offices, 56, 882, 1144, 1516; power resources in, 639; practice of medicine in, 1349; prairie chicken distribution, 1043; preachers, 1482; press associations, 1045; prison reform, 395; prisons, 567, 639, 1101, 1214; professional associations, 639; prohibition, 50, 639, 726, 989, 1163, 1214; public health, 587, 639; racism, 639; radio history, 1453; railroad development, 507; railroads, records of, 1057 (*see also* railroads); ranches, 1516; reapportionment, 1200; reformatories, 1101; religion, 639; Republican Party, 1114; retirement systems, 1025; Rhodes Scholars, 639; right-to-work issue, 1059; rivers, 639; roads, 639, 831, 1516; rodeos, 639; rural life, 34, 657; schools, 176, 526, 639, 888, 1161, 1467, 1477, 1516; schools, sale of lands, 416; schools, science fairs, 639; Selective Service registration, 587; Senate rules, 915; settlement of, 1, 1039, 1210, 1467; sites, historic, 639; Socialist Party in, 177, 1524; social welfare, 340; sports, 639; stage stops, 1516; state auditor, 915; statehood, 27, 402, 860, 886, 938, 1124, 1189, 1262, 1487; statehood celebrations, 381, 1049; state records inventories, 1517; Supreme Court, cases tried before, 1124; Supreme Court, clerks of, 206, 948; Supreme Court justices, salaries of, 802; taxes and taxation, 639, 1016, 1055, 1118; teachers, 656; teachers' retirement, 509; telephones, 639; television, 1453; Toll Bridge Wars, 639; tornadoes, 639; tourism, 639, 1241; trade associations, 639; trading posts, 1516; traffic safety, 1047; trails, 639, 1516; transportation, 639; unemployment, 1235; U.S. Army, 45th Infantry, 639; universities and colleges, 639; utilities, public, 639; utility rates, 650; veterans, 639; water resources, 639; weather conditions, 600, 639; wildlife, 570, 639, 1043; Wilson's Creek, Battle of, in 1861: 639; women, 639; workers compensation cases, 788; World War II price controls, 1018; zoology of, 138

Oklahoma Academy of Science, **1023**, 1463; records of, 365

Oklahoma Advertiser, The, 1284

Oklahoma Agricultural & Mechanical College (Stillwater, Okla.), 434, 633; bond issues of 1903: 757

Oklahoma Almanac, publication of, 465

Oklahoma Anti-Saloon League, 1163

Oklahoma Association for Old Age Security, 978

Oklahoma Association for Teachers Retirement, **1025**

Oklahoma Association of College History Professors, **1024**

Oklahoma Authors Club, publications of, 1382

Oklahoma Aviation Commission, 1265

Oklahoma Bankers' Association, 688

Oklahoma Bar Association, board of governors records, 341

Oklahoma Boys State convention, 1378

Oklahoma Chapter of the Society of the Sigma Xi, **1026**

Oklahoma Children's Sooner Orchestra, 405

Oklahoma City, Ada, and Atoka Railway Company, 375
Oklahoma City, Okla.: anniversaries, 923; attorneys, 802; banks and banking, 813, 923, 1028, 1030; businesses, 1324; city charter, 878; city clerks of, 1293; city councilmen, papers of, 592; civic leaders, 1293; clubs, 861, 881, 1247; development of, 1108; drug stores, 739; Episcopal churches, records of, 1245; First National Bank Building, 610; Fox-Vliet Drug Store, 1438; funeral homes, 822; history of, 571; housing, 104; mayors, 610; medical care, 104; Methodist Episcopal church in, 1281; Miss Oklahoma City contest, 1453; orchestras, 1029; oil fields, 479; Overholser Theatre programs, 1324; physicians, 795, 872; politics, 27; publications regarding, 923; public library, 878; rooming houses, 1180; streetcar system, 1395; weather reports for, 1463
Oklahoma City Boy Scout Collection, **1027**
Oklahoma City First National Bank, **1028**
Oklahoma City Junior Symphony Orchestra, **1029**
Oklahoma City National Memorial, 639
Oklahoma City Railway Co., records of, 1395
Oklahoma City Symphony, 405
Oklahoma City *Times* Company, report of earnings, 27
Oklahoma City Tradesmens National Bank, **1030**
Oklahoma City University, students, 962, 1020
Oklahoma Civil Liberties Union, 736
Oklahoma Club, program from, 861
Oklahoma Commissioners of Charities and Corrections, report, 350
Oklahoma Corporation Commission, **1031**, 1235
Oklahoma County, Okla., 639
Oklahoma County Consumers Council, records and publications of, 104
Oklahoma County jail, 708
Oklahoma County Medical Society, 1002
Oklahoma Daily, special St. Patrick's Day issue, 1157

Oklahoma Democratic Party, **1032**
Oklahoma Department of Pardons and Parole, 1214
Oklahoma Department of Public Safety, **1033**
Oklahoma Department of Public Welfare, physicians for, 788
Oklahoma Diamond Jubilee Commission, records of, 381
Oklahoma Education Association, legislation supported by, 356
Oklahoma '89ers Association, membership certificate, 1376
Oklahoma Equal Rights Amendment, 626
Oklahoma Farm Bureau, **1034**
Oklahoma Farmers Union, 1294; publications, 484; records of, 399
Oklahoma Federation of Music Clubs, history of, 638
Oklahoma Fish and Game Council, 1463
Oklahoma Genealogical Society, **1035**
Oklahoma Geological Survey, 141, **1036**; expedition of 1900: 561
Oklahoma Goodwill Industries, Inc., 720
Oklahoma Grain Growers Association, records of, 562
Oklahoma Hall of Fame, 864, 951
Oklahoma Heritage Association, 1468
Oklahoma Highway Commission, 1363
Oklahoma Highway Patrol, 1033
Oklahoma Historical Society, 343, 639
Oklahoma Imprints, 579
Oklahoma Indian Baptist Association, 984
Oklahoma Indian Rights Association, **1037**
Oklahoma Jim. *See* Shears, James
Oklahoma Junior Academy of Science, records of, 1023
Oklahoma-Kansas Natural Gas Company, records of, 730
Oklahoma Labor Studies Collection, **1038**
Oklahoma Library Association, 1168
Oklahoma Library Commission, 1168
Oklahoma McCarthy for President Committee, 876
Oklahoma Medical Research Foundation, 617
Oklahoma Memorial Association, 951
Oklahoma Memorial Union, 1387; records of, 828
Oklahoma Museum Project Collection, **1039**

[417]

Oklahoma Music Educators Association Collection, **1040**
Oklahoma National Guard, 899, 1214
Oklahoma Natural Gas Company, 650
Oklahoma Natural Mutoscene Company, **1041**
Oklahoma Normal School, bond issues, 1903: 757
Oklahomans, biographical information, 640
Oklahomans For The Right To Work, Incorporated, **1059**
Oklahoma Odd Fellow, 1214
Oklahoma Ornithological Society, **1042**
Oklahoma Outdoor Council, **1043**
Oklahoma People's Lobby, 496
Oklahoma Pharmaceutical Association, constitution of, 816
Oklahoma Pioneer Physicians Oral History, **1044**
Oklahoma Press Association, **1045**
Oklahoma Public Services Corporation, records of, 730
Oklahoma Railway Co., records of, 1395
Oklahoma Republican Party, **1046**
Oklahoma Safety Council, **1047**
Oklahoma School of Religion, **1048**
Oklahoma Semi-Centennial Exposition, **1049**
Oklahoma Soil Conservation Service, **1050**
Oklahoma State Archaeological Society, records of, 79
Oklahoma State Board of Medical Examiners, 807
Oklahoma State Council of Defense, report of, 1469
Oklahoma State Democratic Convention of 1968: 876
Oklahoma State Department of Agriculture, 1034
Oklahoma State Federation of Labor, **1051**
Oklahoma State Federation of Women's Clubs, **1052**; reports of, 1412
Oklahoma State Grange, **1053**
Oklahoma State Highway Department, 755
Oklahoma State Legislative Council, reports of, 177
Oklahoma State Medical Association, 436, 807, **1054**, 1185, 1203; constitution and bylaws, 891; membership lists, 166; proceedings, 463; publications of, 463, 1062
Oklahoma State Planning Board, reports of, 177
Oklahoma State Public Health Department, report of 1910–1912: 587
Oklahoma State University, loyalty oaths, 236
Oklahoma State Writers, Inc., directories of, 1081
Oklahoma Student Librarians Association, 636
Oklahoma Supreme Court, proceedings of, 1235
Oklahoma Symphony Orchestra, 1412
Oklahoma Tax Commission, **1055**; reports of, 177
Oklahoma Territorial Board of Pharmacy, records of, 816
Oklahoma Territorial Medical Association, **1056**
Oklahoma Territorial Supreme Court, justices of, 1266
Oklahoma Territory: annual reports, 452; attorneys, 1212; banks and banking, 953, 998; cattle brands used in, 1510; college bond issues in 1903: 757; courts, 564; courts, records of, 1418; crime and criminals, 54, 1418; description of, 847; economy of, 1411; forts, 1516; fraternal organizations in, 694; frontier and pioneer life, 524, 543, 599, 621, 656, 696, 711, 744, 924, 1015, 1174, 1195, 1210, 1247, 1305, 1319, 1339, 1373, 1390, 1400, 1411, 1440, 1452, 1467, 1522; governors, 53, 54, 392, 451, 452, 770, 1229; governors, personal papers of, 1266; history, 236, 618, 639; holiday proclamations, 1199; judges, 53, 564; labor unions in, 1320; land claim litigation, 857; land records, 1499; letterheads, 808; maps of, 387; Masonry (Scottish Rite) in, 1211; medical societies, records of, 1056; military posts, 458; No Man's Land, 639, 744; opening of Indian lands, 54; place names, 639; politics, 306, 1229, 1266, 1411; post offices, 1144; preachers, 1482; schools, 1467; settlement of, 696, 1174, 1467; statehood, 430, 886, 938; statehood, Indian opposition to, 860; supreme court justices, 1266; territorial

records, inventories, 1517; townships, 1452; vigilante groups, 35; women, 1174
Oklahoma Territory Dental Association, 1441
Oklahoma Transportation Company, **1057**
Oklahoma Tuberculosis Association, 288
Oklahoma Turnpike Authority, 1200
Oklahoma University Pharmaceutical Association, publications of, 1424
Oklahoma Wheat Growers Association, **1058**
Oklahoma Wildlife Conservation Commission, records of, 312
Okmulgee, Okla.: banks, 83; clubs, 1061; medical care, 91
Okmulgee Abstract and Title Company, **1060**
Okmulgee Civic Improvement Club, **1061**
Okmulgee County, Okla., 639; abstracts of title, 1060; martial law in, 236
Okmulgee County Medical Society, **1062**
Okmulgee-Youngstown Oil Company, 1151
Oktaha, Okla., physicians, 670
Olds, Frederick, 640
Olds, Leland, **1063**
Olinger, Paul T., **1064**
Oliver, Jennie Harris, 640
Omaha, Nebr., vigilante committee at, 1137
Omaha Indian Mission (Nebr.), 297
Oneide Indians, 1124
Onondaga Indians, 1124
Oochalata, **1065**
Opler, Morris Edward, **1066**
Opothleyaholo, 224, 369, 640, **1067**
Oral histories: Indian Territory, 696; Indians, 400; Oklahoma Territory, 696; physicians, 1044
Orchestras (Okla.), 1029
Order of the Coif, 652
Order of the Eastern Star, **1068**
Oregon Territory, massacres, 1137
Oregon Trail, travel accounts of, 205. *See also* Overland journeys to the Pacific
Organized labor, 188, 480, 747, 1422, 1470; Oklahoma, 11, 135, 227, 351, 639, 675, 978, 1051, 1057, 1320
Ornithologists, 811, 1003; papers of, 1359
Ornithology: Mexico, 1359; Oklahoma, 1359; Oklahoma, research, 73, 1003; Oklahoma, societies, 1042
Orphanages for Indians, 504
Orr, Kenneth, 79
Ortenburger, Arthur Irving, **1069**
Osage Arrow Oil Company, 925
Osage County, Okla., 639; oil and gas leases, 1021
Osage Indian Agency, history of, 459
Osage Indian Papers, **1070**
Osage Indians: allotment of land, 1070; attorneys of, 1006; Civil War, 303; encounters with whites, 837; funds, 1124; history, 459; lands, 1124; oil and gas leases, 459, 479, 1124; per capita payments, 1124; relations with U.S. government, 1070, 1326; relations with whites, 1070; songs, 342; trade, 1124; traditions, 342; tribal council, 1070; tribal roll, 1070; writings about, 1451
Osborne, Kans., founding of, 67
Osborne, Lyle, **1071**
Osceola, 640
Oskison, John Milton, **1072**
Other Film Club Collection, **1073**
Oto Indians, land, 1124; schools, 366; trade, 1124
Ottawa County, Okla., 639; history of, 1007; treasurer's records, 300
Ottawa County (Okla.) Semi-Centennial Committee, 1007
Ottawa County Medical Society, **1074**
Ourada, Patricia K., **1076**
Our Monthly Collection, **1075**
Outlaw Mountains (Ark.), 1486
Overholser, Henry, **1077**
Overholser Theatre (Oklahoma City, Okla.), showbills, 861
Overland journeys to the Pacific, 107, 205, 371, 501, 1097, 1137, 1352, 1482
Overton, Benjamin F., **1078**
Owen, Robert Latham, 461, 640; correspondence, 1224; speeches of, 1527
Owen, Thomas H., 640
Owens family, 517
Owings, Donnell MacClure, **1079**
Owl, Della Irene Brunsteter, **1080**

Packet boats, account of travel on, 1176
Paden National Bank (Paden, Okla.), records of, 1148
Padgett, Ora, 952
Page, Charles, 640, 677

[*419*]

Pah Se To Pah, Dora, 342
Paine, Mary Graham Giles, **1081**
Paiute Indians: claims against U.S. government, 1508; depredations, 1124; wars, 698
Paleontologists, papers of, 1351
Palmer, Benn G., **1082**
Palmer, Don L., **1083**
Palo Pinto County, Tex., history of, 543
Pamunkey Indians, 1124
Pan American Airways, 490
Pantoja, (Father), **1084**
Parade, military, 411
Paris, Ill., history of, 1513
Paris, Tex.: history of, 11; medical care, 60
Parker, Cynthia Ann, 640
Parker, Everett C., **1085**
Parker, Franklin, **1086**
Parker, George Burton, 134, 1356
Parker, Harry, **1087**
Parker, Isaac C., 640, 718, 758, 1202, 1417
Parker, Quanah, 386, 618, 640
Parker, Robert, **1088**
Parker, Thomas, **1089**
Park Hill, Indian Terr., 446
Park Hill, Okla., banks and banking, 443
Parking meter, 639; invention of, 162
Parks (Okla.), 639
Parks, Lucile Snider, **1090**, 1319
Parman, James Franklin, **1091**
Parnell, Charles, **1092**
Parrington, Vernon Louis, 90, 561, **1093**
Patchell, O. W., **1094**
Pate, J. D., **1095**
Patent medicines, 291, **1096**, 1143, 1533
Patrick, James, biography of, 1305
Patrick, Lee, 1321
Patrick, William, **1097**
Patrol, 933
Patterson, L. E., 543
Paul, Haskell, **1098**
Paul, Smith, 109; genealogy of, 1098
Pauls Valley, Indian Terr.: banks and banking, 1100; cemeteries, 109
Pauls Valley, Okla.: attorneys, 1198; banks and banking, 1100; history of, 183, 1099; medical care, 196; newspapers, 133; physicians, 819; Presbyterian church in, 596; reformatory for boys, 1101; social clubs, 1348; telephone directory, 1099; women's clubs, 1081
Pauls Valley Chamber of Commerce, **1099**
Pauls Valley First National Bank (Okla.), **1100**
Pauls Valley State Training School for Boys, **1101**
Pavlova, Anna, 165
Pawhuska, Okla.: history of, 459; medical facilities, 838
Pawnee, Okla., description of, 644
Pawnee, Okla. Terr., description of life in, 1319
Pawnee County, Okla., 639
Pawnee Indians: allotment, 1124; culture, 1258; relations with Kaw Indians, 553; relations with U.S. government, 1326; reservation, 1124; social life and customs, 1466; trade, 1124; weaving, 1466
Payne, David Lewis, 236, 640, **1102**
Payne, Mattie Beal, 640
Payne, Okemah, **1103**
Payne, Tom, 1103
Payne County, Okla., 639; medical care, 643
Payne County, Okla. Terr., homesteading in, 1174
Pea Ridge, Battle of, 639
Pearl Harbor, Hawaii, attack by Japanese, 1432
Pearson, Drew, 640
Pearson, John Cannon, Sr., **1104**
Pearson, Lola Clark, **1105**
Pearson, Ralph, **1106**
Pearson, Robert Shelton, Sr., **1107**
Pearson Funeral Home (Walters, Okla.), 1106
Peck, Herbert Massey, **1108**
Peek, George, 464
Peeler, Paul, **1109**
Pender, Winnfield Russell, **1110**
Pendleton, Robert Henry, **1111**
Penney, Grace S. Jackson, **1112**
P.E.O., publications of, 1348
Peoples, William T., murder trial of, 841
Peoria Indians, litigation by, 695
Performers: dancers, 254; musicians, 924; storytellers, 462; wild west shows, 817, 925, 1121, 1365
Perren, Donna Lea, **1113**
Perren Garage (Pond Creek, Okla.), records of, 1113
Perry, Adolphus Edward, **1114**
Perry, John C., **1115**
Perryman, Joseph M., 324, **1116**

Perryman, Legus Chouteau, **1117**
Perryman family, 640
Pershing, John J., 861; correspondence, 1411
Peru, missionaries in, 606
Peters, Kay, **1118**
Peters, Susan, 1453
Peterson, Horace Cornelius, **1119**
Peterson, Robert V., **1120**
Petroleum companies (Okla.), 304
Petroleum geologists: papers of, 214; personal narratives, 1085
Petroleum industry: conservation, 760; corporate history, 260, 763; corporate records, 316, 479, 730, 763, 890, 1186; development of (Okla.), 639, 1031, 1298; equipment, 1175; flooding, 760; geology reports, 396, 573; history of, 459; history of in Oklahoma, 459, 479, 551, 624, 760, 1168, 1516; investigative reports (Okla.), 1242; labor relations, 1038; literature about, 486, 536; natural gas industry, investigation of, 1497; oil and gas leases (Choctaw Nation), 1535; oil discovery (Okla.), 479, 624, 1168; oil field contractors, 760, 1175; oil field workers, 17, 847, 1516; oil field workers, injuries to, 1409; oil leases, 631, 802, 925; oil production in, Louisiana, 890; oil production in Middle East, 573; oil production in Oklahoma, 389, 479, 536, 573, 760, 890, 925, 1031, 1516; oil production in South America, 573; oil production in Texas, 890; oil reserves in California, 536; oil well logs, 1485; pipelines, development of, 1502; poster art, 1393; price controls, 337; private investment, 33, 250, 200, 204, 287, 721, 1151; professional associations, 760; publications, 1259; refineries, records of, 337; storage tanks, 337; World War II and rationing, 337
Pettingill, Olin Sewell, 1359
Pettyjohn, (Mrs.) John, **1121**
Pharmacies, records of, 59, 124, 383, 739, 778. *See also* Drug stores
Pharmacists, 1402, 1438; Indian Territory, 754; Oklahoma, 48, 59, 98, 124, 393, 725, 739, 816; professional societies, 499
Phelan, Camille Nixdorf, 640

Phi Beta Kappa, 202, **1122**
Phi Beta Kappa Key, 911
Phi Delta Theta, **1123**
Philatelists, 98, 137, 1297
Phillips, Frank, 316, 640, 925; Woolaroc Museum, 1512
Phillips, George Wendel, **1125**
Phillips, John Allen, 640
Phillips, Leon Chase, 640, **1126**, 1489
Phillips, Waite, 640; company of, 925
Phillips, William A., 243, 640
Phillips Pamphlet Collection, **1124**
Phoenix Union High School (Ariz.), diplomas, 1142
Photographers, 291, 607, 1226
Photography: galleries, Rogers, Ark., 101; studio in Chelsea, Okla., records of, 620; studios, 441;
Physicians, 127, 190, 485, 546, 552, 1282, 1285, 1338, 1392; Arkansas, 969; Colorado, 1004; Indian Territory, 180, 212, 299, 547, 1044, 1136, 1230, 1442; Indian Territory, personal narratives, 91, 949, 965; Indian Territory, records of, 681, 714, 1388, 1409, 1439, 1457; Midwestern, 122; military, 299, 857, 1009, 1152, 1181; Missouri, 1203; Oklahoma, 82, 104, 157, 164, 212, 330, 436, 463, 545, 587, 639, 651, 659, 807, 929, 940, 993, 995, 1002, 1020, 1044, 1115, 1185, 1203, 1205, 1221, 1263, 1430, 1448, 1525; Oklahoma, biographical information, 1054; Oklahoma, cooperative medicine, 1276; Oklahoma, correspondence, 1278; Oklahoma, lecture notes, 218, 362; Oklahoma, obstetricians, 719, 993, 1310; Oklahoma, personal narratives, 91, 210, 670, 676, 865; Oklahoma, publications of, 196, 218, 360, 684, 788, 792, 872, 1009, 1190, 1239; Oklahoma, records of, 28, 31, 69, 72, 75, 106, 125, 168, 196, 198, 201, 221, 237, 266, 269, 281, 350, 360, 362, 388, 428, 460, 494, 500, 512, 600, 601, 617, 637, 643, 667, 714, 715, 716, 734, 761, 767, 788, 792, 793, 795, 796, 804, 809, 810, 872, 880, 901, 942, 987, 1013, 1095, 1125, 1230, 1310, 1317, 1336, 1337, 1347, 1367, 1368, 1388, 1409, 1461, 1503; Oklahoma, reference books, 722; Oklahoma, research, 684, 792, 955; Oklahoma, wives of, 819; Okla-

[*421*]

homa, women, 281; Oklahoma, World War I service, 218; Oklahoma, writings, 311, 500; Oklahoma, x-ray use, 1239; Oklahoma Territory, 1044; Oklahoma Territory, records of, 795, 826; Texas, records of, 60, 62
Physics, research, 482
Pianists, 924
Piburn, Anne Ross, **1128**
Pickard, Clyde C., **1129**
Pickens County, Indian Terr., 639
Pickett, Bill, 640, 925
Pickett, Joe, 925
Piegan Indians, 1124
Pierce, Thomas Franklin, Sr., 640, **1130**
Pierson, Iowa, government of, 1104
Pi Kappa Alpha, 74, **1127**
Pike, Albert, 224, 386, 1131
Pilgrims of the Plains, 800
Pima Indians, 1124
Pioneer Club (Chickasha, Okla.), 49
Pioneers, personal narratives, 408. *See also* Frontier and pioneer life
Pitchlynn, E. P., 683
Pitchlynn, Ernest, 640
Pitchlynn, John, 1131
Pitchlynn, Lycurgus P., 1131
Pitchlynn, Peter Perkins, 115, 257, 489, 578, **1131**; correspondence, 1224
Pitchlynn family, 489, 1224; records of, 1131
Pitman shorthand, nineteenth-century examples of, 550
Pittman, F. D., **1132**
Pittman, Oakley H., 1040
Pitt River Indians, 1124
Pittsburg County, Okla., 639; land titles, 506; mine explosion, 1930, 1470
Pittsburg County Medical Society, **1133**
Place names: Indian Territory, 1516; Oklahoma, 639, 1305, 1516
Planned Parenthood Association, **1134**
Playbills, 609, 1083, 1208
Playwrights, 1207, 1208
Plummer, William A., **1135**
Plummer family, correspondence, 1135
Poetry Society of Oklahoma, publications of, 1382
Poets and poetry, 108, 288, 385, 386, 420, 486, 515, 537, 539, 577, 578, 601, 724, 748, 751, 898, 935, 938, 946, 972, 983, 1088, 1130, 1152, 1207, 1261, 1311, 1322, 1346, 1402, 1432

Poinsett, Joel R., 386
Political appointments (Okla.), 351
Political campaigns, 92, 182, 220, 268, 317, 331, 345, 484, 534, 584, 728, 852, 948, 982, 1449; Democratic Party of Oklahoma, 1032; pamphlets and brochures, 876, 957, 1032; posters, 1143, 1188, 1235; presidential, 876; ribbons and buttons, 559, 1105, 1202; U.S. Senate, 1411
Political conventions: Democratic (Okla.), 1032; publications, 1126
Political memorabilia, 629
Political organizations (Indian Terr.), 629
Political pamphlets and brochures, 188, 317, 484, 584, 592, 626, 672, 1046
Political parties (Okla.), 1032, 1046
Political posters, 1341
Political theory, 435
Politics: agricultural, 689, 1294; cartoons, 1126; Equal Rights Amendment, 626; Ku Klux Klan, 1458; Missouri, 770; municipal, 84, 290; national, 250, 306, 776, 804, 1114, 1046; Oklahoma, 12, 335, 567; publications, 290, 345, 491; state, 92, 136, 220, 268, 288, 290, 317, 331, 484, 576, 588, 626, 728, 1005, 1046, 1114, 1126, 1214, 1235, 1341, 1386, 1411, 1449, 1455, 1487, 1508; territorial, 306, 1229, 1266
Pollard, Tildue H., **1136**
Pomeroy, Henry Martyn, **1137**
Pomona College (Calif.), 888
Ponca Indians, history, 599; reservations, 1124
Pond, Nina Louise Phillipi, **1138**
Pond Creek, Okla.: garages, 1113; high school students, 751; physicians, 1336
Pontotoc County, Okla., 639; political campaigns, 182
Pony Express, 639
Popé, 275
Porter, Indian Terr.: general stores, 253; physicians, 714
Porter, Joseph L., **1140**
Porter, Okla.: banks and banking, 1139; physicians, 714
Porter, Pleasant, 544, **1141**
Porter First National Bank (Okla.), 1139
Portillo, Jack, 342
Posey, Alexander Lawrence, 640, 938
Posey, Irving, **1142**

Post, Wiley, 165, 640
Postage stamps, 98, 137, 1297
Postal service, airmail, 861
Post cards, 99, 411, 495, 704, 1204, 1251, 1367, 1404; leather, 1163; Virginia scenes, 1168
Poster Collection, **1143**
Posters: disarmament, 1226; football games, 1177; Norman Rockwell, 1386; petroleum industry, 1393; political campaign, 1235; World War I, 1469
Postmasters: Oklahoma, 200, 255, 1144; Oklahoma Territory, 1357
Postmasters of Oklahoma Collection, **1144**
Post offices: Indian Territory, records of, 166; Oklahoma, 56, 1516; Oklahoma, records of, 255, 992, 1144; Oklahoma Territory, records of, 1144
Potawatomi Indians, 1124; art, 332; history of, 93; land quality, 781; litigation by, 695; living conditions, 781; treaties, 93; Wisconsin, 1124
Potaway, 640
Poteau, Indian Terr., physicians, 1457
Poteau, Okla., African-Americans, 963
Pottawatomie County, Okla., 639
Pottawatomie County Medical Society, **1145**
Pottery, manufacture of, (Okla.), 1251
Potts, Harry Walton, **1146**
Potts, Rhoda Gunn Colbert, 1313
Powell, Peter J., **1147**
Powell, Susan, 640
Power resources (Okla.), 639
Prague National Bank (Okla.), **1148**
Prairie Oil Company, 200
Pratt, Horace, **1149**
Pray, Joseph, **1150**
Presbyterian Church, 639, 1196; communist infiltration of, 1531; Indian Territory ministers, 1523; Indian Territory missionaries, 446; Indian Territory, records of, 1523; Norman, Okla., 1048; Oklahoma, history of, 638, 1526; Oklahoma ministers, 662; Pauls Valley, Okla., history of, 596
Presidios, history of, 954
Prevost, Charles Albert, **1151**
Price, Charles Gary, **1152**
Price, Walter, **1153**
Price controls (Okla.), World War II, 1018
Prickett, Theodocia Cralle, **1154**

Princess Wenona, 925
Printers (Okla.), 70, 652
Printing, examples of, 70
Prisoner of war camps, **1155**; American, 92; Fort Reno, Okla., 1492; German, 1492
Prison reform (Okla.), 395, 736
Prisons: New York, 1161; Oklahoma, 14, 567, 639, 1101, 1516
Proclamation Collection, **1156**
Proctor, C. L., **1157**
Proctor family, 640
Professional societies: pre-medical, 19; sciences, 1023; women's, 20. *See also* Medical associations and societies
Progressive Party, 1114, 1256
Prohibition, 50, 317; Oklahoma, 50, 639, 1163
Propaganda, Nazi, 1297
Propaganda Collection, **1158**
Protestant Episcopal Cathedral Foundation (Diocese of Oklahoma), 1245
Proxmire, William, 78
Pruitt Gin Company, **1159**
Pryor, William W., **1160**
Public buildings (Okla.), 639
Publishers and publishing: academic, 139, 1425; Indian Territory, 1303; Oklahoma, history, 279
Pueblo Bonito, Mexico, 743
Pueblo Indians, 275, 1124
Pugmire, Donald Ross, **1161**
Pulitzer Prize Board, 592, 1396
Pulitzer Prize winners, 1396
Pumpkin, Thomas, **1162**
Purcell, Okla., realtors, 631
Purdum, Helen, **1163**
Pushmataha, 640, 1516
Pushmataha County, Okla., 639
Putnam City, Okla., Methodist Episcopal church in, 1281
Puyallup Indians, 1124

Quakers. *See* Society of Friends
Quantrill, William Clarke, 307, 640
Quapaw, Okla.: mining equipment stores, 95; municipal records of, **1164**
Quapaw Indians: claims against U.S. government, 1508; farm leases, 378; schools, 378; tribal government, 378
Quigley, Michael, **1165**
Quinton, Indian Terr., land titles, 506
Quong, Jennie Lou Grey, **1166**

[423]

Rachlin, Carol, 856, **1167**
Racism (Okla.), 639
Rader, Fanny, 1169
Rader, Jesse Lee, **1168**, 1169
Rader, Katherine, **1169**
Radio: advertisements, 753; operators, amateur, 376; scripts, 799, 827, 996, 1047; scripts, "Great Men and Books," 827; scripts, "Labor's Side of the News," 799; scripts, "Museum of the Air," 1518; scripts, "Wake Up to Yesterday," 799; shows, 1453; shows, educational, 996; stations, WNAD (Norman, Okla.), 1112
Railroads: books, 458; Chicago, Rock Island, and Pacific, 247, 1219; Denver and Salt Lake, 372; depots and stations, 247; equipment, 247; federal ownership of, 1235; Fort Smith, Subiaco, and Eastern, 476; freight train permits, 939; health and pension plans, 500; history of, 458; Indian Territory, 130, 885, 1124; interurban, 1395; Kansas, Oklahoma and Gulf, 375; labor relations of, 1219; land, sales and transfers, 77, 247; leases, 802; litigation, 454; Midland Valley, 375; mines and mining, 1470; Missouri, Kansas, and Texas Railroad Company, 788, 804, 1340; modeling groups, 507; Oklahoma, 639, 1124, 1395; Oklahoma City, Ada, and Atoka, 375; Oklahoma Transportation Company, 1057; operations, 1219; physicians, 463, 788; records of, 247, 476, 634, 1057, 1219, 1224, 1267, 1395; rights-of-way, 579; rolling stock, 247; street, 1395; strikes, 1219; timetables, 458
Rainey, George, **1170**
Rainey family, 1170
Rainy Mountain Baptist Mission (Okla.), 1255
Ralls, Joseph G., Sr., **1171**
Ramona, Indian Terr., 1361; retail trade, 40
Ramsay, J. J., **1172**
Ramsay, James Ross, **1173**
Ramsey, Flora Belle Simmons, **1174**
Ranches and ranching, 322, 403, 493, 632, 721, 1362, 1400, 1428; Cherokee Outlet, 1184; Dakota Territory, 575; Indian Territory, 709, 1516; Kansas, 1184; Oklahoma, 479, 604, 628, 639, 817, 925, 1104, 1379, 1516; Oklahoma Territory, 744, 1087; Sonora, Mexico, 765; Texas, 488, 568, 575, 604
Randall, William B., **1175**
Ransom, Will Hewitt, **1176**
Ransom family, 1176
Rape, Lewis E., 316
Rascoe, Burton, 461, 640
Rasmus, William F., 671
Rathbone, Okla. Terr., 1357
Rawlinson, Sally, **1177**
Ray, Dee Ann, **1178**
Ray, Grace Ernestine, 956, **1179**
Ray, Jessie Dimple Newby, **1180**
Reagan, Nancy, 690
Reagan, Ronald, 690
Reagles, James, Jr., **1181**
Real estate (Okla.), 1, 160, 200, 1104, 1298
Realtors: personal papers, 588, 631, 957, 1103, 1129; records of, 966
Ream, Ruth K., **1182**
Reapportionment (Okla.), 1200
Reaves, Samuel Watson, **1183**
Recipes, 49, 627; ink, 660; medicines, 251, 612, 681, 709, 778, 810, 907. *See also* Cookbooks
Records, L. S., 1184
Records, Ralph Hayden, **1184**
Rector, (Mrs.) Newton, 1185
Rector, Newton, **1185**
Red Bird, 640
Red Buck, 640
Red Cross chapters (Okla.), records of, 25, 26
Red Fork, Okla., discovery of oil at, 624
Red Moon Indian Boarding School, 1264
Red Rabbit Oil Company Collection, **1186**
Red Rock Indian Agency (Indian Terr.), schools, 366
Red Store Trading Post (Fort Sill, Okla. Terr.), 377
Redwine, Wilburn Nash, **1188**
Redwine Trading Company Collection, **1187**
Reed, Gertrude Clark, **1189**
Reed, Horace, **1190**
Reed, Joannah Floyd, 895
Reed, Milo T., **1191**
Reed, Nathaniel (Texas Jack), 640
Reed, William J., 895
Reeds, Chester Albert, **1192**

Reeds, Clarence, **1193**
Rees, Margaret, 640
Reese, Jim E., **1194**
Reeve, Lelia Hudson, **1195**
Reeves, Bass, 640
Referendum News, 1214
Reformatories (Okla.), 1101
Relief organizations, (Okla.), records of, 1520
Religion (Okla.), 639
Religious Denominations of Oklahoma Collection, **1196**
Religious viewpoints, 583
Religious writings, 582
Remington, Frederic, 640
Renfro, Isaac, 814
Renfrow, William C., correspondence, 1229
Renner, John W., **1197**
Rennie, Albert, **1198**
Renze, Dolores C., **1199**
Repplier, Agnes, 461
Republican Party: national convention of 1920: 1105; Oklahoma, 588, 957, 1114, 1508; Oklahoma campaigns, 1487, Oklahoma convention proceedings in 1908: 1114; United States, 1114
Republican Party of Oklahoma, **1046**
Retail stores: Indian reservations, 772; Indian Territory, 40, 51, 203, 253, 310, 341, 377, 671, 732, 871, 1187, 1224; Indian Territory, records of, 1535; Missouri, records of, 516; Oklahoma, 95, 160, 203, 225, 278, 293, 300, 572, 663, 679, 753, 772, 816, 846, 912, 917, 928, 975, 1187, 1224, 1287; Oklahoma, history of, 1330; Oklahoma, records of, 520, 1535; Oklahoma Territory, 383, 816; trade tokens, 284, 663
Retirement systems, Oklahoma teachers, 1025
Revolutions, American, 397; description of, 374
Rewards, payment of, 802
Reynolds, James E., 640, 1417
Reynolds, Norman E., Jr., **1200**
Rhoads, Earl Roaine, **1201**
Rhoads, Sherman, 1201
Rhoads family, 1201
Rhodes, Charles B., **1202**
Rhodes Legal History Collection, 835
Rice, Clyde Vernon, **1203**
Richards, Aute, **1204**
Richardson, David Phillip, **1205**
Richardson, John, 640
Riddles, Leonard, 640
Ridge, John Rollin, 243, 640; correspondence, 740
Ridge family, 386, 1481; papers of, 243
Riedt, G. A., **1206**
Riggs, Rollie Lynn, 87, 640, **1207**, 1208
Right-to-work issue (Okla.), 1059
Riley, Rob, **1208**
Rinsland, Henry Daniel, **1209**
Ripley, Okla., development of railroads, 507
Rister, Carl Coke, **1210**
Rittenhouse, Frank A., **1211**
Rittenhouse, George B., **1212**
Ritzenthaler, Robert E., **1213**
Rivers (Okla.), 639
Roads (Okla.), construction of, 831, 1363
Robberts, Attie B., 640
Roberts, E. N., 835
Roberts, John, 835
Roberts, Oral, 640
Roberts, Rush, 640
Robertson, Alice, 67
Robertson, Ann Eliza Worcester, 640, 1215
Robertson, James Brooks Ayers, 53, **1214**
Robertson, Samuel W., **1215**
Robertson, William S., 1215
Robey, Roberta, **1216**
Robinson, Ella Coodey, 640
Robinson, Jim Lee, **1217**
Rockefeller, Nelson A., 78
Rockefeller, Winthrop, 640
Rock Island, Illinois Collection, **1218**
Rock Island Technical Society, **1219**
Rockport, Tex., description of, 575
Rockwell, Norman, posters by, 1386
Rocky Ridge Farm (Mo.), 794
Rodeos (Okla.), 639
Rodger Mills Company Cooperative Association, records of, 1109
Roger Mills County, Okla., 639
Rogers, Betty (Mrs. Will), 1121
Rogers, Charles S., 297
Rogers, Clement Vann, 243
Rogers, Harrison, 1309
Rogers, Henry Collins, **1221**
Rogers, John Powell, **1222**
Rogers, Roy, 640; songs recorded by, 1529
Rogers, Will (William Penn Adair Rogers), 12, 165, 137, 640, 752, 786, 935, 1121, 1498

[425]

Rogers, William Charles, **1223**
Rogers County, Okla., 639
Rogers County Medical Society, 667, 1220
Rogers-Neill Collection, **1224**
Romback family, genealogy, 371
Roodhouse, Frank S., **1225**
Roosevelt, Eleanor, correspondence, 104, 1105
Roosevelt, Franklin D., 844, 1294; correspondence of, 227, 268, 685, 1108
Roosevelt, Theodore, 521, 640, 1105, 1168; correspondence of, 270
Roosevelt Junior High School (Oklahoma City, Okla.), 888
Rose, Noah Hamilton, 640, **1226**
Rosenthal, Elizabeth (Betty) Clark, **1227**
Ross, Daniel H., 243
Ross, John, 243, 386, 640, **1228**
Ross, Leslie P., Sr., **1229**
Ross, Lewis A., 243
Ross, Robert B., 243
Ross, Samuel Price, **1230**
Ross, William Penn, 243
Ross, William Potter, **1231**
Ross family, 243; genealogy of, 134
Rotary International of Oklahoma, **1232**
Rough Riders, 1301; memorabilia, 521; reunions (Okla.), 54, 270
Routh, Guy, 641
Rowe, David, 1507
Rowe, Thomas, 1027
Roxana Petroleum Corporation (Ardmore, Okla.), 304
Ruggiers, (Mrs.) Paul Eddleman, **1233**
Ruggiers, Paul George, **1234**
Russell, Campbell, **1235**
Russell, Charles Marion, 640, 1237, 1240
Russell, Earl C., **1236**
Russell, Gordon, 1487
Russell, Nancy, Trust Collection, **1237**
Russell, (Mrs.) U. S., **1238**
Russell, William Green, 640
Russia: description and travel, 726; propaganda posters from, 1105. *See also* Soviet Union
Russo, Peter E., **1239**
Ruth, Charles P., **1240**
Ruth, Kent, **1241**
Rutherford, David Ross, 45
Rutherford, Isaiah, 1191
Rutherford, L. Morton, II, **1242**
Rutherford, Mary, 1191

Ryan, Jesse Willis, **1243**
Ryan family, 1243

Sacajawea, 835
Sac and Fox Bank (Stroud, Okla.), records of, 1354
Sac and Fox Indian Agency (Okla.), 294, **1244**, 1321
Sac and Fox Indians: agriculture, 294; banks, 1354; biography, 1167; customs, 1321; dances, 1321; depredations, 1244; education, 1244; employment, 1244; land leases, 294; lands, 313; land transfers, 1244; per capita payments, 1244; police force, 1244; relations with U.S. government, 1326; trade, 1244; treaties, 959; women, 1167, 1321
Sacred Heart Abbey (Okla.), 115
Sacred Heart Mission, Indian Terr., 1527
Sago palms, Marianas Islands, 117
Sailors, 1316
St. Catharine's Convent (Lehigh, Indian Terr.), 1527
St. John's Protestant Episcopal Church Collection, **1245**
St. Joseph's Convent (Krebs, Indian Terr.), 1527
St. Louis and San Francisco Railway Company, 579
St. Louis College of Physicians and Surgeons, 546
St. Mary's Academy, 1527
St. Michael's Catholic Church (Henryetta, Okla.), 227
Salasovic, Robert J., **1246**
Sallisaw, Okla., history of, 782
Saloons, 551, 814, 939; Indian Territory, records of, 116
Salter, Lewis Spencer, **1247**
Sam, Alfred Charles, 640
Samples Coal Mining Company, 1470
San Antonio, Tex., description of, 575
Sanborn Fire Insurance Company maps, 387
San Carlos, Ariz., description of in 1880s: 698
Sand Creek Massacre, 835
Sanders, Stella E., **1248**
Sanders family, 516; genealogy, 466
Sandheimer, Samuel, 1527
San Francisco, Calif., description of, 1137

Santa Fe Trail, 1195
Santos-Dumont, Alberto, 490
Sappa Creek, Battle of, 1875 (Kans.), 642
Sapulpa, Indian Terr.: Euchee Boarding School, **1250**; history of, 1286; records of, 1286
Sapulpa, James, 1249
Sapulpa, Okla.: Frankoma Pottery Company, **1251**; history of, 1301; physicians, 810; Presbyterian church, 1531
Sapulpa Collection, **1249**
Sarokin, Pitirim, correspondence, 104
Sassoon, Sigfried, 461
Satank, 640
Satanta, 640
Sattler, Helen R., **1252**
Saudia Arabia, training of educators, 230, 614
Savage, William Woodrow, Jr., **1253**
Saxon, Mary Esther, **1254**
Schaefer, Hedwig, **1255**
Schaper, William August, **1256**
Schermerhorn, H. R., 1064
Schmidt, Robert W., **1257**
Schmidt family, correspondence, 1257
Schmitt, Iva, **1258**
Schmitt, Karl, 640, **1258**
Schonwald, Fred P., Sr., 640, **1259**
Schools: Carter County, Okla., 639; commencement programs, 606, 1180, 1182; diplomas, 1175; Germany, grade books, 427; Grant County, Okla., 1273; Hennessey, Okla., 616; Illinois, 1496; Indian, 243, 504, 535, 1346; Indian boarding, 1250, 1264; Indian mission, 446, 470; Indian Territory, 243, 297, 366, 378, 430, 446, 508, 746, 884, 940, 1472, 1477, 1514; Kingfisher County, Okla., 1271; Kiowa County, Okla., 56; leasing of school lands (Okla. Terr.), 1499; Noble County, Okla., 1273; Norman, Okla., 187; Oklahoma, 526, 639, 1161, 1467, 1477; Oklahoma, construction of, 574; Oklahoma, immunization programs, 555; Oklahoma, sale of lands in, 416; Oklahoma Territory, 1467; orphans, 1472; Poland, 319; religious, 1048; report cards, 1182; Spiro, Indian Terr., records of, 1187; student term papers, 1284; student writing assignments, 616; superintendents of, 100; textbooks, 54, 766; Tulsa, Okla.,

public schools, history of, 1406; Wanette, Okla., 359; women's, 1346
Schuster-Barbour Collection, **1260**
Schwegler, Caroline, **1261**
Science education, 1197
Scientific societies, 1026
Scott, Angelo C., 640
Scott, George W., **1262**
Scott, Howell A., **1263**
Scott, William R., 630
Scrapbooks, 549, 1369
Scripps, E. W., 1396
Scroggs, Joseph W., 1514
Sculptors, 1369
Seal, notary public, 559
Sealey Chapel Methodist Church, history of, 470
Seamans Oil Company, 170
Searcy, Emmett Coldwell, **1264**
Searcy, Kate, 1264
Sears, Alfred Byron, 1119, **1265**
Sears, Helen, 1265
Sears, Roebuck and Co., profit sharing certificates, 1355
Seay, Abraham Jefferson, 392, 434, **1266**; correspondence, 770
Seay, Edgar W., Jr., **1267**
Seay family, 1266; history of, 770
Sebastian County, Ark., 836
Secretaries, 690
Seed stores (Okla.), records of, 753
Seger, Meta Chestnutt, 640
Seger Indian Agency (Colony, Okla.), 209
Selby, (Mrs.) Bruce, **1268**
Selden Codex, 1331
Self Help Exchange, bylaws of, 1235
Sellers family, 11
Seminole County, Okla., 639; crime and criminals, 1191; history of, 341
Seminole (Okla.) High School, yearbooks, 1407
Seminole Indians: allotment of land, 341; censuses, 1288; chiefs, 159, 354, 591, 745, 919; crime and criminals, 693; freedmen, 426; land disputes, 354, 1269; medical care, 91, 1173; military service, 426; mining and grazing leases, 159; missionaries to, 815, 1173, 1313; slavery, 815; tribal factionalism, 815; tribal government, 159
Seminole Nation: allotment, 1124; attorneys of, 1006; Civil War, 1173; crime

[427]

and criminals, 693; description of, 693, 815; funds, 1124; general council records, 1269; lands, 1124; lawsuits, 1124; missions, 745; oil wells, 479; per capita payments, 1124; tribal government, 354, 919, 1269; tribal politics, 1269

Seminole Nation Papers, **1269**

Semore, Enos, 640

Senate Literary Society (University of Oklahoma), 1180

Seneca-Cayuga Tribe (Okla.), 1124

Seneca Indians: farm leases, 862; green corn festival of, 67; legends, 55; schools, 746

Seneca Indian School, 746

Seneca Nation: allocation of land, 1270; tribal government, 1270; tribal politics, 1270; wars, 1124

Seneca Nation Papers, **1270**

Seneker, George Washington, **1271**

Sentinel, Okla., drug stores, 124

Sequoyah (George Guess), 56, 640, 1231; death of, 523

Sequoyah Convention, 1141

Sequoyah Movement, 1223

Seran, A. M., **1272**

Servant indentures, 821

Serviss, Irma Porter, **1273**

Seven Days Battle, in 1862 (Va.), 874

Shackelford, F. P., **1274**

Shackelford, Marshall, Jr., **1275**

Shackelford, Robert L., correspondence, 1275

Shadid, Michael Abraham, **1276**

Shaffer County, Okla., 639

Sharp, Paul F., **1277**

Shattuck, Okla., land sales and rentals, 425

Shaw, Elizabeth, 379

Shawnee, Kans., 768

Shawnee, Okla.: city charter of, 1225; missionaries, 712; physicians, 676; retail stores, 753; teachers, 1301

Shawnee (Okla.) Fanciers Association, records of, 753

Shawnee Indians, 1124; biography, 1167; claims against U.S. government, 1508; daily life and culture, 768; women, 1167

Shears, James (Oklahoma Jim), 640, 1260

Sheridan, Philip H., 1210, 1326

Sheriffs, 208

Sherman, William T., 1210, 1326

Sherrill, Rufus Hansen, **1278**

Shetland ponies, 181

Shilling, Marvin, **1279**

Shippey, E. E., **1280**

Shirk, George H., 640

Shirley, Glenn, 640

Shirley Trading Post, 678

Shoemakers (Iowa), records of, 660

Shoemaking, 391

Shook, Lottie Lee, 1281

Shook, William Vance, **1281**

Shorbe, Howard B., **1282**

Short, George F., **1283**

Short, Julia A. (Julee), **1284**

Shorthand, examples of, 550

Shoshone Indians, legends, 55

Shriners, 665. *See also* Freemasonry; Masonry

Shull, Russell Johnson, **1285**

Shumard, Evelyn Hughes, **1286**

Shumate, Enola, **1288**

Shumate and Sons, **1287**

Shumate Department Store (Pauls Valley, Okla.), records of, 1287

Shunatona, Baptiste, 640

Sidney, Ohio, 411

Sigler, Earle Marion, **1289**

Sigma Alpha Epsilon, **1290**

Sigma Delta Chi, **1291**; award, 1396

Sigma Gamma Epsilon, 365

Sigma Nu, **1292**; publications of, 1168

Silkwood, Karen, 496, 640, 763

Siloam Springs, Ark., postcard views of, 1404

Simmons, J. J., 640

Simon, Earle Marvin, **1293**

Simons, L. J., correspondence, 1041

Simpson, John Andrew, 640, **1294**

Simpson, (Mrs.) Morris S., **1295**

Sinclair, Upton, 461, 1519

Sino-Japanese Conflict, 1937–1945: 685, 1226

Sioux Indians, 207, 1124; wars, 207, 1414

Sisseton Indian reservation, survey of, 599

Sisseton Indians, depredations, 1124

Sittell, Fritz, 1224

Sittell family, 1224

Sitting Bull, 207, 640

Sixkiller, Samuel, 243

Skeleton, The, 767

Skelly, William Grove, **1296**

Skinner, Esthmer H., **1297**

Slavens, T. H., 698

Slaves and slavery, 386; bills of sale for, 1534; Cherokee Nation, 1216, 1427; contract for sale of, 883; description of (S.C.), 1334; missionaries attempting to free, 1216; receipt of sale, 602
Slick, Thomas Baker, **1298**
Slover, James Anderson, Sr., **1299**
Slovic, Eddie D., 924
Small, John, 825
Smalley, Joseph A., 640, **1300**
Smalley, Marjorie Beard, **1301**
Smallpox, among Cherokee Indians, 243
Smallwood, Ben F., **1302**
Smead, Elizabeth, 379
Smiser, (Mrs.) Butler Stonestreet, **1303**
Smith, Al, presidential campaign in Oklahoma, 1386
Smith, (Mrs.) E. P., **1304**
Smith, Franklin Campbell, **1305**
Smith, H. P., **1306**
Smith, Isabel Foster, **1307**
Smith, James Morton, **1308**
Smith, Jedediah Strong, **1309**
Smith, Joseph G., **1310**
Smith, Joseph R., 837
Smith, Maggie Aldridge, **1311**
Smith, Merle G., **1312**
Smith, Merle G., Jr., 1312
Smith, Micah Pearce, **1313**
Smith, Nell Achsah, 1319
Smith, Orville, correspondence, 599
Smith, Samuel Walter, **1314**
Smith, Stewart K., **1315**
Smith, Woodrow W., **1316**
Smithe, P. A., **1317**
Smithville, Okla., Indian school at, 470
Snake Indians, claims against U.S. government, 1508; depredations, 1124
Snider, Denton Jacques, **1318**
Snider, Luther Crockett, 640
Snider, Nell Achsah Smith, **1319**
Snodgrass, Bill, **1320**
Snow, Jerry Whistler, **1321**
Snyder, Lawrence H., 640, **1322**
Sober, Gertrude Selma, 640
Socialist Party: Oklahoma, 177, 1524; publications of, 1509
Socialists, papers of, 1509
Socialized medicine, 104
Social work (Okla.), 340
Society of Friends (Quakers), **1323**; locations of records of, 1323; missionaries, 71, 548; relations with Indians, 1323

Sociologists, writings of, 395, 858
Sod houses, 668, 1314; descriptions of, 599
Sohlberg, George Gustar, **1324**
Soil conservation programs (Okla.), 1050
Songbooks, religious, 359
Songs: country and western, 1529; Oklahoma Territory, 668
Songwriters, 144, 358, 478, 519
Soucek, Apollo, 640
South America, description and travel, 676
South Dakota: description and travel, 877; governors, 464
Southeastern Oklahoma Medical Association, **1325**
Southern Plains Indian Agencies, **1326**
South McAlester, Okla., settlement of, 1355
Southwest Davis Zinc Field, 447
Southwestern Association of Naturalists, **1327**
Southwestern Oklahoma Survival Association, **1328**
Southwest Merchandise Company (Mo.), records of, 516
Southwick, (Mrs.) Harl F., **1329**
Soviet Union: foreign relations during 1939–1946: 685; history of, 1389. *See also* Russia
Space flight, 581; human, 370; moon landings, 1243
Spain: colonial institutions in America, 954; colonial records of, 701; description and travel in 1901–1902: 1306; immigration of authors from, 1519; soldiers' service records, 916
Spanish-American War, 1305; personal narratives, 299; U.S. Army in, 1414
Spaulding Female College (Indian Terr.), 505, 1346
Spelling, research on teaching of, 1209
Spencer, Maude Clinkenbeard, **1330**
Spencer Academy (Indian Terr.), 297, 1131
Spinden, Herbert Joseph, **1331**
Spiro, Indian Terr.: cotton gins and ginning, records of, 1187; funeral homes, records of, 1187; general stores, records of, 1187; school district records, 1187
Spiro, Okla.: attorneys, records of, 1188; cemeteries, 1399; churches, 1399;

[429]

cotton gins and ginning, records of, 1187; funeral homes, records of, 1187; general stores, records of, 1187; physicians, 942
Sports (Okla.), 639
Spring, Otto F., **1332**, 1486
Springstead, Clarence S., Jr., **1333**
Springston family, 386
Stafford, B. S., **1334**
Staggs, Carrie Edna, **1335**
Stalker, Harry, **1336**
Standifer, John E., **1337**
Standifer, Orion C., **1338**
Standing Bear, 67
Standley, J. B., 640
Stansberry, Robert, 516
Stanton, Anna Amelia Doubleday, 147
Stapler and Son funeral home, 671
Starr, Belle, 498, 640
Starr, Ellis, 243
Starr, Emmett, 243, 640, 1313
Starr, Henry, 640
Starr family, 243
State Capitol Printing Company, history of, 279
Steed, Tom, 640
Stephens, Margaret Clark, **1339**
Stephens, Spencer S., 243
Stephens, Waldo, 640
Stephens College (Mo.), 1335
Stephens County, Okla., 639
Stephenson, Thomas J., 77
Stevens, Robert S., **1340**
Stevens family, 1340
Stevenson, Adams, 4
Stevenson, Adlai E., 78
Stevenson, Henry, 4
Stevenson, Robert Louis, 635
Stewart, Elijah King, **1341**
Stewart, Paul, 640
Stewart, Roy Pittard, **1342**
Stigler, Oren, **1345**
Stigler First National Bank (Okla.), **1343**
Stigler Masonic Lodge No. 121 (Okla.), **1344**
Stillwater, Okla. Terr., history of, 236
Stillwater, Oklahoma Woman's Relief Corps, 315
Stilwell, Giles (Jack), 640
Stilwell, Joseph, correspondence, 685
Stith, Mary E., 640
Stith, Ruth Brewer, **1346**
Stock certificates, 170

Stockyards National Bank (Oklahoma City, Okla.), 813
Stokes, Montfort, 223
Stone, DeWitt, **1347**
Stone, Lucile Oliver, **1348**
Stonewall County, Tex., 1274
Storms, 468
Story, William, 836
Stough, D. F., Sr., **1349**
Stovall, John Willis, **1351**
Stovall Museum, **1350**, 1351. *See also* University of Oklahoma, museum
Stover, Samuel Murray, **1352**
Street, Allen, 640
Stromstad, Ralph J., **1353**
Stroud State Bank (Okla.), **1354**
Struble, (Mrs.) Howard, **1355**
Student's Echo, 1092
Stumbling Bear, 640
Sturgeon, (Mrs.) Thomas H., 640
Sturgis, James Wellings, **1356**
Sturm's Oklahoma Magazine, 36, 1272
Sullivan, (Mrs.) Jim L., **1357**
Sulphur Chautauqua (Indian Terr.), 357
Sunbeam Farms Cattle, 493
Sunday schools (Indian Terr.), 1523
Sun River, Mont., 1240
Summer Institute of Linguistics Collection, **1358**
Suquamish Indians, 699
Surveyors, 703
Sutter, John A., 10
Sutton, George Miksch, **1359**
Swain, John, 640
Swank, David, **1360**
Swanson County, Okla., 639
Swearingen, Martha T., **1361**
Sweezy, Carl William, 640; art of, 207
Sweezy, Paul, 641
Swett, Morris J., 640
Swimmer, George Washington, 243
Swink, Indian Terr., physicians, 949

Taft, William H., signature of, 406
Tahlequah, Indian Terr.: description of, 466; notaries public, records of, 671; telephones in, 1511
Tah Sa Co Fah Ahwee. *See* Pumpkin, Thomas
Tait, J. H., **1363**
Tali Hekia Presbyterian Church, records of, 1523
Tallchief, Maria, 459, 640

Tamagno, Francesco, 87
Tanghe, Jerry, **1364**
Tanning of leather, 391
Tantlinger, D. Vernon, **1365**
Tantlinger, Edith, **1365**
Tarleton State University (Tex.), 256
Tarpley, Bloyce, **1366**
Tasaday Indians, 447
Tatum, Lawrie, 1326
Taxation (Okla.), 639
Taxes, state and county (Okla.), 1055, 1118, 1172, 1217
Taylor, Frank W., 875
Taylor, Guy William, **1367**
Taylor, John C., **1368**
Taylor, Joseph Richard, 640, **1369**
Taylor, Maxwell D., 640
Taylor, William Merritt, **1370**
T-Bone Ranch, 403, **1362**
Teachers: Arkansas, 349; Indian Territory, personal narratives, 71, 366, 1130, 1132; Oklahoma, 656, 1301, 1377, 1468; Oklahoma, African-American, 347; Oklahoma, contracts for employment, 176, 192, 349, 492; Oklahoma, directories and programs, 194; Oklahoma, lecture notes, 1477; Oklahoma, personal narratives, 187, 413, 1130, 1176; Oklahoma, personal papers of, 176, 183, 549, 594, 1293, 1477; Oklahoma, retirement systems, 1025; Oklahoma Territory, personal papers, 646
Tecumseh, 184
Tecumseh, Okla., drug stores, 778
Teehee, Houston Benge, 640
Teeter, Mary Bachelor, **1371**
Telegraph code books, 495
Telephone directories: Oklahoma, 17; Texas, 17; Union, City, Okla. Terr., 1205
Telephone service: Indian Territory, 618; Oklahoma, 861
Television personalities, 1453
Television shows: "The Open Window," 799; scripts and publicity, 799, 946, 1047
Television stations: Oklahoma, 1453; operating records of, 1521; programming, 1521
Temperance societies: publications of, 1264; records of, 193, 1505; songs of, 193
Temple First State Bank (Okla.), **1372**

Tenenbaum, Morris, 640
Tennessee, land records, 1484
Terrill, A. W., 386
Territorial Board for the Leasing of School Lands (Okla.), 1467
Territorial Oklahoma Manuscripts Collection, **1373**
Territory of Kansas Collection, **1374**
Texas: attorneys, 936; biographies of Texans, 1226; cattle brands, 226; frontier and pioneer life, 735, 1440; homesteading in, 867; Indian wars, 834; state records inventories, 1517
Texas A&M College, 103
Texas County, Okla., 639
Texas Jack. *See* Reed, Nathaniel
Texas Road, 1304
Textbooks: Choctaw Indian language, 492; *McGuffey's Eclectic Reader*, 176; mathematics, 176; nineteenth-century, 1264; spelling, 54; theological, 1064; used in missions, 548
Thames, Battle of the, 184
Thanksgiving, proclamations of, 1156, 1199
Theatrical productions and performances: playbills, 861, 1207; posters, 1143, 1153; programs of, 412, 672
Thoburn, Joseph, 1332
Thomas, Elmer, 640, 1294; correspondence, 1108
Thomas, Henry Andrew (Heck), 640; correspondence regarding, 718; diaries of, 718; stories regarding, 718
Thomas, Matie Mowbray, stories by, 718
Thomas, Norman, correspondence, 1119
Thomas, Okla. Terr., frontier and pioneer life, 1019
Thompson, Alfred M., Sr., **1375**
Thompson, B. F., 883
Thompson, Charles, 243, 1065
Thompson, Harry Edgar, **1376**
Thornton, Agatha R., **1377**
Thornton, Hurschel Vern, **1378**
Thorpe, Jim, 640
Three Forks Ranch, **1379**
Tibbs, Burrell, **1380**
Tiger, Moty, **1381**
Tilghman, William Matthew, 207, 640, 927, **1382**
Tilghman, Zoe, 1382
Tillman County, Okla., state senators, 576
Timmons, Alice, 640, **1383**

[*431*]

Timmons, Boyce, **1383**
Tinker, Clarence L., 640
Tipis, 207
Tishomingo, Indian Terr., description of, 175
Tittle, Leon H., **1384**
Tittle, Samuel H., 640
Tobias, Henry Jack, **1385**
Tolbert, James Randolph, **1386**
Tolbert, Raymond A., **1387**
Toll Bridge Wars, 639
Tolleson, William Alfred, **1388**
Tolleson family, 1388
Tolson, Arthur L., 640
Tolson, Melvin B., 640
Tomer, John, correspondence, 811
Tompkins, Charles Harland, 640
Tompkins, Stuart Ramsay, **1389**
Tonkawa, Okla.: history of, 1390; public library, **1390**; Sunny Side Club, **1391**
Tonkawa Indians: allotment, 1124; culture, 1066; history, 599
Topeka, Kans., description of, 66
Tornadoes, 468, 639, 1015
Torrey, Charles C., 409
Torrey, John Paine, **1392**
Totco, Incorporated, **1393**
Tourism (Okla.), 639
Towaconie Indians, 1124
Townsend, E. D., 1326
Tracy, Fred, **1394**
Tradesmens National Bank (Oklahoma City, Okla.), records of, 1030
Trade tokens, 284, 663
Trading posts (Okla.), 459, 1516
Traffic safety (Okla.), 1047
Trails (Okla.), 639
Trails: Santa Fe, 1195
Transcontinental Oil Company, 730
Transportation (Okla.), 639
Trapp, Martin Edwin, 640
Travel: accounts of, 271, 1176, 1241; brochures, 99, 495, 916, 1204; publications regarding, 271, 1241
Travis, Merle, songs recorded by, 1529
Treat, Guy Bradford, **1395**
Tri-County Medical Society (Okla.), 1503
Trimble, Vance, **1396**
Truman, Harry S., 78
Truss, Sam M., **1397**
Truss family, history, 1397
Tubb, Ernest, songs recorded by, 1529

Tucker, Amelia A., **1398**
Tucker, Barren E., **1399**
Tucker, Fred V., **1400**
Tucker, Hampton, **1401**
Tucker, Marshall A., 1398, **1402**
Tucker, R. Truman, **1403**
Tucker, Wanda, **1399**
Tuggle, C. E.:,**1404**
Tulsa, Okla.: Lions Club, 273; physicians, 995, 1448; public school system, history of, 1406
Tulsa County, Okla., fauna, 1003
Tulsa County Medical Society (Okla.), **1405**; publications of, 1115
Tulsa Public Schools, **1406**
Tunica Indians, language, 558
Turbyfill, Harper Subert, **1407**
Turbyfill, Mark, 640
Turley, Louis Alvin, **1408**
Turlington, Marcellus Martin, **1409**
Turnbo, Silas C., **1410**
Turner, Frederick Jackson, 640
Turner, Martin Luther, **1411**
Turner, Roy Joseph, 640; inauguration of, 1032
Turpin, Carl J., **1412**
Turpin family, 1412
Turtle, Willie, **1413**
Twain, Mark, 272
Twentieth-Century Club (McAlester, Okla.), 1206
Two Feathers, Abraham Isaac, 640

Ulster County, N.Y., 32
Umpqua Indians, depredations, 1124
Unger, Marion Draughon Murray, **1420**
Union City, Okla. Terr., telephone directories, 1205
Union Equity Coop Exchange, **1421**
Union Mutual Insurance Company, records of, 399
United Auto Workers, **1422**
United Daughters of 1812 (Okla.), publications of, 783
United Methodist Church (Okla.), ministry to the deaf, 1138
United Mine Workers Local #1864 (Okla.), records of, 135
United Nations, 1531; delegates to, 755
United Scholarship Service, Inc., 1227
United States: African-Americans, 395; ambassador, 844; bicentennial celebrations, 231; centennial, 327; civil

[432]

rights, 491; conservation of grasslands, 990; Constitution, 327; courts, 718; description and travel, 1241; ecology, 491; education, trends, 391; foreign policy, 392, 776; foreign relations, 844; foreign service officers, 513; frontiers, comparative studies, 1253; government, foreign policy, 1939–1946: 685; government, Indian policy of, 22, 80, 93, 130, 223, 386, 475, 952, 1124; government, subversive organizations, 1158; history of, 1170; Indian relations, 1124; international relations, 776; maps of, 387; marshals, 208, 639, 718, 978, 1202, 1224, 1382, 1416, 1418; medical care, 104; national parks, 743; patents, 1434; presidential cabinets, 690; presidential inaugurations, 1431; southwest, exploration of, 501; southwest, history of, 551; Spanish borderlands, history of, 954; tourism, 1241; trade expositions, cotton, 511
U.S. Army, 1st Volunteer Infantry Regiment (Indian Terr.), 1247; 5th Iowa Cavalry, 15; 10th Cavalry, 1181; 10th Infantry Regiment, **1414**; 11th Indiana Volunteer Infantry, 325; 23rd Iowa Infantry, 431; 31st Ohio Infantry, Company I, 1071; 33rd Infantry Association, 958; 45th Infantry Division, 639, 899; 95th Training Division, 864; 357th Infantry Regiment, 286; Air Force, personal narratives, 623, 731; Air Force, Seymour Johnson Field (N.C.), 731; Air Force, Peterson Field (Colo.), 731; Air Force, Will Rogers Field (Okla.), 731; basic training, 731; Department of the West, 373; Indian Territory, correspondence, 475; Indian troops, 426; Indian wars, 472, 698, 834, 835, 1414; land acquisition, Wichita Mountains (Okla.), 1473; military payment script, 878; officers, articles regarding, 843; officers, correspondence, 371, 1479; officers, personal narratives, 382, 752, 1390; officers, personal papers of, 864, 888, 899; Oklahoma, enlistments, 1414; physicians, 857, 1181; posts, 473; publications for, 764, 843; records and correspondence, 197, 475, 501, 1414; recruitment posters, 1143; reserve affairs, 864; scouts, 264, 442; soldiers, correspondence, 481, 845; soldiers, papers of, 1370; Spanish American War, 1414; special orders, 1285; Texas, posts, 473; Union forces, 171, 481

U.S. Board of Indian Commissioners, 445; annual reports, 469, 1124

U.S. Board of Tax Appeals, opinions of, 384

U.S. Cavalry Association, 843

U.S. Circuit Court (Indian Terr.), records of, 866

U.S. Civil Aeronautics Administration, medical reports, 788

U.S. Commissioner of Education, 590

U.S. Commission on Civil Rights, 261

U.S. Congress, nepotism scandal, 1396

U.S. Court of Claims, 1006

U.S. Department of Agriculture, publications of, 562

U.S. Department of Interior, Bureau of Indian Affairs, 22, 553, 603, 781, 832, 848

U.S. Department of the West, 373

U.S. District Court: Central District of Indian Territory, **1415**; Northern District of Indian Territory, **1416**; Western District of Arkansas, 404, 836, **1417**; Western District of Oklahoma, **1418**, 1435

U.S. Indian Service, 944, 952

U.S. Marines, 1201

U.S. Naval Air Station (Norman, Okla.), history of, 530, 991

U.S. Naval Air Technical Training Center (Norman, Okla.), history of, 530, **991**, 1246

U.S. Naval bases, 991

U.S. Navy: battleships, 1419; expedition to Darien, Panama, 547; physicians, 547; sailors, 1316

U.S. Secretary of War, correspondence, 685

U.S. Selective Service, directives of, 454

U.S. Supreme Court, justices of, 165; lawsuits tried before, 1006, 1124

U.S. Treasury Department, publications, 440

U.S. Veterans Bureau, physicians, 667

University Improvement Association (Lawton, Okla.), 1295

University of Arkansas, faculty, 396

[433]

University of California (Berkeley, Calif.), postcard views of, 1404

University of Denver, Denver and Gross College of Medicine diploma, 1004

University of Minnesota: faculty attitude toward World War I, 1256; political science department, 1256

University of Nashville, 552, 1185

University of Oklahoma: academic organizations, 1122; accreditation reviews, 230; Achievement Day at, 1296; administrators, 74, 126, 554, 614, 1451; African-Americans, admission of, 347; alumni, 126, 219, 393, 614, 656, 678, 751, 752, 1192, 1312, 1423; Alumni Association, 113, 554, 1387; American Indian Institute, 932; annual reports, 1451; art and artists, 1369; athletes, 752, 864; athletic association, bylaws of, 997; athletic directors, 733; athletic event programs, 752; athletics, football, 126, 769, 784, 840, 1177; Athletics Council, 230; biology department, 1204; bond issues in 1903: 757; *Books Abroad*, 554, 664, 1492 (*see also World Literature Today*); Budget Council, 230; buildings, 126, 189, 215, 363, 386, 412, 1312, 1387, 1433; campus master plan, 1093; carillons, 250; Carpenter Hall, 215; centennial celebration, 229; Center for Studies in Higher Education, 230, 614; chemistry building, 363; civil defense preparations, 707; class of 1910: 1180, 1423; class of 1913: 565; clubs and societies, 296, 457, 797, 1168, 1180, 1247, 1426, 1462; College of Arts and Sciences, 437, 448, 619, 656; College of Business Administration, 177; College of Education, 1197; College of Fine Arts, 215, 762; College of Law, 943; College of Pharmacy, 725, 1012, **1424**; commencement exercises, 126, 853; commencement programs, 606, 1020; Commission on Curriculum, 448; committees and councils, 1451; course catalogs, 997; curriculum, 448, 561, 1451; dance cards, 1312; deans, 437, 647, 762, 943, 1451; DeGolyer Committee, 1425; Delta Delta Delta, 1169; Department of Communication, 799; Department of English, 207, 561, 1093; Department of Geography, 622, 1036; Department of Geology, 1036; Department of History, 343, 1389, 1451; Department of Political Science, 85; Department of Sociology, 103; Department of Zoology, 1463; diplomas, 931; Distinguished Service Citation Committee, 1425; dormitories, 412; Extension Division, 1112, 1451; faculty, 16, 29, 85, 87, 102, 103, 118, 134, 169, 207, 215, 314, 343, 345, 363, 365, 395, 435, 437, 448, 482, 526, 561, 595, 611, 614, 619, 622, 647, 664, 707, 784, 799, 827, 828, 850, 858, 880, 902, 943, 951, 954, 955, 961, 967, 972, 1014, 1079, 1086, 1093, 1119, 1150, 1155, 1168, 1179, 1197, 1204, 1210, 1253, 1265, 1277, 1360, 1369, 1389, 1451, 1463, 1485, 1492, 1496; faculty club, 296; Family Life Institute, 1112; finances, 561; fine arts events, 134, 534; fraternities, 368, 429, 1123, 1127, 1168, 1290, 1291, 1292; Galen Society, records of, 499; grade books, 29, 450, 1210, 1389; graduates of 1897–1908: 1093; history of, 126, 134, 169, 526, 561, 614, 997, 1377; hospital, 1387; Independent Men's Association, 457; Indian Education Center, 932; integration, 347; Interschool Speech Service, 1112; Korean students, 962; lecture notes, 435, 762; librarians, 336, 450, 1168, 1169, 1254; library, 4, 554, 1254; literary societies, 245, 455; maps of campus, 386, 997; medals and pins, 565; memorabilia, 126, 1193; museum, 554, 639; musical performances, programs, 412; newspaper, 951; Oklahoma Memorial Union, 386, 412; Other Film Club, **1073**; Owen Field, 1177, 1387; PE-ET, 1451; Phi Beta Kappa, 202, **1122**; Phi Delta Theta, 1123; Phi Eta Sigma, 1451; presidents, 88, 103, 126, 134, 139, 154, 169, 343, 430, 464, 997, 1150, 1154, 1168, 1222, 1277, 1496, 1524; President's Class, 828; Press, 139, **1425**; professional societies, 19, 20, 246, 365, 429, 499; professional writing program, 207; publications of, 99, 134, 189, 229, 607, 1168, 1193; radio station WNAD, 1112, 1451; regents, 182, 363, 551,

614, 784, 1222, 1387; registrars, 997, 1451; research centers, 230; Rockefeller Foundation Committee, 1425; School of Fine Arts, 647, 997, 1369; School of Journalism, 314, 619; School of Law, 1387; School of Medicine, 955; School of Music, 595; School of Social Work, 347; seal of, 230, 835; Semi-Centennial Committee, 1425; Sigma Gamma Epsilon, 365; social events, 908; songs and music, 134, 519; *Sooner Magazine*, 229; sororities, 1169; special collections, library, 47; sports, 126, 134; sports information directors, 752; staff, 614; statues on campus of, 1369; student life, 90, 187, 370, 678, 1085; students, 34, 39, 219, 269, 437, 833, 864, 343, 526, 619, 751, 752, 789, 913, 931, 962, 997, 1012, 1168, 1233, 1308, 1312, 1345, 1402, 1407, 1433, 1451, 1453, 1485, 1496; students, medical, 19; student senate, constitution and bylaws, 997; student union, 1387; Summer Institute of Linguistics, **1358**; theatrical performances and programs, 412, 1193; University and Town Committee, 1425; university constitution, 448; Vance Hall, 1433; veterans organizations, 24; Websterian Literary Society, 1462; Westheimer, Max, Air Field, 554; Will Rogers Scholarship Fund, 1483; women's association, **1426**; Women's Club, 296; Women's History Project, 1506; *World Literature Today*, 1519 (*see also Books Abroad*); World War I, 154; World War II, 1451; yearbook, 951; YMCA branch, event programs, 126, 134; YMCA branch, records of, 1451, 1530; YWCA branch, event programs, 126, 134; YWCA branch, records of, 1451, 1530
University of Oklahoma Association, **1423**
University of Tulsa, Phi Beta Kappa, 1122
University of Washington, map of, 1093
University Women's Association, **1426**
Updegraff, Ruth, **1427**
Urschel, Charles F., kidnapping case, 287
USS *Caelum*, 933
USS *Oklahoma*, 1316, **1419**

Utah, Territory of, Indian attacks, 970
Utterback, Bert R., **1428**

Valentines, 672
Valliant, Okla., medical care, 269
Van Ausdal, Harvey G., **1429**
Vance, Leon C., 640
Vance, Leon Robert, Jr., **1433**
Van Cleave, William E., **1430**
Vanderbilt University medical school, 552
Van Dorn, Fred, **1431**
Van Dyke, Gerald Mason, **1432**
Vann, Joseph, 640
Varderburg, Henry, 825
Vaudeville, posters, 1143, 1153
Vaughan, Floyd Lamar, **1434**
Vaught, Edgar Sullins, Sr., 422, 640, **1435**
Venereal diseases, 72, 311
Vera, Indian Terr., missions, 548
Verdi, Giuseppe, 87
Vestal, Stanley. *See* Campbell, Walter Stanley
Veterans (Okla.), 639
Veterans' organizations: records of, 24; 33rd Infantry Association, 958
Vian, Okla., census of 1910: 386
Vidal, Gore, 640
Vietnam War, 491
Vigilante committee (Omaha, Nebr.), records of, 1137
Vigilantes (Okla. Terr.), 35
Vinita, Indian Terr., history, 243; housing, 1460; political organizations, 629
Vinita, Okla.: Lions Club, **1436**; physicians, 940, 993
Virden, John M., **1437**; correspondence, 551
Vliet, Gertrude M., 1438
Vliet, Richard M., **1438**
Von Keller, Frederick Philander P., **1439**

Waco Indians, 1124
Wagner, J. E., **1440**
Wagoner County, Okla., 639
Wagoner, Indian Terr., medical care, 91
Wagoner, Okla.: health care, 69; real estate, 588
Wagon trains, attacks upon, 970
Wahpakoota Indians, depredations, 1124
Wahpeton Indian Reservation, survey of, 599

[435]

Wahpeton Indians, depredations, 1124
Walker, Andrew Beattie, **1441**
Walker, Charles F., **1442**
Walker, Christopher Columbus, **1443**
Walker, John Riley, **1444**
Walker, Tandy C., 1131, **1445**
Walker, Thelma Brown, **1446**
Wallace, Cecile Boone, **1447**
Wallace, Henry, correspondence, 685
Wallace, Jesse E., **1448**
Wallace, Sidney, 640
Wallis, Indian Terr., physicians, 681
Wallock, Anthony Mark, 502
Walter, Fred C., 517
Walters, Okla.: funeral homes, 1106; high school teachers, 549; retail stores, 912
Walters, Okla. Terr.: history of, 1375; store in, 7; townsite controversy, 1375
Walton, John Calloway (Jack), 265, 534, 640, 861, 1386, **1449**
Walton, Sam, biography of, 1396
Wanette, Okla.: history of, 359; post office, 992; schools, 359
Wantland, Lewis Cass, 640
Wapanucka, Okla., Presbyterian church in, 1523
Ward, D. C., **1450**
Wardell, Morris L., 1155, **1451**
Wark, George H., 50
Warm Springs Apache Indians, missions, 233
Warne, Rhoda Foster, **1452**
Warner, Carolyn Rexroat, **1453**
Warner, Okla., Jacob Johnson Library, 308
Washington County, Okla., 639
Washita, Battle of the, in 1868: 382, 771, 1264
Washita County, Okla., 639; map of, 1021
Washita County, Okla. Terr., pioneer life, 413
Wassaja: Freedom's Signal for the Indian, 944
Watchorn Oil and Gas Company, 925
Watchtaker, George Smith (Woogie), 640
Watergate scandal, 348
Water resources (Okla.), 639
Waters, Jim, 640
Watie, Charles E., 243
Watie, Jacqueline, 243
Watie, Ninnie, 243
Watie, Saladin, 243
Watie, Sarah C., correspondence and papers of, 243

Watie, Stand, 285, 578, 640, 740, 752, 1284, 1299; correspondence and papers of, 243
Watie, Watica, 243
Watie family, 243, 386
Watonga, Okla.: financial institutions, 661; funeral homes, 975; retail stores, 975
Watson, Archer Hunter, Sr., **1454**
Watson, Harold, 640
Watt, Florence Ellen Haynes, 904
Watt, James, **904**
Watts, Charles Gordon, Sr., **1455**
Waugh, Evelyn, 355
Waynoka Commercial Bank (Waynoka, Okla.), **1456**
Wear, John B., **1457**
Weather (Okla.), 639
Weaver, Carlton, **1458**
Weaver, Claude Dickens, Sr., 640, 841, **1459**
Webbers Falls, Indian Terr., **1460**
Weber, S. G., **1461**
Websterian Literary Society (University of Oklahoma), 1168, **1462**
Weese, Asa Orrin, **1463**
Weith, Charles C., 640
Welch, Okla.: crime and criminals, 1464; municipal records, **1464**; Van Ausdal Drug Store, 1429
Wells, Wayne, 640
Welsh, Jack D., **1465**
Weltfish, Gene, **1466**
Wenner, Fred Lincoln, 640, **1467**; map collection of, 387
Wenona, Ill., newspapers, 327
Wentz, Lewis Haines, 179, 640
West, Beth, **1468**
Western History Collections, 1425; history of, 47
Western National Bank (Oklahoma City, Okla.), records of, 1028
Western Writers of America, 174
Westerners International, Indian Territory Posse, 1259
Westfall, Chester Harold, **1469**
West Virginia, mines and mining, 747
Wetumka, Okla., medical care, 91
Wewoka, Indian Terr.: history of, 341; Masonry (Scottish Rite), 341; retail stores, 341
Wewoka, Okla., 1272
Wewoka Masonic Lodge, records of, 341

Wewoka Trading Company, 341
Wheat Grower's Advocate, 1058
Wheatley, Thomas W., **1470**
Wheeler, Homer W., 442
Wheeler, J. Clyde, **1471**
Wheeler, John F., 782
Wheeler, Roger M., 640
Wheeler family, 782
Wheelock Seminary (Indian Terr.), **1472**
Whistler, Don, 640
Whistler, Maude Mayes, 1321
Whistler, Pearl Mayes, 1321
Whistler family, 1321
Whitaker, Lovie, **1473**
White, Greenup, 525
White, Hal H., **1475**
White, (Mrs.) J. R., **1476**
White, Lida, **1477**
Whitebead, Indian Terr., cemeteries, 109
White Bull, Joseph, 207
Whitehill, Walter Muir, **1478**
White Shrine of Jerusalem (Okla.), **1474**
Whitmore, Ellen, 640
Whitney, Charles W., **1479**
Wichita, Kans., description, 1135
Wichita Indian Agency, **1480**
Wichita Indians, 1124; attorneys of, 1006; claims against U.S. government, 1508; culture, 1258; land transfers, 54; relations with U.S. government, 1326
Wichita Mountains (Okla.), mines and mining, 621
Wichita Mountains Easter Pageant, 1375; history of, 502
Wichita Mountains Wildlife Refuge, 1473
Wickersham, Victor, 1341
Wickmiller, Charles, 640
Wilcox family, history of, 156
Wild Cat, 815
Wilder, Laura Ingalls, 794
Wilder, Thornton, 1519
Wildlife conservation (Okla.), 639
Wild west shows, 1321; memorabilia, 925; performers, 817, 925, 1121, 1365; posters, 1143; publications of, 54; records of, 817, 925
Wilkins, Thurman, **1481**
Wilkinson, Charles Burnham (Bud), 640, 752
Wilkinson, James B., correspondence, 1070
Wilkinson, Otha, **1482**
Wilks, James, 1357

Willard, Melissa Kate, **1484**
Willey family, 532
Willford family, genealogy of, 1330
Williams, Arthur James, **1485**
Williams, Charles H., **1486**
Williams, John Robert, **1487**
Williams, Mary Clay, **1488**
Williams, Meredith Newton, **1489**
Williams, Robert L., 1490
Williams, Roger, 1284
Williams, Samuel, **1490**
Williams, Stephen, **1491**
Williamson, Halsell, Frasier Company, 571
Willibrand, William Anthony, **1492**
Willis, Robert F., **1493**
Willis, Wallace, 640
Willour, J. A., **1494**
Will Rogers Memorial Commission, records of, 592
Will Rogers Scholarship Fund, **1483**
Wills, 386
Wills, Bob, and the Texas Playboys, 627
Wilson, A. Florence, 640
Wilson, Andrew R., **1495**
Wilson, Charles, 703
Wilson, Charles Banks, 640
Wilson, Milbourne Otto, **1496**
Wilson's Creek, Battle of, in 1861: 639
Wimberly, Harrington, **1497**
Winchester Store (Winchester, Okla.), history of, 1330
Wingate, Beni, 717
Winnebago Indians, depredations, 1124
Wister, Okla., insurance agents, 1280
Witcher, Esther, **1498**
Witte, (Mrs.) Juan R., **1499**
WKY-TV (Okla.), 1453
Woden Club (Norman, Okla.), history of, 1011
Wolf, Euline Capshaw, 640
Wolf, Jonas, **1500**
Wolf, Leland, **1501**
Wolfe, Oscar, **1502**
Wolfe, Reed E., **1503**
Wolfe, Richard M., 1507
Womack, John, 640, **1504**
Woman's Christian Temperance Union, **1505**
Woman's Relief Corps, Stillwater, Okla., chapter, 315
Women: anthropologists, 854, 856; athletes, 267; authors and writers, 67,

[437]

132, 309, 314, 452, 486, 490, 502, 515, 680, 776, 800, 806, 854, 856, 946, 1081, 1286, 1382, 1511; charitable organizations, 1474; clothing, 291; college professors, 846, 850, 926, 951; college students, 63, 67, 422, 881; editors, 1105; equal rights (Okla.), 626; historians, 364; illustrators, 1322; Indian Territory, 805, 815, 1230; journalists, 288, 452, 720, 776, 951; Ku Klux Klan membership, 787; librarians, 527, 846, 850; Oklahoma, 639; ornithologists, 1003; photographers, 291; physicians, 104, 281; physicians' wives, 819, 1230; pioneer narratives, 653, 711, 735, 815, 1019, 1090, 1174, 1195, 1216, 1230, 1247; playwrights, 1519; poets, 288, 724, 1322; societies and clubs, 49, 246, 352, 497, 783, 787, 790, 1052, 1068, 1081, 1105, 1138, 1145, 1382, 1412; suffrage, 288; teachers, 169, 347, 492, 549, 594, 1176, 1477; temperance societies, 1505
Women of '89 Club, publications of, 1382
Women's History Project, **1506**
Women's Society of Christian Science, 1138
Wood, Anna K., 1247
Wood, Charles L., 374
Wood, Edwin K., **1507**
Woodard, Fred Barton, **1508**
Woodard Ranch (San Antonio, Tex.), 575
Woodrow, Thomas W., 640, **1509**
Woods, E. K., **1510**
Woods, Samuel Newitt, 640
Woods County, Okla., 639
Woodward, Grace, **1511**
Woodward, Grace Steele, 640
Woodward County, Okla., 639
Woolaroc Museum (Bartlesville, Okla.), **1512**
Wooton, Esther A. Reed, **1513**
Worcester, Samuel A., 243, 640, 1131
Worcester, Sarah, 67
Worcester Academy, **1514**
Workers Alliance (Okla.), 708
Workers' compensation cases (Okla.), 788
Works Progress Administration, 639; Archaeological Survey Project, **1515**; Federal Writers Project, **1516**; Historical Records Survey, **1517**; Historic Sites Project, **1516**; Indian-Pioneer Papers Project, 343, **696**; Oklahoma, 1382; Oklahoma, records of, 1351; project records, 1515, 1516, 1517, 1518; Statewide Projects, **1518**
World Assistance, records of, 1520
World fairs, memorabilia, 1264
World Literature Today, **1519**. *See also Books Abroad*
World Neighbors, Inc., **1520**
World War I, 1914–1918: American Legion certificate for participation in, 1285; American participation in, 27; artillery, role of, 899; attitude toward, 1256, 1375, 1404; civil defense, 707; correspondence with U.S. soldiers, 594; Creel Committee publications, 328; Germany, 1509; Liberty Bond sales (Okla.), 1028, 1490; Liberty Loan records, 1100, 1490; newspaper clippings regarding, 707; Oklahoma participation in, 1469, 1490; patriotic society, records of, 1391; peace treaty, 1119; personal narratives, 154, 1389; posters, 1143, 1469; propaganda, 430, 1119; relief of sick and wounded, 26; selective service registration, 587; soldiers' correspondence, 1027, 1268
World War II, 1939–1945: 639; battle scenes, 896; blockade of Germany, 345; China–Burma–India campaign, 764; civil defense, 707; diaries, 149; Far Eastern theater, 685, 764; German prisoners of war, 1155, 1492; Japanese-Americans, internment of, 1166; Medal of Honor recipients, 1433; military newspapers, 933; musical compositions about, 502; news clippings regarding, 165, 349, 405, 594, 1204, 1243; officers' correspondence, 888; origins of, 392; Pacific theater, 896; pacifist publications, 1005; personal narratives, 149, 286, 623, 926; posters, 1143; price controls, 1018; propaganda, 1158, 1297; Purple Heart medals, 1201; ration books, 17, 128, 937, 1069, 1168, 1201, 1268, 1413; rationing, gasoline, 337; soldiers' correspondence, 752, 924, 1201; U.S. involvement in, 1005
Woyna, Fritz Willie, **1521**
Wright, Albert Daniel, **1522**
Wright, Allen, 640, **1523**
Wright, Eliphalet Nott, 640
Wright, Frank Lloyd, correspondence, 529

Wright, Harriet Bunce, 67
Wright, J. George, 243
Wright, Michael P., **1524**
Wright, Muriel Hazel, 640
Wright, R. G., 883
Wright, Rush L., **1525**
Writers: freelance, papers of, 1241; travel, 1241. *See also* Authors
Wyandotte Indians: depredations, 1124; hymnals, 976; language, example of, 976
Wyatt, Robert Lee, III, **1526**
Wyatt, Rose Mary Burt, **1527**
Wyncoop, Frank M., 835
Wynnewood, Okla., Eskridge Hotel, 1495

XIT Ranch, Tex., 1

Yakima Indians, claims against U.S. government, 1508; depredations, 1124; treaties with the U.S., 699
Yale First National Bank (Yale, Okla.), **1528**
Yaller Dawg Saloon (Tex.), 939
Yavapai College (Prescott, Ariz.), 275
Yazoo land frauds, 29

York, Bill, **1529**
Young, Glen Olen, **1531**
Young, Hiram, **1532**
Young, James Harvey, **1533**
Young, L. A., 1532
Young Men's Christian Association, 134, **1530**
Young Women's Christian Association, 134, 296, **1530**
Youpe, Louis Allen, 640
Yowell, Lillian J., **1534**
Yuchi Indians, 161. *See also* Euchee Indians
Yugoslavia, description of life in, 531
Yukioma, 275

Zabloudel, Jake, 640
Zetaletheans (University of Oklahoma), 1180
Ziegfield Follies, program, 1083
Zofness, Martin I., 1385
Zoologists: personal papers of, 1463; research of, 138, 1069, 1204
Zuni Indians, 275
Zweigel Mercantile Company, **1535**

www.ingramcontent.com/pod-product-compliance
Lightning Source LLC
Chambersburg PA
CBHW020728160426
43192CB00006B/149